INSIDERS'GUIDE® to
North Carolina's Mountains

*Including Asheville, Biltmore Estate,
Cherokee, and the Blue Ridge Parkway*

ELEVENTH EDITION

CONSTANCE E. RICHARDS AND
KENNETH L. RICHARDS

Globe
Pequot

GUILFORD, CONNEC

D0880478

All the information in this guidebook is subject to change. We recommend that you call ahead to obtain current information before traveling.

Globe Pequot

An imprint of The Rowman & Littlefield Publishing Group, Inc.
4501 Forbes Blvd., Ste. 200
Lanham, MD 20706
www.rowman.com

Distributed by NATIONAL BOOK NETWORK

Title page image, Fly fishing at Biltmore, used with permission from The Biltmore Company, Asheville, North Carolina

British Library Cataloguing in Publication Information available

Library of Congress Cataloging-in-Publication Data available

ISBN 978-1-4930-4346-0 (paperback)
ISBN 978-1-4930-4347-7 (e-book)

♾️ ™ The paper used in this publication meets the minimum requirements of American National Standard for Information Sciences—Permanence of Paper for Printed Library Materials, ANSI/NISO Z39.48-1992.

Contents

Appendix: Living Here

Directory of Maps

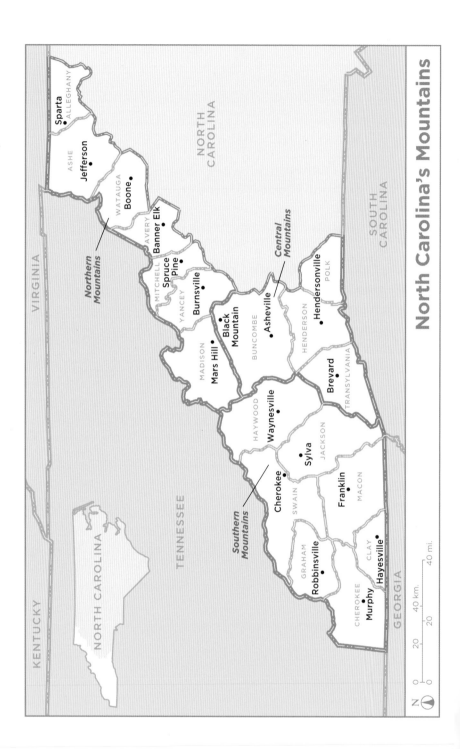

North Carolina's Mountains

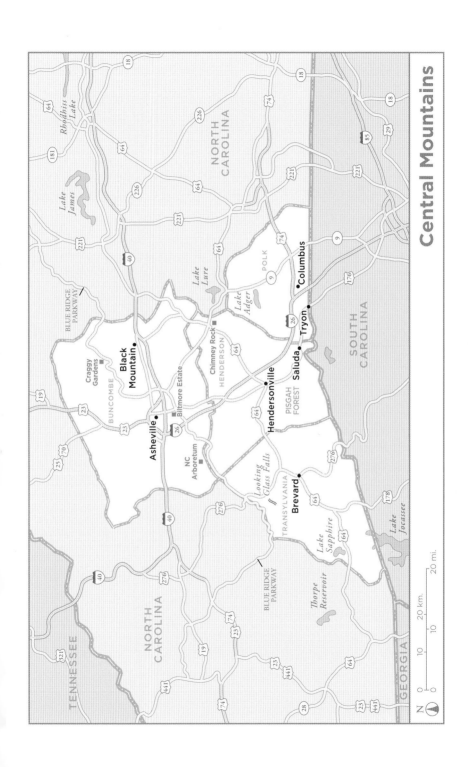

Central Mountains

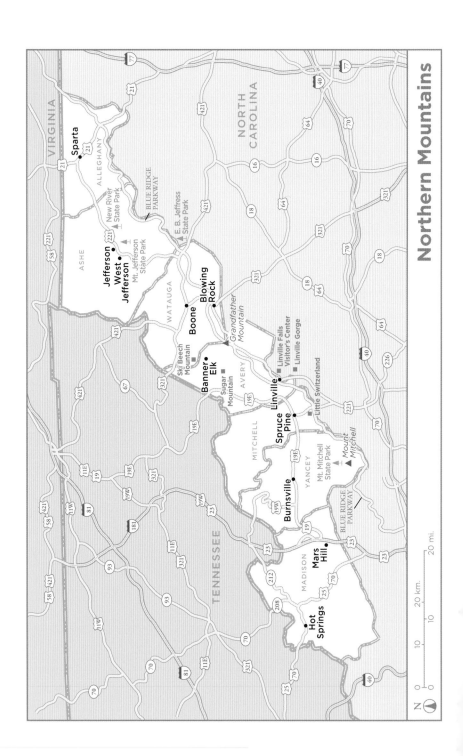
Northern Mountains

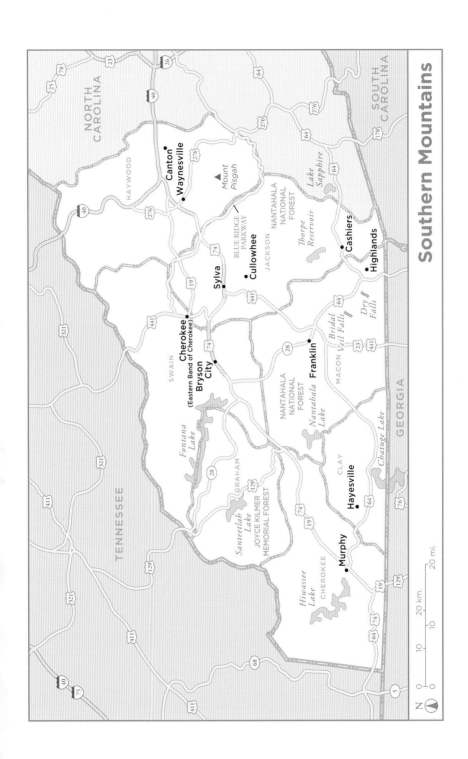

Southern Mountains

About the Authors

Constance E. Richards is a journalist, author, and curator based in Asheville, North Carolina. She grew up in Europe, where her American parents worked as educators for 25 years, but spent her childhood summers in these North Carolina mountains. A graduate of Georgetown University, in international studies and languages, she began her career in Berlin, Germany, and then in Russia. In Moscow she first worked for ABC News, then reported for *Time* magazine, *LIFE*, *People*, and Time-Life Books. She also wrote for *Moscow* magazine, the *Moscow Times*, the *London Daily Telegraph*, *Sports Illustrated*, *Fortune*, and *Conde Nast Traveler*. Back in the United States she continued to contribute to *Time*, *People*, Reuters News Agency, the *New York Times*, *Washington Flyer* magazine, *GO* magazine, *Southern Living,* and others. She authored *Artful Asheville—Along the Urban Trail*, *Creative Giftwraps*, *Making Books and Journals*, and co-authored *Bloom's Literary Places: St. Petersburg*. She has been an arts columnist, culinary writer, and is contributing editor for *WNC* magazine. When not writing, she is a fine-art curator for galleries and private collections.

Kenneth L. Richards entered the Big Ivy Community of Buncombe County in Western North Carolina in the early 1960s. He and his wife, Irene Dillingham Richards, were married in Switzerland after first meeting in London. Irene is from Dillingham, North Carolina, in the Big Ivy Community. Living in Europe for 25 years they were involved with international education in Europe. They have worked as school administrators, university teachers, authors, wine masters, conference organizers, and lecturers throughout Europe. They also published the journal *Education World*. Ken has written about wine, food, and opera for numerous European and American publications. He was director of education at Biltmore Estate and is considered by former *Asheville Citizen-Times* entertainment editor Tony Kiss to be "Asheville's Bon Vivant." He is former North Carolina State Coordinator for Sister Cities International and is a popular lecturer and tour guide.

Acknowledgments

Thank you to the publishers of *Insiders' Guide* for choosing me all those years ago to continue the journey of this book. It is what kept me Stateside and sent me on a new life's journey of my own. A very special thank you and much love to my parents, Irene Dillingham Richards and Ken Richards, for instilling in me a love of travel at a very young age, as well as an understanding that all places can be delightful and interesting if you just look. Turns out, I'm a Mountain Girl after all! Thank you to my colleagues at *WNC magazine*, who have been partners in my discoveries around North Carolina's mountains, particularly in the culinary arts world. Eternal love to my late husband, international sculptor and painter Vadim Bora, who adopted these mountains as his own, becoming a son of the Appalachians as he was of the Caucasus.

—Constance E. Richards

We all have a story to tell. By way of *Insiders' Guide* we share ours welcoming you to these ancient Appalachian Mountains of Western North Carolina. It's our wish to make you feel at home by following our suggestions of places to stay, restaurants, enjoying the great outdoors, and attractions. Thus adventure and comfort can be found in the largest city in the area, Asheville, as it can in one of the classic towns such as, Loafers Glory and far reaching Murphy, NC. This glimpse of the adventure awaiting you will assist you to see it with your own eyes. My thanks go to all those who have shared with me the best of what we offer you, our guests. So a tip of the hat and thanks to our colleagues from Biltmore Estate, Grove Park Inn, Chimney Rock Park, Eastern Band of the Cherokee, motor coach companies, travel connections and the multitude of restaurants, B&B's, and Chambers of Commerce throughout the area. And especially to the many guests we have hosted over the years, a huge thank you and welcome.

I must always be grateful to my coauthor, my daughter, Constance, for sharing this opportunity. She has given me a "Father's Day" for life. And to my wife, Irene, in addition to all you are, you opened the world and the people of these mountains to me. In proofing all I do, you live up to your legacy of being my "refiner." I love you both.

—Kenneth L. Richards

How to Use This Book

High adventure unites with the serenity of the majestic Appalachians in North Carolina's mountains. This might be reason enough to journey into the ancient land of the Cherokee, yet what draws people to these mountains again and again is manifold. Nature, tradition, and culture merge in a beautiful display of mountain living in this westernmost part of the state.

You will often see us refer to this area as Western North Carolina. The WNC moniker refers to the mountainous part of the state and is used interchangeably, actually more so, as a regional identifier in the state. Because the book covers such a large area (there are more than 70 towns with populations over 10,000) we have divided Western North Carolina into the following three sections: the Northern Mountains, Central Mountains, and Southern Mountains. While counties aren't usually important to travelers, they are a major *local* identifier, and where needed, we've listed the counties alphabetically. Under those county headings, we've put most listings in alphabetical order, but we also highlight some of the larger towns as starting points for your journey.

Asheville is the largest city (and growing) in Western North Carolina, with some 92,000 in population. Thus, much of the book concentrates on the Asheville area, which has been a tourist draw for over a century, and certainly at an all-time high at this point in time.

Naturally, a good place to begin this book is with the **Welcome** chapter. From there you can jump around to subjects that specifically interest you. The area is growing so quickly, it's often hard to keep up with openings and closings

Asheville at dusk. ExploreAsheville.com

of business, so here you'll find a guide with historical and practical information and entries of tried-and-true places, events, and activities that we recommend. For the most up-to-date local listings for events, opening hours, and such, be sure to consult hyper-local websites, as well as local newspapers and freebie magazines for up-to-the-minute listings.

Speaking of relocation, are you moving to the Western North Carolina region or just arrived? Be sure to check out the blue-tabbed pages at the back of the book, where you will find the **Living Here** appendix that offers information on relocation and retirement.

We've included maps so you can orient yourself to each region. Just FYI, the *town* of Cherokee is on the Cherokee Indian "Reservation" (the Qualla Boundary, actually) in the northwestern part of the state in Jackson and Swain Counties, while the *county* of Cherokee is some miles away in the far reaches of southwest North Carolina (its county seat is Murphy). They are two entirely separate entities.

Up front, we've provided area maps to help you get your bearings here in Western North Carolina. We give you brief vital statistics, Insiders' Tips (indicated by 🛈), information that is particularly interesting, unusual, and distinctly Western North Carolina. In "Close-up" boxes throughout this *Insiders' Guide* we point out scenic views and feature places, local lore, personalities, and other insider knowledge in greater depth.

You'll also find listings accompanied by the symbol ⭐ —these are our top picks for attractions, dining, accommodations, and everything in between that you shouldn't miss while you're in the area. You want the best this region has to offer? Go with our Insiders' Choice.

With population movements, new roads and highways, development, relocating industries, and other factors of a transient world, change is evident everywhere. Nothing stays the same but the great and rugged peaks of this oldest mountain range in the world.

ExploreAsheville.com

WELCOME TO **North Carolina's Mountains**

Join us on a journey through mossy coves and hollows, over wildflower-studded pasture lands and dewy forest trails, past gurgling mountain streams and mellifluous waterfalls, into the green valleys and onto the misty blue ridges that comprise this glorious mountain range. Too much? Well you'll be waxing poetic as soon as you experience this nature in its fullest. This is the land of the Cherokee. These Appalachians are the oldest mountains in the world (one of which is the highest mountain in the US east of the Mississippi —Mount Mitchell, elevation 6,684 feet) and one of the oldest rivers in the world (ironically, named the New River) runs right through them. Magnates and entrepreneurs, artists and writers, seekers and dreamers have been drawn to join those who were born here, to swell our population centers into exciting, humming places of culture and growth.

In this chapter we offer "thumbnail sketches" of the area's counties and their largest population centers (noted in parenthesis) as well as notable towns nearby. We'll also give you a rundown on the best way to get here, and how to get around!

NORTHERN MOUNTAINS

Alleghany County (Sparta)

Tucked up against the border of Virginia is rural **Alleghany County**, the northernmost of North Carolina's mountain counties. Only 230 square miles, Alleghany is one of the smallest counties in the state. It was once known as "the lost province," and for good reason, because it can only be reached by winding two-lane roads. Snow is not uncommon here, but the elevation, which ranges from 2,500 to 4,000 feet, does not sustain the winter sports more common in neighboring counties.

The geographic remoteness of this county is more a blessing than a hindrance, for Alleghany County's natural isolation has preserved the rural America of more than 40 years ago. The pace is gentler in this small county of some 11,000 residents. Many in Alleghany County still live on family land that has been handed down for generations. And in tiny **Sparta**, the county seat with a population under 2,000, Main Street is not just a location but an atmosphere.

Seven percent of the county's labor force works in agriculture-related businesses, such as tobacco, beef cattle, corn, and hay. Christmas tree production is the fastest growing farm industry in the county. Economic development continues in Alleghany County, especially with the improvement of the county's roads.

Just a few minutes to the east is the **Blue Ridge Parkway**, which had its historical beginning in 1935 at nearby Cumberland Knob and forms some 30 miles of the eastern boundary of the county. A little farther south on the Parkway is Doughton Park, with its network of hiking trails and camping facilities. The easily accessible New River, well known among canoeing enthusiasts, provides easy and inexpensive opportunities for outdoor recreation. For more information contact the Alleghany County Chamber of Commerce, 58 South Main St., Sparta, NC 28675; (336) 372-5473; sparta-nc.com.

Christmas Tree Country

Western North Carolina is Christmas tree country. Families have been farming Christmas trees here for generations. The Fraser fir is a dark green color and one of the most desirable trees on the market. Even heavy ornaments can be hung from its strong boughs. The silvery undersides of the soft needles are pleasant to the touch, and the tree retains them throughout the holiday season. The white pine is also an excellent Christmas tree. The White House has called upon North Carolina mountain tree farmers for its official tree at least nine times.

Ashe County (Jefferson)

Ashe County, the extreme northwestern mountain county bordered by Tennessee and Virginia, is marked by the curling length of the New River, one of this country's few north-flowing rivers. The New River's pervasive presence in Ashe is responsible for much of the unique character of this remote North Carolina county. The county is named after Thomas Jefferson, and only a mile from the separately incorporated town of **West Jefferson**. A combination of Christmas tree farms, golf, and tourism add continued growth to this rural area. Ashe's pristine landscape and less-complicated lifestyle also attract not only visitors, but also retirees.

The prominence of the New River in Ashe County and New River State Park make canoeing and camping popular activities in the area. Mount Jefferson, at an altitude of 4,683 feet, rises majestically out of a 474-acre state park, filled with easy-to-moderate hiking trails abundant with wildflowers. A cave near the top of the mountain is said to have sheltered runaway slaves during the Civil War. The Churches of the Frescoes in West Jefferson and Glendale Springs have gained national attention and bring visitors to the remote hilltops of Ashe County.

State parks provide plenty of opportunities to get outside and enjoy nature.
ExploreAsheville.com

With only 10 percent of the county population of 27,000 living in the towns of **Jefferson** and West Jefferson, Ashe County is still largely rural. Villages cluster at crossroads, and individual farms crown the hillsides. Its proximity to bustling Boone, just 30 minutes away, makes Ashe County an appealing destination for the city person with a country heart.

For more information contact the Ashe County Chamber of Commerce, 1 N. Jefferson Ave., West Jefferson, NC 28694; (888) 343-2743; ashechamber .com.

> **i** You can see three states from Mount Jefferson in Ashe County. This vantage point is especially breathtaking at sunset. Take US Highway 221 from Jefferson, turning onto SR 1152, and drive all the way to the top to the parking area. The Summit Trail is just a fraction of a mile from the highest point on Mount Jefferson.

Avery County (Banner Elk)

Avery County, with a population of roughly 17,500 today, is a curious mix of peaceful rural life and sophisticated tourism. This high mountain land is harsh in winter, but its clear air and cool summer temperatures attracted tourists as early as the 1870s. Many visitors have returned for generations and maintain beautiful second homes in the exclusive areas of Grandfather Mountain, Elk River, and Linville Ridge. **Banner Elk**, home of Lees-McRae College and the famous Woolly Worm Festival, is also a popular skiing and golf resort community. Beech Mountain, the mile-high winter sport community, straddles Avery and neighboring Watauga Counties. These two communities are the more populated, tourism-driven parts of Avery County, while outlying areas of rural farmland continue much as they were early in the century.

The county has a strong tradition in crafts, ranging from pottery and quilts to jewelry and furniture. Today Avery County also boasts the South's highest ski slopes, nine major golf resorts (public and private), and a number of natural landmarks. The only notable changes in the rural landscape of Avery County in a half-century, perhaps, are the geometric patterns of green that cover the hills around Linville, a sign of Avery County's successful Christmas tree industry, in which over 900 families are active. For more information contact the Avery County Chamber of Commerce, 4501 Tynecastle Hwy., Banner Elk, NC 28604, (828) 898-5605, averycounty.com; or the Beech Mountain Chamber of Commerce at (828) 387-9283, beechmtnchamber.com.

"Tar Heels"

The "Old North State" is self-descriptive. "Tar Heels" is another matter. Some versions have the term birthed during the Revolutionary War at the battle of King's Mountain. Others claim that it derives from the tar pits found in the eastern part of the state.

Those in Western North Carolina give credit to Zeb Vance, who claimed that his North Carolina troops had "stick-to-itiveness" during the War Between the States. He once chided Virginians of the Grand Army, saying that if they had had "Tar on your heels, you would have stuck yesterday in the fight, instead of running."

Madison County (Mars Hill)

The rugged terrain of this western county, bisected by the powerful French Broad River, reflects the self-reliant spirit of the local folk and their industrious predecessors. **Madison County** lies northwest of Buncombe County, bordered by Haywood and Yancey Counties and the state of Tennessee. Formed in 1851 from parts of Buncombe and Yancey Counties, Madison County is named for America's fourth president, James Madison. The county is largely rural and has a population of about 22,000, with 48 percent of that population living on farms (the highest percentage in the state). Small towns in the area are Mars Hill, Hot Springs, and Marshall, the county seat.

Agriculture—wheat, cattle, corn, and tobacco farming—is still the primary source of income here, but some small manufacturing has also moved into the county. In the last 25 years, an increasing number of artisans and craftspeople have made Madison County home, finding the solitude of the county's heavily wooded mountains conducive to their work. After 11 years of planning and construction, I-26 opened a corridor through Madison County in 2003, connecting South Carolina to the Ohio Valley.

Mars Hill, the county's largest town, lies 20 minutes northwest of Asheville. As the home of Baptist-affiliated Mars Hill University, it is defined both by its scholastic roots and by the rugged individualism of Madison County's heritage. Attractive old brick storefronts face Main Street, a two-lane artery so narrow you could almost jump over it. Being a college town, the ubiquitous coffeehouse, pizza joint, and diner also compose the tidy downtown. Mars Hill is home to the Rural Life Museum and the Southern Appalachian Repertory Theater, and there is skiing nearby at Wolf Laurel. Still, this town remains a charming old-fashioned hamlet that is kept dynamic by the presence of the university.

Marshall, about 15 minutes west of Mars Hill, straddles the narrow hillsides cut by the French Broad River. Established around 1851, this town is much as it was at the turn of the 20th century. The river has seen to that. Its ebb and flow, and frequent overflows, seem to have suspended the city in time—this is Marshall's charm. Homes hug the hillsides surrounding the town. The cupola-topped courthouse, designed by Richard Sharp Smith of Biltmore Estate fame, commands a position at a crossroads within walking distance of the river. Marshall's arts community is also thriving, with artisans moving to the area and setting up home studios, often participating in downtown art markets.

As early as the 1830s, **Hot Springs** was host to wealthy visitors in search of the healing powers of its springs. A number of hotels, taverns, and boardinghouses sprang up, only to fade away in later years. Well . . . they're ba-ack! Today the town is experiencing a revival as travelers, day-trippers, and hikers hot off the Appalachian Trail do their laundry, load up on groceries, and soak in the reinvigorating Hot Springs Spa fed by natural warm mineral springs (see our **Attractions** chapter). Easy access to the French Broad River makes whitewater rafting an important part of the town's tourist economy.

For more information contact the Madison County Visitor Center, 56 S. Main St., Mars Hill, NC 28754; (828) 680-9031, (877) 262-3476; visit madisoncounty.com.

Mitchell County (Spruce Pine)

Mitchell County was formed in 1861 from portions of five counties: Yancey, Burke, Caldwell, McDowell, and Watauga. With a population of some 15,000 today, this county of only 220 square miles was named in honor of Dr. Elisha

Mitchell, explorer of famed Mount Mitchell, the highest peak east of the Mississippi. The county is bordered by Tennessee and Avery, Yancey, and McDowell Counties. Mining of quartz, feldspar (used in the famous cleaning powder Bon Ami), and mica are major industries here. In fact the Spruce Pine Mining District is recognized the world over for its ultra-pure quartz, which is vital to the computer industry. Agricultural products such as tobacco, corn, apples, and more recently Christmas trees are also important in the county.

Spruce Pine is the largest town in the county with a population close to 2,100. **Bakersville**, the county seat, is surrounded by the long-established communities of Rock Creek, Cane Creek, Mine Creek, and Toe Cane. These tiny towns, nestled in the twisting mountain coves of Mitchell County, are home to generations of families. The proliferation of gem mines in Mitchell County has long made this county popular with rock hounds. The North Carolina Museum of Minerals is just off the Blue Ridge Parkway. Mitchell County is also home to the Penland School of Crafts. Sitting atop a mountain ridge, this internationally acclaimed school of the arts draws talented craftspeople and artists from all over the world.

For more information contact the Mitchell County Chamber of Commerce, 11 Crystal St., Spruce Pine, NC 28777; (828) 765-9033; mitchellcounty chamber.org.

Watauga County (Boone)

This county of 55,000 lies at the heart of North Carolina's high country. Formed in 1849, Watauga's 320 square miles are bordered by Tennessee and Avery, Ashe, Wilkes, and Caldwell Counties. It was named for the Watauga River, which rises near Grandfather Mountain and flows north into Tennessee, where it converges with the Holston River. Watauga is an Indian word for "beautiful water."

The county was largely rural until 1899, when the Dougherty brothers founded the Watauga Academy in Boone, the forerunner of Appalachian State University. Part of the University of North Carolina system, ASU plays an important role in the growth of the area, with thriving Boone, the county seat, at its heart. Boone's permanent resident population of 19,200 doubles with the addition of the students and swells even more with the arrival of tourists throughout the year. The cultural base of the university and the town's tourist-geared entertainment offer something for everyone. Boone has become a magnet for tourism and related industries. Its many restaurants, for example, have turned the city into a dining destination. The climate is suited for both winter and summer sports, with golf and skiing the prime diversions in the county.

Blowing Rock, 15 minutes south of Boone, is a picturesque mountain town perched on a ridge overlooking the John's River Gorge. The town takes its name from the rock formation over the gorge that creates an unusual current of air spiraling up from the valley below. The view from the Blowing Rock is breathtaking, as is the scenery from nearly every vantage point in town. Charming specialty stores and fine restaurants line Main Street, and excellent bed-and-breakfast inns are scattered along Blowing Rock's side streets, just a few steps from downtown. You can walk to almost everything here, including the town square, which is the scene of concerts and art shows in summer.

Foscoe, on Highway 105 leading into Boone, has become known for its selection of craft and antiques shops. The community is blessed with a glorious view of Grandfather Mountain in nearby Avery County. Valle Crucis, in central Watauga County, is also off Highway 105 at the junction of Dutch Creek and the Watauga River. Established as an Episcopal mission in 1842, it retains a largely rural character and has become a popular site for summer homes, unique restaurants, renowned inns, and unusual shopping. Despite the busy pace of the tourist meccas, **Watauga County** offers plenty of quiet countryside. Heading toward Tennessee you can see some of the most scenic farmland in Western North Carolina. US Highway 321 winds up, down, and around hillsides studded with craggy rocks and threaded with lazy, meandering creeks.

For more information contact the Boone Area Chamber of Commerce and Convention & Visitors Bureau, 870 W. King St., Boone, NC 28607, (828) 264-2225, visitboonenc.com; High Country Host, (828) 264-1299, highcountryhost.com; or Blowing Rock Chamber of Commerce, 132 Park Ave., Blowing Rock 28605, (828) 295-7851, blowingrocknc.com.

Yancey County (Burnsville)

The county's largest community and county seat, **Burnsville** is anchored by a classic town square with a statue in honor of its namesake, Captain Otway Burns, a privateer during the War of 1812 and also a member of the North Carolina General Assembly. Life in the town still revolves around the square, and homes are nestled on the mountains rising on one side. A visit to coastal North Carolina in Beaufort will reveal many legends about Otway Burns; he is also buried there.

Agriculture—tobacco, corn, dairy products, and cultivated berries—still plays a vital part in the county's economy, as it did in pioneer times. Mining has always been important here: The excavation of mica and feldspar and sand and gravel operations are found in the northern part of **Yancey County**, near Mitchell County. The county has a population of just under 18,000.

The rich traditional local arts heritage has always drawn creative people, nurtured by the support of the dynamic Toe River Arts Council. The oldest summer stock playhouse in North Carolina—over 50 years old—is located in Burnsville, too.

Yancey County is blessed with seasonal changes and a topography that lends itself to outdoor recreation. The presence of the South Toe and Cane Rivers makes camping, tubing, canoeing, and kayaking easily accessible. The nearby Nolichucky River, flowing into Tennessee, is extremely popular with white-water enthusiasts. Over 100 miles of trails of varying degrees of difficulty, make this area a hiker's dream. The Black Mountain Range in Yancey County features Mount Mitchell, at 6,684 feet the highest peak east of the Mississippi. You can reach this majestic peak from the Blue Ridge Parkway, which runs the length of Western North Carolina's mountains.

For more information contact the Yancey County Chamber of Commerce, 106 West Main St., Burnsville, NC 28714; (828) 682-7413, (800) 948-1632; yanceychamber.com, exploreburnsville.com.

> **i** Mount Mitchell in Yancey County is the highest peak in the eastern United States at 6,684 feet. Take Highway 128, off the Blue Ridge Parkway at milepost 355.4. On a clear day the observation tower at the top of the mountain affords a 70-mile view.

CENTRAL MOUNTAINS

Buncombe County (Asheville)

Sitting high on a plateau surrounded by mountains, **Buncombe County**, population an estimated 258,000, has enjoyed a history of good fortune due to its position as a geographical crossroads. Today's appeal and growth of Asheville and its suburbs echoes the original boomtown era of the late 1880s. You can't say **Asheville** (the county seat) without noting in the same breath "Biltmore," the largest private home in America that George Vanderbilt constructed as such a visitor in the late 1800s. Today this palatial estate (including gardens and a winery) draws over 1 million visitors a year through its gates.

Asheville's growth has swelled its population by 20,000 in just under 20 years, to 92,000. It was numbered second in a list of the most quickly gentrifying towns in the US after Charleston, SC, in a 2017 realtor.com article. Nashville, Austin, Portland, and Denver all came in the top-10 after Asheville.

That small-town mountain charm wrapped in big-city sophistication has not gone unnoticed by national and international travel media, which frequently include Asheville in top-10 listings and feature the town as a premier travel destination. And it is! We've got it all—great dining, a thriving art and craft community, happening nightlife, performing arts, an exciting downtown with shops, cafes, condos, hotels, bookstores, breweries (and growing), distilleries, farmer's markets, music venues—and all this just minutes away from hiking and biking trails, splendorous waterfalls, camping, and other magic from the natural world. Much of the growth has been fueled by the influx of beer tourism. Don't laugh! With Asheville's 33 craft breweries, national heavyweights

Take a bike tour around the Biltmore Estate.

New Belgium and Sierra Nevada made Asheville and nearby Mills River their East Coast headquarters, with massive compounds that contain the breweries, bottling and barreling facilities, tasting rooms, restaurants, performance spaces, and other features that give them a large footprint here.

Top chefs, many of which are James Beard nominees, flock to Asheville to open eateries or collaborate on projects. The new Chow Chow, a wine and food festival being organized by culinary industry heavyweights in town, has its inaugural run in 2019.

Other parts of Asheville are changing, too. The River Arts District—a series of old warehouses turned into artist studios—has gotten fresh coats of paint, way-finding signs, new traffic patterns—basically a shiny new veneer thanks to a city development plan for that area. It's still gritty and authentic, but changes are afoot.

Nearby, the French Broad River divides **West Asheville** from downtown,. Before being incorporated into the city of Asheville, West Asheville was very much its own town. Haywood Road, the main thoroughfare there, is reminiscent of mid-century America, with appliance shops, barbers, mechanics, green grocers, churches and schools. A revitalization of the area today mingles those entities with bakeries, tea rooms, dive bars, restaurants, music clubs, and coffee shops. You'll find secondhand shops near an old-fashioned pharmacy, gas and a few remaining old storefront offices. A vacuum repair shop just made way for a hip new cocktail bar, and there's no turning back now.

And not only is Asheville thriving, but also the smaller towns nearby. With rising real estate prices, people are moving farther out of the city limits to charming small towns like **Weaverville**, mere minutes away, but with a relaxed hipster-meets-hippy-meets-soccer mom vibe cloaked in an old-fashioned Main Street exterior. Want to build a homestead? Leicester, Haw Creek, Alexander— all these "suburbs" just west, east, and north of Asheville, respectively, have small neighborhoods, homes on large plots of land, as well as sizable chunks for farmland. South Asheville is the county's fastest growing section of ready-made neighborhoods, townhomes and planned community shopping commons.

But no matter where you are in Asheville and its suburbs, it gives peace of mind to know that the French Broad River, Pisgah National Forest, and the Blue Ridge Parkway are just a short drive away.

For more information contact the Asheville Visitors Center, 36 Mont-ford Ave., Asheville NC, 28801, (828) 258-6129, exploreasheville.com; or the Black Mountain-Swannanoa Chamber of Commerce, (828) 669-2300, (800) 669-2301, exploreblackmountain.com.

Henderson County (Hendersonville)

From almost any place you happen to be in **Henderson County**, you can see mountains, yet much of the land consists of rolling hills. There are also marshes here similar to those in the lowlands, and some of the rich river valleys are surprisingly flat. That's because the county rests on a high plateau between the Blue Ridge and the Great Smoky Mountains. Elevations here range from 5,000 feet on Little Pisgah Mountain down to 1,400 feet at Bat Cave. This translates into fantastic hiking. Henderson is also apple country. Approximately a million trees—a sight to behold during spring bloom—make the county the largest apple producer in the state and seventh in the nation. This glorious harvest is celebrated each September with a three-day Apple Festival, the largest and most popular of the many annual events held in Henderson County.

Hendersonville, the prosperous county seat, sits at an altitude of 2,200 feet, almost smack-dab in the middle of the county. This bustling and ever-growing little city, with its beautifully-landscaped downtown area, charming shops, and culinary boom, is just off I-26 and is actually closer to the Asheville Airport than Asheville is. Also, the Flat Rock Playhouse (North Carolina's state theater) brings culture in the form of musicals, riveting dramas, and brilliant comedies.

In the 20th century a number of well-known personalities visited or estab-lished homes in Henderson County, including **F. Scott Fitzgerald**, Buffalo Bob and Howdy Doody, and **Carl Sandburg**. The Sandburg home in Flat Rock is now a National Historic Site open to the public. Such part-time residents almost double the population of this area each summer. Today Henderson County has nearly 115,799 full-time residents. Hendersonville proper has a population of nearly 14,000, with approximately 30,000 in the Greater Hendersonville area.

Henderson County's economy is a diverse mix of light manufacturing, tourism, agriculture, and retirement. The county goes out of its way to fulfill the needs of its many senior citizens.

The drive through apple country is dramatic for reasons other than spring apple blossoms and the fall harvest. Just down the road from the center of fruit production at **Edneyville** (about 8 miles from Hendersonville), you'll cross the crest of the Blue Ridge. Then, for the next 5 miles or so, the highway takes a precipitous dive through perpendicular peaks to Bat Cave and Hickory Nut Gorge. It's a quick reminder that Henderson is, indeed, very much in the mountains.

For more information contact the Hendersonville Visitors Information Center, 201 South Main St., Hendersonville, NC 28793; (828) 693-9708; visithendersonvillenc.org.

Polk County (Tryon)

This is horse country. **Polk County**'s 234 square miles lie within the Blue Ridge foothills. The western edge, the area that's covered in this book, is mountainous. Saluda, with a population of approximately 600, is on the county's western border at an elevation of 2,095 feet. It sits at the top of the steepest standard-gauge railroad grade in the eastern United States, known as the Saluda Grade. It's a small and winsome village that has long been a vacation and retirement spot and is home to quite a few artists and craftspeople.

Columbus and **Tryon** are "twin towns," separated by I-26, which goes northwest to Hendersonville and Asheville and southeast to Spartanburg and Charleston. It also connects at this point to US Highway 74, which is a four-lane highway to Charlotte. Columbus, sitting at an elevation of 1,131 feet, is the smaller of the two towns. Its population is only around 1,000. It is the county seat amidst the township, which has a population of 4,000. The town is now a mix of late-19th-century homes, buildings, and churches, combined with condominiums, a modern hospital, a high school, and a college campus. The county population is now approaching 20,500.

Neighboring Tryon has a population of 1,600 full-time residents, more than half of whom moved here from some other part of the country. Tryon's original attraction was its climate, and for years the sick came here to improve their health. There's a well-publicized weather phenomenon in this area of the mountains known as the isothermal belt, or thermal belt, which provides a more equitable climate than other areas in the region. Caused by inversions of warm air, particularly in the spring and fall, this mini-climate enables apple growers in the region to produce abundant crops, and grapes and peaches thrive in the botanically rich Tryon area.

In this storybook town, you'll find a number of charming antiques and gift shops and other family-owned businesses. The Tryon Theater on Trade Street was originally a 1920s vaudeville theater that now shows first-run movies and occasionally hosts theatrical performances. A bronze sculpture of famed songstress (and Civil Rights movement icon) **Nina Simone** makes note that she was born here. The modest clapboard home where she was born was named a National Treasure by the National Trust for Historic Preservation, and plans are underway to fully restore her home.

Today the Tryon area is well known to horse lovers all over the nation for its large equestrian estates, steeplechases, fox hunts, and miles of bridle trails. In 2018 the new Tryon International Equestrian Center (tryon.coth.com) opened in nearby Mills Spring, NC. It hosted the prestigious World Equestrian Games that year.

For more information contact the Carolina Foothills Chamber of Commerce, 2753 Lynn Rd., Ste. A, Tryon, NC 28782; (828) 859-6236; carolina foothillschamber.com.

Transylvania County (Brevard)

This county, with a population of 33,900, has the distinction of being the only one in America called Transylvania. The name naturally leaves the residents open to some teasing about vampires and makes for wonderful T-shirt slogans and Halloween festivals. However, the name, which comes from the Latin for "across the mountains/woodlands," is more than appropriate because 80 percent of this fair county's 378 square miles are covered by forests, almost half of which are managed by the US Forest Service. Elevations in the county range from 1,020 feet at Horsepasture to 6,025 feet on Chestnut Ridge.

One of the most popular entrances to **Pisgah National Forest**, with all its beauty and recreational possibilities, is just outside **Brevard**, the county seat. From this entrance the two-lane US Highway 276 climbs 16 miles to the Blue Ridge Parkway. Along that route you'll pass such alluring attractions as Looking Glass Falls, the Fish Hatchery, Sliding Rock (a natural water slide), and the Cradle of Forestry. (See our chapters on **Arts and Culture**, and **Forests, Parks, and Waterfalls**.)

The county has more than 150 large waterfalls, hence its nickname, "The Land of Waterfalls." It could also be called "The Land of Music" because, in addition to the music of falling waters, rivers, and more than 200 miles of streams, it's the home of the international Brevard Music Festival. Also, Brevard College, a liberal arts institution within the town limits, is known for its fine music department, and the college hosts numerous events in all the arts. This creativity is contagious: Performing groups, artists, writers, and talented craftspeople contribute to the area's cultural milieu of art and music festivals, film festivals, craft shows, and other events that are an accepted part of daily life here.

Transylvania County itself wasn't established until May 20, 1861—the same day North Carolina seceded from the Union—when it was carved out of an eastern section of Henderson County and a western part of Jackson

County. Brevard, Transylvania's county seat, was incorporated in 1868 with only 70 residents and seven registered voters. The town was named after Dr. Ephraim Brevard, a physician and the author of the Mecklenburg Declaration of Independence, which preceded the national Declaration of Independence by a year. Brevard's first post office was in the Red House, which is now a bed-and-breakfast inn. From those humble beginnings, Brevard, with a population of nearly 8,000 full-time residents, has blossomed into a lovely flower of a town, known also for its abundance of summer camps nearby. A five-lane connector to I-26 and the Asheville Airport, less than 20 miles away, make it an easy trek to Transylvania's other small municipalities of Rosman and Lake Toxaway, as well.

For more information contact the Brevard/Transylvania Visitors Center Chamber of Commerce, 175 East Main St., Brevard, NC 28712; (828) 884-8900; explorebrevard.com.

SOUTHERN MOUNTAINS

Cherokee County (Murphy)

Cherokee County, the westernmost county in this region, is bordered by both Georgia and Tennessee, with **Murphy**, its county seat, only 20 minutes from either state and just a two-hour drive from either Chattanooga or Atlanta. It's a rural county of fertile river valleys lined with glorious mountain ridges. One of the most beautiful is the 10-mile-long, 2-mile-wide Valley River Valley, with the Snowbird Mountains soaring on one side and the Valley River Mountains on the other. Cherokee County's other small municipality, **Andrews**, lies near the head of this valley. Both it and Murphy are surrounded by the **Nantahala National Forest**, which takes up 92,363 acres of the county's 300,100 acres, offering facilities for all kinds of outdoor recreation, including off-road vehicle trails. (See our **Forests, Parks, and Waterfalls** and **Recreation** chapters for more on the Nantahala.) Another 37,000 acres are under the control of the Tennessee Valley Authority. This includes the 22-mile-long Lake Hiwassee and its connecting and much smaller Appalachia Lake, which together cut diagonally across the center of the county. They were created when the Hiwassee River was dammed in 1936 for both electricity and flood control, providing the county with a source of water-based recreation.

The first of Cherokee County's four ill-fated courthouses, a brick structure built in Murphy in 1844, was burned in a raid near the end of the Civil War. A second was torn down and replaced; two more burned. Understandably concerned citizens, and especially the local lawyers, urged that the next courthouse be "as totally fireproof as possible." So the fifth—a very beautiful structure— was built in 1927 of a regal blue marble found only in the Valley River Valley. You can visit the town of **Marble** (home of the blue marble) on Highway 141.

In 1891 the Southern Railroad reached Murphy from Asheville, and a logging boom began. Not much remains from the pioneer and antebellum days of 1838 to 1870, but Cherokee County has a substantial number of buildings and homes dating from the prosperous era that began in the 1880s. You can see examples of Greek Revival, Federal, Neoclassical, Victorian, and Queen Anne architecture here, and the residents have taken great pains to preserve this heritage. You'll also find an even larger slice of history preserved in the interesting Cherokee County Museum next to the courthouse. The cultural preservation and influence of the John C. Campbell Folk School at Brasstown on the line between Cherokee and Clay Counties can't be overestimated. Many festivals and fairs also take place in the region, including an old wagon train tradition, which is a highlight of the Fourth of July celebration in Andrews. Notoriously, this is also the area where Eric Robert Rudolph, one of the FBI's "10 Most Wanted," hid out for five years and was subsequently apprehended in the town of Murphy, by rookie officer Jeff Postell, in 2003.

We think you'll love this rural and remote, but far from isolated, county. For more information contact the Cherokee County Visitor Center, 20 Tennessee St., Murphy, NC 28906; (828) 557-0602; visitcherokeecountync.com.

Clay County (Hayesville)

This county in the southwestern-most corner of the state is as uncluttered and unpolluted a place as can exist on this planet today while being two hours, more or less, from Atlanta, Chattanooga, and Asheville. Stretched along its southern border, you'll find beautiful, mountain-encircled Lake Chatuge and its 132-mile shoreline. It's called the crown jewel of the Tennessee Valley Authority's (TVA's) many lakes because of its lovely setting. The lake, which North Carolina shares with Georgia, is not only pretty to look at. It's also a prime area for fishing and other water sports. The county, with a population of 11,000, has 65,650 acres of federal land, 43,400 of which make up part of the Nantahala National Forest, including the Fires Creek Bear Sanctuary in the high mountains of the northeastern corner of the county.

Much of **Clay County** is at an altitude of 1,900 feet, but peaks here can soar as high as 5,400 feet. Even up into this century, Clay was an isolated area. It didn't become a county until 1861, when it was separated from Cherokee County. Its first industry, in fact, was a tanning company that sold its tanned deer hides at 12.5 cents per pound. Local folk used the hides to make shoes because there was no market where they could buy footwear.

Hayesville was named after state representative George Hayes, who had helped establish the new county.

No place reflects the spirit of Clay County's magical preservation better than the John C. Campbell Folk School at **Brasstown**. Both the school and Brasstown straddle the Cherokee-Clay county line and both counties claim it.

This homegrown, do-it-yourself spirit is obvious in other areas of life here, such as the Mountain Valley Farmers' Market, which takes place every Sat of the growing season from 7 to 11 a.m. on the square in Hayesville. Everything sold at this market is guaranteed to be homegrown or handmade, including vegetables, flowers, eggs, herbs, honey, ornamentals, baked goods, and crafts. It's also alive in the many festivals held on the town square.

For more information contact the Clay County Chamber of Commerce, 96 Sanderson St., Hayesville, NC 28904; (828) 389-3704; claycounty chambernc.com.

Graham County (Robbinsville)

There are sections of any county in Western North Carolina that can be called "rugged," but in 1872, when this area became a county, it was described by early explorers as "the most rugged, isolated, inaccessible land in all Eastern America." This 274-square-mile county is literally walled off by the Snowbird Mountains, the Cheoah Range, the Yellow Creek Mountains, and the western range of the Great Smoky Mountains, called the Unicoi. Elevations in the county range from 1,777 feet to approximately 5,560 feet at the western end of the county, which adjoins eastern Tennessee.

Graham County, with a population of 8,000, is at the southwestern boundary of the **Great Smoky Mountains National Park**. Approximately 60 percent of the county is in the Nantahala National Forest, including the 3,800-acre Joyce Kilmer Memorial Forest of virgin timber. Here you'll find trees that are hundreds of years old and grow 150 feet tall. Some are 20 feet in circumference at their bases. This memorial forest is a part of the 14,000-acre Joyce Kilmer–Slickrock Wilderness Area, which offers more than 60 miles of wilderness hiking trails. A 27-mile portion of the Appalachian Trail also crosses Graham County.

In addition to other wildlife, the woods here are famous for their "Rooshians," German wild boars that were mistakenly thought to be from Russia. An English company that planned to establish a high-priced hunting preserve in the mountains shipped them, along with other exotic game, to America. The preserve was a failure. The boars escaped, multiplied, and are still hunted here and in other sections of the mountains where they are notorious for rooting up the native habitat. Graham also contains more than 100 miles of clear mountain streams and 14,000 acres of lakes, including the fjord-like Calderwood and Cheoah Lakes, 2,800-acre Lake Santeetlah, and 30-mile-long Lake Fontana. On the last you'll find Fontana Village, a former town for the workers who built Fontana Dam in the early 1940s, now a large and lovely resort.

Now a number of excellent highways enter the area from south, east, and north. Graham County's borders are 79 miles from Knoxville, Tennessee, and 88 miles from Asheville.

For more information contact Graham County Travel and Tourism Authority, 474 Rodney Orr Bypass, Robbinsville, NC 28771; (828) 479-3790), (800) 479-3790; grahamcountytravel.com.

Haywood County (Waynesville)

No one knows exactly when the first European settlers moved into the area that now makes up **Haywood County**, but some came more than 200 years ago, lending their names to many of the geographic points of interest here, such as Mary Gray Mountain. Others whose names stuck to the areas that they settled—Allens Creek, Francis Cove, Stamey Cove, and Ratcliffe Cove—have descendants whose names help fill the Haywood County phone book today.

Today Haywood County has approximately 61,000 residents and consists of 546 square miles of craggy mountains, rolling foothills, and deep valleys. The county is surrounded by the Great Smokies on the north, the Newfound Mountain Range on the east, the Pisgah Ridge on the south, and the Balsam Mountain Range on the west. Elevations range from 1,400 feet at Waterville on the Pigeon River to 6,621 feet on top of Mount Guyot. Nineteen peaks in the county are higher than 6,000 feet. The most noted is 6,030-foot Cold Mountain, the star of Charles Frazier's best-selling novel, *Cold Mountain*. Almost 40 percent of land is under the protection of the National Forest Service (Pisgah National Forest) and the National Park Service (24 miles of the Blue Ridge Parkway run through the county).

I-40 and a number of other highways, including US Highway 19, US Highway 23, and US Highway 276, serve the county seat of **Waynesville**, 27 miles from Asheville. Haywood has three other incorporated towns: Canton, Clyde, and Maggie Valley. Waynesville is one of the county's oldest towns, established in 1809 as a voting precinct in an area that had been called Mount Prospect. When the county courthouse and jail were built here in 1810, the town's name was changed to Waynesville. A charming, arty town with its pretty Main Street, Waynesville is perched on top of a small plateau and has striking views in all directions. It has a population of nearly 10,000 full-time residents.

One of North Carolina's top 20 annual events is "Folkmoot," founded and hosted in Waynesville. This international extravaganza features the nations of the world every July with two weeks of street dances and performances conducted in Waynesville and throughout the mountains. (See our chapter on **Festivals and Annual Events**.)

Canton is the next largest town, with a population of 4,200. Nearby Lake Logan is the site of the Boy Scouts of America Daniel Boone Council Camp, the Episcopal diocese, Lake Logan Episcopal Center, and the National Forest Service. Of the other two municipalities, **Clyde**, the home of the excellent Haywood Community College, has a population of 1,189; and **Maggie Valley**, named for the young daughter of its first postmaster, has just 354 people. However don't let Maggie Valley's small size fool you. This popular resort town

7 miles west of Waynesville draws thousands of visitors with its many attractions, music, and dancing at the Stompin' Ground and the Cataloochee Ski Area, North Carolina's oldest ski resort.

For more information contact Visit NC Smokies Visitor Center, 1110 Soco Rd., Maggie Valley, NC 28751; (828) 926-1686, (800) 334-9036; visit ncsmokies.com.

Jackson County (Sylva)

Jackson County has a growing population of more than 43,000. Here the Blue Ridge Mountains, with their dramatically shattered and steep rock faces, roll in long, forested ridges toward the southwest. Elevations in the county range from 1,850 to 6,450 feet, with many 5,000-foot summits, and cool, high valleys that sit at 3,000 to 4,000 feet. Rainfall and waterfalls are abundant in the region and, along with the 28,000 acres of national forests, lend a lush beauty to the landscape.

Three of them—Sylva, Dillsboro, and Webster—are incorporated and three others—Cashiers, Cullowhee, and Whittier—are not.

Sylva, at 2,039 feet in the northwestern section of the county, has more than 2,000 full-time residents. Most of the area's businesses and industries are here. The courthouse, which is reached by climbing 107 steps, was built in 1914 when the county seat was moved to Sylva. From its hilltop vantage point, the courthouse overlooks the river and the bustling town that stretches down two long streets. Sylva is the county seat.

A mile away, **Dillsboro**, founded in 1884, has a population of only 270 but its 50 or more shops have become home to the works of hundreds of artists and craftspeople. Thousands of visitors come here to ride the Great Smoky Mountains Railroad's excursion trains and to shop and spend time in this pretty and creative place. (The GSM Railroad operates out of Bryson City only.)

Webster, the former county seat and the site of a number of historic homes, has a population of 385. The town was built on an Indian mound, and the surrounding area offers sweeping views of the Tuckasegee River.

Cullowhee, situated in the scenic Tuckasegee River basin and surrounded by mountains, forests, and streams, is the home of Western Carolina University. With a new performing arts and fine art museum and galleries, it is the center of arts and culture in the county. The university also has the **Mountain Heritage Center**, with its museum and programs that preserve and promote this region's unique heritage. The annual Mountain Heritage Day, a festival of traditional music, crafts, food, and fun that attracts thousands, is also held in Cullowhee.

Whittier lies at Jackson County's lowest elevation, 1,839 feet, in farming country on the border of Swain County. Dr. Clark Whittier of California, a relative of the Quaker poet John Greenleaf Whittier, established it. Nearby is the site of the Cherokee town of Stikohi or Stecoee, destroyed in 1776 in a preemptive strike after the Cherokee sided with the British at the beginning of the Revolutionary War. Later Col. William H. Thomas, white chief and friend of the Cherokee, established his home here and used treaty funds to buy land that became the Qualla Boundary, the home of the Eastern Band of Cherokee.

The town of **Cashiers** sits high up in a mountain valley at an elevation of 3,478 feet, not far from spectacular Whiteside Mountain, whose sheer rock faces are the highest vertical drops in the east. Right outside town, you'll find the historic High Hampton Inn, which maintains its old traditions and a fine golf course, currently being renovated until 2020. In the early 1900s several other inns were established in the area to serve Southern gentry escaping lowland heat and humidity. Many of these visitors ended up building summer homes, and the area has continued to attract vacationers and those who serve them. Nearby, for example, is Sapphire Valley, a huge community resort with all the amenities. Lake Glenville, right on the highway between Cashiers and Cullowhee—along with other small lakes in the Cashiers area—offers fishing, boating, canoeing, and other water sports.

For more information contact the Jackson County Chamber of Commerce, 773 West Main St., Sylva, NC 28779, (828) 586-2155 or (800) 962-1911, mountainlovers.com; and the Cashiers Chamber of Commerce & Visitor Center, 202 Highway 107 South, Cashiers, NC 28717, (828) 743-5191, cashiersareachamber.com

Macon County (Franklin)

Named after Nathaniel Macon, who served in the US Congress for 36 years, Macon County was formed in 1828. The land here is rich in minerals and gemstones. The large territory that made up the original county was later broken up eventually to form all or parts of Cherokee, Jackson, Clay, Swain, and Graham Counties. Macon now covers 517 square miles and has a full-time population of about 34,700, though vacationers and second-home owners more than double that number every summer.

The town of **Franklin**, with a permanent population of around 4,000, was named after Jesse Franklin, one of the men who surveyed the town in 1820 and became governor of North Carolina within the year. Franklin sits at the convergence of three major highways—US Highway 441, US Highway 64, and Highway 28—at an elevation of 2,800 feet. Elevations in Macon County overall range from 1,900 feet in the Little Tennessee River basin to 5,500 feet at Standing Indian Mountain.

Macon County's other town is **Highlands**, which sits atop a mountain plateau at 4,118 feet, making it the highest incorporated town east of the Mississippi. Driving the narrow, curving stretch of US 64 along the Cullasaja Gorge that connects the two towns is an adventure in itself and offers some of the mostphotographed waterfalls in the mountains, including Lower Cullasaja Falls, Bridal Veil Falls, and Dry Falls. Highlands was purposely created in 1875 by Samuel T. Kelsy and Clinton C. Hutchenson, who bought the land from the Dobson family of Horse Cove, a small community south of Highlands. A year later the two men sent flyers all over the country advertising the climate and altitude of the new "town," and by 1883 Highlands had 300 residents and was incorporated. Now its winter population hovers around 1,000, but that grows from 20,000 to 25,000 during the summer, not counting all the visitors who arrive to shop and take in the attractions of the surrounding area.

Where Franklin is rich in gemstones, Highlands is rich in botanical treasures. Macon County as a whole gets 50 inches of rain a year, but Highlands averages 70. This contributes to its unique plant life and led to the establishment of one of the oldest research centers in the country, the Highlands Biological Station, where scientists from all over the world study the area's flora and fauna. Highlands also has some of the most expensive real estate in the mountains.

Macon County loves its visitors, and tourism is its leading industry, but the county is not solely dependent on it. Forestry products, farming, and ranching are still a large part of the local economy, and managers of new, nonpolluting industries are finding that this is an area where business and outdoor pleasure can be easily combined.

For more information contact the Franklin Area Chamber of Commerce, 44 Georgia Rd., Franklin, NC 28734, (828) 369-9606, visitsmokies.org; and the Highlands Area Chamber of Commerce, 108 Main St. or PO Box 404, Highlands, NC 28741, (828) 526-2112, highlandschamber.org.

Swain County (Bryson City)

Swain County was created in 1871 out of parts of Jackson and Macon Counties and was named for David L. Swain, a former governor and president of the state university. The cabin in which he was born is in Asheville, incorporated in the Beaverdam Run condominium complex.

Eighty-five percent of the county's 553 square miles is federal land, which means it's mostly mountains, forests, streams, rivers, and wilderness. Yet this unspoiled, unhurried, unpolluted piece of paradise is just 60 miles from Asheville and 85 miles from Knoxville, Tennessee. The southern part of the Great Smoky Mountains National Park comprises 216,662 acres of the county; the Nantahala National Forest manages another 21,000 acres. And the Blue Ridge Parkway finally comes to an end—or originates, depending on which way you're traveling—in Swain County and takes up 709 acres of county land. In addition, 29,000 acres of the **Cherokee Indian Reservation**, including the town of Cherokee with its many diversions, is also within the county. The reservation is known as the "Qualla Boundary." The boundary begins in the north at Soco Gap, which connects into Maggie Valley. The town of Cherokee lies within that boundary. This includes the authentic Museum of the Cherokee and the Qualla Arts and Crafts Center. Leading from those centers are the directionals pointing the way to the outdoor theater where *Unto These Hills* drama is presented throughout the summer, and the 17th-century prototype of a living Cherokee village, Oconaluftee Village, stands.

The elevation at **Bryson City**, the county seat, is only about 1,800 feet, while just a dozen miles away, as the crow flies, the mountains soar to 6,643 feet at Clingmans Dome.

Some of the state's most scenic rivers—the Nantahala, Oconaluftee, and Tuckasegee—add their beauty and recreational possibilities to all the other attractions. The Nantahala River alone draws thousands of rafters and kayakers, and many white-water outfitters, including the well-known Nantahala Outdoor Center, are in or near Bryson City. Some great mountain biking trails in the area attract such events as Knobscorcher, one of the state's most popular series of mountain bike races. Fontana Lake stretches into the county just a few minutes west of Bryson City.

Bryson City, population 1,455, is a lively, attractive town on the banks of the Tuckasegee River, with parks both along the river and on its islands. It's a popular stop for passengers on the Great Smoky Mountains Railroad, which offers train excursions through the area. As if that weren't enough, annual river festivals, high-school band competitions, chili cook-offs, and other celebrations are held throughout the year. Needless to say, if you like the outdoors, you're going to love it here, because the 14,300 full-time Swain County residents have quick access to some of the largest expanses of wilderness areas in the eastern United States.

What's in a Name?

The Cherokee referred to their mountain home here as *Sa-koh-na-gas*, which means "blue," after the mountains' blue haze, which is created when sunshine and warm, humid air combine with the hydrocarbons produced by the region's thick forests. This single word was later elaborated into "the great blue hills of God" and "land of the blue mists."

The Great Smoky Mountains, on the other hand, were named for the fog that forms as a result of the temperature differences between the air and the mountains' many water sources. This cloudlike mist curls up from valleys and mountain peaks like smoke from a fire, particularly in the early morning, around sunset, and after rains.

This blue mist and curling "smoke" are integral parts of the landscape of both the Great Smokies and the Blue Ridge Mountains, as well as all the lesser-known cross ridges, such as the Graham, Nantahala, Snowbird, Balsam, and New Found Mountains.

The Land of the Sky, a more recent description, was culled from the title of an 1876 romantic novel set in this tranquil region.

For more information contact the Swain County Visitor Center and History Museum, 255 Main St. or PO Box 509, Bryson City, NC 28713; (828) 488-7857; swainheritagemusuem.com; (800) 867-9246, (828) 488-3681, greatsmokies.com.

CLIMATE

Western North Carolina is also known as the Land of the Four Seasons for it is the long-lasting springs and autumns, plus mild winters and (increasingly hot!) summers, that have attracted tourists and new residents to the area for nearly two centuries.

Crocuses and daffodils start pushing up through the earth in late Feb, and the false spring that usually occurs around this time of the year can have you hiking or playing golf in your shirt sleeves. In Mar, tulip magnolias, yellow forsythia, and other early-spring flowers bravely brighten the landscape despite the real possibility of a late snowfall. By the end of Apr, dogwoods and silverbell trees are blooming everywhere. In May, mountainsides are afire with flame azaleas, and the dense thickets of several species of native rhododendrons begin their bloom bursts, a show that lasts right into July. May is also the time when a large portion of the mountains' spring wildflowers reaches its peak, including pink and white mountain laurels that coat the slopes and overhang roadways, rivers, and boulder-strewn creeks.

By June, summer greens up the region with all the lush, ferny beauty of a rain forest. Daytime temperatures are mostly in the 70s and 80s, but as summer plays out, a good month of heat and humidity requires air conditioners and electric fans, at least until a cooling thunderstorm comes along. Even then, by late evening the thermometer drops into the 70s, cooler still at higher elevations, and it's an extremely rare night when it could be considered too hot to sleep.

At any time you can find vast temperature differences by a quick change in elevation. For example, you can stretch spring by several weeks if you follow the bloom from the valleys to the tops of the mountains, and in the fall the color changes begin at the top elevation and slowly work their way downward. The first hints of the colorful autumn to come are seen tinting some of the leaves at higher elevations as early as late Aug. In Oct, visitors by the thousands arrive to enjoy the brilliant red, yellow, and gold foliage display (see our sidebar on autumn leaves in the **Blue Ridge Parkway** chapter).

By mid-Nov, the barren branches of deciduous trees give mountain ridges a crew-cut look, and previously unknown lodgings peer from their wooded perches enjoying "winter views." But, while nights may bring freezing temperatures, days can be pleasantly warm. It's usually not until Christmas that the first frigid Alberta clipper roars south out of Canada. On those occasions temperatures can plummet to zero or below for a short period of time, and from then until well into spring, short spurts of bitterly cold weather, along with occasional snow or ice storms, alternate with surprisingly pleasant winter days. In most places the average snowfall in a typical year is around one foot, and even heavy snows usually disappear in a matter of days.

> **i** Temperature changes are drastic in the mountains. Always take a sweater or jacket when driving from low altitudes to higher ones. We once experienced a sunny, warm day in downtown Asheville, which turned into a windy, icy hailstorm only 2,000 feet higher at a picnic area on the Blue Ridge Parkway.

Rain, on the other hand, is a year-round event. Slightly more falls in the summer than the winter. (Winter wet fronts, rising up from the Gulf of Mexico, actually warm things up.) In summer, rain often takes the form of sudden crashing late-afternoon and evening thunderstorms, sometimes with damaging winds and lightning. While such storms can spoil picnics and other outdoor activities, most residents enjoy these natural light-and-sound shows, knowing the mountains offer protection from destructive tornadoes and hurricanes found elsewhere.

On the average, rainfall totals from 40 to 55 inches per year, depending on the location. But in the rain belt, which includes a large part of Transylvania

Not even rain can dampen the spirits of visitors. DAVID HUFF CREATIVE

County and the southern sections of Jackson and Macon Counties, 80 inches or more can fall in a typical year. All that water has to go somewhere, and much of it tumbles off cliffs and down mountainsides. Transylvania, which dubs itself the Land of Waterfalls, has more than 150 of these splendid water shows. Even so, the county hasn't cornered the waterfall market. Cascades and waterfalls, some of which plunge hundreds of feet, can be found in abundance throughout the region. (See our **Forests, Parks, and Waterfalls** chapter.) So can springs, creeks, rivers, ponds, and lakes. In fact, homes with such water sources are almost more the rule than the exception, and real estate ads touting "bold streams" are common, even inside the boundaries of some towns.

Hazy Days

Some days the mountain vistas don't go on forever. Smog and haze are a growing concern in the Blue Ridge Mountains. Not only are views sometimes obscured by smog, but the pollution also poses a threat to people with asthma and other health concerns. The local newspapers and broadcast media give a daily "air quality" report with a scale that ranges from green to red. Those with respiratory concerns, the very young, the elderly, and pregnant women should stick to lower elevations and/or stay inside when levels reach high orange and red.

GETTING HERE, GETTING AROUND

A natural charm and mystery surrounds many parts of the North Carolina mountains, which are still considered to be fairly wild and remote. Over time, the paths traveled by bears, mountain lions, deer, bison, and elk became hunting trails for Native Americans. These trails became the dusty and muddy roads used by early settlers. As time flowed with the tides of progress, the roads became paved, curvy two-laners. Today, the magnificent highways of America bring travelers into these mountains on beautiful scenic drives. Not the least of these is the Blue Ridge Parkway. The Parkway winds its way southwest at an average elevation of 3,000 feet through the northern and central mountains, finally turning northwest in the southern mountains. It ends at Cherokee at the southern entrance to the Great Smoky Mountains National Park. Yet there's still a wealth of wilderness to be found. And within this wilderness you can access nature preserves, waterfalls, hiking trails, and the area's other attractions.

National and state highways now crisscross this ancient land of the Cherokees. Two busy interstate highways—I-40 and I-26—intersect in Asheville, and just an hour or so south, I-26 crosses I-85 at Spartanburg, South Carolina, on that interstate's busy leg between Atlanta and Charlotte.

Getting to many of the best hiking trails, the prettiest waterfalls, and some of the most beautiful areas of the woods can involve taking Forest Service (FS) or unpaved secondary roads (SR). Many of these are steep, curvy, narrow, graveled, and often one lane with only small pullouts to get around oncoming traffic. Passing is mostly impossible and certainly inadvisable. But, if your vehicle is in decent shape and its tank filled with gas, we encourage you to explore these adventuresome byways. It's also a good idea to stop by the closest ranger station (the numbers are listed in the **Forests, Parks, and Waterfalls** chapter) and ask about road conditions. Bad weather sometimes washes out whole sections of these roads or creates landslides.

The Asheville Regional Airport, adjacent to I-26 and strategically located between Asheville and Hendersonville, is connected to Brevard by a five-lane highway. The jetport located at the Asheville Regional Airport handles corporate and private air traffic. Some prefer to drive to Greenville-Spartanburg International Airport or Charlotte-Douglas International Airport.

When this wilderness first opened, few rail lines reached the region. Eventually the highest railroad point in the southeast was in North Carolina. Thomas Wolfe wrote of the nostalgia of hearing the train whistle at night. But alas, passenger trains into the mountains are now part of history. Today a number of railroads provide freight service to the mountains, and Amtrak serves nearby Greenville and Clemson, South Carolina, but rail passenger service in Western North Carolina is limited to a railroad excursion company, the Great Smoky Mountains Railroad. It is based in Bryson City, North Carolina (see our **Attractions** chapter).

Driving in the Mountains

While airports and interstate highways make arriving in the North Carolina mountains extremely easy, you'll be taking other highways and byways in order to enjoy all the scenery and attractions this region offers. Driving in the mountains can require patience, but it's usually not the kind demanded by bumper-to-bumper traffic jams. In many areas you'll have the roads mostly to yourself, yet you may need to allow double the time it would normally take to drive a set distance. The very nature of these steep-graded, twisting roads demands slower speeds. The top speed allowed on the Blue Ridge Parkway, for example, is 45 miles per hour, and some hairpin curves, even on major routes, require that you slow down to 15 miles per hour. In addition, sudden weather changes can bring blinding fog or downpours. In winter, unexpected ice, snow, and freezing rain can bring travel to a dangerous crawl.

Another thing that can—and probably should—cut into your traveling time is the incredible scenery you'll encounter along the way. Smoky mist curling out of a deep valley, a sunset turning a lake to rosy pink, a waterfall cascading down a mountainside, a highway pull-off offering a green-dappled vista that stretches for miles will tempt you to stop for a look. For those who enjoy the journey as well as the destination, the North Carolina Scenic Byways project covers 1,600 miles of picturesque North Carolina back roads, free of man-made eyesores. Each route was chosen for its particular attractions, based on historic significance or natural beauty, such as waterfalls, rivers, or land formations.

> **i** The state maintains more than 77,000 miles of primary and secondary roads. North Carolina also has the largest state-maintained road system in the United States. North Carolina is commonly called the Good Roads State.

Here in the mountains of North Carolina, we are fortunate to have nine of these scenic byways, which cover 410 miles. You can identify the road you're traveling as a scenic byway from the distinctive white sign decorated with green mountains and blue waterways and the title NC SCENIC BYWAY emblazoned at the bottom. The North Carolina Department of Transportation has issued a helpful, 91-page guide booklet for the entire state system of scenic byways. You can get a copy at most North Carolina welcome centers and DOT offices or online at ncdot.com.

Most notably, be prepared to share our mountain roads with pedestrians, bicyclists, horseback riders, and a variety of wildlife. The last is particularly prevalent at night.

Here are a few other rules you should be aware of:

A new resident must apply for a driver's license within 30 days of moving here. Bring your out-of-state license, proof of insurance, and proof of residency to a driver's license office of the North Carolina Department of Motor Vehicles; you'll have to pass a written exam and an eye exam. Each county has a DMV office. Most offices are open from 8 a.m. to 5 p.m.; some close for lunch from noon to 1 p.m.

New residents also must register their vehicles and purchase license tags within 30 days. Vehicles must also be inspected within 10 days of the registration date.

The North Carolina Safe Roads Act forbids drivers to drink alcohol or to have an open container of an alcoholic beverage in the passenger area. All front seat passengers are required to wear seat belts. Children younger than four must ride in child safety seats. All children younger than 12 must wear seat belts. There is no longer an exemption for vehicles registered outside the state. Children younger than 12 may not ride in the open beds of pickup trucks except when an adult is present to supervise

Close-up

The Interstate 26 Connector

After 11 years of planning and building, I-26 now connects Charleston, South Carolina, with the Ohio Valley, and what a road it is! In addition to underpasses for wildlife, there are run-off ramps for runaway trucks with special traps for containing hazardous waste spillage. An automated spray, triggered to de-ice the bridge approaching notorious Sam's Gap, which peaks at the North Carolina–Tennessee line, has been built as a winter safety feature. Even monarch butterflies have been given special consideration with the development of a special preserve filled with their favorite flowers and milkweeds high above the interstate.

A unique visitor center offers comfort and assistance as well as a gallery of traditional crafts native to the region. The center has vast picnic areas and offers great scenery. Photo opportunities abound all the way from Asheville north through Tennessee.

This corridor connects directly with I-81 at Johnson City and provides access to the culturally rich town of Abingdon, Virginia, with its grandiose Martha Washington Hotel and the Abingdon Theatre.

Along the way on I-26 West, one encounters the university town of Mars Hill. Heading east on US Highway 19 just past Mars Hill, enter into Yancey County to the quaint town center of Burnsville, North Carolina. Located along US 19 are the historic Penland School of Craft, the town of Spruce Pine, and the Appalachian State University town of Boone.

the child, or the child is secured or restrained by an approved seat belt. The state requires that headlights be on whenever windshield wipers are on. Motorcyclists are required to wear helmets and use their headlights at all times. It is illegal to send text messages on a cell phone while driving in North Carolina.

> **i** If you're sightseeing at a leisurely pace, road etiquette asks that you pull over, when you can do so safely, and let those in a hurry pass by. The more popular mountain roads and highways actually have pull-off or passing zones.

Commercial Airports

Central Mountains

ASHEVILLE REGIONAL AIRPORT, 61 Terminal Dr., Fletcher, NC; (828) 684-2226; flyavl.com. Western North Carolina's only commercial air service is centrally located on Highway 280, just 15 miles south of Asheville, and is easily accessed from I-26. The airport is tourist friendly and not far from all the most popular vacation destinations. Hendersonville is 8 miles from the Asheville airport; Brevard only 20; Waynesville, 36; Sylva, 57; Cashiers, 58; and Highlands, 69. This airport is the fourth largest in the state. With frequent daily flights to major hubs (Atlanta, Charlotte, Chicago, Dallas, Philadelphia, Washington, DC), year-round service to New York (Newark), and seasonal service to Denver, New York (LaGuardia), Vero Beach, Florida, and the Washington, DC, area (Baltimore), as well as year-round service to these Florida destinations: Ft. Lauderdale, Orlando, Punta Gorda, Sarasota, St. Pete-Clearwater, and Tampa, Asheville Regional Airport is rated one of the best connected regional airports in America. New nonstop destinations are being added frequently. Allegiant, American, Delta, Elite, Spirit, and United serve the airport currently. Also on hand are four auto rental services: Hertz, Avis, Budget, and National. (Alternate airport transfer services are listed at the end of this chapter.)

Plenty of short and long-term spaces, a cafeteria, bar, restaurant, sundries and newspaper/ magazine shop, and lounge provide a pleasant seating area for those seeking sustenance. An art gallery features rotating exhibitions by local artists. The latest addition to the airport is the pop-up concert series, in partnership with Ashvegas.com, providing local musicians of various genres in concert.

> **i** A special photo exhibit of World War I and II airmen from Asheville is located at the Asheville Airport. Among the many photos is one of Kiffin Rockwell, ace of World War I. A character playing his role was in the early film Layette Escadrille. Also among the photos is that of Robert Morgan, World War II pilot of the B-17 Memphis Belle fame. The story of that plane and crew was featured in both a book and a movie.

ASHEVILLE REGIONAL AIRPORT GROUND TRANSPORTATION, Airport Rd., Fletcher, NC; (828) 209-3660. Transportation from the airport can be contracted at the facility located in the baggage claim area. There is no taxi stand at the Asheville Regional Airport, although taxis are available. Most

Uber and Lyft-type companies currently provide services. (Other transportation systems are listed at the end of this chapter.)

General Aviation - Private Airports

Northern Mountains

ASHE COUNTY AIRPORT, 639 Airport Rd., Jefferson, NC; (336) 982-5144; airnav.com/airport/KGEV

> **i** If you plan to fly your own plane, it would be a good idea to call the airports at which you intend to land and refuel. Smaller airports may not offer all the services to which you are accustomed.

AVERY COUNTY AIRPORT, 400 Brushy Creek Rd., Spruce Pine, NC; (828) 733-8200; airnav.com/airport/7A8

BOONE AIRPORT, 346 Bamboo Rd., Boone, NC; (828) 265-3598; airnav.com/airport/NC14

ELK RIVER AIRPORT, 643 Banner Elk Hwy., Banner Elk, NC; (828) 898-9791; airnav.com/airport/NC06

Central Mountains

HENDERSONVILLE AIRPORT, 1232 Shepherd St., Hendersonville, NC; (828) 693-1897; hendersonvilleairport.com

Southern Mountains

WESTERN CAROLINA REGIONAL AIRPORT, 5840 Airport Rd., Andrews, NC; (828) 321-5114, (404) 695-110 (after hours); westerncarolinaregional.us

JACKSON COUNTY AIRPORT, 626 Airport Rd., Sylva, NC; (828) 586-0321; airnav.com/airport/24A

MACON COUNTY AIRPORT, 1241 Airport Rd., Franklin, NC; (828) 524-5529; maconcountyairport.com

Bus Lines

Central Mountains

APPALACHIAN STATE UNIVERSITY, 168 Hardin St., Boone, NC; main:
(828) 268-0555, tickets: (828) 268-0555, (800) 231-2222; greyhound.com.
Located curbside at Phil's Citgo Service Station.

APPLE COUNTRY PUBLIC TRANSIT, 526 7th Ave. E., Hendersonville,
NC; (828) 698-8571; henderson.lib.nc.us/county/planning/actransit/main
.html. Transportation operates throughout the city of Hendersonville, town of
Fletcher, and Laurel Park with three bus routes running from 6:30 a.m. to 6:30
p.m., Mon through Fri. Routes originate from the transfer site located at the
corner of 4th and Grove Streets in downtown Hendersonville (next to the 1995
Henderson County Courthouse).

ASHEVILLE REDEFINES TRANSIT SYSTEM (ART), 49 Coxe Ave.,
Asheville, NC; (828) 253-5691; ashevillenc.gov/departments/transit. This
municipal agency provides service from 5:30 a.m. to 10:30 p.m. Mon through
Sat; and from 8:30 a.m. to 6:30 p.m. on Sun and holidays. The standard fare is
$1.The main terminal is beside the downtown post office on Coxe Avenue. For
real time information on your next bus, download the Transit app or Google
Maps, or dial the number above and press #1. It serves 49 stations in and
around Asheville.

GREYHOUND BUS LINE, 2 South Tunnel Rd., Asheville, NC; (800)
231-2222; greyhound.com. The Greyhound Bus Line is the only bus company providing long-range scheduled motor coach service from this area. The
Buncombe County terminal is located east of the tunnel that connects downtown Asheville to Tunnel Road. The Greyhound facilities provide passenger
and package service to all major US destinations. The terminal opens at 8 a.m.,
but closing times vary so call ahead.

Touring Companies

ACCENTS ON ASHEVILLE, 290 Macon Ave., Asheville, NC 28804; (828)
251-9013, (800) 627-1185; accentsonasheville.com. Provides guide and transportation services to local areas and beyond for larger groups. Services include
airport pickups, transporting groups from hotels throughout western North
Carolina, upstate South Carolina, and eastern Tennessee, and tours of historic
Asheville, Cherokee (Qualla), Great Smoky Mountain Railroad, mountains
artisan studios, and Biltmore Estate, plus white-water rafting. Featured tours
may be customized according to groups.

BREWS CRUISE, Asheville Brewing Company, 77 Coxe Ave., Asheville, NC; (828) 545-5181; brewscruise.com. Experience a behind-the-scenes glimpse of the glory of beer with visits to many of the area's famed breweries. The tasting and entertainment tour with experienced guides engage everyone to sample a wide variety of beers, understand the brewing process, the history of beer, and the way to taste and pair beer with food.

CAROLINA LIMOUSINE, 2019 Smoky Park Hwy., Asheville, NC; (828) 258-2526; wnctransportation.com. Provides first class limousine service in and around Western North Carolina since 1999. Offers a large fleet of luxury limousines, town cars, and stretch SUVs.

DILLINGHAM-RICHARDS INTERNATIONAL, INC., (private address) Asheville, NC; (828) 253-3943. Custom-tailored tours are led by Western North Carolina's premier historian, lecturer, tour guide, wine master, and author—Insiders' Guide's own Ken Richards.

ELITE LIMOUSINE, 3833 North Mills River Rd., Mills River, NC; (828) 890-2424; elite-limousine.com. Serving the Asheville area since 1992, the company has a fleet of vehicles ranging from motor coaches to stretch limos, Hummers, Lincoln Navigators, a party bus, a Rolls or two, Cadillac convertibles, and other snazzy rides for special occasions.

GRAY LINE TROLLEY TOURS, Asheville Visitor Center, 36 Montford Ave., Asheville, NC; (825) 251-8687, (866) 592-8687; graylineasheville.com. Enjoy a preview of the city with a "Hop-On/Hop-Off Trolley Tour," combining an informative and entertaining narration with the convenience of unlimited "hop-on/hop-off" privileges at several stops located along the tour route. The "Haunted History & Murder Mystery Ghost Tour" and the "Holly Jolly Christmas Trolley Tour" with live music and caroling round out the fun offerings with this company.

LAZOOM TOURS, 76 Biltmore Ave., Asheville, NC; (828) 225-6932; lazoomtours.com. The quirky 40-passenger purple art buses run a variety of themed tours through Asheville's downtown area and historic Montford. The wild, fun, and outrageous Comedy, Haunted, and Band and Beer Tours are not for the timid, and include acting, storytelling, singing, and some passenger participation. The sometimes rowdy and completely idiosyncratic tours begin and end at the LaZoom Room, where you can wait for your tour on velvet sofas with a drink.

PEGASUS AIRPORT LIMOUSINE, Asheville, NC; (828) 281-4600; pegasusairport.net. Pegasus has been servicing passengers for over 20 years,

LaZoom Comedy Bus Tours. David Huff Creative

> **i** You can park for free in many of WNC's small towns. Not so in Asheville. Parking at meters is strictly monitored (new meters feature credit card slots), and if time runs out on the meter where you're parked, you'll be slapped with a ticket. Also, parking in private business lots around town means almost certain towing. So save yourself a lot of headaches and inconvenience and park in one of the city garages centrally located downtown, or try some of the self-service private lots now set up, but be sure to monitor your time.

employing professional drivers for taxi, shuttle, or limousine service, ranging beyond the Asheville area to Charlotte/Douglas International Airport, Atlanta, Greenville/Spartanburg Airport, Knoxville, and Tri-Cities Airports.

SPECIAL OCCASIONS LIMOUSINE, Asheville, NC; (828) 681-2811, (888) 288-9915; specialoccasionslimo.com. Their motto is "Anywhere, Any Time" and they offer 24-hour service. Their variety of premium class vehicles ranges from sedans to vans, Black Car Service (black stretch limousines) to luxury stretch limousines.

WALKING TOURS OF HISTORIC ASHEVILLE, Asheville, NC; (828) 777-1014; history-at-hand.com. Explore the history of Asheville through its fascinating stories and architecture. There are three separate walking tours offered: Downtown Asheville, Historic Montford, Riverside Cemetery, and Family Store Tours. Learn about Asheville's vibrant Jewish community during the 1.5 hour Family Store Tour pointing out locations of some of the 400-plus Jewish businesses that supported the early economy of Asheville. All tours by appointment. Enhance your tour experience with a copy of *The Family Store: A History of Jewish Businesses in Downtown Asheville, 1880–1990.*

YOUNG TRANSPORTATION & TOURS, 843 Riverside Dr., Asheville, NC; (828) 258-0084; youngtransportation.com. Through the creativity of Ralph Young Sr., this company became "people-movers" by bolting theater seats to a truck and transporting folks from Western North Carolina to the Chicago Exhibition in the 1930s, during the Great Depression when money was scarce. Again in 1982, with the World's Fair just down the road in Knoxville, Tennessee, the Young fleet was enlarged to provide transportation. Today they have a large fleet of mini-coaches and highway coaches with seating for 22 to 55 passengers. They offer receptive tour services, shop services, charter tours, and executive vans. Step-on guides are also available.

History

If these silent sentinels of this ancient mountain chain could only speak we'd learn of the formation of the earth when they were higher than the Himalayas. In geologist-speak the Appalachians, within eons, will be river bottom when mountains such as the Rockies erode to half their current size.

These trails we hike, the roads we travel, and the cities and towns of Western North Carolina hide the first footsteps of the Paleo-Indians of more than 12,000 years ago. Within the last 2,000 years their descendants, the Cherokee, established their villages, fished these rivers, and hunted the land. They grew crops using this flora for foods and medicines.

The giant hardwoods of beech, iron wood, chestnut, hickory, ash, and others were painstakingly turned into huge canoes by burning out the core. Today, the descendants of this virgin timber can be found in a remote corner of Western North Carolina at the Joyce Kilmer Memorial Forest.

In due course the monarchies of Europe reached out for land expansion, searching for earth minerals and all the bounty of the land. Thus, by 1540 Hernando de Soto led his Spanish Conquistadors into the wilderness of what became the Carolinas.

Within the next century the French were working their way to the Atlantic from the Mississippi. When French explorers arrived, they renamed the Cherokee river whose name translated to "the long man" to the French Broad River. The Cherokee had also called the mountain streams "Chattering Children." In current times these streams are called "Raging Adolescents" due to the floods of 1916 and as recent as 2004 when the French Broad River, Swannanoa River, and others crested their banks to flood parts of Asheville and other communities.

North Carolina authors of note have captured the history of these early beginnings. The late author Wilma Dykeman's book, *The French Broad*, covers the history of the civilizations that developed along this longest river in Southeast United States. West Asheville's, John Ehle followed the government removal of the Cherokee to the Oklahoma Territory in 1838 in his tome *Trail of Tears*. The bestseller and eventual movie *Cold Mountain* by Asheville's Charles Frazer bring us into the War Between the States.

NATIVE TO THESE MOUNTAINS—THE CHEROKEE

Somewhere back in time, American Indians built a mound known as Nik-wa-si along the banks of the Little Tennessee River. A town council house was built on its top, and the lodges of the city were spread up and down the valley.

This site formed the government and spiritual center of the Middle Cherokee tribe. According to Cherokee tradition, the "Immortals" remain deep within the mound. They are the defenders of their people. A marker at the mound is now on East Main Street in Franklin, Macon's county seat.

In de Soto's search for gold here in 1540 his expedition totally overlooked the wealth of gemstones for which this area is now so famous. De Soto's visit, however, was relatively peaceful compared with what came later. In 1760 war broke out between the Cherokee and encroaching settlers, and the ancient town of Nik-wa-si was attacked by the British on several occasions and eventually destroyed. Finally, in the Treaty of 1815, the Cherokee gave up the land east of the Nantahala Mountains. Nantahala, meaning "land of the noonday sun," was so named by the Cherokee because only at midday does sunshine reach the bottom of the deep Nantahala Gorge.

This newly conquered territory became a part of Haywood County, and in 1817 Jacob Siler and William Britton journeyed from Buncombe County to set up a trading post, thus becoming the first white settlers in the area. They were not, however, the first to get to know it well. Botanist William Bartram had been hospitably received by the Cherokee during his stay at Nik-wa-si in 1777, and today's Bartram Trail, second in popularity only to the Appalachian Trail, actually passes through the city limits of Franklin.

Graham County was the home of Chief Junaluska, the Cherokee leader who saved Gen. Andrew Jackson's life in the Battle of Horseshoe Bend in the War of 1812. Ironically the same Andrew Jackson, as president of the United States, issued the order to round up and send the Cherokee to Oklahoma. Junaluska walked all the way back to North Carolina from that territory and was ultimately successful in his struggle to keep the remaining Cherokee people in the mountains, thus maintaining the Eastern Band of the Cherokee. He was more than 100 years old when he died. His grave is in Robbinsville (population 750), Graham's quaint county seat. The first road into Graham County was built in 1838 for the specific purpose of removing the Cherokee from their native land.

The prehistoric hieroglyphics made by ancient Native Americans who long predate the Cherokee on Judaculla Rock, between Cashiers and Cullowhee, give mute evidence that the area has attracted humans throughout the ages. However, it wasn't until 1828 that the first white settlers moved into the area. Yet by 1850 there were enough people in this broad depression between two mountain ranges drained by the Tuckasegee River to warrant a new county. Both Haywood and Macon Counties consented to part with some territory to form a new one. The county stretches between the Balsam and Cowee Mountains and runs from the top of the Blue Ridge on the south to the Great Smoky Mountains in the north. In today's Swain County, the town of Cherokee and the Qualla Boundry (what our Cherokee Indian Reservation is also called), you can visit a restored Oconaluftee Indian Village of the 17th century, walk through Cherokee history in the Museum of the Cherokee, and during summer months be overwhelmed by the outdoor drama of the Cherokee, "Unto these Hills."

THE SCOTS AND ENGLISH ARRIVE

We know that the English arrived in New Amsterdam replacing the Dutch rule with that of England and renaming that area New York. King Charles II of England claimed these colonies as belonging to England. Among them was the colony of Carolina as derived from the Latin name *Carolus*, translated as "Charles." The state was named in honor of King Charles I and King Charles II of England, as the Cherokee first found themselves allying with the English, and eventually the colonists, when the early wars of the nation ensued.

One such battle was at Horse Shoe Bend in Alabama when Gen. Andrew Jackson would not have brought down the British fort had it not been for Chief Junaluska and his Cherokee braves who stormed the fort from the swamp land in the rear and thrust open the gates for Jackson to advance and capture the fort.

As Western North Carolina was divided into counties, the area of the Cherokee became part of Jackson County, named after General Jackson who had become president of the United States. The Cherokee nation blends into Swain County named after the Asheville pioneer, Swain, who eventually became the governor of the state and president of the University of North Carolina.

History has recorded the rugged individualism of Andrew Jackson. One such story was following his inauguration as President of the United States. The celebration accompanied by many barrels of whiskey and rough-shod celebrants came close to burning down the White House.

The Western North Carolina story goes like this: Waightstill Avery was a lawyer in peacetime. In one heated debate with Andrew Jackson, these two combatants elected to settle their differences with a duel. A quirk of the law in North Carolina read that one could make a challenge, but the duel could not be fought within the boundaries of the state. So at sunrise on the selected morning, the men met on the field of valor in Jonesborough, Tennessee, just over the state line. Even stranger, neither wished to harm the other. Thus they fired their dueling pistols into the air, shook hands, and had a beaker of whiskey to celebrate their newborn friendship. Jackson even offered a gift to Avery. The whole problem had arisen from the so-called Bacon Law. Wrapped like a book, the package contained a slab of bacon. And that's how NC's Avery County earned its name.

In late September one can join the reenactors who begin their trek through the Orchard just off the Blue Ridge Parkway near McKinney Gap. It was here that the mountain men gathered for their one week march south to Kings Mountain on the North and South Carolina border, to confront the British

Army commanded by Lord Cornwallis. His plan was to bring his troops south from New Jersey and New York, and his troops north from Charleston to catch the colonist in a vice and burn them out, hanging all those who remained. The plan was foiled when British Major Patrick Ferguson was surprised at Kings Mountain by this ragtag army of colonists. Being defeated in that battle at King's Mountain the following day, Ferguson rallied his troops in the Battle at Cow Pens in SC where they suffered another defeat and Ferguson lost his life.

In 1809 Haywood County was formed from a section of Buncombe and named for John Haywood, North Carolina's state treasurer from 1787 to 1827. Because the Cherokee moved west of the Tuckasegee River after the Revolutionary War, the new county was made up of 2,500 white residents. Land grants were given to numerous English, Scotch-Irish, German, and Dutch settlers. Waynesville is this county's seat.

ARTS AND EDUCATION

As recent as the mid-20th century many communities in North Carolina's mountains were somewhat isolated for lack of modern roads and the decline of rail passenger service to these remote areas. It was the railroads that opened these mountains for economic reasons supporting mining and logging.

The Scots brought with them Calvinism and the Presbyterian Church. They established visiting teachers, mostly women missionaries. Thus one-room school houses proliferated. One such missionary teacher was known as "Kristy." Her daughter was Catherine Marshall, who wrote books and a movie about her mother's experiences. Catherine Marshall was the wife of Washington, DC, Presbyterian minister Peter Marshall. She also wrote books about Marshall when he was the chaplain to the United States Senate. She regularly spent her summers at the Presbyterian established community of Montreat, NC. Today it is a township, has a conference center, and is home to Montreat College. This coed four-year college began as a grammar school for girls.

In 1890 when Yale graduate Frances Goodrich moved to Buncombe County to do missionary work for the Presbyterian Church, she located women weaving traditional coverlets, scarves, and blankets. She gave the women work, creating a cottage industry that would help mountain families financially. She founded the Allanstand Cottage Industries in 1897 in Madison County, and it would later become Allanstand Craft Shop. Goodrich moved the business into downtown Asheville in 1908. Eventually the Southern Highland Craft Guild developed from Allanstand, which became a leader of the Southern Arts and Crafts movement.

Founded in 1929 by Lucy Morgan, Penland School was originally an outgrowth of a craft-based economic development project she had started several years earlier. Bishop Junius Horner, director of the Episcopalian Appalachian School, supported her efforts. Thus, the British brought with them to the mountains the Church of England, American Episcopal of the Transfiguration, which supported this crafts program in the northern mountains.

In 1859 Mars Hill College was founded by supporters of the Baptist Church. Joe Anderson was a slave in Mars Hill. Anderson, his wife and his children were owned by J.W. Anderson, one of the founders of Mars Hill College (now Mars Hill University).

The price of $1,100 was owed to a financial group in Asheville. Three years later, the formative college had not paid its debt. Whatever the case, in 1859, a sheriff from Buncombe County rode north to collect. The debt had to be paid, if not in money, in property. Thus, the slave Joe Anderson was taken as collateral for the financial burdens of the college, shackled, and led off to the prison. Oral tradition relates that the board of trustees had five days to come up with the $1,100 before Anderson would be sold to a new owner. J.W. Anderson raised the money so he wouldn't be sold off. Following the Civil War, Joe became a free man. At 17, Oralene Simmons of Asheville was the first African-American to attend Mars Hill University. That was in 1961. Oralene was Joe Anderson's great-great-granddaughter.

THE BUNCOMBE TURNPIKE AND BEYOND

Trade with the Cherokee Indians was established as early as 1673 along the well-worn Indian paths that crossed at the site of present-day Asheville. The natural riches of the region and the flow of commerce soon drew large numbers of settlers. Samuel W. Davidson and his family were the first to settle in the region in 1784, along Christian Creek in the Swannanoa Valley. Trade continued to boom, and the county was officially formed in 1791. The business of government brought in scores of new settlers, traders, speculators, and adventurers. With this influx of new citizens, the well-traveled Indian paths soon became thoroughfares for traders and stock drovers from Kentucky and Tennessee moving through the French Broad Valley on their way to the open markets in South Carolina. The construction of the Buncombe Turnpike from 1824 to 1828 further secured this steady stream of trade.

From the early 1800s to 1880, Buncombe County settled into a period of bucolic bliss. Recovery from the Civil War was slow, and it was not until completion of the railroad in 1880 that the county came into its own. The railroads brought the moneyed class, which was attracted to the healthful climate, crisp mountain air, and sparkling social atmosphere. One young visitor, George Vanderbilt, vowed to return, and when he did he changed the county forever. After purchasing 125,000 acres, he set about building a castle. The construction of his Biltmore Estate in 1895 brought a legion of artists and craftspeople whose legacy remains as an influence on the area's architecture.

By the close of the 1800's Asheville had become a beehive of activity as the land bridge of this massive Asheville Plateau, which connected the Blue Ridge

Mountains sweeping down from Virginia and the south Great Smokies of the Appalachian chain. The city became the playground of the wealthy who rode their luxurious private train cars from the North to overwinter in the warmer climate, and from the South and coastal regions, to cool off in the summer. Some visitors stayed and became the castle builders. Today more than a million visitors arrive annually to visit George Vanderbilt's private home, Biltmore. Two other castles still stand today overlooking Asheville. They, too, are privately owned, as is Biltmore, but not open to the public.

Asheville was dubbed "Land of the Sky" and "Paris of the South". Realtors set up shop and advertised widely. The investors came and a building boom was created. A wealthy pharmacist and businessman, E.W. Grove, arrived from Paris, Tennessee, and in 1913 opened his grand hotel, the Grove Park Inn (today owned by Omni).

In his 1928 novel, *Look Homeward Angel*, Asheville author Thomas Wolfe wrote of the many sanatoriums established by world-famous doctors in his literary city of Altamont. And indeed, Asheville was encircled with clinics, hospitals, and research centers.

The 1920s were Buncombe County's boom time. The architectural character of Asheville was formed during these glory days, giving it the unique cosmopolitan flavor that continues to attract visitors as well as new residents. Not only barons and wealthy socialites were coming to the mountains, though. Artists, writers, and philosophers also found a home here.

Black Mountain is often referred to as "The Front Porch of Western North Carolina." Throughout the community you will find decorated rocking chairs that celebrate the region's beauty and history. ExploreAsheville.com

Close-up

Historical Place Names of Western North Carolina

- **Smoky Mountains** is derived from the Cherokee word "Shaconage" (*Sha-Kon-O-Hey*), which means "land of the blue smoke."
- **Buncombe County**, the largest county in Western North Carolina, was named after Revolutionary War Col. Edward Buncombe. Its county seat is in Asheville. Congressman from Buncombe Felix Walker established the legend of the name to symbolize, "buncombe" or "bunk," i.e. foolish talk, when he filibustered congress with nonsensical diatribe.
- **Asheville**, established in 1797, was named after then governor Samuel Ashe.

Twenty miles east of Asheville, Black Mountain (which had been established in 1893 as a quaint summer resort town originally known as Grey Eagle) attracted visitors looking for relief from the heat of the low country. But then, avant-garde Black Mountain College opened and operated from 1933 to 1956 as an experimental place of higher education. It attracted artists, teachers, and thinkers of renown, many of whom were refugees from Nazi Germany. Josef and Anni Albers, Cy Twombly, Robert Rauschenburg, John Cage, and Buckminster Fuller were only some of the recognizable names that made this area their home for a time. A museum capturing the school's glory is located in downtown Asheville.

The boomtown excitement of this modern age couldn't last, though, and it didn't with the financial crash ushering in the Great Depression. The city was heavily in debt but vowed to pay off all it owed. This commitment was fulfilled when Mayor Eugene Oxenrider burned all the paid bills in a public ceremony in 1975. Therefore, many of Asheville's old buildings were never razed for building new mid-century modern "masterpieces" and today, downtown Asheville boasts the finest collection of art deco buildings this side of Miami Beach.

Asheville and the towns within two hours' drive of the largest city in the NC mountains, continue to grow, prosper, and experience a contemporary "boom" all over again. As you read along, you'll find the history of these mountains and communities invariably tied to its present. The inscription on one of the great boulders at the Grove Park Inn on Sunset Mountain says it all: "SO LATE YOU CAME; SO SOON YOU MUST LEAVE; BUT COME BACK YOU MUST; AGAIN AND AGAIN . . . AND STAY!"

Funny Town Names

The origins of other delightfully named hamlets such as Loafer's Glory, Relief, Ledger, Bandana, and Altapass are worthy of note. Loafer's Glory, about 3 miles north of Bakersville on Highway 226, was christened by the wives of the community after they observed the unabashed loitering of their men on the front porch of the community store. Relief is named for a once-popular cure-all tonic, Dr. Hart's Relief, which was sold in the community at Squire Peterson's Store around 1870. No doubt the popularity of the tonic came from the large volume of alcohol it contained.

The community of Ledger was named for the ledger book sent to Washington, DC, by community residents who were trying to establish the amount of mail passing through the area and their need for a local post office.

The railroad played a part in naming two Mitchell County hamlets: Bandana got its name from the bandana a railroad brakeman used to locate a proper site for a railroad station. The Clinchfield Railroad, passing over these mountains from Tennessee, reached its highest point at the aptly named community of Altapass before heading down the mountain.

Accommodations

Where to stay? Resorts have been a part of this region for as long as some of the towns have been here. Which came first, then—resorts or towns? For instance, the town of Cashiers in the Southern Mountains developed around the High Hampton Inn. Another example is the Eseeola Lodge, which was built first, followed by the development of the town of Linville around it.

Besides boarding houses or travelers' inns at the crossroads of mountain trails, hotels began cropping up not just for the weary traveler, but also the moneyed classes traveling via railroad from the north and the south, taking in the curatorial airs and water of the mountains.

The first resorts were nowhere near as elaborate or elegant as some of the vacation spots we have now, but, just like today, they drew flocks of visitors seeking the relaxing and restorative beauty of the mountains.

The unique allures of Western North Carolina's mountains as a resort area are the same as they have been for more than a century: a mild, healthful climate with four distinct and equally lovely seasons, botanical diversity unmatched in America, rock-strewn rivers and streams that'll sing you to sleep, mountains older than time stretching out to forever, more unspoiled wild areas than you could ever explore, and people who take the time to be polite.

Some of us like the anonymity or pure convenience of an obscure roadside motel, but there are other times when real creature comfort and a bit of coddling would be more preferable. In fact, for many, it's the only way to travel. North Carolina's mountains are blessed not only with natural beauty but with scores of charming and graceful inns. The establishments we recommend to you in this chapter are some of the finest examples of the bed-and-breakfast inns and country inns North Carolina's mountains have to offer. Some have lavish surroundings and interiors worthy of a museum estate, and some sport the more simple comforts of home. We've chosen each one—be it unique or traditional—because it offers the traveler a memorable stay. All are devoted to making your stay as pleasing as possible. We've given you the choice of large or small, elegant or rustic, in the heart of town or secluded in the countryside. Use this as a guide and strike out on your own to find out what's so special about Southern hospitality.

There are dozens of reasonably priced, family-owned motels and cabins in and around our towns, and all the big chain hotels are represented throughout the region at locations very convenient to our attractions.

Price Code

Most of the accommodations in this chapter will accept major credit cards. Rates are based on double occupancy.

$	less than $120
$$	$120 to $200
$$$	$200 to $300
$$$$	$300 and higher

RESORTS

Northern Mountains

Avery County

ESEEOLA LODGE, Linville Golf Club, 175 Linville Ave., Linville, NC; (800) 742-6717; eseeola.com; $$–$$$. Eseeola Lodge is noted as a Mobil Four Star resort for its tradition of excellence. It is "hunting-lodge" rustic on the outside, adorned with great barked slabs of mighty chestnut, and "English manor" comfort on the inside, with a fireplace and sections for lounging. One wing of the room houses the cozy, well-stocked library. Leading on through the double doors is a great hall, adorned with flags depicting the states and countries of those holding membership in the Eseeola Golf Club. Pristine white tablecloths grace the tables in the dining hall where the staff is attentive from start to finish. In order to enjoy the full range of the talented chef, one needs to book an extended stay, as the menu changes daily.

Other available services include tennis courts, an outdoor heated swimming pool, croquet greensward, fully equipped exercise room, and, at this family-friendly resort, a children's playground and day camp. A day spa provides everything from massage and wellness packages to full salon hair and mani-pedi services.

The 18-hole championship golf course was designed by Donald Ross in 1924, and the Linville Golf Club has been recognized by *Golf* magazine as a silver medalist for Best Golf Resorts in America. Many golf legends have played on this award-winning course.

The course is open to members of the Linville Golf Club and to those staying at the Eseeola Lodge.

Watauga County

CHETOLA RESORT, North Main St., off US Hwy. 221, Blowing Rock, NC; (828) 295-5500, (800) 243-8652; chetola.com; $$–$$$$. Chetola is the Cherokee word for "haven of rest." This fine resort just outside Blowing Rock (off the Highway 321 bypass) has a long history. The estate was first purchased by Lot Estes back in 1846 for a mere $5. He called it Silver Lake. The property changed hands and served the next 50 years primarily as a way station for coach traffic. Then at the turn of the 20th century, as roads improved, the inn became a fashionable accommodation for lowlanders escaping the oppressive heat of the Deep South. One such lowlander, Alabama lumberman W. W. Stringfellow, fell in love with the High Country, purchased the Silver Lake property, renamed it "Chetola," and built the fine manor house that remains today. The property was sold once again, in 1924, to J. Luther Snyder, known as the "Coca-Cola King of the Carolinas." Snyder bought additional adjoining property and continued to improve the estate. He built houses on the property for his children and their families and added a swimming pool and bowling alley.

The marvelous manor house is now home to **Timberlake's Restaurant**, with a menu inspired by world-renowned North Carolina artist and designer Bob Timberlake's culinary favorites. The restaurant features three dining rooms, an intimate wine room, and waterfront dining on the patio. The charming and warmly outfitted Headwaters Pub is just inside Timberlake's main entrance. The Chetola Lodge and Conference Center includes spacious suites and professional meeting and conference space.

The resort offers a wide variety of diversions: boating on 7-acre Chetola Lake, hiking on the trails of Moses Cone Memorial Park just over the hill, cross-country skiing on the nearby Blue Ridge Parkway, and tennis on Chetola's courts. A full spa for relaxation treatments and beautification is steps away from the indoor pool and fitness center at Highlands Sports & Recreation Center at Chetola. Premier golf and skiing resorts are just minutes away in nearby Blowing Rock, Boone, and the Banner Elk area. You can fill your days and nights entirely with the luxury of Chetola.

WESTGLOW SPA, 2845 US 221 S., Blowing Rock, NC; (828) 295-4463, (800) 562-0807; westglow.com; $$$$. This year-round resort and European-style spa set in an elegant, historic plantation-style mansion looms large with significance to the area. This lovely Greek Revival mansion served as home to the artist and writer Elliott Daingerfield. Plush bedrooms and suites, luxurious Aqua di Parma bath accessories, the fabulous Rowland's dining experience, grand breakfasts, and charming evening wine and cheese meetings and music in the drawing room are among the many reasons to take respite here.

The spa's program includes a variety of treatments—body sloughing, aromatherapy, herbal body wraps, Parisian body polish, facials, foot reflexology, and body massage. Fitness programs are also a large part of the schedule. Weekly weight management programs that include nutrition and diet assessment are also offered. The "resting room" has some of the best views in the High Country, awash in neutral colors, a glass-enclosed fireplace, and contemporary art.

Choose from a day sampler to all-inclusive overnight stays. Rates vary according to the kind of treatment and length of stay.

Close-up

Crossnore Makes History

The mountain town of Crossnore, North Carolina, bears the name of its first postmaster. John Crossnore ran a general store where the post office was established. A name was needed for it and his was used.

This little town is located off US Highway 221, 8 miles south of Grandfather Mountain. The Crossnore Weavers and Gallery is a working museum. Profits from sales are used to support the Crossnore School.

It was in the early 1900s that Dr. Mary Martin Sloop arrived in the mountains and began to carve a legacy of hope for an impoverished but proud people. She fought against child marriages and moonshining. She revitalized the almost forgotten art of handweaving. With some help, she built the Crossnore School, a beacon of light in caring for children, and then in 1951 she was named American Mother of the Year. Dr. Sloop died in 1962 and is buried in the cemetery adjoining the Crossnore Presbyterian Church.

This complex is worth a visit. In addition to the Weavers Gallery, the Sloop Chapel is a beautiful edifice comprised of wormy chestnut paneling on the interior housed by rocks from the Linville River.

A Ben Long fresco, "Suffer the Little Children," personifies the mission of the Crossnore School. For more information, visit crossnoreschool.org.

YONAHLOSSEE RESORT & CLUB, 226 Oakley Green, Boone, NC; (828) 775-5018, yonahlosseeinnresort.com; $$$$. *Yonahlossee* is Cherokee for "trail of the bear." This former girls' camp with its spectacularly lush, secluded 300 acres is the perfect setting for outdoor activities for the entire family, yet it's very close to downtown Blowing Rock for in-town shopping and dining. Large viewing decks surround the seven clay tennis courts at the Racquet Club here. Bad weather doesn't stall tennis enthusiasts: Three indoor Deco-Turf courts with large climate-controlled viewing areas assure tennis play summer or winter, rain or shine.

You can also take advantage of the outdoors at Yonahlossee's small lake, an ideal place for canoeing, fishing, and swimming. Or swim inside in the lovely 75-foot indoor swimming pool. Other golf and ski areas are about 20 minutes in either direction.

Guests may stay in an intimate inn room, a cozy studio cottage, court-side condominium, or spacious townhomes. Private homes up to five bedrooms in size can accommodate larger groups. Each residence is unique and all of the

Blowing Rock resort rentals in Yonahlossee feature convenient paved access, especially helpful during winter weather.

The Gamekeeper Restaurant nearby has a tempting menu studded with exotic wild game dishes and other fine cuisine.

Central Mountains

Buncombe County

OMNI GROVE PARK INN RESORT & SPA, 290 Macon Ave., Asheville, NC; (828) 252-2711, (800) 438-5800; groveparkinn.com; $$$–$$$$. The Grove Park Inn is one of the premier landmarks of the city of Asheville. Kings, US presidents, inventors, golf legends, famous actors, and writers (Eleanor Roosevelt, Franklin Roosevelt, Harry Houdini, George Bush, Henry Ford, Thomas Edison, and Mikhail Baryshnikov, to mention a few) have all passed through the massive stone portico of the Grove Park Inn.

The inn, built in 1913 from tremendous boulders blasted out of nearby Sunset Mountain, was an engineering marvel and the personal vision of dynamic entrepreneur E. W. Grove, who invented Grove's Chill Tonic, a drink claiming to have "medicinal" value for many aches and pains. He came to Asheville during the city's turn-of-the-20th-century boom period, attracted by the natural beauty of the area and the city's possibilities. With the Grove Park Inn, E. W. Grove left not only an architectural legacy to the city of Asheville, but, by example, a spirit of business foresight and daring that continues to define the unique character of our small mountain city.

The Sammons Corporation acquired the Grove Park Inn in the 1950s, and the resulting growth and innovation spearheaded by this ownership developed two new wings. They were designed to maintain the architectural integrity of the original structure, dated between 1984 and 1988, culminating in a total of 513 guest rooms, including an adults-only club floor. It is now owned by Omni Hotels.

The inn is furnished with antique pieces from the Arts and Crafts style so popular in the early 1900s, in addition to the Omni contemporary touches. Soak in some grandeur in the Great Hall, dominated by fireplaces at either end measuring 6 feet deep, 6 feet high, and 12 feet wide.

With gift shops, clothing boutiques, and a variety of eateries from very formal to coffee shop–style, the inn is alive with activity. Don't miss Sunset Terrace with a view of Asheville and the mountain ridges beyond. Vue 1913 is the ultimate in dimly-lit, formal dining and Edison's is perfect for socializing with a sandwich and cocktail. The outdoor sofas by the fireplaces are a great place to sip and take in the view again.

Golf has always played a major role in the history of the Grove Park Inn. The 18-hole course, designed in the 1920s by renowned golf architect Donald Ross, has hosted many of golf's greats: Bobby Jones, Arnold Palmer, Jack

Nicklaus, Ben Hogan, Sam Snead, Fuzzy Zoeller, and Doug Sanders, to name a few. A comprehensive golf program is administered by the inn's golf professional. There is also a well-stocked sports shop for your convenience. Other recreation at the inn includes a pool, racquetball and squash courts, tennis courts, and gym on the grounds. Don't miss the 40,000-square-foot, world-class spa, built partially underground between the two residential wings. If you are here during the holidays, don't miss the National Gingerbread House Competition, with these architectural confections displayed through the hotel. Other big events and conventions are held here throughout the year.

Henderson County

THE GREYSTONE INN, 220 Greystone Ln., Lake Toxaway, NC; (828) 966-4700, (800) 824-5766; greystoneinn.com; $$$$. Pampered comfort awaits you at Greystone. First, a little history: A hundred years ago, a group called the Lake Toxaway Company built a 640-acre lake in the high mountains between Brevard and Cashiers that they called "America's Switzerland." There they created a five-story, 500-room hotel out of the finest woods and with the most modern conveniences, such as electric lights, bathrooms, elevators, steam heat, refrigeration, and long-distance telephone and telegraph service. They offered European cuisine, full orchestras for dancing and lavish balls, and all those outdoor sports we enjoy today: tennis, horseback riding, sailing, fishing, and more. The lake attracted Savannah native Lucy Armstrong Moltz. In 1915 she moved into her "small summer place" on the lake—a magnificent six-level, 16,000-square-foot Swiss chalet. However, weakened by a flood, the Toxaway dam broke in 1917. It took until 1960 to restore the dam and the lake. In 1985 the Moltz home, which is now on the National Register of Historic Places, was elegantly renovated and opened as the Greystone Inn.

Thirty rooms and suites are housed in the elegant mansion, the Lakeside Cottage, which was built in 1995, and the Hillmont Building (where rooms have private balconies overlooking the lake). The latter was built in 1988 blending with the architectural style and furnishings of the mansion. All these rooms have Jacuzzis, wet bars, sitting areas, and gas fireplaces.

The rates, which are on a Modified American Plan, include your room, an incredible High Country breakfast menu from which you can order anything you desire, and dinner with a varied menu. The rates include soft drinks and complimentary hors d'oeuvres; mid-afternoon tea, coffee, and cake served on a wicker-filled sunporch; a daily newspaper; water skiing, hydrosliding, and tubing with the boat, equipment, and driver provided; a daily champagne cruise on a canopied electric boat; use of a bass boat and fishing equipment; tennis court time; croquet, volleyball, and other outdoor sports; swimming in the pool or off the dock at the lake; and evening turndown service. A spa and sauna are on the grounds.

Close-up

The Mystery of the Pink Lady

It's been said that there is a sad but gentle ghost residing within the gray granite walls of Asheville's historic Grove Park Inn, known as the Pink Lady. She has been seen, felt, and experienced by hotel employees and guests for more than a half-century. The mystery centers around Room 545 in the Main Inn, where employees, guests, and repair workers have seen or heard ghostly phenomena, including unexplained chills and rushes of cold air and the feeling of a presence of some type, prompting the hotel's engineering facilities manager in 1995 to write: "I was on my way back to check a recent bathtub resurfacing in Room 545. As I approached the room, my hair suddenly lifted from my scalp and stood on end on my arms. Simultaneously I felt a very uncomfortable cold rush across my whole body." His words echoed those of a painter who had worked in the hotel in the 1950s. Neither of these employees knew of the other's experiences.

Other employees as well as guests have mentioned that they have seen the luminous form of a lady dressed in pink party clothes, whisking around corners of the grand hotel. The legend dates back to senior employees' recollections of a young woman, dressed in pink, who fell to her death in the Palm Court Atrium around 1920, several stories below Room 545. The manager of the Grove Park Inn, who has seen the Pink Lady several times, explains: "It's like a real dense smoke—a pinkish pastel that just flows. It's a real gentle spirit, whatever it is."

HIGHLAND LAKE INN AND RESORT, 86 Lily Pad Ln., Flat Rock, NC; (800) 635-6101; hliresort.com; $$–$$$. Highland Lake Inn was founded in the early 1900s by a group of visionary gentlemen and has taken many different forms over the years—from a military academy to a summer camp. Nowadays the country retreat offers 26 acres of cottages, a historic lodge and inn, gardens, forested trails, and a 40-acre lake for fishing, boating, and other joyful outdoor activities. Its award-winning restaurant **Season's** offers breakfast, lunch, and dinner with seasonal menus based on the flow of produce from the organic gardens. You might find special events scheduled monthly as well as a sought-after Sunday brunch. The *Wine Spectator*'s Award of Excellence is only one of the many accolades heaped upon the restaurant and inn over the years. If you stay in one of the 47 rooms or suites, expect a full Southern breakfast. The six poolside cottages have kitchens for cooking with family or friends. You may not wish to leave the lovely environs here, but just down the road you'll also find the Carl Sandburg Home, St. John in the Wilderness church, and the Flat Rock Playhouse (see our **Attractions** chapter).

Transylvania County: The Pretty Place

This is one of those spots known more by locals than by tourists. Well-attended Easter sunrise services are held here, as are many weddings. The waves-of-mountains vista is framed by an open-sided chapel, called Symmes Chapel, with steeply sloping tiers of seats fitted to the side of the mountain. The view is—we aren't exaggerating—truly breathtaking.

To find the Pretty Place, which is part of the facilities of Camp Greenville, a summer camp, take US Highway 276 out of Brevard toward Greenville, South Carolina. Drive 12 miles until you see the turnoff at the YMCA Camp Greenville sign on the left. Follow the signs for about 4.5 miles, enter the camp, and drive to the chapel. It's a side trip well worth taking. However, no picnicking is allowed in the area.

Southern Mountains

Graham County

HISTORIC FONTANA VILLAGE RESORT, 300 Woods Rd., Fontana Dam, NC; (800) 849-2258; fontanavillage.com; $–$$$$. Fontana is more than a resort. It's actually a small, secluded, self-contained town that's a fascinating part of our nation's history. The Tennessee Valley Authority (TVA) built a 480-foot-tall dam, the highest in the eastern United States, across the Little Tennessee River. Overnight a village for workers and their families sprang up; the village included a school, a 50-bed hospital, churches, and space to play. Work on the dam went on around the clock, seven days a week. On November 7, 1944, the project was complete; Fontana Lake's 10,600 acres filled with water, and electricity began to zip through the wires to Oak Ridge not far away over the mountains. After the war there was power to spare for rural electrification, and the dam proved itself in flood control. Not long after that the village was transformed into a year-round resort.

On the southern border of the Great Smoky Mountains National Park, Fontana Village offers guided hikes, arts and crafts shops, three swimming pools (one indoor), a giant waterslide, an exercise spa, horseback and bike riding, miniature golf, volleyball, basketball, softball, tennis, a playground, trout pond, church, post office, village store, ice-cream parlor, restaurant, small museum, and a host of activities, including traditional Smoky Mountain dances and other entertainment. It also operates the Fontana Marina on Fontana Lake, where you can take a lake cruise or rent all kinds of boats. The fishing is great in both the lake and nearby trout streams. As for accommodations, you're almost sure to find something to fit your budget and group size. There are rooms at the inn (some with fireplaces), cottages with kitchenettes (some as large as three bedrooms and three baths with a fireplace and whirlpool), and campground sites.

> **i** Graham County's Maple Spring Observation Point is the highlight of a 900-foot loop trail, designed for wheelchair use that includes a deck that opens to a sweeping view of mountain peaks and valleys. It is on Wagon Train Road (SR 1127) approximately 4.5 miles beyond the entrance road to the Joyce Kilmer Recreation Trail.

Haywood County

CATALOOCHEE RANCH, 119 Ranch Dr., Maggie Valley, NC; (828) 926-1401, (800) 868-1401; cataloocheeranch.com; $$–$$$$. For more than 75 years Cataloochee Ranch has welcomed guests to its 1,000-acre resort that's a mile high in the Great Smoky Mountains. In 1934, when the area was still a pristine wilderness, Tom and "Miss Judy" Alexander acquired what had been a rugged sheep and cattle farm and turned it into this mountain legend. Third generation family members still run the ranch. The name Cataloochee comes from the Cherokee *ga-da-lu-sti*, which has been translated as "standing up in a row" or "wave upon wave," a reference, no doubt, to the range upon range of mountains—the Blue Ridge and the Smokies—that are visible here. The ranch itself has three major peaks: Fie Top, Moody Top, and Hemphill Bald, with elevations from 4,700 to 5,680 feet. Cabins sleep two to eight people (two of the cabins were originally pioneer log homes), several with cozy living rooms and fireplaces, some with Jacuzzi tubs.

The historic main Ranch House, once a large barn, also has guest rooms, a great room, and dining hall. The furnishings throughout the resort feature colorful quilts and primitive or classic antiques that reflect the ranch's pioneer heritage. The resort is pet-friendly, with a pet fee.

Daily rates include breakfast and dinner. These are family-style feasts you'll never forget. There are also frequent outdoor cookouts and a beer and wine service. Other amenities include a trout pond, a 20-foot heated swim-spa, horseshoe pits, Ping-Pong tables, a croquet court, and hiking paths, and of course, horseback riding. Half-day guided rides last two to three hours. Cataloochee

Ranch is also the closest facility to the Cataloochee Ski Resort, just a mile over the hill, which has winter ski packages.

MAGGIE VALLEY CLUB & RESORT, 1819 Country Club Rd., Maggie Valley, NC; (828) 926-1616, (800) 438-3861; maggievalleyresort.com; $–$$$. The mountains, as is typical in this particular area, soar almost straight up around the valley where this resort is nestled. They also shelter it from extremes in temperature. One of this resort's main attractions is its golf course. Beginners and even the most seasoned players will find the 6,500-yard course a unique challenge. On-site amenities include a heated pool, hot tub, tennis courts, driving range, a short game practice area, walking trails, yoga, and fitness room. There's also easy access to numerous hiking and biking trails, fishing, rafting, and zip-lining adventures. Dine at **Pin High Bar and Grill**, the resort's restaurant. Rates are reasonable here, and the resort also offers money-saving golf packages that include greens fees and use of the tennis courts and pool. Rooms in the guest lodges are spacious, and each has its own balcony. Guest villas are on the golf course's back nine. Each villa has a living room, dining area, and furnished kitchen, and both one-bedroom, one-bath and two-bedroom, two-bath units are available.

WAYNESVILLE COUNTRY CLUB INN, 176 Country Club Dr., Waynesville, NC; (828) 452-2258, (800) 627-6250; twigolfresort.com; $–$$$$. A 270-foot-long main terrace overlooks the manicured acres of the expansive golf course. As in the old days, it's lined with rocking chairs—just one hint of the Southern hospitality you'll find here. Nestled between the Blue Ridge and the western ridges of the Great Smokies, this resort offers 27 picturesque holes of golf with fairways winding like ribbons through the mountain valley (see our **Recreation** chapter). Accommodations are gracious and varied with 111 rooms in the main lodge or its Woodcrest wing. The Brookside or the Fairway lodges have porches or balconies within putting distance of the golf course. There is also a swimming pool and tennis courts, plus the Balsam Spa. Numerous golf, holiday getaway, and special winter packages are available. Cork and Cleaver provides wholesome meals from traditional Southern favorites like biscuits and gravy, grits, and bacon and eggs to lighter fare. Breakfast is served as a buffet through the spring, summer, and fall months, while cooked-to-order during the winter.

Jackson County

HIGH HAMPTON RESORT, 1525 Hwy. 107 S., Cashiers, NC; (828) 743-2411, (800) 334-2551; highhamptonresort.com; $$–$$$$. In the early 1800s Wade Hampton II, a South Carolina upcountry planter and owner of Millwood, a Columbia, South Carolina, plantation that was the social center of Southern aristocracy, bought 450 acres in Cashiers. The property served as

Close-up

The White Owl of High Hampton

As we mentioned in the listing for High Hampton Inn, Dr. and Mrs. Halsted, the second owners of the High Hampton property, gradually increased their holdings by buying out adjoining farms. In the process Dr. Halsted made an offer for a 50-acre homestead owned by Mr. Hannibal Heaton and his wife. He wanted to sell, but Mrs. Heaton adamantly refused.

"I'll kill myself if you sell our home," she supposedly told her husband.

But Dr. Halsted must have made an offer that Hannibal felt he shouldn't refuse, so off he went to close the deal. But when he returned home with the bill of sale, he found his wife hanging from an oak tree, and the story goes that there was a white owl flying around her head screeching like a crying woman. Some said it was the spirit of the woman herself.

Shortly after his wife's death, Hannibal Heaton disappeared from the Cashiers area and was never heard from again. Mrs. Heaton, a woman of her word, was buried in the Upper Zachary Cemetery, just a short distance from where the High Hampton Inn stands today. And it's still said by some that the owls heard at night around High Hampton are Mrs. Heaton, still crying over the home she loved and lost.

a farm and hunting preserve and provided escape from heat, humidity, and malaria. Hampton's son, Wade Hampton III, spent a lot of time here before he went on to become a general in the Confederate army and, later, South Carolina's governor and a US senator.

In the 1880s the Hampton Place in the mountains, which by now had a seven-bedroom "cottage," a kitchen building, servants' quarters, and outbuildings, was sold to Dr. and Mrs. Halsted (Wade Hampton III's niece). Her husband had been the first professor of surgery at Johns Hopkins Hospital, and she had briefly served as head of nursing. They called the place High Hampton, from the title of his ancestral estate in England, known as High Halsted. The couple gradually increased the property to 2,200 acres (see "**The White Owl of High Hampton**" Close-up). They are responsible for many of the lovely trees and shrubs that are still seen on High Hampton's current 1,400 acres.

After the Halsteds' deaths in 1922, E. Lyndon McKee of Sylva, the father of the present owner, William D. McKee, purchased the estate. The present High Hampton Inn was completed in 1933. The resort is closed for major renovations until 2020.

WYNDHAM RESORT AT FAIRFIELD SAPPHIRE VALLEY, 70 Sapphire Valley Rd., Sapphire, NC; (828) 743-3441; fairfieldsapphirevalley.com; $$–$$$$. It all began back in 1896 with the opening of Fairfield Inn on Fairfield Lake. Although the inn is gone, the pristine scenery and a distinctive way of life remain. Enjoy the fitness center or a swim in one of the indoor or two outdoor swimming pools. There's a game room and two restaurants, and diversions like miniature golf or tennis at one of the 10 courts. Accommodations range from hotel rooms to three-bedroom condominiums. Three- and four-bedroom homes are also available.

BED-AND-BREAKFASTS AND COUNTRY INNS

Northern Mountains

Alleghany County

DOUGHTON HALL BED & BREAKFAST, 12668 Hwy. 18, Laurel Springs, NC; (336) 596-2468; facebook.com/Doughton-Hall-Bed-Breakfast; $$$. Less than a mile from the Blue Ridge Parkway's exit to rural Laurel Springs is Doughton Hall. Open year-round, this lovely Queen Anne–style home, built in the 1890s, was once home to former Congressman Robert L. Doughton, an influential figure in Congress during the 1940s. Listed on the National Register of Historic Places, the inn has marvelous woodwork, high ceilings, and old-fashioned sitting rooms. Some of the antiques are original to the house. Photos of Congressman Doughton during his term in Washington decorate the sitting room walls. You have a choice of three guest rooms, two with private baths that include Jacuzzis. One room has a splendid queen-size brass bed. The buffet breakfast is generous enough to serve a crowd—eggs cooked to order, several kinds of fresh bread, country ham, sausage, bacon, croissants, and more—even if the house isn't full of guests. Doughton is the perfect spot for events and hosts many weddings, even featuring event rentals. The inn does not have a website, only a Facebook page currently.

Ashe County

RIVER HOUSE, 1896 Old Field Creek Rd., off Hwy. 16, Grassy Creek, NC; (336) 982-2109; riverhousenc.com; $$$–$$$$. The innkeepers have taken pains to re-create and maintain the gentler pace of a time past at River House, an elegant 1870 farmhouse that was once home to a local physician. The home has been meticulously restored and tastefully furnished with period antiques. River House sits near the Virginia border on 125 beautifully rolling acres, a mile of which hugs the New River. The inn, open year-round, offers a dozen uniquely-decorated guest rooms, with private baths, Jacuzzis, and Wi-Fi. Breakfast, served from 8:30 to 10:00 a.m., is popular among the locals here, too! River House is also home to an exceptional restaurant with a unique menu.

Avery County

THE AZALEA INN, 149 Azalea Circle, Banner Elk, NC; (828) 260-9528; theazaleainnbb.com; $$$–$$$$. Originally owned by members of one of Banner Elk's founding families, the house has been restored under new ownership as of 2018. In the heart of town, the inn is within walking distance of the village shops and many fine restaurants. A full French-influenced breakfast completes your stay, but you might also opt for French cooking classes, taught by manager Chef Missy, known as the French Magnolia.

BANNER ELK INN B&B AND COTTAGES, 407 Main St. East, Banner Elk, NC; (828) 898-6223; bannerelkinn.com; $$$–$$$$. This small, charming inn is convenient to Boone and the ski resorts of the northern mountains. The tasteful decor here has the flavor of both the Victorian era and Old World Europe in the original inn that was once known as the Shawneehaw Inn. It now also offers three new luxurious cottages and a wonderful cabin for families, with private baths, whirlpools, fireplaces, down comforters, and soft sheets, as well as modern conveniences. Breakfasts including banana nut muffins, Parmesan omelette soufflé with cheddar cheese sauce, and pumpkin bread might be on the weekend menu. Weekday breakfasts are full service but a bit simpler. Enjoy gardens with a bubbling stone fountain in the spring and summer. The Coffee & Tea Room is open to guests 24 hours a day with small snacks and beverages.

ESEEOLA LODGE, 175 Linville Ave., Linville, NC; (828) 733-4311, (800) 742-6717; eseeola.com; $$$$. This wonderful old inn is central to the history of Linville as well as to the development of the High Country as a tourist destination. The original Eseeola Lodge, destroyed by fire in 1936, had its beginnings at the turn of the 20th century with the advent of the railroad in these long-remote mountains. As a result of the railroad's coming, Eseeola Lodge and Linville soon became a fashionable watering place for the wealthy of the Southeast. Golf became a passion at the lodge, and a premier 18-hole course designed by renowned golf architect Donald Ross was added in the 1920s. In

i Many bed-and-breakfasts and inns package their own coffee blends, jams, herbs, and other goodies. These small souvenirs make lovely gifts for friends, or the house sitter, back home . . . or for yourself as a reminder of a heavenly vacation.

those early years Eseeola Lodge was the center of community activity and lively entertainment for the village of Linville.

Madison County

MARSHALL HOUSE BED & BREAKFAST INN, 100 Hill St., Marshall, NC; (828) 649-6445, (844) 400-1903; marshallhouseinn.com; $–$$. Marshall House is nestled in the hillside above the town of Marshall, thirty minutes northwest of Asheville. Noted society architect Richard Sharp Smith built this home in 1903 as the private residence of James H. White, a prominent Madison County community leader and political figure. The distinctive pebble-dash exterior is typical of the homes Smith built in the Asheville area and the cottages of Biltmore Village, commissioned by George Vanderbilt. Marshall House fosters the serenity of that simpler time, characterized by the town of Marshall itself, just below on the banks of the French Broad River. Choice antiques decorate the house. Two rooms have private baths; the others have shared baths. A sumptuous breakfast of pancakes, French toast or waffles, eggs, and homemade breads or bagels is served to guests in the formal dining room.

MOUNTAIN MAGNOLIA INN, SUITES & RESTAURANT, 204 Lawson St., Hot Springs, NC; (828) 622-3543, (800) 914-9306; mountainmagnoliainn.com; $$$–$$$$. The Rumboughs were the founding family of Hot Springs, which was originally called Warm Springs. The name emanated from the natural springs boiling from the ground. Confederate Col. James H. Rumbough built Rutland House in 1868 so that it had the space necessary to accommodate a family of 10. In the 1950s the last of the Rumboughs downsized Rutland by removing its tower and upper two floors. Pete and Karen Nagle of Charlotte, North Carolina, purchased the remains of this once-glorious estate in 1997, planning a minor renovation as their retirement home. But as the work got under way, they discovered that they had a mission to bring Rutland House back to its Victorian glory. They literally raised the roof, returning the upper floors and the tower to their former positions, and reclaimed the grounds from the overgrowth. Amidst this restored luxury, along with contemporary ventilation and heating, the Nagle family has continued Pete's legacy and turned the facility "green" with kitchen composting, recycling, and no fertilizers or herbicides to be as chemical-free as possible. The dining room and porch are open to the public for Sunday brunch and superb nightly dining. Nearby are the hot tubs for dipping and massages. The Appalachian Trail crosses nearby at Max Patch, and trails of lesser mileage also crisscross this mountain valley paradise.

Mitchell County

THE SWITZERLAND INN, 85 High Ridge Rd., Little Switzerland, NC; (828) 765-2153, (800) 654-4026; switzerlandinn.com; $$$–$$$$. The

Switzerland Inn is a landmark in the northern mountains. Perched high on a ridge, it straddles Mitchell and McDowell Counties and commands one of the most spectacular views in the region. North Carolina State Supreme Court Judge Herriot Clarkson was the first to be inspired by the Swiss-like atmosphere of this knob, and he determined to make it his own, buying 1,100 acres in 1910. The charm of the place is its unchanging personality, remaining much as it was almost 100 years ago.

The Blue Ridge Parkway exit at Little Switzerland is the only one on the parkway that leads to private land. The Jensen family, longtime seasonal residents who are now permanent mountaineers, purchased the inn in the 1980s. They have maintained the 55-room lodge and its surrounding grounds with the same devotion Judge Clarkson brought to Little Switzerland so long ago.

The Switzerland Inn is a veritable kingdom unto itself with quaint lodging, fine dining, a pub, and on-site shopping. Guests mingle in the great hall, playing a friendly game of checkers, relaxing by the fire, listening to the charming strains of a Victorian-era music box, or just burrowing into the comfortable armchairs to watch the mists roll in over the mountain ridge. Switzerland Inn has an outdoor swimming pool, hot tub, tennis court, and fitness room. It's also a smoke-free facility.

Watauga County

GIDEON RIDGE INN, 202 Gideon Ridge Rd., Blowing Rock, NC; (828) 295-3644; gideonridge.com; $$$–$$$$. Guests at Gideon Ridge are charmed by the magnificent family antiques throughout the house, the views from the rooms, the porches, and the gardens. Paths running through graduated banks dotted with rich yellow black-eyed Susans, rhododendrons, ivy, and a pergola make up the lush gardens. But the small touches will capture your heart here— afternoon tea was spread before us on the dining room island as we arrived. A pot of Earl Grey, which the innkeepers import from England, sat beside plates of light homemade shortbread and finger sandwiches.

Made of cedar and the red stone of Grandfather Mountain, the building itself hugs the ridge. The nephew of Moses Cone, a textile magnate who built mills in Greensboro with the money from his Cone Export & Commission Company in New York City, constructed the home as a mountain cottage in 1939. Carpets and Central Asian kilims lend the hall and dining room their natural earthen warmth. The walnut dining table, a fourth-generation family heirloom, is surrounded by high-back chairs. Four Russian impressionist paintings in muted hues decorate the walls. The artist was a friend of the innkeepers.

The butler's pantry is stocked for guests with cold juices and sodas, a kettle, and plenty of tea and coffee. Guest rooms have gas fireplaces, luxury linens, and plush bathrobes. Think mahogany four-poster beds, marble sinks, and antique furniture in every room. Our favorite is the Sunrise View, set apart from the others with its own private entrance. The king-size bed, piled high with thick pillows and quilts, offers a view out the picture window of the sun rising over 90 miles of mountain peaks. Under the beamed cathedral ceiling is a Franklin iron stove, an open whirlpool tub surrounded by a stone wall, and a bathroom designed with an exposed stone wall in the shower. Each room has a private bath.

Breakfast, set at individual wooden tables in a glass-enclosed terrace above the gardens, can include stuffed French toast, cornmeal pancakes, muffins, waffles, sausage, and numerous other edibles, all attractively presented with fresh fruit.

> **i** October is the busiest month in the mountains and visitors make their reservations as far as a year in advance. Rates are higher, too. It's the most beautiful time to be in the mountains, but plan ahead for the most pleasurable and restful stay.

THE INN AT RAGGED GARDENS, 203 Sunset Dr., Blowing Rock, NC; (828) 295-9703; ragged-gardens.com; $$–$$$$. This grand old inn surrounded by a stone wall and lovely English cottage–style flower gardens is covered by the rustic chestnut bark siding frequently found on fine older homes in the High Country. Built as a seasonal summer "cottage," the estate has been remodeled to accept guests all year long in its 12 distinctive rooms. These rooms include five suites designed in the Arts and Crafts period style. Each has separate sitting areas, whirlpool baths for two, fireplaces, and balconies or patios looking into the formal rock-walled garden.

Each room is uniquely decorated in earthy, soothing tones. The central focus of the Inn at Ragged Gardens is its magnificent stone staircase in the grand hall. Another excellent touch is the butler's pantry on the second floor, always furnished with sodas, juices, coffee, tea, mints, hot chocolate, and rich home-baked cookies presented under a glass dome. If the cookies haven't spoiled your breakfast appetite, pull close to the lace-covered table for eggs to order, fresh fruit cups, omelettes, pancakes, waffles, and sausage, only after you have helped yourself to the buffet of muffins, bagels, and breads. Candles glow on the mantel on misty cool mornings, while summer days allow for breakfast out on the porch overlooking the brilliant variety of flowers of the Ragged Gardens. Don't miss the excellent **Best Cellar** restaurant that is part of the inn and a Blowing Rock tradition.

LOVILL HOUSE INN, 404 Old Bristol Rd., Boone, NC; (828) 264-4204; lovillhouseinn.com; $$$–$$$$. This historic home, built in 1875, was the residence of Captain Edward Francis Lovill, a decorated Confederate officer,

North Carolina state senator, and a founding trustee of the Appalachian Training School, later Appalachian State University. In fact it was in the front parlor of Lovill House, the captain's occasional law office, where he and B. B. Daugherty drafted the papers establishing the university. The home continued as a Lovill family residence well into the 1970s.

You'll wake to the rich aroma of home-baked muffins and coffee outside your door. Enjoy a full gourmet breakfast, including seasonal fruit, home-baked breads, Belgian waffles, eggs Benedict, garden vegetable strata, and omelettes, accompanied by country ham, sausage, or bacon. The informal evening social hour is popular with guests of Lovill House. Groups gather outside by the stream, in the rockers on the front porch, or around the cozy front parlor fireplace.

The inn is furnished in a casually elegant country style, with a mix of antiques and quality reproductions. The wormy chestnut paneling was discovered during restoration and supplemented by matching refinished wood recovered from old, abandoned barns. The inn offers guest rooms, each with a private bath, television (discreetly tucked away in a wooden cabinet), and telephone. Beds at the Lovill House are spread with down comforters. The innkeepers encourage you to let them know if you have special dietary requirements, if you'll be celebrating a special occasion, or if you require any other service to make your visit more enjoyable. You can hike the trails on the lovely grounds, or the innkeepers can recommend the best local restaurants.

MAST FARM INN, SR 1112, off Hwy. 105, Valle Crucis, NC; (828) 963-5857, (888) 963-5857; mastfarminn.com; $$$$. The Mast Farm Inn has been a landmark and vital part of the history of the High Country since 1885. It was operated as an inn by Finley Mast and his wife, Josephine, in the early 1900s. The Masts were known far and wide for their mountain hospitality, not to mention the bounty of their table.

In 1972 the Mast Farm Inn was included on the National Register of Historic Places. It remains one of the best examples of a self-contained mountain homestead in the state. The rambling 18-room Victorian farmhouse is the center of the inn and is open year-round. The main house has nine cozy guest rooms, all with private baths. All rooms have queen- and king-size beds. Original outbuildings—the Blacksmith Shop, the Woodwork Shop, and the Loom House—have been converted to additional, comfortably furnished guest cottages. Rates include a bountiful two-course gourmet breakfast, offering something different on the menu every day. The combination of period farmhouse antiques and modern conveniences at the Mast Farm Inn allows guests to easily enjoy the charm of turn-of-the-20th-century mountain life in North Carolina. Mast Farm is a true tradition of the Northern Mountains and deservingly, additional accolades include Historic Hotels of America and Select Registry Inn designations.

TAYLOR HOUSE INN, 4584 Hwy. 194, Valle Crucis, NC; (828) 963-5581, (800) 963-5581; taylorhouseinn.com; $$$$. This lovely, two-story farmhouse, with double chimneys and a wraparound porch, was built in 1911 for the family of C. D. Taylor. Today it has been transformed into a sophisticated European-style inn with farmhouse flair. Guests enjoy the inn's mountain escape for family reunions, wedding and anniversary celebrations, special luncheons or dinner parties, art shows, cooking classes, and flower shows.

Taylor House Inn is decorated with a mix of European and American country antiques, Oriental rugs, and original artwork. There are 10 spacious rooms in the inn, all offering private baths and goose-down comforters. Three of the rooms are suites, complemented by comfortable sitting rooms. A gourmet breakfast usually includes seasonal fruit, pancakes, fresh vegetables, and specially prepared egg dishes.

Yancey County

TERRELL HOUSE BED AND BREAKFAST, 109 Robertson St., Burnsville, NC; (828) 682-4505, (888) 682-4505; terrellhousebandb.com; $$–$$$. A little off the beaten path in the friendly township of Burnsville, historic Terrell House is surrounded by mountains, offering its guests vistas of the Blue Ridge Mountains, the Bald and Unaka Ranges, and Seven Mile Ridge. The nearby Black Mountains are capped by the majestic Mount Mitchell. The 1900 Colonial-style home was built as a girls' dormitory for the Stanley McCormick School. Six country-style rooms with bath, each with its own personality and furnished with a queen- or full-size bed, allow for a comfy night's sleep in this quiet town. The owners lived in London for over a decade before taking over the inn-keeping.

Central Mountains

Buncombe County

ALBEMARLE INN, 86 Edgemont Rd., Asheville, NC; (828) 255-0027; albemarleinn.com; $$$–$$$$. This large Neoclassical Revival mansion was built as a private residence in 1909 at the foot of Sunset Mountain for Dr. Carl V. Reynolds, City Health Officer. It later became a prestigious private girls' school for a brief time and a school of the arts. The classic Southern mansion once hosted Bela Bartok, during which time he wrote a symphony subtitled, "The Asheville Symphony" [he composed the Sonata for Solo Violin there], based on the birdsong he'd hear outside the windows. The home became a bed-and-breakfast in 1980, with gardens now as lush and lovely to invite much birdsong. Its present owners have created an elegant atmosphere in 11 classically-decorated rooms and a sumptuous gourmet breakfast. Elaborate high tea and other special packages make this a space for truly memorable celebrations.

BLACK MOUNTAIN INN, 1186 Old Hwy. 70, Black Mountain, NC; (828) 669-6528; blackmountaininn.com; $$–$$$$. Nestled in the forest, the inn was built originally as a stagecoach stop approximately 170 years ago. At the turn of the 20th century, the home was owned by Martha Mallory, who operated the inn as a tuberculosis sanitarium until her untimely death. She was killed on the railroad tracks on her way home from town. The house fell into ruin and became a squatter's camp, complete with cows stabled in the dining room! In the 1940s the house was refurbished and opened as the Oak Knoll Art Studio, which served primarily as a summer retreat. Ernest Hemingway, John Steinbeck, Norman Rockwell, and Helen Keller were among the guests attending the garden parties that were common events all summer long. In 1989 the house, badly in need of further restoration and updating, began its new life as the Black Mountain Inn.

Each room has its own private bath and ceiling fans keep the mountain breezes circulating. Some rooms are pet-friendly, and one room features an antique claw-foot tub right in the room. Another has two sections large enough to sleep a family of four.

BLACK WALNUT BED AND BREAKFAST INN, 288 Montford Ave., Asheville, NC; (828) 254-3878; blackwalnut.com; $$–$$$$. The current innkeepers, who are in the process of selling, operated specialty bakeries at Martha's Vineyard and in West Palm Beach, Florida, for years before settling in Asheville. They provide many tantalizing breakfast moments for their guests as well as a wine and cheese hour upon arrival. The Black Walnut Inn stands out significantly from its surroundings as a Shingle-style house built in 1899 by architect Richard Sharp Smith. The mayor of Asheville in the 1930s, Ottis Greene, made this his home. His former one-horse barn is now the updated and modernized Cottage.

It was restored as a bed-and-breakfast in 1992. Only a short walk from downtown, the inn is surrounded by a lushly landscaped garden of flowers, black walnut trees, conifers, ivy, perfectly trimmed shrubbery, and a burbling koi pond. Four guest rooms in the main house are filled with antiques. A large front porch with rockers allows you to enjoy a balmy summer evening.

CEDAR CREST, 674 Biltmore Ave., Asheville, NC; (828) 252-1389; cedarcrestinn.com; $$$–$$$$. Less than a mile north of the entrance to Biltmore Estate sits a stunning Victorian beauty. Rising from a flower-bedecked hill on lower Biltmore Avenue, Cedar Crest commands the ascent from Biltmore Village. The traffic scurries uphill toward downtown Asheville, but this exquisite bed-and-breakfast seems forever poised in the Gilded Age. The opulent Queen Anne–style home was built in 1891 for prominent Asheville businessman William E. Breese. Breese played host to Asheville society, but as the century passed and the prosperous 1920s waned, Cedar Crest fell into disrepair. Through the years the home took on the guise of a sanitarium and, much later, a boarding-house. Then the founding innkeepers answered an ad in *Preservation News* and came all the way from Wisconsin to rescue this lovely, faded lady. Careful restoration followed, much of it just removing decades of grime and ill-conceived decoration. What emerged was the amazing beauty of rich oak woodwork, intricately carved mantels, and solid Victorian construction. The inn has been lavished with period antiques: claw-foot tubs, delicate lace, brass beds, and Victorian collectibles.

CHESTNUT STREET INN, 176 East Chestnut St., Asheville, NC; (828) 285-0705; chestnutstreetinn.com; $$–$$$$. Enjoy a candlelit breakfast at Chestnut Street Inn in this historic district. Late afternoon tea and Fri evening social hour allow you to meet other guests in the antiques-filled parlors. Artworks by local artists provide extra interest. Large four-poster beds satisfy the need for downy comfort, as does the fluffy bathrobe provided for your stay. Several rooms have gas fireplaces and there's Wi-Fi throughout the inn. Cookies and hot tea served on the porch provide an afternoon pick-me-up, and the kitchen is vegetarian-friendly and will work with your dietary needs (lactose- or gluten-intolerant, diabetic, etc.) as long as the inn knows your needs upon making reservations.

THE GRAND BOHEMIAN HOTEL, 11 Boston Way, Biltmore Village, NC; (828) 505-2949; kesslercollection.com/bohemian-asheville; $$$–$$$$. A luxurious and unique 104-room boutique hotel in Biltmore Village just outside the gates of the Biltmore Estate, the Grand Bohemian was built in a pebble-dash Tudor style that fits into its surroundings in 2009. The hotel is anything but usual on the inside—from a fireplace open on four sides in the lobby, to mosaic-covered check-in desks where guests are seated in leather chairs upon arrival—everything is a little different here. The privately owned Kessler Collection hotel (affiliated with Marriott through the Autograph Collection) has original artwork on every floor and a full-fledged art gallery with local and international art that holds artist receptions once a month. Piano music is played almost nightly in the bar, carved wood from Bali and India are placed in the ceilings and around doorways, sculptures dot the guest room hallways, and the ballroom on the top floor is filled with sparkling Swarovski crystal chandeliers. A Rosewood Bosendorfer piano resides in the eponymous salon by the ballroom. A spa and fitness center are in the main building, as well as the rustic **Red Stag Grill**, while an entire private gallery is located in the smaller, but no less-charming, Manor House across the street.

THE INN AROUND THE CORNER, 109 Church St., Black Mountain, NC; (828) 669-6005; innaroundthecorner.com; $$–$$$. The Inn Around the Corner features seven lovely guest rooms in a restored 1915 Four Square

Victorian House. The upstairs porch, with porch swings and rockers, slows time to a standstill. All rooms have private baths. A lovely view of the mountains awaits outside the private entrance to the second-story porch. A bountiful breakfast is served to guests in the dining room or on one of the porches, weather permitting. The innkeepers are amenable to special dietary requirements or requests, but be sure to tell them ahead of time. The inn is close to Black Mountain's quaint downtown shopping area, with a variety of dining possibilities. The inn is also a short distance from a walking trail around Lake Tomahawk.

THE INN ON MILL CREEK, 3898 Mill Creek Rd., Old Fort, NC; (828) 668-1115; innonmillcreek.com; $$$. Secluded among mountain laurel near the top of the Ridgecrest Pass, the inn's seven scenic acres are hidden in the Pisgah National Forest between the historic villages of Black Mountain and Old Fort. Outdoor decks, gardens, and an orchard suspend time for a bit here. Two buildings, the Main House and the Deck House, feature guest rooms decorated in soothing sage green and mushroom tones, and rough-hewn wood accents. There's AC throughout the main building and individual units in the latter, with Wi-Fi everywhere. Nature lovers on a getaway to the Black Mountain area love the 400-square-foot Mountain Laurel Room, located on the northern side of the Deck House, and it works well for families. (It has a full kitchen, for example.) The room's king bed has a hand-crafted headboard. A hand-painted tree mural over the bed was inspired by the inn's location inside Pisgah National Forest. A lush herb garden supplants a former pool. Innkeepers serve breakfast on the sunny solarium glassed-in porch in two seatings, and will honor special dietary requests if given advance notice. Their recipes are featured on the inn's blog. You might opt for their yoga weekend or other special retreats.

Mount Pisgah

Mount Pisgah is the highest peak on the Asheville Plateau. Standing at 5,700 feet, this mountain overlooks western Buncombe County. Nudging it from the south is "The Sleeping Rat." On its face, after a fierce snow, one can see "The Bride and Groom."

Some folks believe Pisgah is a Cherokee word, but it is found in the Old Testament in Deuteronomy 34:1: "Then Moses went up from the plains of Moab to Mount Nebo, to the top of Pisgah . . . from there he saw the promised land." Assumedly the early settlers of this wilderness of Western North Carolina must have hoped they had reached the Promised Land after all the hardships they faced in carving trails and homes out of it. They were either Bible-believing people or as survivors became such—thus naming the symbol of their hope Mount Pisgah.

THE LION AND THE ROSE, 276 Montford Ave., Asheville, NC; (828) 255-ROSE; lion-rose.com; $$$. Listed on the National Register of Historic Places, The Lion and the Rose is a simplified Queen Anne– or Georgian-style residence built in 1898. High embossed ceilings, oak woodwork, and leaded- and stained-glass windows are just a few of the architectural details that give distinction to the Lion and the Rose. Each room has a private bath.

RED ROCKER INN, 136 North Dougherty St., Black Mountain, NC; (828) 669-5991; redrockerinn.com; $$–$$$$. Not much has changed at the Red Rocker over the years, showcased by the measured pace of the red rock- ers on the enormous porch overlooking the gardens. Tucked away in a quiet residential neighborhood in the quaint village of Black Mountain, just 14 miles east of Asheville, life here is determinedly slow-paced. The inn was a boarding- house known as Dougherty Heights back in 1927. It became the Red Rocker Inn in 1964. The tranquility of the place is its hallmark, and the 17 exquisite guest rooms (each with private bath) reflect this search for inner peace. The warm fireplace and lovers' window seat in Elizabeth's Attic, the inspired stained glass of the Preacher's Room, and the white lace canopy bed in the romantic Anniversary Room are just a few of the thoughtful efforts to give visitors an island of calm. The inn is centrally heated and air-conditioned and has Wi-Fi. The dining room is a celebrated spot for guests as well as the community. With the generous bounty provided by the innkeepers, the dining room seems to be the only place where guests might exhibit a lack of self-restraint in this peace- ful domain. The family-style meals, served on lace-clothed, candlelit tables, are robust and hearty Southern selections heaped on in generous proportions. The Red Rocker Inn is open almost year-round (Feb through Dec).

SOURWOOD INN, 810 Elk Mountain Scenic Hwy., Asheville, NC; (828) 255-0690; sourwoodinn.com; $$$–$$$$. Located just off the Blue Ridge Parkway on 100 acres, this is what a country inn is all about. Walking trails crisscross the forested land, but even just sitting in your room looking out over the mountain through the dense foliage below, you will know you have truly "gotten away from it all." Sourwood Inn is finely constructed of cedar trimmed with stone. The entire structure sits on hilly terrain at an elevation of 3,200 feet. Easily accessible to downtown Asheville, it is nonetheless in the country- side and can feel like wilderness, with densely growing trees and birdsong all around. Each of the inn's 12 guest rooms has a private balcony overlooking the Reems Creek Valley, a woodburning fireplace, and a tub with a view! When you turn on your faucet to draw a bath, you will be amazed with the ensuing waterfall, thanks to Scandinavian faucetry. The French doors that open onto the guest room balconies let mountain breezes drift in at night. Decorated in muted forest and meadow colors, the rooms are as peaceful within as the idyllic countryside outside. The inn also maintains numerous public areas—porches with rocking chairs, a lobby with plush chairs in front of a crackling fireplace, and a library stocked with books for your leisure time. There's also a game room downstairs with a billiard table, and a very nice small restaurant that serves inn guests fantastic farm-to-table cuisine.

WHITEGATE INN & COTTAGE, 117 East Chestnut St., Asheville, NC; (828) 253-2553; whitegate.net; $$–$$$$. The first things you'll notice about this 1889 inn are the unique gardens and greenhouse that surround it. Deliciously landscaped with lush foliage, waterfalls, a koi pond, and a patio with a gas-log fire pit, the WhiteGate Inn makes it hard to want to come inside. But once you do, delight in the large rooms decorated with elegant antiques and Oriental rugs. Saunter downstairs after reading the complimentary morning paper to a three-course breakfast in the dining room. Monogrammed robes and down comforters have allowed you to revel in comfort the night before. A guest refrigerator remains stocked, and a library has a selection of DVDs, books, and CDs.

> **i** With so many bed-and-breakfasts in the area, we are hard pressed to mention them all. Therefore we urge you to explore on your own the member inns listed on the Asheville Bed & Breakfast Association website, ashevillebba.com.

Henderson County

ECHO MOUNTAIN INN, 2849 Laurel Park Hwy., Hendersonville, NC; (828) 693-9626; echoinn.com; $$–$$$. This massive stone-and-frame inn 3 miles from Hendersonville was built in 1896 on a mountainside that overlooks the whole area—a spectacular view that's visible from many of the guest rooms and the dining room. The view is particularly pretty at night with the city lights twinkling below. Once a home, then a tea-room for the public, and then "Camp Happiness" for teenage girls for four seasons before becoming an inn and restaurant, this structure has an interesting past. The interior now has a mix of those eras from the 30s, 60s, and on up, but with basic river stone and wood dominating the decor. The Main House has 40 rooms and Little Echo houses 25 efficiency rooms with kitchenette that might be compared to a motel. The entire place hearkens back to another era. There are no elevators, so be ready for stairs. Some rooms have fireplaces, all have AC and Wi-Fi, and a continental breakfast has two sittings every morning.

MELANGE BED & BREAKFAST, 1230 Fifth Ave. West, Hendersonville, NC; (828) 697-5253; melangebb.com; $–$$$$. "Luxuriously cosmopolitan" best describes this bed-and-breakfast, just a 15-minute walk from downtown Hendersonville. The mansion, complete with a pony barn and a dollhouse with six-foot ceilings, was designed and built by North Carolina's famous architect Erle G. Stillwell, in 1920. In the 1960s its owner added marble mantels from Paris, crystal chandeliers from Vienna, and hand-painted porcelain accessories from Italy. The old grandeur is still represented by the 11-foot, ornamented ceilings, ornate mirrors, and marble fireplaces, now graced by contemporary comfort, fine tiles, Turkish rugs, books, candles, and flowers. Four guest rooms occupy the second floor, and a full-floor suite with two bedrooms is on the third. Each is named after its predominant color scheme: Rose, Pearl, Cinnamon, Green, and Red. Each room has a private bath or Jacuzzi, hardwood floors, air-conditioning, and a TV. A large collection of videos and books is available for guests. At the time of publication, the B&B was up for sale, but still in operation.

WAVERLY INN, 783 North Main St., Hendersonville, NC, (828) 693-9193; waverlyinn.com; $$–$$$. For a stay in pretty Historic Downtown Hendersonville, you can't find more handy accommodations than at the three-story Waverly, the oldest surviving inn in town, which is listed on the National Register of Historic Places. It's a two-block walk to Hendersonville's dynamic downtown with its wonderful shops and restaurants and frequent art shows and festivals. Open year-round, the Waverly is a large and gracious inn, even though it now faces a street whose steady stream of traffic reflects the popularity of the town. The Queen Anne–style bed-and-breakfast was built as a two-and-a-half-story guest house with dormer windows on the third floor and a wraparound porch at street level.

You'll get a good view of all this activity from the inn's long, wide veranda, which holds about 20 rocking chairs; there are almost that many on the upstairs porch, too. Polished wood, four-posters, and turn-of-the-20th-century fittings fill the guest rooms and three suites, all of which come with private baths and cable TV. There are sitting rooms on all three floors.

A hearty breakfast, cooked to order, begins the day. You can preorder "inn-dulgences" like flowers, in-room hors d'oeuvres, chocolate-chip cookies, and the like.

Polk County

GREENLIFE INN AT THE MIMOSA, 65 Mimosa Inn Dr., Tryon, NC; (828) 436-0097; greenlifeinn.com; $$. This rambling bed-and-breakfast inn with its column-lined veranda has 200 years of history behind it. In the 1700s King George granted John Mills 90,000 acres of land in this area. He and his son operated Mill's Inn here along the trading trail that would become Howard Gap Road. After the Civil War, a Pennsylvania Presbyterian minister named Dr. Leland McAboy bought the inn, named it the McAboy House and, like the Millses, became known as a hospitable host. In 1903 Aaron French and David Sterns bought and modernized the property with innovations such as gaslight and hot and cold running water, added a casino/bowling alley, and renamed it the Mimosa Inn. Fire destroyed most of the building in 1916, sparing only the casino/bowling alley, which was remodeled into the current inn. New innkeepers are presently renovating the stately beauty as of this writing and christened it GreenLife Inn at the Mimosa.

THE OAKS BED & BREAKFAST, 339 Greenville St., Saluda, NC; (828) 749-2000; theoaksbedandbreakfast.com; $$$. Built by a local banker as a private residence in 1894, this arresting, turreted house was a boarding home from 1905 until the 1940s. Tall trees set off the exterior, which features a wraparound porch with seasonal hanging baskets, wicker furniture, and a swing. Inside you'll discover an inviting library with a fireplace and a large, airy living room. The center of the house is the gracious dining room where delicious gourmet breakfasts are served family style. Each of the inn's distinctively decorated guest rooms has a private bath and cable TV, and the place is pet-friendly. The property also has a separate and self-contained guest house, the Carriage House, which boasts a nice view of the ivy-filled woods below and two suites with kitchens. The Oaks, which closes in Jan, is just a short walk from the antiques, arts, crafts, and old-time stores of Saluda.

Polk County: White Oak Mountain

Polk County's topography varies from rolling foothills to level plains on one side and high timber-clad mountains on the other. You can see a great example of all this from what has been called "the greatest view east of the Rockies." Drive east on Highway 108 for just less than 5 miles to Houston Road (SR 1137). Turn left and drive a half-mile to a fork. Bear right for just more than a half-mile, turn left onto White Oak Mountain Road, and drive 2 miles to "The Brow," fronting the White Oak Condominiums near the top of Shunkawauken Falls. From this height of 3,000 feet on a clear day, you can see fields and farmlands stretching for 50 miles, and it's very pretty at night with all the lights twinkling below. Another great vista lies across the relatively flat mountaintop westward to the base of the last incline of Tryon Peak, which is the highest of a number of summits on the White Oak Mountain massif. It's called Sunset Rock, and it's a popular Polk County picnic spot with a view of rugged, steep mountain ranges flowing into each other.

THE ORCHARD INN, 100 Orchard Inn Ln., Hwy. 176, Saluda, NC; (828) 749-5471; orchardinn.com; $$$–$$$$. This inn, sprawled with plantation-like elegance on a ridge, was built by the International Brotherhood of Railway Clerks and Engineers as a mountain getaway in the early 1900s, near the terminus of the steepest railway grade east of the Rockies. That engineering feat is a marvel even today, and a stay in this tranquil place is just as marvelous. In addition to the nine guest rooms in the imposing main building, there are three remodeled cottages with fireplaces, whirlpool baths, and private decks. Each room and cottage has a personality of its own, from the delicate patterns on the wallpaper to its paintings, prints, stenciling, and quilts. The entire guest quarters are furnished with period pieces and antiques. Wide porches and a shaded deck hold swings, rockers, ferns, and blooming plants. You can relax on swings out on the grounds, too.

An airy, glassed-in porch that runs the length of the inn is Newman's Restaurant, serving award-winning fare on a prix-fix menu. From here a stunning view of the mountains stretches all the way into South Carolina. Full breakfasts and French Provincial dinners "with a country flair," say the hosts, are served, and dinner is open to the public by reservation. You do need to keep in mind that Saluda is a "dry" town as far as alcoholic beverages go, but you may bring your own spirits. There's ice in the rooms.

PINE CREST INN, 85 Pine Crest Ln., Tryon, NC; (800) 633-3001; pinecrestinn.com; $$–$$$. In 1918 a hotel owner from Michigan, Carter P. Brown, created the charmingly rustic Pine Crest Inn. Later, in the 1920s, Brown played a leading role in establishing the Tryon Riding and Hunt Club that helped make Tryon the equestrian center it is today. The Pine Crest Inn is still thriving. It's full of fireplaces, wide porches, tranquil gardens, bright lawns, and wooded grounds. The inn has 35 air-conditioned rooms, most with fireplaces and all with televisions and fluffy robes for guests. Rates include a full continental breakfast. Both suites and cottages are available (some pet-friendly), along with the intimate Fox and Hounds Bar and a small restaurant, Carter's Tavern and Wine Cellar. The complex also has a conference center available for retreats, seminars, or other gatherings.

Rutherford County

LAKE LURE INN & SPA, 2771 Memorial Hwy., Lake Lure, NC; (888) 434-4970; lakelure.com; $$$–$$$$. This stately inn overlooking beautiful Lake Lure has been a tradition in Hickory Nut Gorge since 1927. In its early days F. Scott Fitzgerald, President Franklin D. Roosevelt, and Emily Post came to Lake Lure Inn. Today the inn, with 50 guest rooms, has been renovated and attracts scores of vacationers. Guests may choose from a variety of rooms—standard with two double beds or one queen, deluxe with a king, or rooms with king- or queen-size bed and a pullout sofa in a large sitting area. Suites and all rooms are furnished with antique historic inn furniture and newer styles, giving the ambiance of a well-loved place from another era. All rooms have cable TV, Wi-Fi, and private baths. The spacious lobby runs the width of the hotel and is furnished with sofas, soft chairs, and area literature and newspapers to help plan your local sight-seeing. Fresh flowers and old photographs of famous former guests complement the decor. Cozy up to the fireplace in the main dining room for the complimentary continental breakfast, which includes cereal, breads, bagels, muffins fresh from the inn's kitchen, juices, coffee, and tea. The Veranda and the Moose & Goose Lounge on the ground floor cater to inn guests as well as the visiting public. The inn's outdoor pool has a sundeck, and a shaded veranda with benches and chairs overlooking Lake Lure at the front of the inn. The newest addition is the Irongate Spa, providing a variety of luxury hair, nail, and body treatments, open Wed through Sun with appointment.

Transylvania County

THE INN AT BREVARD, 315 East Main St., Brevard, NC; (828) 884-2105; theinnatbrevard.com; $$–$$$. This elegant, columned inn, listed on the National Register of Historic Places, is within easy walking distance of all the great shops and restaurants in downtown Brevard. The inn has a distinguished history. It was built in 1885 as the private home of Mrs. Woodbridge, a wealthy widow from Virginia who entertained the nobility of the Victorian era here, including her good friend, Lady Astor. Woodbridge bequeathed the house to her only daughter, Rebecca, who married William E. Breese, a prominent attorney and mayor of Brevard. In 1911 Breese hosted a reunion of the Confederate troops who served under Stonewall Jackson (Jackson's widow attended). The house was sold in the 1940s and operated as the Colonial Inn for many years. Folks rave about the bountiful breakfasts.

KEY FALLS INN, 151 Everett Rd., Pisgah Forest, NC; (828) 884-7559; keyfallsinn.com; $–$$$. Formerly known as the Patton House after its original owner, John Patton, this 1868 Victorian farmhouse bed-and-breakfast has four guest bedrooms and a two-room suite furnished with antiques. All have private baths and there's Wi-Fi throughout. The house's porches are popular for reading, relaxing, and enjoying the view. The Pisgah Forest Cabin can sleep four and has a full kitchen. A sumptuous breakfast is included in the price, and complimentary refreshments are served in the afternoon. The inn is only 4.5 miles from Pisgah National Forest and 10.3 miles to DuPont State Forest where miles of hiking and biking trails and be found. Key Falls Trail begins on the grounds and climbs up to Key Falls, one of the many waterfalls in Transylvania County. The inn's small restaurant, the Pavilion, serves reasonably-priced, lovely small plates, local beers, and quite a nice variety of wines.

The White Squirrels of Brevard

In 1986 the Brevard City Council declared the city a squirrel sanctuary because some of the squirrels around here are super-special—they're white! We enjoy our gray squirrels, too, but the white variety, which you can see darting throughout the town, has become a symbol of Brevard. These squirrels are not albinos, as they have normal dark eyes and a dark stripe down their backs. The white squirrels have been migrating to the countryside around the town, probably because of Brevard's increased urbanization.

THE RED HOUSE INN AND BED AND BREAKFAST, 266 West Probart St., Brevard, NC; (828) 884-9349; brevardbedandbreakfast.com; $–$$$. Four blocks from the center of town and on the road next to the Brevard Music Center, you'll find Brevard's oldest house. It was built as a trading post/general store in 1851 after the first 1848 house burned. The house survived years of neglect and several attempts to destroy it during the Civil War. The trading post closed in 1861, and the structure then became the W. P. Poor Tavern, which had four rooms for boarders. The street at that time was also called Poor Street, but the residents understandably didn't cotton to that! Hence the name was changed to Probart Street, after Poor's middle name, and so it remains today.

Since its days as a tavern, the building has been used as a residence, a railway station, the county's first courthouse, Brevard's first post office, a boardinghouse, a hotel, and briefly as a school. It's been added to and altered over the years, but the original foundation is still firm, and its four-corner chimneys are still functioning.

The inn has been refurbished and the five rooms showcase the art of local painters, photographers, and sculptors. Two cottages and five self-sustaining vacation houses all have Wi-Fi like the inn. A cooked-to-order fab breakfast comes with the rooms and cottages, but not the vacation houses which have kitchens. And, yes, the main house is painted red—the trim on its wide upstairs and downstairs porches is a bright contrast in white. The story goes that in the days when the streets had no numbers, the houses all had names. As the New England branch of the family had several homes, each called Red House, the family in Brevard decided to use that name, too.

Southern Mountains

Cherokee County

HAWKESDENE HOUSE, 381 Phillips Creek Rd., Andrews, NC; (828) 321-6027, (800) 447-9549; hawkesdene.com; $$$–$$$$. What was once a quaint English-style manor has developed into a 54-acre private residential village adjoining the Nantahala National Forest. Interconnected by roads and trails, Hawkesdene has cottages, homes, and the 10,000-square-foot three-story original house for accommodations for vacations, special events, and work retreats. Estate dining at Hawkesdene is farm-to-fork with Appalachian highlights, including use of local produce and Carolina-grown wheat for baked goods.

Graham County

SNOWBIRD MOUNTAIN LODGE, 4633 Santeetlah Rd., Robbinsville, NC; (828) 479-3433, (800) 941-9290; snowbirdlodge.com; $$$–$$$$. Built of native stone and chestnut logs, the lodge has 15 rooms, cozy with wood paneling and floors made from trees harvested from the surrounding forest in 1938. The lush forest has grown back in around this inn, which is on the National Register of Historic Places, and the rooms boast views of either the woods or the mountains. A massive stone fireplace dominates the main lodge room, which is paneled in butternut, and another warms up the dining room, paneled in cherry. The main lodge, with its historical, creaking floors, is paneled in a variety of native woods, with furniture to match. Handmade quilts, many in-room amenities, and private baths complete the comfort. None of the rooms have televisions or telephones. Overall, Snowbird has 22 rooms, with more in two historical cottages on the property.

From its spacious flagstone terrace, the inn offers a panoramic view of the Snowbird Mountain Range, and in the valley below are glimpses of Lake Santeetlah and the homes and fields of the Snowbird Indians. The lodge has an interesting 2,500-volume library. There are 2.5 miles of hiking trails on the property. You can swim in a mountain pool fed by a cool stream or spend the day fishing in any number of blue-ribbon trout streams nearby. Canoes and kayaks are available for rent at the lodge and are a great way to explore nearby Lake Santeetlah.

The rates at Snowbird are on the Full American Plan, which includes a fine buffet-style breakfast, a hearty picnic lunch, and an exquisite full-menu dinner prepared by the staff with fresh, seasonal ingredients.

Haywood County

GRANDVIEW LODGE, 466 Lickstone Rd., Waynesville, NC; (828) 456-5212; grandviewlodgenorthcarolina.com; $–$$. Grandview has 10 year-round guest rooms that are wood-paneled country-cozy in a suburban area a short drive to downtown Waynesville. All guest rooms have a king- or queen-size bed and a second bed, a private bath, and cable TV. They are a bit dated but the perfect price-appropriate respite if you plan to be out hiking and sightseeing most of the day. There's Wi-Fi and some pet-friendly rooms. Full farm-to-table/

country breakfast is included in the rates, served family style, and some special dietary needs can be accommodated. The public may dine here by making advance reservations.

THE SWAG, 2300 Swag Rd., Waynesville, NC; (828) 926-0430, (800) 789-7672; theswag.com; $$$$. When the founders of The Swag, which refers to a dip in a ridge, call theirs a mountaintop inn, they mean it! This inn sits on 250 acres at 5,000 feet on a private mountain with 50-mile views. Dan and Deener Matthews built what was to be a private family retreat using native stone and hand-hewn logs from old buildings, including a century-old church. They ended up turning the retreat into this highly praised inn. Now retired (Dan is Rector Emeritus of Trinity Church, Wall Street, in New York City), they sold the inn to former guests, who continue the tradition of this authentically rustic atmosphere with handmade quilts, woven rugs, and unique pieces of North Carolina art.

The 14 guest rooms have private baths (some with whirlpools or steam showers, all with terry robes), and many feature balconies to bring that 50-mile view right indoors. Some rooms have fireplaces. There are also three cabins with separate sitting rooms and private porches, and an extensive library to satisfy most literary tastes.

Outside a split-rail fence marks the boundary of the Great Smoky Mountains National Park with its many hiking trails, reached by The Swag's own private entrance. The lavish meals are farm-to-table, many with local produce and on-site garden herbs, lovingly prepared in multiple courses. The sumptuous dinner begins with hors d'oeuvres on the porch (non-inn guests may also make reservations), while tea time with cookies, nuts, and savory snacks at 3 p.m. sharp and a buffet breakfast for inn guests only are equally lovely.

> **i** Historic inns and B&Bs vary in quality and upkeep, which can change quickly (even within just a year or two), like with personal homes. We recommend consulting a variety of recent online reviews to get a feel for the most up-to-date news. Be a smart traveler!

THE YELLOW HOUSE, 89 Oakview Dr., Waynesville, NC; (828) 452-0991; theyellowhouse.com; $$$$. The Yellow House sits at 3,000 feet on top of a hill looking out to the ever-changing colors of the Blue Ridge Mountains. Located just a mile from Waynesville, the 100-year-old home has no distractions like televisions in this quiet rural setting. There are eight rooms total. All rooms feature a charming fireplace, coffee service, terry robes, and controlled music. The rates include your choice of a breakfast served in your quarters, in the dining room, or on the front veranda. Other amenities include appetizers and conversation in the evening and a refrigerator stocked with soft drinks.

Jackson County

INNISFREE VICTORIAN INN, 108 Innisfree Dr., Glenville, NC; (828) 743-2946; innisfreeinn.com; $$$$. As the name implies, this is a gabled Victorian. Wide porches run around two floors of this superb building overlooking Lake Glenville. The nine guest rooms are named in keeping with its era, such as the Prince Albert Suite, with French doors leading to a private veranda; the sensuous Cambridge Room, which has a parking place next to its private entrance; and the cheerful Canterbury Room, with a bay-windowed love seat that affords a view of flower gardens and mountains. The Garden House, which follows the style of the main house, has two feminine boudoirs—the Elizabeth Barrett and Emily Brontë Suites—each with a four-poster bed made up in French lace, a private veranda, and two fireplaces, one in the bathroom. There is also an ornate suite and a room with its own entrance. All the accommodations in the Garden House have wet bars, TVs, and private phones. Rates include the candlelit breakfast in the Tower, a 5:30 p.m. hospitality hour with hors d'oeuvres served on the sweeping upper veranda, and Irish coffee and hot chocolate by the parlor fire each evening.

> ℹ There is a 3-mile round-trip hike in Jackson County that takes you through a lovely mile-high meadow with superb views of the Pisgah National Forest. It is not a difficult hike. For part of the walk, you will be on sections of the Mountains-to-the-Sea Trail. Be sure to take a sharp left at the trail junction about 15 minutes from the start of your walk. To reach the trail, drive to the Bear Pen Gap parking overlook at milepost 427.6 on the Blue Ridge Parkway in Jackson County. The trail begins at the lower end of the parking lot.

THE JARRETT HOUSE; 219 Haywood St., Dillsboro, NC; (828) 477-4958; jarretthouse.com; $. The Jarrett House is one of the oldest inns in Western North Carolina with a storied history, but has undergone a change in ownership and is still finding its "sea legs" as of this writing. While we recommend waiting until much-needed repairs have taken place, here's the history: William Allen Dills, founder of the town of Dillsboro, built it in 1882, just two years after the railroad came through. Because the train from Asheville stopped here at noon, the Mount Beulah Hotel, as the Jarrett House was called then, became the place for passengers and railroad employees to eat lunch. By 1894 the hotel was serving "comers and stayers" from great distances away, including two women from Edenton, North Carolina, who were the first females to be seen smoking cigarettes in these parts. As Mrs. Minnie Dills Gray, one of William Dills's daughters, recalls in her History of Dillsboro, the two smokers "set the countryside agog and gave zest to the neighborhood gossip."

Dills sold the hotel to R. Frank Jarrett of Franklin in 1894. Jarrett, capitalizing on a sulfur spring that bubbled up into a soapstone basin at the rear of the hotel, renamed the place the Jarrett Springs Hotel. However the busy owner left the running of the hotel mostly to his wife, Miss Sally. After his death in 1950, a hotel operator from Gainesville, Georgia, bought the hotel and renamed it the Jarrett House.

Macon County

THE CHALET INN, 285 Lone Oak Dr., Whittier, NC; (828) 586-0251, (800) 789-8024; chaletinn.com; $$–$$$. Nestled on 22 acres in a mountain cove, The Chalet provides gracious lodging and combines the traditions and congeniality of an Alpine *gasthaus* with rustic surroundings. It's also the closest B&B to the main entrance of the Great Smoky Mountains National Park. The guest rooms have private balconies with carved wood railings festooned with flowers. European furnishings and German-Swiss windows continue the theme. From the Chalet's great room, you can view Doubletop Mountain, which dominates 19 miles of forested ridges. The Romantic Suite has a sitting room with a fireplace and whirlpool tub, a private entrance, and a private patio. Guests at the Chalet Inn can enjoy its hiking trails, lawn games, and picnic area with a grill. A candlelit breakfast is served in the sweet dining room or on the covered patio along the brook. It's a breakfast that satisfies all tastes. For the health conscious there's always plenty of fresh fruit, juices, and yogurt; for the world traveler with a hearty appetite longing for memories of the Alps, the German-style meats are fresh, and German wholegrain breads and Swiss muesli are imported. Also included are a variety of cheeses, fresh-baked *brotchen* (rolls), and soft-boiled eggs or an egg casserole.

COLONIAL PINES INN, 541 Hickory St., Highlands, NC; (828) 526-2060; colonialpinesinn.com; $$$. Large pillars framing a gigantic colonial American flag and a porch that stretches across the front of the house are a statement of eloquence and grace. This quiet country guest house was once home to several original Highlands families.

Within the inn is the warmth of knotty pine, antiques, and an eclectic mix of books, accessories, a playable grand piano, and a cozy fireside for chilly mountain evenings. The inn is surrounded by two acres of giant old rhododendron, hemlock, maple, and oak. Mountain views are spectacular from all rooms. There is also a guest house apartment on the property and a private cottage known as

"Miss Rebecca's Cottage," which is a short distance away. The cottage is very special, sleeping two to six in three bedrooms, and it has two baths.

Breakfast for guests in the main inn is sumptuous. You will usually find freshly made jams from the berry bushes on the property.

THE MAIN STREET INN, 270 Main St., Highlands, NC; (828) 526-2590; mainstreet-inn.com; $$–$$$. The Main Street Inn, built in the Federal Farmhouse style in 1885, has welcomed guests with Southern hospitality for more than a century, and was formerly known as the Phelps House. The original hand-hewn beams in its adjacent Guest House were exposed through the addition of cathedral ceilings, and many of the original sand-forged windows were saved and reinstalled in the rooms as interior windows for the enjoyment of guests. The inn, which is a block from Main Street shopping, features small rooms, all with private baths, individual heating and air-conditioning, direct-dial telephones, and a TV. Some rooms have sitting areas or balconies. In a pricy town, it's a good option. Room rates include a continental-style breakfast and afternoon tea.

THE OLD EDWARDS INN AND SPA, 445 Main St., Highlands, NC; (828) 526-9319; oldedwardsinn.com; $$$–$$$$. This gloriously-renovated hotel was established in 1876. The decor throughout has been carefully researched and restored in an elegant European country–manor style with dark wood paneling, exposed beams, and brocade furniture. Sink into the soft leather chairs for tea or cocktails in the splendid wood-paneled library, or spend some time in the state-of-the-art spa to be truly transported away. A Romanesque mosaic-filled soaking room adjacent to the dry and wet saunas is perfect for decompressing, as are individual massage and treatment rooms, each with its own crystal chandelier. The inn is truly a small village unto itself on a hill in Highlands, with first class service in the old-school tradition. The inn's premiere restaurant, **Madison's**, overlooks the courtyard gardens. It is surrounded by a hedge that wards off traffic noise and passersby on Main Street, and cascading waterfalls and a koi pond provide an idyllic atmosphere for relaxation and dining.

Swain County

FRYEMONT INN, 245 Fryemont St., Bryson City, NC; (828) 488-2159; fryemontinn.com; $–$$. Two generations of Browns have served as innkeepers at this comfortable 37-room inn that sits on a mountain shelf overlooking the Great Smoky Mountains National Park. Everything about the inn, which has had a tradition in hospitality here since 1923, is "woodsy:" its rustic exterior and lustrous hardwood floors; its chestnut-paneled bedrooms; the mountainous view from its tree-top rocking-chair porch; its lovely 80-degree swimming pool nestled in a grove of hemlock, dogwood, and poplar. The large lobby is more than matched by a giant stone fireplace that can hold logs 8 feet long. There is also a full-service lounge and a library. All rooms have private baths, but no two are alike, except for their many-paned pocket windows that slide back to let in the mountain air. Adjacent to the main lodge are cottage suites, each with a living room, a bedroom with a king-size bed, a wet bar, and a working fireplace. Some suites have loft bedrooms; others have private decks. Fryemont Inn's rates are reasonable and include both a solidly Southern breakfast and dinner. The public can enjoy meals by reservation. Fryemont Inn is open from Apr through Nov, but the cottage suites are open year-round.

> **i** For over 50 years, an inn's inclusion in the Select Registry of Distinguished Inns of North America has assured the traveler of consistently high standards. It is comparable to the Relaise de Chateaux of Europe in expectations. Of the 200 member inns across the United States, 11 are found in North Carolina's mountains. All select registry inns are included in this chapter.

HEMLOCK INN, 911 Galbraith Creek Rd., off US Hwy. 19, Bryson City, NC; (828) 488-2885; hemlockinn.com; $$–$$$$. This is an unpretentious place, but there's nothing unpretentious about the view. Hemlock Inn is built on a small mountain that overlooks three valleys, backed up by big mountains. Sitting on the front porch with a steaming cup of coffee in hand and watching the sunrise is something worth getting up early for! The inn opened in 1952 with nine rooms; its popularity grew, and the owners added 12 rooms and four cottages to meet the demand. The rooms and cottages (one very secluded and popular with honeymooners) are furnished in antiques and pieces made by mountain craftspeople. The rates include family-style breakfasts and dinners and all gratuities. Meals for the public are by reservation only and the innkeepers always feature fresh foods native to the area. There's a published cookbook, too.

MCKINLEY EDWARDS INN, 208 Arlington Ave., Bryson City, NC; (828) 488-9626, (888) 285-1555; mckinleyedwardsinn.com; $$–$$$. Originally the 1922 home of prominent Bryson City lawyer and the Honorable McKinley Edwards, a decorated WWI Marine war hero, the inn's main house provides cozy common areas for conversation, board games, reading, television, and breakfast. The judge's wife, Annie Angel Edwards, a prominent business woman, designed and oversaw construction of the adjacent Edwards Apartments in 1940, which she managed for 46 years. Those apartments were later transformed into the inn's spacious bedrooms. A sweet cabin with full kitchen works well for families on the grassy, forested grounds.

HOTELS AND MOTELS

Northern Mountains

Alleghany County

ALLEGHANY INN, 341 North Main St., Sparta, NC; (336) 372-2501, (888) 372-2501; alleghanyinn.com; $–$$. Not far off the Blue Ridge Parkway's milepost 217 west of Sparta, the Alleghany Inn provides reasonably priced rooms. There's an efficiency apartment-style accommodation for families and a small conference center.

Ashe County

GREENFIELD RESORT, 120 Greenfield Circle, West Jefferson, NC; (336) 246-9106; greenfieldcampgroundnc.com; $–$$. Greenfield Resort is spread over approximately 100 rolling acres of pasture, originally part of the Rufus McNeil farm, ca. 1847, at the foot of Mount Jefferson. Open Apr through Oct, the "campground" has rustic rental cabins, camping, and RV facilities with bathhouse and laundry for a bare-bones, casual, and fun stay. There's a clubhouse for groups, live music almost nightly, two stocked fishing ponds, a playground, and miles of hiking trails that wind around Mount Jefferson.

JEFFERSON LANDING LODGE; 184 West Landing Dr., Jefferson, NC; (800) 292-6274; visitjeffersonlanding.com; $$$–$$$$. Jefferson Landing is perfect for romantic getaways, golf outings, weddings, business retreats, and just plain relaxation. The Lodge accommodations offer comfortable rooms with panoramic views of the championship golf course from the balcony. Jefferson Landing Lodge is open year-round, and townhome rentals and golf packages are also available. The colonial-style Manor House has seven bedrooms for family or small group rental.

Avery County

BEECH ALPEN INN, 700 Beech Mountain Pkwy., Beech Mountain, NC; (828) 387-2252; beechalpen.com; $$–$$$$. Beech Alpen Inn is a country inn under the same management as its neighbor, Top of the Beech Ski Lodge, just down the road. Together they are known as Beech Mountain Inns. The Beech Alpen Inn is open year-round, offering a cool retreat in the summer and ski opportunities in the winter. Some of the rooms in this rustic, European-style inn have fireplaces and balconies, and all rooms have exposed-beam ceilings as well as great views of the mountains and ski slopes at nearby Ski Beech.

King- and queen-size beds are available. The Alpen Restaurant & Bar offers a menu of fine dining, featuring New York strip, filet mignon, superb crab cakes, and mountain trout prepared by their award-winning chef.

> **i** Call ahead if you need a refrigerator in your room for picnic food or leftovers if you'll be staying a while. Not all hotels have them in every room.

PARKVIEW LODGE, 10345 Linville Falls Hwy., Newland, NC; (828) 765-4787; parkviewlodge.com; $$–$$$. Right off the Linville Falls exit of the Blue Ridge Parkway, this lodge has a relaxed atmosphere hearkening back to quieter times. In addition to its 16 rooms, the complex has several cottages with kitchenettes and a suite on the picturesque grounds that back up to the parkway. You'll find plenty of wooded privacy and a swimming pool banked by cultivated wildflower beds. Parkview is popular with the parkway's hikers and campers, who occasionally stop in for a dose of civilization, especially hot showers. Parkview Lodge is open seasonally.

Mitchell County

BIG LYNN LODGE, 10860 NC Hwy. 226 A, Little Switzerland, NC; (828) 765-4257; biglynnlodge.com; $$$–$$$$. Just off the Blue Ridge Parkway milepost 332.5 is delightful Big Lynn Lodge, a welcome sight after a long drive. This rustic inn is a combination of individual rooms and cottages in a woodland setting. Some rooms offer a spectacular view of the valley below. An exceptionally nice feature here is the complimentary inclusion of breakfast and dinner with all accommodations. There's an early-bird discount if you make reservations prior to the busy fall season. Enjoy a fireplace and player piano in the living room. The lodge sits at 3,100 feet, so bring a sweater for evening.

Watauga County

THE ALPINE VILLAGE INN, 297 Sunset Dr., Blowing Rock, NC; (828) 295-7206; alpine-village-inn.com; $$–$$$. The Alpine Village Inn is in the heart of Blowing Rock, within walking distance of Main Street and all the shops and restaurants. This homey motel offers many of the detailed amenities of a bed-and-breakfast inn: 100 percent cotton towels, percale sheets, magazines and flowers in the rooms, individual heat and air-conditioning controls, flat-screen TVs, and complimentary newspapers and morning coffee. Antique furnishings and collectibles complement the homespun decor. Room refrigerators are available. The rocking chairs in the gazebo on the grounds are an invitation to take it easy. Rooms with a hot tub and fireplace are also available.

FALL CREEK CABINS, 1105 Fall Creek Rd., Purlear, NC; (336) 877-3131; fallcreekcabins.com; $$–$$$$. Surrounded by miles of lush forest on all sides, a gurgling creek, and a small waterfall, Fall Creek Cabins seem far removed from civilization. The cabins, built from fragrant western red cedar, house two bedrooms, two baths, a living room, loft, and kitchen. The full kitchen, with dishes and washer/dryer, enables you to be completely self-sufficient once you've done your initial grocery shopping. An enormous stack of firewood sits just outside the cabins for the fireplace inside, and a gas grill on the front porch means grilling those steaks and sausages will be a snap, leaving more time for outdoor activities or a longer soak in the hot tub on the covered porch—whichever your inclination may be. During the day be sure to explore the extensive hiking trails, streams, waterfalls, and a trout stream stocked by the state. You'll have to purchase a fishing license, which you can find at any hardware store, fishing and bait shop, or even large superstore.

HEMLOCK INN AND SUITES, 134 Morris St., Blowing Rock, NC; (828) 295-7987; hemlockinn.net; $$. For those of you who don't like to fool with the intimacy of a bed-and-breakfast, who prefer to be left to your own devices, or who prefer to spend your money on sightseeing, gifts, and food rather than your accommodations, the Hemlock Inn is for you. This motel-style inn is just off Blowing Rock's main street. It offers tidy rooms with double, queen-, or king-size beds, air-conditioning, private baths, and the added plus of a kitchenette in every room. A microwave, coffee pot, and refrigerator enable you to be quite independent in your travels here. Or if you plan on heavy-duty cooking, suites are available with fully equipped kitchens.

HILLWINDS INN, 315 Sunset Dr., Blowing Rock, NC; (828) 295-7660, (800) 821-4908; thevillageinnsofblowingrock.com; $$–$$$. This delightful little motel-style inn offers a relaxing respite from a day of shopping and dining. Choose from a variety of rooms with two double beds, or queen- or king-size bed, private bath, and TV. No pretensions here—it's relaxed and close to shopping and restaurants in downtown Blowing Rock. Flowers and benches decorate the exterior of the inn and maintain cozy seating in the lobby for sorting through the vast amount of information on the surrounding area, provided by the owners. A modest complimentary continental breakfast and wine and cheese reception are offered daily.

THE MEADOWBROOK INN, 711 Main St., Blowing Rock, NC; (828) 295-4300; meadowbrook-inn.com; $$–$$$. This gracious inn offers numerous amenities in elegant surroundings. Rooms and suites are furnished in a traditional decor, and deluxe accommodations include fireplaces and oversize whirlpool baths. A serene pond is bordered by landscaped grounds. The Meadowbrook Inn has an indoor heated pool and whirlpool and a fitness center. A glass-enclosed room adjacent to the pool area is used for meetings, conferences, and private dining.

SMOKETREE LODGE, 11914 Hwy. 105 South, Foscoe, NC; (828) 963-6505, (800) 422-1880 in NC; smoketree-lodge.com; $–$$. Tucked away off Highway 105 leading directly into Boone, it's the perfect no-frills stop-off when you plan to be spending most of your time out and about.

> **i** Blowing Rock is tiny, so you won't find huge hotel chains here. Instead, the area has an array of small, clean, and cozy motels too numerous to mention here. Many of these smaller motels are happy to take walk-ins if you are not quite sure of your travel plans beforehand.

SWISS MOUNTAIN VILLAGE, 2324 Flat Top Rd., Blowing Rock, NC; (828) 295-3373, (888) 785-1188; swissmountain.com; $$–$$$$. The mountain cabins and chalets of Swiss Mountain Village offer the homey charm of a bed-and-breakfast with the privacy of your own home away from home. Set on lovely landscaped grounds, surrounded by a forest filled with native rhododendron and mountain laurel, these rough-hewn timber Swiss-style chalets have a loft and stairway over a native-stone fireplace, and each comes furnished with everything you'll need to feel at home, right down to the towels, linens, stoneware, pots, and utensils. Hiking trails and a fishing pond are on the property for your outdoor recreation. Studio and one-, two-, and three-bedroom units are available, each with queen-size beds and queen-size sleeper sofas. Some have extra twin beds or bunks, so bring a crowd.

THE VILLAGE INN, 7876 Valley Blvd., Blowing Rock, NC; (828) 295-3380; thevillageinnsofblowingrock.com; $$–$$$. One third of the Village Inns of Blowing Rock, this pet friendly inn features guest rooms, suites, and cottages, situated on two landscaped acres with a brook, lake, gardens, and small orchard. Rooms have private decks. A complimentary continental breakfast and wine and cheese reception are offered daily in the Nickajack Lodge with wood-burning fireplace. Check with the front desk for complimentary "s'more" fixings for the fire pit outside.

Yancey County

ALPINE VILLAGE RESORT TOWNHOMES, 40 National Forest Dr., Burnsville, NC; (727) 389-3404; alpine-village-resort.com; $$$–$$$$. Set high back in the mountains in the shadow of spectacular Mount Mitchell,

Alpine Village is a cluster of private one- and two-bedroom, chalet-style condominiums with all the amenities of home, each accommodating four to six people. Most cabins are equipped with a kitchen, a dishwasher, a washer/dryer, a telephone, a whirlpool bath, linens, private decks, cable TV, and gas grills. A heated pool and a tennis court are on the grounds, and golf is available at a special discount to guests at nearby Mount Mitchell Golf Club (see our **Recreation** chapter). You can rent these cabins by the night, week, or month. A two-night minimum stay is usually required and availability runs May through Oct.

Central Mountains

Buncombe County

AC MARRIOTT, 10 Broadway St., Asheville, NC; (828) 259-2522; achotels .marriott.com/hotels/ac-hotel-asheville-downtown; $$–$$$$. One of the newest hotels on the downtown Asheville skyline, the AC features mountain or downtown views from almost every room. The sophisticated, clean design continues up to the rooftop restaurant, Capella 9, serving a European-style breakfast in the mornings, and rustic hot tapas and fine cocktails in the evening, slung by fedora-wearing mixologists. Well-known local chef Peter Pollay teamed up with AC to craft the menu of small plates. The stylish bar often features live music and art exhibitions.Outdoor seating on either side of the building is perfect for stargazing or watching the sun set over the town and mountains.

ALOFT HOTEL, 51 Biltmore Ave., Asheville, NC; (828) 232-2938; marriott.com/hotels/travel/avlal-aloft-asheville-downtown; $$–$$$. You can't get any more central than this. Located on one of downtown's main thoroughfares, the Aloft is a mix of sleek rooms, many with mountain views, featuring local contemporary art and well-loved common areas, such as the W XYZ Bar and its seating area with a concrete-surrounded fireplace and a large outdoor patio overlooking the main drag. Order tapas from the bar or something from the Starbucks grab-and-go cafe corner. A pool for guests only on the upper level overlooks the mountains.

CAMBRIA SUITES, 5 Page Ave., Asheville, NC; (828) 255-0888; cambria downtownasheville.com; $$–$$$. One of the newest downtown hotels, Cambria has rooms with plenty of mountain and city views, a modest valet parking price with unlimited in-and-out privileges, and a fantastic upper-level terrace and restaurant called Hemingway's. Here, you'll be treated to outdoor lounging, chic fire bowls on cool nights, and plenty of Cuban-style delicacies in the modern glass and concrete restaurant.

CROWN PLAZA ASHEVILLE, 1 Resort Dr., Asheville, NC; (828) 254-3211, (800) 733-3211; ashevillecp.com; $$–$$$$. This 120-acre resort and conference center caters to all, from small families to corporate and tourist groups. Located three minutes from downtown Asheville, the comfortable resort offers patios and balconies off almost every room. The resort's 34,000 square feet of meeting space accommodates a wide variety of functions, including ballroom banquets, sunset receptions, and boardroom meetings. Located on-site at the Crowne Plaza Resort Asheville, the Asheville Racquet Club (ARC) offer guests and members tennis, fitness, nine-hole golf course, indoor saltwater lap pool, heated outdoor pool, Adelaide Spa and Salon, Jacuzzi, hot tub, and sauna. In addition to the aforementioned, the four season resort also offers guests adventures like zip-lining among 100 year-old oak trees to mountain biking at the Asheville Adventure Center, adjacent to the Crown Plaza.

THE DOUBLETREE BILTMORE HOTEL, 115 Hendersonville Rd., Asheville, NC; (828) 274-1800, (800) 228-5151; biltmoreinns.com; $$$–$$$$. Wood-paneling and dramatic lighting in the hotel lobby complement the elegance of the lush furnishings. A photo exhibition of Biltmore Village and Biltmore Estate between the lobby and meeting rooms tells the story of the area. That space is often used for local artist exhibitions as well. The hotel caters to corporate businesses, with several flexible meeting rooms and on-site advance coordination of catering, audiovisual equipment, and entertainment. It's also a good choice for those spending much time on Biltmore Estate and in the south end of town.

FOUNDRY ASHEVILLE, 51 South Market St., Asheville, NC; (828) 552-8545; foundryasheville.com; $$$–$$$$. This chic hotel is the newest in downtown Asheville and is an imprint of Hilton's Curio Collection. Cozily tucked into what was historically downtown's African American business district, the new building has modern decor with classical touches, a hardwood floor lobby with sleek gas fireplace, a lounge, and house jazz orchestra that plays Thurs. A small shop there stocks local grab-and-go products. The hotel restaurant, Benne on Eagle, is led by locally-famed chef John Fleer, offering a unique elevated 'soul food' style dining experience.

FOUR POINTS BY SHERATON, 22 Woodfin St., Asheville, NC; (828) 253-1851; starwoodhotels.com; $$–$$$. Just off I-240, which loops around the city, Four Points by Sheraton is walking distance to most downtown attractions. Clean lines and light colors mark the interior, and an outdoor pool, meeting rooms, and a restaurant and lounge work for both families and folks in town for biz.

HAYWOOD PARK HOTEL, 1 Battery Park Ave., Asheville, NC; (828) 252-2522, (800) 228-2522; haywoodpark.com; $$$–$$$$. The Haywood Park Hotel was a prominent flagship in the resurgence of downtown Asheville in the

1980s. A full-service hotel in the heart of downtown was a risky business at that time, but the renovation of the historic Ivey's Department Store at the corner of Battery Park Avenue and Haywood Street into the sleek hotel was backed by strong business commitment. The success of this undertaking brought a level of sophistication to the inner city that set the tone for the upscale mood and cultural renaissance enjoyed by downtown Asheville today. The hotel renovation is an interesting use of space, opening up and reshaping the former boxy retail building. The adjoining atrium space, which houses shops, restaurants, and offices, brings the sky inside the heart of this city block with its vaulted ceiling, skylights, and gleaming glass elevator. Haywood Park has also hosted a number of celebrities, whose photos line the lobby walls. Bright and airy, Isa's Bistro occupies the street front corner of the hotel, serving brunch on Sun, fine lunches, and dinners. A stylish bar anchors the indoor wall to one side, and outdoor seating wraps around the front of the space for dining al fresco.

PRINCESS ANNE HOTEL, 301 East Chestnut St., Asheville, NC; (828) 258-0986; princessannehotel.com; $$–$$$. This charming historic hotel was built in 1924 and served in many different incarnations. It's now a 16-suite hotel that acts much like a small B&B. An in-house chef creates unique dinners Fri and Sat that are open to the public. All rooms include a hot, made-to-order breakfast each morning in the dining room and a wine and hors d'oeuvres reception each afternoon.

RENAISSANCE ASHEVILLE HOTEL, Thomas Wolfe Plaza, Asheville, NC; (828) 252-8211; marriott.com/hotels/travel/avlbr-renaissance-asheville-hotel; $$$–$$$$. The 12-story Renaissance Asheville Hotel, a prominent feature on the skyline of downtown Asheville, provides guests with a breathtaking view of the city and the mountains beyond. It's a great choice for those wishing to walk to concerts or musical venues, since it's within walking distance of Pack Square, restaurants, shopping, and downtown galleries. The AAA Three Diamond hotel has a pool and fitness center and the lobby contains a locally-owned gift shop with Appalachian crafts and jewelry, a bar, and a restaurant. The hotel also has a large ballroom, and a number of meeting rooms with state-of-the-art conference planning and support.

WINDSOR HOTEL, 36 Broadway St., Asheville, NC; (844) 494-6376; windsorasheville.com; $$$–$$$$. Constructed in 1907, The Windsor underwent several incarnations before becoming the beautiful 14-room chic hotel it is now (including a stint as apartments and a boarding house). An 18-month historical renovation completed in 2014 created these charming downtown suites with private bedroom, bath, washer/dryer, fully equipped kitchen, and living room. It has won several historic preservation awards and in 2019 was given special historical protections by the city.

Polk County

PISGAH INN, 408 Blue Ridge Pkwy., Waynesville, NC; (828) 235-8228; pisgahinn.com; $$–$$$. The Pisgah Inn is a landmark on the Blue Ridge Parkway, and authorized to provide services on the parkway under a concessions contract with the National Park Service. Open Apr through Oct, the inn provides cozy simplicity with double beds, private bath, and private porches or balconies directly overlooking Pisgah Ledge and the ever-changing play of lights and shadows on the mountain peaks below. Situated at 5,000 feet and just a hike down a trail from Mount Pisgah itself, Pisgah Inn is all about nature, so don't expect exceptional phone reception or Wi-Fi. The restaurant serves great country-style food at very reasonable prices for breakfast, lunch, and dinner, and the view from the dining room is spectacular. A new viewing deck and the ever-recent rockers below are also serviced by window for ordering take-away

A couple and their four-legged friend enjoy views from Slate Rock on Mount Pisgah. ExploreAsheville.com

snacks, wine, and beer. If you want to get out in all this beauty, you can hike on a number of trails—interconnecting with many other Pisgah Forest trails—that begin practically at the inn's door. During fall-foliage days, early reservations are essential.

Rutherford County

WYNDHAM RESORT AT FAIRFIELD MOUNTAINS, 747 Buffalo Creek Rd., Lake Lure, NC; (828) 625-9111, (866) 701-3950; $$$–$$$$. Taken over by Wyndham, this resort offers efficiencies, condominiums, rentals, and time-shares for travelers wishing to enjoy the scenery of Lake Lure and Chimney Rock and the recreation of two golf courses on the 2,400-acre resort property (Apple Valley Course and Bald Mountain Course). Several of Fairfield's units sit on the banks of the lake, opposite the town of Lake Lure. Others offer views of mountain ridges and foliage. Guests have access to an indoor and outdoor pools and a Mountain Kids Club Activity Program keeps everyone in the family busy.

Southern Mountains

Clay County

CHATUGE MOUNTAIN INN, 4238 US 64, Hayesville, NC; (828) 389-3000, (800) 948-2755; chatugemountaininn-nc.com; $. Super simple rooms east of Hayesville on US 64 going toward Hiwassee, Georgia. All rooms have air-conditioning, TV, and Wi-Fi. Although it's much like a typical 1960s-style roadside motel, small creature comforts like rocking chairs in front of the rooms, a gas grill for cooking out, and suites available with full kitchens, make this a perfectly fine little respite.

Haywood County

CHALET MOTEL AND APARTMENTS, 48 Holland Dr., Maggie Valley, NC; (828) 926-2811; mvchalet.com; $. Nestled up and off US 19 in a secluded and quiet spot, Chalet Motel rents apartments, efficiencies, and rooms. The average apartment has a living-dining room combination, a bedroom with two double beds, and a separate full kitchen. Many have private patios with pretty mountain views, and the chalet architecture is just charming.

TWINBROOK RESORT, 230 Twinbrook Ln., Maggie Valley, NC; (828) 926-1388, (800) 305-8946; twinbrookresort.com; $$. Set on 20 acres, this four-season facility features 14 one-, two-, three-, and four-bedroom, individually-crafted cottages with fireplaces, phones, and cable TV. The cottages are scattered among tall hemlocks. On site are an indoor pool, a hot tub, a game area, horseshoe pits, a volleyball court, and a playground. A heated indoor pool and hot tub function year-round. The lawn is flat and expansive and has shade trees, picnic tables, and grills; there are trails and trout streams close by.

Jackson County

MOUNTAIN BROOK COTTAGES, 208 Mountain Brook Rd., Sylva, NC; (828) 586-4329; mountainbrook.com; $$$. Midway between Sylva/Dillsboro and Franklin, these dozen charming brookside cottages offer fireplaces, equipped kitchens, and Wi-Fi, as well as rockers and porch swings! Some have bubble tubs/saunas and king-size beds. There is also a spa/sauna bungalow, but make note that the entire place closes for the winter. Mountain Brook offers a game room, a stocked trout pond, and a nature trail.

Macon County

SKYLINE LODGE, Flat Mountain Rd., Highlands, NC; (828) 526-2121; skyline-lodge.com; $$$. At an altitude of more than 4,000 feet, Skyline is housed in a Frank Lloyd Wright–designed, tastefully furnished building with 50 acres of grounds that have streams, lakes, waterfalls, and nature walks. Other attractions include a swimming pool, tennis courts, restaurant with ultra-traditional fine-dining, and spa with sauna, steam room, and whirlpool. The facility also offers facials, full-body massages, and foot- and hand-care sessions, along with guided fitness walks, aerobics, yoga, and seminars on healthful living (seminars are offered only to guests participating in the lodge's "Holiday Health" specials). Skyline Lodge is open year-round.

Swain County

HARRAH'S CHEROKEE CASINO AND HOTEL, 777 Casino Dr., Cherokee, NC; (828) 497-7777; caesars.com/harrahs-cherokee/hotel; $–$$$$. An enterprise of the Eastern Band of Cherokee Indians, this luxurious hotel and casino has an indoor heated pool, whirlpool, fitness center, and 10 restaurants! The lavish 21-story hotel provides luxury lodging that creates an upscale experience with 1,108 spacious rooms that include breathtaking views. The casino has 150,000 square feet of gaming space and offers 3,800 slot machines and over 100 traditional table games such as black jack, roulette, and craps. Harrah's also features a 3,000-seat event center, the luxurious 18,000-square-foot Mandara Spa, and eight retail shops. In addition to the 56-acre property, guests have privileged access to the Eastern Band of the Cherokee Nation–owned Sequoyah National Golf Club, named one of *Golf Magazine*'s best new golf courses.

CAMPGROUNDS

You can pitch a tent in the woods, down a creek prong of a wilderness area, or within a designated forest campground here in the mountains of North Carolina.

Backcountry Camping

A free backcountry permit is required for all persons spending the night in the park's backcountry. (Day-hikers are not required to register or to obtain permits.) Backcountry permits are available at most park campgrounds, ranger stations, and at the Sugarlands and Oconaluftee Visitor Centers. Registration areas at ranger stations and campgrounds are accessible 24 hours a day. Visitor center registration stations are open from 9 a.m. to 5 p.m.

Camping is permitted only at designated sites and shelters. The few backcountry campsites and all shelters require advance reservations. A Great Smoky Mountains Trail map for backcountry campsite locations and information is available at visitor centers for a small fee. To make a reservation call (423) 436-1231 from 8 a.m. to 6 p.m. seven days a week.

(For more information on the Great Smoky Mountains National Park, see our **Forests, Parks, and Waterfalls** chapter.)

National Forest Camping

Most national forest campgrounds have no hookups, but all developed campgrounds have at least one 25-foot parking spur, and many campgrounds have one or more campsites that can accommodate a large motor home or trailer that's 35 feet long or longer. Some sites provide pull-through drives. Primitive camps that are scattered all over the forests, including the wilderness areas, are for tents only. A few of those that offer some amenities, like drinking water, are listed below.

In addition to these listed campgrounds, there are also 10 group camps designed for organized groups of 25 to 100 people: Rattler Ford in the Cheoah District; Apple Tree and Kemsey Creek in the Wayah District; Kuykendall, Cove Creek, and White Pines in the Pisgah District; Silvermine and Harmon Den Horse Camp in the Appalachian French Broad District; Briar Bottom in the Appalachian Toecane District; and Boone Fork in the Grandfather District. Group camps are available only by reservation through the district office where the site is located. (See our list of district offices in the **Forests, Parks, and Waterfalls** chapter.) The exceptions are the campgrounds located in the Pisgah District. Call toll-free (877) 444-6777 at least 10 days, but no more than 360 days, in advance for group camping, and no more than 240 days in advance for family camping.

Blue Ridge Parkway Region

CRABTREE MEADOWS CAMPGROUND, Mile 339.5, Blue Ridge Pkwy., Micaville, NC; (828) 675-5444; www.blueridgeparkway.org/camping. Seventy-one tent sites and 22 RV sites lie close to large grassy clearings. The lawn of wildflowers runs up to the forest edge, with mountains visible in the distance. The campground has the requisite picnic tables, grills, and tent pads, but no showers. Water fountains and hand water pumps are centrally located.

This is a quiet, peaceful area awash with rhododendrons and hardwood trees and a good base camp for hiking in the Pisgah National Forest; trails lead to scenic falls on Crabtree Creek. Crabtree Falls Trail, a strenuous 2.5-mile loop, begins near the campground entrance. A camp store, gas station, and restaurant/gift shop are also nearby.

DOUGHTON PARK CAMPGROUND, Mile 239.0, Blue Ridge Pkwy., Laurel Springs, NC; (336) 372-8877; www.recreation.gov/camping/camp grounds/233369. No reservations are needed here. It's first come, first served; about $10 per adult, $5 for Golden Age Passport holders, and youths younger than 18 stay for free. There are 110 tent sites, including tent pads, picnic tables, grills, and lantern posts scattered in wooded areas and around a grassy hillside. A smaller area with 25 RV sites lies across the road, though none of the sites have hookups.

Restrooms and water spigots are available, but no showers. This is camping as it was meant to be! The park itself covers approximately 6,000 acres in Alleghany and Wilkes Counties and is the largest park on the parkway. It was named after Robert Lee Doughton, a US representative who served from 1911 to 1953 and who was an advocate for the construction of the parkway.

JULIAN PRICE CAMPGROUND, Mile 297.0, Blue Ridge Pkwy., Laurel Springs, NC; (828) 963-5911; www.recreation.gov/camping/campgrounds/234037. Reservations aren't required for Julian Price. Like Doughton Park, it's first come, first served; about $10 per adult, $5 for Golden Age Passport holders, youths younger than 18 free. This campground sprawls across both sides of the parkway near Price Lake. One hundred twenty-nine tent sites lie fairly close together, divided by blossoming rhododendron bushes. Sixty-eight RV sites are also available, though with no plug-ins. Tent pads, picnic tables, grills, and spigots provide adequate comforts.

There are restrooms, but no showers. Firewood can be purchased nearby. The park is marked by mild terrain, covered by a dense hardwood forest. Poplars, chestnut trees, and maples make a pleasant canopy for hikers and campers. Canoes may be rented at the lake, and hiking trails nearby lead to two smaller lakes and creeks.

LINVILLE FALLS CAMPGROUND, RV PARK & CABINS, 717 Gurney Franklin Rd., Linville Falls, NC; (828) 765-2681; linvillefalls.com. Primitive tent sites, full hook-up RV sites, and eight furnished cabins are available in the campground of this 440-acre wooded park. Tent site 15 is the most secluded. The surrounding forest seems almost primordial with moss-covered trees and waterfalls that plunge through the granite walls of Linville Gorge. Fishing in the nearby Linville River is allowed, and a visitor center and bookstore provide campers with plenty of area information.

MOUNT PISGAH CAMPGROUND, Mile 408.8, Blue Ridge Pkwy., Balsam Gap, NC; (828) 648-2644; www.recreation.gov/camping/campgrounds/234182. The entrance to Mount Pisgah Campground with its 70 tent sites and 70 RV sites lies directly across from Pisgah Inn on the parkway. Small sites, close together, are arranged in three landscaped loops. A dense forest adds privacy. There are no showers, but central hand water pumps and individual picnic tables, grills, and lantern posts are provided. Maps of the area, including hiking trails, are available at the camp. A picnic area lies in a meadow bordered by rhododendron.

Great Smoky Mountains National Park

Of the 10 developed campsites in this national park, five are in Tennessee and five are in North Carolina. All have tent sites, picnic tables, fireplace grills, and bathrooms with cold water and flush toilets but no showers. There are a limited number of trailer sites but none of them have hookups. Sewage disposal stations are located at the Smokemont, Cades Cove, Deep Creek, and Cosby Campgrounds and across the road from the Sugarland Visitors Center about 5 miles south of Gatlinburg, Tennessee, on US 441. The stations aren't available for use in winter.

Three of the campgrounds—Elkmont and Cades Cove on the Tennessee side and Smokemont on the North Carolina side—take reservations from May 15 through Oct 31, which can be made by calling (800) 365-2267 up to five months in advance. All other campgrounds are on a first-come, first-served basis.

No more than six people may occupy a site (two tents or one RV and one tent). Group camping sites are available at Big Creek, Cades Cove, Cataloochee, Cosby, Deep Creek, Elkmont, and Smokemont. Reservations at group camps are required and can be made by calling (800) 365-2267 or (423) 436-1266.

There is a seven-day limit at any campground between May 15 and Oct 31 and a 14-day limit between Nov 1 and May 14. Pets are allowed in the campground as long as they are on a leash or otherwise confined.

The following list of camping areas shows the number of campsites, fees per night, open/close dates, and maximum RV lengths. To locate these camps, pick up a map or ask for directions at any of the park visitor centers listed in our **Forests, Parks, and Waterfalls** chapter, which also contains additional information on the Great Smoky Mountains National Park. Most sites have overnight fees. All of the sites below can be accessed online at www.mysmokymountainpark.com/where-to-stay-camp-eat/where-should-i-camp-in-smoky.

ABRAMS CREEK CAMPGROUND, Abrams Creek Rd., Gatlinburg, TN; (865) 448-4103. There are 16 camping sites at the Abrams Creek Campground on the northwestern edge of the park. It is reached from US 129 as the road circles the eastern end of the scenic Chilhowee Reservoir in Tennessee. Some sites will take RVs up to 12 feet long and are open from Mar 21 to Nov 3.

BALSAM MOUNTAIN CAMPGROUND, Balsam Mountain Rd., Cherokee, NC; (877) 444-6777. When you camp here be sure to have a sweater handy even in the summer, because at 5,310 feet it's the highest and coolest of the park's developed campgrounds. To reach it, turn off the Blue Ridge Parkway onto Balsam Mountain Road. Here you'll find 46 sites (some will take 30-foot RVs) and a 1-mile, self-guided nature trail through alpine woods. Balsam Mountain is open from May 23 through Sept 29.

BIG CREEK CAMPGROUND, Big Creek Entrance Rd., Newport, NC. This campground is just 2 miles off I-40. It has a ranger station and 12 tent-only campsites, and is open from May 21 through Nov 3. A very narrow, graveled, one-lane road leads from this area to the Cataloochee Campground some 15 miles away, but should the Cosby Campground be full, don't attempt this road with trailers or RVs or in the dark. In fact no RVs are allowed at Big Creek.

CADES COVE CAMPGROUND, 10042 Campground Dr., Townsend, TN; (877) 444-6777. One hundred fifty-nine sites capable of handling 35-foot RVs are available at this popular campground in Cades Cove, home to 700 people in the last century. (See our **Forests, Parks, and Waterfalls** chapter.) A few of these early buildings are still preserved, and the areas they originally cleared for farming are wonderful places to spot all kinds of wildlife, particularly in the early morning and late evening. This campground is open year-round.

CATALOOCHEE CAMPGROUND, Cove Creek Rd., Waynesville, NC. This is another campground in the area of two pioneer communities, Little Cataloochee and Big Cataloochee. With a combined population of 1,200 people, it was the largest settlement in the Smokies. Some buildings are still there (see our **Forests, Parks, and Waterfalls** chapter), and this area, too, is a good place to see wild turkey and deer.

The pretty campground, tucked into tall evergreens, has 27 sites and will take some 31-foot RVs. To reach it take partly paved/mostly graveled Cove Creek Road off of US 276 for nearly 12 miles. We think you'll find the rather rough trip and sharp curves worth it. Cataloochee is open from Mar 21 through Nov 3.

COSBY CAMPGROUND, 127 Cosby Entrance Rd., Cosby, TN. Even if you don't want to camp, this is a good place to go to hike. In addition to a self-guiding nature trail, there are trails that will take you through lovely woods and to waterfalls. (Ask folks at the camp office for some suggestions.)

If you do want to camp, you are likely to find room at one of the 175 campsites here when other campgrounds are full. You can reach Cosby Campground by taking US 321 and cutting south on Tennessee Highway 32. Turn onto Cosby Park Road. The campsites will take 25-foot RVs. Cosby is open Mar 21 through Nov 3.

DEEP CREEK TUBE CENTER & CAMPGROUND, 1090 West Deep Creek Rd., Bryson City, NC; (828) 488-6055; deepcreekcamping.com. The Deep Creek Campground, just outside Bryson City, rests on the site of yet another pioneer community and is a great place to go even if you don't want to camp here. It's only a short walk from the campground to Toms Branch, Juney Whank, and Indian Creek Falls. In addition Deep Creek is a popular place to go tubing.

The campground has 189 sites, some of which are suitable for 26-foot RVs. In the summer, programs that are advertised on the camp's bulletin board are offered at the camp's amphitheater. The campground is open from Apr 11 through Nov 3, but is open to picnickers and hikers year-round.

ELKMONT CAMPGROUND, 434 Elkmont Rd., Gatlinburg, TN; (877) 444-6777. The Elkmont Campground lies 1 mile off Little River Road, one of the easiest (except for the traffic) and most popular drives in the park. Early in this century Elkmont itself was a summer resort with dozens of cottages. Today it has 120 campsites, some suitable for 32-foot RVs. There is a self-guiding nature trail here, and park rangers offer programs for campers and noncampers alike. Elkmont is open from Mar 21 through Dec 1.

SMOKEMONT CAMPGROUND, Newfound Gap Rd., Gatlinburg, TN. The site of this popular campground was once a small pioneer settlement and then a booming logging village. It was operated by Champion Fibre, which owned 93,000 acres of timber here prior to 1931. Today, second-growth timber has hidden old lumbering scars, but a stroll from the parking area will bring you to Mingus Mill, where corn has been ground into meal since 1886.

There is a short, self-guided nature trail along the stream in the campground that contains 140 sites, some suitable for 27-foot RVs. Smokemont is open year-round.

Nantahala National Forest Camping

To make reservations for the campgrounds below, call 877-444-6777 or visit www.recreation.gov.

CABLE COVE RECREATION AREA, FR 520 off Hwy. 28 E., Robbinsville, NC; (828) 479-6431. Near Fontana Lake, this camping area that's open from Apr 15 through Oct 31 offers 26 sites, restrooms with flush toilets, a picnic area, water, fishing, trails, and a boat ramp.

CHEOAH POINT CAMPGROUND, 1373 Thunder Bird Mountain Rd., Robinsville, NC; (828) 479-6431. At this area on Lake Santeetlah, you'll find 26 sites, restrooms with flush toilets, water, a picnic area, a boat ramp, swimming, fishing, and trails. It is open from Apr 15 through Oct 31.

ACCOMMODATIONS

HORSE COVE CAMPGROUND, FR 415, Robbinsville, NC; (828) 479-6431. Located almost 13 miles from Robbinsville and open from Mar 31 through Oct 31, Horse Cove has 18 sites, water, flush and vault toilets, fishing, and trails. There are also five sites open in winter at no fee, but there is no water available at that time.

HURRICANE CREEK HORSE & PRIMITIVE CAMPGROUND, FR 67, Otto, NC; (828) 524-6441. This is a primitive camp with undesignated sites and no drinking water. However, it offers vault toilets, fishing, and horse and hiking trails. It is open from Mar 15 through Jan 1, depending on the weather.

JACKRABBIT MOUNTAIN CAMPGROUND, 464 Jack Rabbit Rd., Hayesville, NC; (828) 837-5152. Open from May 1 through Oct 31, this large camping area on Chatuge Lake has 103 sites and provides a dump station, a picnic area, flush toilets, amphitheater, showers, drinking water, swimming, a boat ramp, fishing, and hiking trails. There are evening programs in season.

STANDING INDIAN CAMPGROUND, access off Forest Development Rd 67 Franklin, NC; (828) 524-6441. There are 84 campsites at this campground located on the Nantahala River, along with a picnic area, restrooms, an amphitheater, shows, drinking water, and hiking trails. Standing Indian is open from Mar 31 through Dec 1. There is a small fee per car for day use.

TSALI RECREATION AREA, FR 521, Robbinsville, NC; (828) 479-6431. Made up of 42 campsites on Fontana Lake, Tsali has a picnic area, flush toilets, showers, drinking water, a boat ramp, fishing, hiking, biking, and horse trails. There is a trail-use fee in this popular area. It is open from Apr 15 through Oct 31.

VAN HOOK GLADE CAMPGROUND, 14014 Highlands Rd., Highlands, NC; (877) 444-6777. Since Van Hook Glade is located just off picturesque and popular US 64 near Highlands and all its attractions, you might have to be a little lucky to get one of the 20 sites in this campground in high season. It has flush toilets, drinking water, and hiking trails. Campers also have access to adjoining Cliffside Lake and can use the showers there. Van Hook is open from Apr 1 through Oct 31.

Pisgah National Forest Campgrounds
To make reservations for the campgrounds below, call 877-444-6777 or visit www.recreation.gov.

The Legend of Standing Indian Mountain

Many years ago, say the Cherokee, a great winged monster swooped down and carried off a child playing near the village and took him to a cave high in the cliffs of a nearby mountain. Frightened people from all around came together and prayed to the Great Spirit for help in getting rid of the huge beast. After days and nights of prayer, a dazzling lightning bolt and a booming thunderclap came out of a clear sky and shattered the mountain, killing the creature and its offspring.

The lightning was so powerful, though, that it destroyed all the trees on the mountain's summit, producing the bald top that it has to this day. It also turned a warrior, who was posted on the mountain to keep an eye on the beast, to stone. Some said it was his punishment for being a poor sentry. Over the hundreds of years since this event occurred, this standing Indian has been worn away to a pillar of stone with an ill-defined head on top. In fact you may even have some trouble distinguishing the stone pillar from the jumble of rock that surrounds it, but you will be able to see the cliffs that were torn asunder by the Great Spirit's lightning bolt.

ACCOMMODATIONS

BLACK MOUNTAIN CAMPGROUND/BRIAR BOTTOM GROUP CAMPGROUND, 50 Black Mountain Campground Rd., Burnsville, NC; (828) 675-5616. This very attractive campground on the South Toe River has 46 sites, flush toilets, drinking water, an amphitheater, fishing, and hiking trails. It's open from Apr 14 through Nov 1. The fee includes guided activities in season.

CAROLINA HEMLOCKS RECREATION AREA, 6000 Hwy. 80 S., Burnsville, NC; (828) 675-5509. Here you'll find flush toilets, drinking water, swimming, fishing, hiking trails, and 32 campsites. There is also a picnic shelter that is available by reservation. The area is open from Apr 15 through Oct 30.

CURTIS CREEK CAMPGROUND, 3799 Curtis Creek Rd., Old Fort, NC; (828) 652-2144. This tents-only campground has no-charge, primitive, undesignated sites. However, there is drinking water, vault toilets, a picnic area, fishing, and hiking trails. It is open from Mar 19 through Dec 31.

DAVIDSON RIVER RECREATION AREA, US 276, Pisgah Forest, NC; (877) 444-6777. One of the most popular campgrounds in North Carolina's mountains, Davidson River (situated along the beautiful river of the same name) has 161 campsites and is just 1.3 miles inside the Brevard entrance to Pisgah National Forest. It offers a dump station, flush toilets, an amphitheater, showers, drinking water, fishing, and hiking trails. There are also guided activities in season. It's open all year. Reservations are advisable.

LAKE POWHATAN RECREATION AREA & CAMPGROUND, 375 Wesley Branch Rd., Asheville, NC; (877) 444-6777. This is another extremely popular campground on Lake Powhatan; it's less than 8 miles from Asheville and has 98 sites, a dump station, a picnic area, flush toilets, showers, drinking water, swimming, fishing, and hiking trails. A lifeguard and guided activities are offered in season. Lake Powhatan is open from Apr 7 through Nov 1.

MORTIMER CAMPGROUND, 8384 Hwy. 90, Collettsville, NC; (828) 652-2144. Mortimer has 23 sites, a picnic area, vault toilets, drinking water, hiking trails, and fishing for a fee. In winter there is no fee, but there is also no drinking water.

NORTH MILLS RIVER RECREATION AREA, 5289 N. Mills River Rd., Mills River, NC; (877) 444-6777. Located on North Mills River, this campground has 28 sites, a dump station, a picnic area, flush and vault toilets, drinking water, hiking trails, and fishing. It is open from Apr 1 through Oct 31, and there is a 50 percent reduction in fees during the off-season.

ROCKY BLUFF CAMPGROUND, 2145 Hwy. 209 S., Hot Springs, NC; (828) 622-3202. This campground on Spring Creek has 30 sites, a picnic area, flush toilets, drinking water, an amphitheater, hiking trails, and fishing. It's open from Memorial Day through Labor Day weekend.

SUNBURST CAMPGROUND, 8820 Lake Logan Rd., Canton, NC; (828) 877-3350. Based at the site of an old logging town, Sunburst has nine primitive sites, a picnic area, flush toilets, and drinking water. It's open from May through Oct.

Dining

Mountain cooking brings to mind visions of fluffy biscuits, thick gravy, corn bread, soup beans, buttery grits, soft-cooked vegetables like okra and squash, fried chicken, molasses-based barbecue, and deep-dish pies of all varieties. You'll find plenty of family-style restaurants specializing in authentic country cooking—especially in smaller communities—and many fine-dining establishments in larger towns are rediscovering and highlighting Appalachian cuisine. Yet in the past decade the dining landscape has changed immeasurably. As the era of food television and blogs, rockstar chefs, and "farm-to-table" sensibilities mixed with hyper-localism blossoms, our mountain towns have risen to the challenge. Particularly Asheville has become a mecca for "food life," with everything from upstart food trucks and pop-up restaurants to James Beard-nominated chefs opening more than one establishment to feed the need. So much so that our own convention and visitors' bureau has dubbed this city *"Foodtopia."*

As our area grows so, too, do the dining choices. You could easily plan a vacation around the culinary options in many of our towns and communities, and many travelers do.

Our selections, which are featured by region, may vary greatly in style, from the smallest coffee shop with the best biscuits, burgers, and chocolate

ExploreAsheville.com

malts in the area to the most elegant haute cuisine from a French master chef. Variety is the spice of life, after all, and mostly we've tried to highlight locales that give you a taste of the region and maintain a proven track record.

Price Code

Most of these restaurants will accept major credit cards for payment. While menu changes may certainly affect the pricing of some restaurants, we've provided a pricing guide for an idea of what you can expect on the check for a basic meal for two (without desserts and alcoholic beverages). This table does not reflect tax or gratuities. Enjoy!

$	Less than $25
$$	$25 to $40
$$$	$40 to $60
$$$$	$60 and higher

Northern Mountains

Alleghany County

STATION'S INN, 14355 Hwy. 18, Laurel Springs, NC; (336) 359-2888; stationsinn.com; $–$$. This country store, motel, and restaurant surrounds itself with everything motorcycle and car. Two dining rooms, porch seating, and a bar are decorated with gadgetry, signs, and items devoted to the all-American enjoyment of the open road. Burgers, hot dogs, pork tenderloin, ribs, steaks, and grilled chicken are the menu choices here. Live music arrives on the weekends.

Ashe County

GLENDALE SPRINGS INN AND RESTAURANT, 7414 Hwy. 16, Glendale Springs, NC; (336) 982-2103; glendalespringsinn.com; $–$$$. Once a general merchandise store, a circuit courthouse, a post office, a chapel, a community center, and a boarding house, the inn features two wood-paneled dining rooms and one white and peach room, while side-porch dining by the garden is also available. (Read more about the inn in our **Accommodations** chapter.) Lazy fans spin overhead in the main dining hall, where creaking wooden floors and an old piano evoke visions of Saturday night country jamborees. The ambience and cuisine are quite sophisticated here, with a seasonally changing menu. Tables are covered in crisp linens, and the menu offers delicacies whipped up by the resident chef. Do call for evening reservations, but feel free to walk in for lunch.

LOUISIANA PURCHASE, 397 Shawneehaw Ave., Banner Elk, NC; (828) 898-5656; louisianapurchasefoodandspirits.com; $$–$$$$. If your heart belongs to the moss-draped avenues of New Orleans and the sultry tones of Bourbon Street, and your palate enjoys Cajun, Creole, or classic French cuisine,

DINING

you'll want to try Louisiana Purchase in Banner Elk. The classy restaurant with over 30 years of bringing the flavor of old New Orleans to the High Country also specializes in classic French, all beautifully presented for an elegant dining experience. The restaurant also has an extensive wine list, and often does wine dinner with visiting vintners. Reservations are suggested.

MOUNTAIN AIRE SEAFOOD AND STEAK HOUSE, 9930 NC Hwy. 16, West Jefferson, NC; (336) 982-3060; mountainaireseafood.com; $–$$$. This friendly restaurant is a welcome sight after working up an appetite traveling the winding two-lanes of Ashe County. (The restaurant is just minutes from Holy Trinity Church, up the road in Glendale Springs, where you can see the exquisite Ben Long fresco of the Last Supper.) The menu boasts a selection of fresh seafood, delivered several times a week from the coast. Fresh stuffed flounder, salt-and-pepper catfish, and stir-fried shrimp are customer favorites. It's a totally casual place with vinyl booths and many fried seafood options, too. You can also order a substantial filet mignon, chicken strips (grilled or fried), and crispy homemade hush puppies.

RIVER HOUSE, 1896 Old Field Creek Rd., Grassy Creek, NC; (336) 982-2109; riverhousenc.com; $$–$$$$. The River House restaurant, part of a lovely 1870 farmhouse bed-and-breakfast inn, is a destination for diners from across the country and abroad. The fare at River House is an unusual mix of European haute cuisine and down-home American style. Unlike the petite-size servings you get in some restaurants, where presentation is the primary goal, generous portions are guaranteed at River House—and the presentation is impressive too. A four-course tasting menu follows the Salon Series entertainment on Sun afternoon.

Avery County

ESEEOLA LODGE, 175 Linville Ave., Linville, NC; (828) 733-4311; eseeola.com; $$–$$$$. This is a rare opportunity for elegant dining at a historic lodge (see our **Accomodations** chapter). Experience a sumptuous breakfast, self-served from the buffet of fresh fruit, cereals, and breakfast breads, or a table service of heartier fare. Lunch and dinner are served at the club just across the road; there is a bar for sitting and sipping. For those not staying at the resort, reservations for dinner are requested.

FAMOUS LOUISE'S ROCK HOUSE RESTAURANT, 23175 Linville Falls Hwy., Linville Falls, NC; (828) 765-2702; facebook.com/louisesrockhouse; $. You can dine in three counties and never step outside the door of Famous Louise's Rock House Restaurant, which is just 3 miles north of Linville Caverns. This quaint family-owned restaurant has the distinction of sitting directly on the spot where Burke, McDowell, and Avery Counties meet. Signs point the way to your dining location—and favorite county—or you can sit near the fireplace, the spot where all three counties come together! Your food will be cooked in Avery County, picked up by your waitress in Burke County, and very often served just over the line in McDowell County. Credit cards are not accepted. Simple, old school home cooking.

STONEWALLS, 344 Shawneehaw Ave., Banner Elk, NC; (828) 898-5550; stonewallsrestaurant.com; $$–$$$. This rustic stone building is home to a restaurant that's been a stalwart of hearty American cuisine in the area since 1985. Now, under new ownership, the restaurant continues the tradition of serving up steakhouse-style cuts of beef found in prime rib, sirloin, rib eye, New York strip, and filet mignon, as well as chicken and ribs, pasta and seafood. They also kept the amazing 50-item salad bar, but added Sunday brunch with chicken and waffles, pulled pork grilled cheese sandwiches, brunch salads, and steak and eggs.

TARTAN RESTAURANT, 31 Coffey Rd., Linville, NC; (828) 733-0779; facebook.com/thetartanrestaurant; $–$$. This unassuming simple family restaurant near Grandfather Mountain serves an array of mountain favorites like country ham, biscuits, burgers, a litany of sandwiches, chicken and dumplings, and other meat-and-three-style meals. The menu offers breakfast, lunch, and dinner specialties.

Madison County

STAR DINER, 115 N Main St., Marshall, NC; (828) 649-9900; $$–$$$. Oh, this is quite the little find. This tiny restaurant, squeezed into a former 1920s service station, delights and surprises with the inspired continental cuisine that comes out of the kitchen of a Johnson & Wales-trained chef who oversaw the expansion of Tupelo Honey's into multiple states. The chef and his wife run this sweet operation, creating the stuff of dreams—brown butter almond-crusted Carolina mountain trout with beurre blanc, braised pork belly with cheesy cauliflower mash, and other locally-sourced fine cuisine. Call for reservations; the place is small and atmospheric.

SWEET MONKEY BAKERY, 133 Main St., Marshall, NC; (828) 649-2489; sweetmonkeybakery.com; $–$$. Much more than a bakery, the cozy cafe in this historical little town, nonetheless, creates great cakes, pastries, cookies, and pies. But stay for a New Zealand lamb chop, clams in white wine cream sauce, or kale, squash, and wild mushroom vegetable lasagna first.

Mitchell County

CHALET RESTAURANT AT SWITZERLAND INN, 86 High Ridge Rd., Little Switzerland, NC; (828) 765-2153; switzerlandinn.com; $$–$$$. The

Caviar from Canton

Caviar from the mountains? It's not so unusual if you look at the early beginnings of fish farming: Dick Jennings founded Sunburst Trout Company in 1946 in the region of Pisgah National Forest. At first Dick supplied farm-raised trout, but then he began experimenting with smoked trout and trout pâté. In more recent years, working with his daughter, Sally Eason, who now heads the business, Dick has worked up the trout eggs, or roe, for eating. Eventually their caviar collection caught on in restaurants throughout the region. As in the case of the pungent mountain onion, the ramp, which found its way to the kitchens of New York chefs, so too has the rainbow trout caviar of the mountains of Western North Carolina caught on. Eason has even taken "coals to Newcastle" by traveling to Armenia, where sturgeon roe from the Caspian Sea reigns as king. She demonstrated to caviar collectors a better way to harvest the eggs. This caviar is best with poached trout or smoked trout, on salads, toasted bagels, or toast corners, and with cream cheese or butter.

views are phenomenal and the menu is varied with a good wine list in this cozy lodge-style locale. Menu items run the gamut from Cajun frog legs to New Zealand rack of lamb and plank salmon.

Watauga County

BISTRO ROCA, 143 Wonderland Trail, Blowing Rock, NC; (828) 295-4008; bistroroca.com; $$–$$$. A true insiders' locale for crispy-crust individual pizzas baked in the wood-fired brick oven, which is the centerpiece of this restaurant. Inspired pork chops, prosciutto-honey-baked figs, robust burgers, pan-seared tuna, and other rustic dishes appeal to those locals who want to reconnect and relax in this cozy place tucked into a bend just past Blowing Rock's Mayview Lake. Sip on a digestif afterwards at Antlers Bar, where part of the decor features photos of patrons' dogs. Antlers is open until midnight.

COBO SUSHI BAR AND CAFE, 161 Howard St., Boone, NC; (828) 386-1201; cobosushi.com; $–$$. CoBo owner and chef Joseph Miller spent five years in Steamboat Springs, Colorado (the "Co" in CoBo), apprenticing in sushi restaurants, and craving that similar sushi experience in his hometown of Boone (the "Bo" in the name) upon his return. More than raw fish and sticky

DINING

rice, CoBo has become a lively late-night downtown hotspot. It's spacious for larger groups and the bar area is perfect for cocktails and quality sushi rolls, and larger hot entrees as well.

> **i** To be clear: in the mountains, folks often refer to the noontime meal as dinner and the evening meal as supper.

DAN'L BOONE INN RESTAURANT, 130 Hardin St., Boone, NC; (828) 264-8657; danlbooneinn.com; $–$$. Since 1959, this old-fashioned, family-style restaurant has been drawing locals and visitors for hearty dining in a historic structure that was Boone's first hospital. For a fixed price, big serving bowls and platters of food are brought to your table, including fried chicken, country-style steak, biscuits, mashed potatoes, green beans, slaw, corn, fresh-stewed apples, dessert, and beverage. In the summer, lunch and dinner are served each day. Winter hours are more limited. Reservations may be made for groups of 15 or more. No credit or debit cards.

THE GAMEKEEPER RESTAURANT, 3005 Shull's Mill Rd., Blowing Rock, NC; (828) 963-7400; gamekeeper-nc.com; $$$–$$$$. The Gamekeeper is in a rustic lodge-style converted house built in 1926 near Yonahlossee Resort on Shull's Mill Road between Boone and Blowing Rock. This elegant (but not stiff!) restaurant with starched linens, impeccable service, and unforgettable fare, accommodates guests in cozy private nooks warmed by a fireplace. Dining here is a culinary experience: The menu is composed entirely of wild game—and not just venison either. Selections often include boar, antelope, bison, and duck. The restaurant has a fine wine selection, a seasonal "apres ski" Bavarian menu, rich desserts, and a boozy dessert beverage menu. Come to the jovial bar for small plates and fun cocktails.

JOY BISTRO, 115 New Market Centre, Boone, NC; (828) 265-0500; joybistroboone.com; $$–$$$. The majority of the bistro's dishes fall into categories of familiar house-made pasta dishes, gnocchi, pork chops, heirloom chicken, and the like (all well-crafted). But pecan-encrusted salmon over black quinoa and parsnips, veal meatloaf, and escargot add an elegance to the menu that belies its setting tucked into the side of a shopping center.

THE NEW PUBLIC HOUSE, 239 Sunset Dr., Blowing Rock, NC; (828) 295-3487; thenewpublichouse.com; $$$–$$$$. Cocktails on the porch and in the cozy bar at the front of the house are what we look forward to most here.

The main dining room in back is all neutral tones and low ceilings. A bountiful menu offers quite a variety, from house-made hotdogs and farm burgers to meatloaf in sorghum BBQ sauce, 24-hour-brined pork chops, seafood gumbo, and local tempeh lo mein noodles. There can be a wait, so try early in the lunch or dinner hour.

OUR DAILY BREAD, 627 West King St., Boone, NC; (828) 264-0173; ourdailybreadodb.com; $. A student and local favorite, ODB, as it's known, serves rustic sandwiches, hearty homemade soups and chilis, and delectable breakfast breads. The sandwiches are imaginative combinations, such as the Jamaican, a generous portion of turkey topped with pepper cheese and sweet relish on a roll from the original menu. Vegetarian and vegan options abound. Leave room for a slice of cake.

THE RED ONION CAFE, 227 Hardin St., Boone, NC; (828) 264-5470; theredonioncafe.com; $–$$. Sitting in the heart of the university district, the restaurant serves creative soups, salads, sandwiches, quiche, pasta, and is considered a staple on the Boone dining scene. Prints, paintings, and sculpture by local and regional artists surround diners, and all of the art is for sale. The plant-draped piazza outdoors is also a popular dining spot, weather permitting.

THE SPECKLED TROUT, 922 Main St., Blowing Rock, NC; (828) 295-9819; thespeckledtrout.com; $–$$. The Speckled Trout has been serving hearty breakfasts, lunches, and dinners since 1986. There's even trout for breakfast. They've stepped up the game with classic cocktails, a list of their local purveyors (there are lots!), and added music on Thurs evenings. Trout and oyster dishes dominate the dinner menu, which also includes a classic selection of steaks and side dishes like Gouda grits and beets and goat cheese. Lunch is the tamer meal here, with standard sandwiches, soups, and salads. A bottle shop allows you take that wine or beer home, too.

VIDALIA, 831-835 West King St., Boone, NC; (828)-263-9176; vidaliaof boonenc.com; $–$$. This sweet space in downtown Boone serves amped up comfort food for dinner and Saturday/Sunday brunches. Spectacular meatloaf shares the menu with yellowfin tuna, chicken and dumplings with braised pork cheeks, chicken and waffles with red curry mussels . . . you get the picture. Definitely a place worth checking out.

THE VILLAGE CAFE; 146 Greenway Ct., Blowing Rock, NC; (828) 295-3769; thecafevillage.weebly.com; $$–$$$. Step off Main Street in Blowing Rock and down the path beside Kilwin's. At its end you'll find a tree-shaded courtyard and the Village Cafe. The restaurant is tucked into the Randall

Memorial Building, a quaint, white-frame cottage on the National Register of Historic Places that housed a mountain crafts co-op in 1907. Later the building served as the Blowing Rock Village Library. Imagine the soft sweetness of Belgian waffles made to order, garnished with plump, fresh raspberries, blueberries, strawberries, and unbelievably light honey syrup. Most memorable are the variety of fresh soups daily: mushroom and hazelnut, sweet corn and green-pepper sauce, tomato, and smoked Gouda. A cafe specialty is the marvelous homemade Argentine fugasa bread, which you may also pick up to take home. You may dine in the courtyard under the trees in fair weather. The Village Cafe is open seasonally, from late Apr to late Oct.

Yancey County

GARDEN DELI, 107 Town Sq., Burnsville, NC; (828) 682-3946; garden-deli.com; $–$$. Deli-lovers who happen upon this great little spot couldn't be more satisfied with typical deli sandwiches, soups, and salads. Heartier evening fare includes flat iron steak, a Greek chicken platter, and fried shrimp baskets. During the summer season many customers prefer to eat on the spacious outside deck shaded by wisteria vines and willow trees. The addition of the nautically-themed Snap Dragon (which is open later than the Garden Deli) introduces exotic cocktails, spring rolls, fish tacos, Thai-glazed market ribs, fried pickles, and other fun flavors.

PIG AND GRITS, 620 W. Main St., Burnsville, NC; (828) 536-0010; pigandgrits.com; $. Open since 2014, this simple, clean space offers a bevy of breakfasts from traditional Southern to kettle-baked French toast, harvest potato bowls, omelettes, eggs or brisket Benedict, and brown sugar-streusled apple cobbler sweet cakes. Lunch and dinner include plenty of barbecue and smoked brisket, but also cast iron chicken, bacon-wrapped meatloaf, and shrimp and grits. Dinner is seasonal only, Apr through Oct, Tues, Thurs, and Fri.

Central Mountains

Buncombe County

THE ADMIRAL, 400 Haywood Rd., Asheville, NC; (828) 252-2541; theadmiralasheville.com; $$–$$$$. This squatty cinderblock building across from an old gas station belies the gustatory delights inside. The interior is decidedly dive-y—but the elegance is on the plate here. Since 2007, one of the most adventurous eateries on the Asheville food scene has delighted serious foodies with popcorn soup, salt-baked celeriac, earthy beef tartare, mussels in preserved tomato broth and crusty grilled ciabatta, and other "New American" classic cuisine that looks as beautiful as it tastes. The house-made ginger syrup makes for an amazing Dark and Stormy, and other cocktails are equally on point. Dine at the bar and watch the kitchen at work.

AUX BAR, 68 N. Lexington Ave., Asheville, NC; (828) 575-2723; auxbar. com; $$–$$$. This irreverent restaurant and late-night dining spot is new and notable, with a bevy of young chefs experimenting expertly in the open kitchen with local provisions. From giant cheeseburgers to smoked pork shoulder on Carolina rice porridge, wild mushroom, smoked jus, soft egg, and cracklings, the restaurant hits the right note with foodies. A lovely patio is pet-friendly. DJ dance parties start at 10 p.m. on weekends for a big young late-night crowd.

BERLINER KINDL GERMAN RESTAURANT & DELI, 121 Broadway Ave., Black Mountain, NC; (828) 669-5255; $–$$$. No nonsense, hearty fare of sausages, schnitzel, sauerbraten (marinated pork), and other German delicacies makes its way to your table at this comfy and simple restaurant. Beers are on tap and in bottles. German deli items and other wares are available at the check-out counter.

BISCUIT HEAD, 733 Haywood Rd., Asheville, NC; (828) 333-5145; biscuitheads.com; $. This husband-and-wife-team, breakfast-and-brunch cafe expanded quickly from its main West Asheville location to three spaces in Asheville and one in Greenville, SC. The simple premise of "put some South in your mouth" is in the form of fluffy cathead biscuits with toppings from the jam buffet, or gravies like espresso red-eye, veggie "chorizo," sweet potato coconut, mushroom, and more. Sides include sausage, bacon, fried chicken, and eggs.

BOMBA, 1 North Park Sq., Asheville, NC; (828) 254-0209; bombanc.com; $. Perfect people-watching space on downtown's main square with counters and a few chairs lining the windows, much like a stylish European snack-cafe. You'll find fantastic coffees and pastries, and Latin cuisine small bites here, including Salvadorian pupusas and breakfast tacos. There are soups and fresh-made sandwiches and breakfast served all day!

BOUCHON, 62 North Lexington Ave., Asheville, NC; (828) 350-1140; ashevillebouchon.com; $–$$$. The menu has a blended greeting of "Bon appetit, y'all." Textbook French tells us that bouchon is a cork; however, the concept behind the name here follows a tradition established in Lyon, France, of clustering neighborhood bistros offering French comfort food in a friendly atmosphere. Here you'll find a convivial atmosphere at the cozy bar and in the courtyard, as well as the brick-walled dining area. Hearty country French dishes are a delight and locals gather for all-you-can-eat mussels-and-frites night on Mon and Tues.

BULL AND BEGGAR, 37 Payne's Way, Asheville, NC; (828) 575-9443; the bullandbeggar.com; $–$$$$. Another exciting addition to the food scene, B & B in the River Arts District serves more farm-to-table Euro-influenced cuisine,

Bouchon, a French bistro in Asheville. DAVID HUFF CREATIVE

with an emphasis on oysters and other raw-bar offerings (they offer those big iced seafood towers like in Paris!). Classic duck liver pâté and rabbit terrine, dry-aged bone-in rib eye, or filet mignon served with the marrow bone are on the satisfyingly heartier end, but don't miss out on the charred octopus starter with lima beans and romesco. Fun sides like hushpuppies served with maple butter or pommes frits in a cone, and a great cheeseburger served on Monday showcase a place that doesn't take itself too seriously. It's located in a former warehouse-turned-artist-studio with industrial high ceilings and a mezzanine to watch over the larger hall. Outdoor seating, too. Same owners as Admiral.

BUXTON HALL BARBECUE, 32 Banks Ave., Asheville, NC; (828) 232-726; $–$$. Buxton Hall brings whole-hog Eastern Carolina BBQ and Southern sides to the new South Slope neighborhood in the midst of all new breweries. There's usually a line, but James Beard nominees Elliott Moss and Meherwan Irani have teamed up to bring plenty of authentic plates of 'cue, fried chicken, and BBQ sandwiches to the discerning masses in this open-hall dining room. Most everything here is locally sourced, and do save room for the mile-high pie from the in-house pastry chef. Sit at the counter for a quick bite and maybe a frozen cocktail churning in the machines here.

CHAI PANI, 22 Battery Park Ave., Asheville, NC; (828) 254-4003; chaipani asheville.com; $–$$. Described as Indian street food–style snacks, the cuisine here is full-on Indian flavors married with locally-sourced fresh innovation, headed by three-time James Beard nominee Meherwan Irani and his wife. Since 2009 this bright, cheerful space has introduced many visitors to crispy okra fries, ground lamb sliders, kale pakoras, and the sloppy jai (think Sloppy Joe but with lamb hash simmered in aromatic flavors, tomato, and ginger). All the Indian favorites are here, concentrating on chaat, foods eaten by hand. So plenty of warm, pliable Indian breads wrapped around chicken tikka, potato dumplings, grilled vegetables, and so much more. There's an extensive cocktail list, hot chai, of course, and sweet and savory yogurt beverages, too. Separate kids' menu also available.

THE CORNER KITCHEN, 3 Boston Way, Asheville, NC; (828) 274-2439; thecornerkitchen.com; $–$$$. In the heart of Biltmore Village, this charming restaurant offers dishes of distinction with new South flavor. The charming cottage interior covers two floors and a lovely courtyard in one of Asheville's cutest neighborhoods. It has a fierce local following, especially for breakfast (which is fun at the bar), and has outdoor seating under umbrellas in the tiny courtyard. There's often a line in high season. Owners also have Chestnut downtown.

CUCINA 24, 24 Wall St., Asheville, NC; (828) 254-6170; cucina24 restaurant.com; $$–$$$. Serving an array of innovative northern Italian dishes, like the delicate first-course pasta-dish leading into meat or complex fish dishes, this sometimes-underrated restaurant will also feed you superb wood-fired brick oven pizzas. Think seared sea scallops and fennel, duck scallopini, braised lamb shanks, and other fulfilling dishes. Enjoy a cheese course instead of dessert in the contemporary wood and black-toned dining room. Cocktails are of-the-moment, and sitting at the bar for dinner is quite lovely, too.

Enjoy watching the chefs work when seated at the counter of Downtown Asheville's tapas restaurant, Curate. CONSTANCE E. RICHARDS

CURATE, 13 Biltmore Ave., Asheville, NC; (828) 239-2946; katiebuttonrestaurants.com; $–$$$. This chic Spanish tapas–style bar was the first of James Beard nominee and powerhouse Chef Katie Button's growing restaurant empire. Trained at elBulli in Spain, she and husband Felix Meana introduced the savory small plates, sherries, ports, Spanish wines, and table-side-constructed sangrias in a well-orchestrated setting in Asheville's downtown. Delicate croquettes, whipped cod puree, molten tortillas, and so much more have quickly made this a foodie haven. So popular, it expanded next door and created a walk-in vermouth bar. Reservations are a must. Sitting at the counter allows you to watch the magic happen with the delicate dance in the open kitchen.

EARLY GIRL EATERY, 8 Wall St., Asheville, NC; (828) 259-9292; earlygirleatery.com; $–$$. This little cutie serves up organic dishes and comfort food favorites. Under new ownership, and having expanded to West Asheville also, this simple-but-so-good eatery still features homemade sausage and jams, stuffed omelettes and pancakes, pumpkin bread, sweet potato pancakes, and black bean cakes for great breakfasts. The light, airy design that overlooks the street is a winner for lunch and dinner dining also. Lunch features sandwiches and wraps, as well as salads with spring-fresh ingredients year-round. Dinner goes heavier, with duck breast over polenta and pan-fried chicken in addition to a menu of innovative specials. There's often a line forming at the door, so be sure to get here early, or be ready to wait. Lots of national exposure makes this a very popular place with in- and out-of-towners.

EN LA CALLE, 15 Eagle St., Asheville, NC; (828) 232-7012; enlacalleasheville.com; $–$$. The younger sister of Limones next door, this long, narrow bar-cafe with murals and atmospheric patina on the walls slings adventurous cocktails and highly enjoyable Latin-style small plate "street food." Lime and chili-coated corn on the cob with crema, free-range chicken tinga nachos, and chorizo hominy chipotle mussels, oh yes!

FIG, 18 Brooke St., Asheville, NC; (828) 277-0889; figbistro.com; $–$$$. Somewhat off the beaten path, just outside Biltmore Village, this small sun-lit bistro serves French-accented cuisine for lunch and dinner. Outdoor seating in warm weather takes place in a charming shared courtyard.

GAN SHAN STATION, 143 Charlotte St., Asheville, NC; (828) 774-5280; ganshangroup.com; $–$$. Set in a former gas station, with rustic patinas left on the walls and other industrial notes (and lots of covered outdoor seating), Gan Shan features full-on, well-defined flavors of ginger, curry, chili pepper, lime leaf, and other notes you'll find in pan-Asian cuisine, served mostly as ramen, noodle, and rice dishes. A recent update to the menu brings dry rub ribs and heartier dishes. Dumplings, too, including a daily vegetarian version. Exotic cocktails at the long bar make this a great North Asheville gathering place. A quick-stop location for ramen is located in West Asheville, called simply Gan Shan West. The spicy beef ramen is a must-try.

HAYWOOD COMMON, 507 Haywood Rd., Asheville, NC; (828) 575-2542; haywoodcommon.com; $–$$$. Rustic and approachable wholesome comfort food served in an elevated community gathering space in West Asheville. Brick walls, old patina, and dark wood accent this light-filled place. The outdoor patio also gets ample sun, just right for sipping on the daily frozen cocktail. It developed from the Belly-Up food truck, and continues to source local farms for great produce to complement pork belly, bibimbap, or the root vegetable bowls, Bavette steak, or the fab chicken and waffles. This innovative kitchen also serves The Wale, a unique imported beer bar that shares the building.

ISA'S BISTRO, 1 Battery Park Ave., Asheville, NC; (828) 275-9636; isas bistro.com; $–$$$$. Bright and airy, Isa's Bistro occupies the street-front corner of the Battery Park Hotel, serving brunch on Sunday, breakfast, fine lunches, and dinners with a European-influenced menu that is still all farm-to-table—typical of Asheville. A stylish bar anchors the indoor wall to one side, and outdoor seating wraps around the front of the space for dining al fresco and people watching.

JARGON, 715 Haywood Rd., Asheville, NC; (828) 785-1761; jargon restaurant.com; $$–$$$. New American cuisine served in an eclectic retro-designed space in West Asheville. Everything here is innovative, from the 'spherical' Manhattan from the bar to the vintage game–themed decor, including artist Maryanne Pappano's intricate wooden word-play installation, funky shadowbox scenes, playful murals, a Scrabble wall in the restroom, and, of course, the continental cuisine with toothsome delicacies like elk meatballs, house-made agnolotti (delicate ravioli), and deep-fried deviled eggs.

JERUSALEM GARDEN CAFÉ, 78 Patton Ave., Asheville, NC; (828) 254-0255; jerusalemgardencafe.com; $. This Middle Eastern restaurant sits directly across from Pritchard Park in the city center. Stepping through the front door is like opening to a page from *The Arabian Nights* with tented ceiling, ornamental brass tables, and silk cushions (and chairs) for seating. The cuisine is a combination of Jordanian and Turkish delights, from falafel sandwiches to mezze platters and juicy grilled kebabs. On weekends there is belly dancing in the tented party room and throughout the restaurant.

LA GUINGUETTE, 105 Richardson Blvd., Black Mountain, NC; (888) 434-7810; laguinguettecreperie.com; $. This special little place serves Latin and French cuisine for lunch, dinner, and brunch. The crepe (both savory and plenty of sweet) is king here, as well as empanadas stuffed with chicken, pumpkin, beef, corn, and other fantastic combos. Tamales, soups, and Cuban sandwiches round out a fun menu, served in this cute cottage and outdoor patio.

THE LAUGHING SEED CAFE, 40 Wall St., Asheville, NC; (828) 252-3445; laughingseed.com; $–$$. Tucked into charming Wall Street this vegetarian restaurant has thrilled plant-based diners for decades, specializing in flavorful international dishes. If you're not accustomed to an entirely vegetarian menu, you will be pleasantly surprised. This is not just rice and beans, mind you. We're talking about exotic and delicious dishes from Morocco to Thailand sharing the extensive menu with old favorites from closer to home. Fresh-pressed juices, smoothies, and protein shakes add to a great menu of Indian variety plates, grilled seitan dishes, veggie lentil burritos, and so much more. (Downstairs Jack of the Wood Pub serves up microbrew beer, enlightened pub grub, and live music.)

LIMONES, 13 Eagle St., Asheville, NC; (828) 252-2327; limonesrestaurant.com; $$–$$$. Part California, part Mexico, the menu here boasts all the freshness, innovation, and piquant flavors of both. A comfortable setting allows visitors to linger over blood orange or pomegranate margaritas and skirt steak with lime and fennel, Rioja slow-braised short ribs, a tangy ceviche, and many other inventive dishes. Ever-popular, it fills up quickly, but try next door at En La Calle by the same owners for small bites.

MAMACITAS, 77 Biltmore Ave., Asheville, NC; (828) 255-8080; mamacitasgrill.com; $. Walk down the line and point to which fresh ingredients you want in your burrito. It's that simple. Icy margaritas, fresh-pressed juices, and a self-serve bar of salsas make this the perfect quick bite before a concert at clubs nearby.

Close-up

Asheville's Restaurant Row

Not only is the historic Grove Arcade a fine example of turn-of-the-century pedestrian shopping passages, it features an entire "restaurant row." Located on the east side of the Arcade, a variety of eateries spill out onto the sidewalk for *al fresco* dining, representing everything from California cuisine to, Italian, Middle Eastern, plus burgers and dogs. Check out the interior and other side of the Arcade for fun boutique shopping as well; (828) 252-7799; grovearcade.com.

Baba Nahm; (828) 572-2075; babanahm.com. A grab-and-go Middle Eastern snack bar with bright, fresh, and flavorful ingredients.

Battery Park Book Exchange and Champagne Bar; (828) 252-0020; batteryparkbookexchange.com. A marvelous place to purchase rare, new, and used books, as well as sip champagne or a glass of wine. Order elegant charcuterie or cheese boards, and croissant sandwiches, too.

Burgerworx; (828) 412-5212; burgerworxavl.com. Choose from a beef, chicken, veggie, or cheese patty and load that burger up with all sorts of incredible toppings.

Carmel's Restaurant & Bar; (828) 252-8730; carmelsofasheville.com. A great locals' hang-out with friendly bartenders, solid elevated pub cuisine, and outdoor seating.

Modesto; (828) 225-4133; modestonc.com. A stalwart Italian-influenced menu with wood-fired brick oven for gourmet pizzas and grilling meats for fine farm-to-table dishes.

Santé; (828) 254-8188; santewinebar.com. Convivial European-style wine bar with wines by the glass or by the bottle, meat and cheese boards, and homemade dips for noshing; also retail bottle sales.

DINING

THE MARKET PLACE, 20 Wall St., Asheville, NC; (828) 252-4162; marketplace-restaurant.com; $$$–$$$$. A symbol of excellence in dining since 1979 in downtown Asheville, the Market Place has amassed accolades from the *New York Times* and *Food & Wine* to *Bon Appétit*, *Southern Living*, and *Wine Spectator*. The transition of new ownership was overseen with blessings and chef-owner William Dissen continues the march toward hand-crafted, innovative, seasonal farm-to-fork cuisine. The restaurant's slate-gray sophisticated, urban look provides a backdrop for classic culinary traditions infused with imaginative, contemporary twists. Dissen continues to innovate and open new restaurants in other North Carolina cities.

MAYFEL'S, 22 College St., Asheville, NC; (828) 252-8840; mayfels.net; $–$$. A meat and three—that's the premise for this cute throwback to old blue-plate-special Southern diners. Here, you'll find local art on the walls and, indeed, blue plate specials, like spicy mac and cheese and crispy coleslaw with a twist. Zesty gumbo and egg Bennies pair well with the build-your-own Bloody Mary bar for brunch, or try the lighter café au lait and beignets. Check out the secret late-night courtyard in back for cocktails from the tiki bar.

MELA, 70 Lexington Ave., Asheville, NC; (828) 225-8880; melaasheville .com; $–$$. This Indian restaurant represents all that is Lexington Avenue—urban chic with a little funkiness thrown in. Authentically prepared curry and tandoori meals are elegantly served in a large saffron-colored dining room with a wood-carved bar.

NINE MILE, 233 Montford Ave., Asheville, NC; (828) 505-3121; nine mileasheville.com; $–$$. A popular neighborhood locale which features Caribbean-inspired spicy pasta dishes, vegetarian plates, and microbrew beers. Mango salsa, coconut curry, and other garnishes are a great part of the cuisine, plus pungent natty bread (garlic) and salad with green goddess dressing with evening meals. The expanded bar is comfy and stylish. Nine Mile has expanded to West Asheville now, and a South Asheville version is planned as well.

POSANA, 1 Biltmore Ave., Asheville, NC; (828) 505-3969; posana restaurant.com; $$–$$$. Stylish and bright with contemporary art installations, lighting, and local artwork (including a sometimes revolving exhibition in the private dining room), this anchor of Pack Square—Asheville's central square—serves dinner and Saturday/Sunday brunches with a special nod to those with wheat and gluten allergies (though you'd never know it). Chef-owner Peter Pollay cut his teeth on big-name restaurants like Spago, and worked with Wolfgang Puck at Granita, but has created his very own brand of quality contemporary American cuisine using the fresh produce and proteins of a phalanx of respected local purveyors. Dining or drinking here truly feels like a night on the town.

RED STAG GRILL, 11 Boston Way, Asheville, NC; (828) 398-5600; kessler collection/red-stag-grill.com; $$–$$$$. A unique dining experience awaits with a menu that reflects European comfort food with tinges of Austrian,

Bavarian, and French influences. Game such as tender elk, duck, quail, and perfectly prepared trout, salmon, scallops, and steaks create a well-rounded menu. While breakfast and lunch are light-filled from the tall windows and very reasonably-priced, evening transforms the Red Stag into an atmospheric special-occasion space—if even just for a date night. Located in the rustically plush Grand Bohemian Hotel, the decor features antlers, elk and deer mounts, twig chandeliers, moody and impressionist art, with dramatic light and music. A bar top made of petrified wood and small area with tables and chairs is cozy for cocktails and live music Thurs through Sat. Free valet parking and a gorgeous four-sided fireplace in the lobby lend to the fantastical atmosphere.

REZAZ, 28 Hendersonville Rd., Asheville, NC; (828) 277-1510; rezaz.com; $$–$$$. A contemporary setting with a chef-owner husband-and-wife team who serve pan-Mediterranean cuisine, delightful desserts, and small plates. A beautiful long bar makes for a good meeting place over wine.

RHUBARB, 7 SW North Pack Square, Asheville, NC; (828) 785-1503; rhubarbasheville.com; $$–$$$. In the heart of downtown Asheville on Pack Square, Rhubarb has a simple, rustic interior with an open kitchen in one dining room and an emphasis on Appalachian cuisine shared amongst friends. Chef and owner John Fleer, named a "Rising Star of the 21st Century" by the James Beard Foundation and a five-time finalist for the James Beard "Best Chef in the Southeast" award, has created a warm gathering place for sampling elevated, fine comfort food such as local trout, quail, pork loin, peanut-braised collard greens, sorghum-glazed sweet potatoes, and so much more. "Sunday Suppers" are convivial events served at community tables with bowls of goodness served family-style and plenty for everyone. A breezy outdoor patio and small cocktail lounge add to this expansive space.

ROSETTA'S KITCHEN, 116 N Lexington Ave., Asheville, NC; (828) 232-0738; rosettaskitchen.com; $–$$. By now an Asheville tradition, this is the place vegans and vegetarians will find a home. The sunny restaurant upstairs features organic tofu incorporated into flavorful stews and sandwiches, fantastic tempeh Reubens and other flavorful sandwiches (options for gluten-free, too), Buddha bowls and other whole-food bowls with rice, sautéed veggies, peanut sauce, herbed-walnut sauce, rice, and other rich flavors. You can order from the same menu downstairs in the Buchi Bar and add cocktails and Asheville's well-known kombucha (fermented probiotic beverage) choices to the meal.

SALSA, 6 Patton Ave., Asheville, NC; (828) 252-9805; salsasnc.com; $–$$. This sassy little downtown restaurant is short on space but big on taste and innovative cuisine. It's a long-time favorite, still filling seats with lovers of pan-Caribbean fare with "mountain" touches, like wild mushrooms, goat cheese, pinto beans, greens, and other offerings. The menu might include herb chicken quesadillas and tacos made Salsa style (fire-roasted pepper tacos and black bean and goat cheese tacos, both served with pico de gallo salsa on any given day.) Restaurateur Hector Diaz, who brought the culinary heritage of his native Puerto Rico to this popular eatery, has opened other downtown eateries since this was but a little take-out window and kitchen.

SMOKY PARK SUPPER CLUB, 350 Riverside Dr., Asheville, NC; (828) 350-0315; smokypark.com; $$$. Built on the banks of the French Broad River and made entirely of shipping containers, this inventive eatery is all about wood-fired dishes, craft cocktails, and slowing down while the river slides by. Open for dinner and Sunday brunch, Smoky Park will grill up things like swordfish with apple-fennel-black-walnut slaw, a local New York strip with black garlic jam, or a juicy cheddar burger. Sides are farm-to-fork goodness. One of the founders of the place is known as the godfather of fine cuisine in Asheville. The vibe is laid-back, though, and the riverside deck and picnic tables are perfect for the warm months.

STONEY KNOB CAFÉ, 337 Merrimon Ave., Weaverville, NC; (828) 645-3309; stoneyknobcafe.com. $–$$$. Sit at the outdoor patio or by the fireplace in the wine bar addition—this former diner (in the family for over 45 years) serves up delightful Greek-inflected dishes in a cozy and creative atmosphere. Set off by itself on the road to Weaverville, Stoney Knob is a local favorite, whether for a platter of grilled chicken gyros, spicy grilled shrimp, or for blackberry brunch crepes.

SUNNY POINT CAFÉ, 626 Haywood Rd., Asheville, NC; (828) 252-0055; sunnypointcafe.com; $. Bright and cheery with a sidewalk cafe, Sunny Point has been a beacon of change in West Asheville. Luscious brunches of organic produce—much of which comes from the garden behind the cafe—meats, homemade breads, and baked goods have achieved perfection at this adorable neighborhood joint. Open seven days and five nights. Come for the food, stay for the people watching, lots of young families from the 'hood, local artists, and relaxed folk.

i West Asheville, a neighborhood divided by a bridge from downtown Asheville, has a Main Street quickly filling up with interesting restaurants, cafes, and boutiques. Check out more about them at onhaywood.com.

TABLE, 48 College St., Asheville, NC; (828) 254-8980; tableasheville.com; $$–$$$. Sparse and sleek design makes this dining room notable. Well-crafted dishes and favorites with a twist, such as pasta carbonara with fava beans and prosciutto, fish dishes, and other innovations attract regulars for a unique, urban experience. Desserts and old-fashioned cocktails are a draw here as well. Try the Imperial Lounge cocktail bar upstairs before or after dinner, owned by the same folks.

TUPELO HONEY CAFÉ, 12 College St., Asheville, NC; (828) 255-4404; tupelohoneycafe.com; $–$$. Indoors or out, the original Tupelo Honey is a delight, from its French toast with mascarpone and sweet potato pecan pancakes to the wholesome homemade tomato soup and choice-of-cheese grilled cheese sandwich. Oyster cocktails, spicy shrimp and grits, and grilled salmon over field greens allude to the Low Country sensibilities here. A basket of biscuits and corn muffins on the white linen–covered tables are a welcome touch. The original, which has now expanded into seven states, usually has a line; open breakfast, lunch, and dinner.

> **i** The Asheville Independent Restaurant Association (AIR) website breaks down eateries by cuisine, price point, and geographic location. Additionally, the site indicates special deals, discounts, and dining trends in the area. Visit airasheville.org.

VERANDA CAFÉ & GIFTS, 119 Cherry St., Black Mountain, NC; (828) 669-8864; verandacafeandgifts.com; $–$$. Wandering down Cherry Street is a delightful treat in Black Mountain. It is adjacent to the historic archives and galleries, where Cherry Street and State Street meet. Dining tables are set up throughout this charming little gift shop as well as on the back porch. Its soups and sandwiches have created long-time fans. Ever tried a warm Bavarian Pretzel Club? Cubans, NOLA-style muffalettas, and other warm sandwiches create memorable lunches (the only meal served here). Fluffy cakes, fresh-baked cookies, and pies for dessert.

WHITE DUCK TACO SHOP, 388 Riverside Dr., Asheville, NC; (828) 254-1398; whiteducktacoshop.com; $. So good you can't stop at one. On the banks of the French Broad in a Quonset with plenty of tables riverside, plus games like corn hole and such, this is a laid-back stop while shopping in the River Arts District. Enjoy tacos of every ilk, the Korean bulgogi and jerk chicken are favorites, and order what's on tap or try the seasonal sangrias, frozen Cheerwine (boozy or not), or top-shelf margarita for an extra happy

DINING

afternoon. There's also a downtown location on Biltmore Avenue in Asheville as well as now in South Asheville.

ZAMBRA, 84 Walnut St., Asheville, NC; (828) 232-1060; zambratapas .com; $–$$$. In a dramatic Spanish/Moroccan–style setting, Zambra offers inspired tapas—a menagerie of small portions of delectable dishes to be shared by the whole table. Calamari are fried to crisp perfection and served with divine lemony salad greens, curried lamb, and mushrooms nestle in a bed of garlic polenta, and dozens of equally-creative dishes are simply too tantalizing to pass up. Spanish and French wines, sherries, and ports tickle the tongue. Stack the table with many small plates or order from the entree-size meals on a smaller menu. On the weekends Zambra invites musicians to make music in the cozy bar area. Some romantic lantern-lit outdoor seating, too.

Henderson County

THE FRENCH BROAD, 342 N. Main St., Hendersonville, NC; (828) 595-979, thefrenchbroad.net; $$$. A fun, bright brasserie-style restaurant serving French-influenced comfort food on two levels. Enjoy the long marble-topped community table that runs the length of the first floor, or the cozy mezzanine level, with linen-covered tables overlooking Main Street and a bar with piano for live music evenings.

NEVER BLUE, 119 South Main St., Hendersonville, NC; (828) 693-4646; theneverblue.com; $–$$$. Inventive cocktails here are colorful and fruity—particularly fun in the courtyard scene and the tiled interior of this happening Cuban-inspired restaurant. Roasted pork and grilled chicken with chopped salsas, plantain dishes, black beans and rice, grilled fish, tacos, tapas, spall dishes, and fresh and zesty accompaniments are the norm here.

POSTERO, 401 North Main St., Hendersonville, NC; (828) 595-9676; postero-hvl.com; $$–$$$. Beautifully-presented New American locally-sourced cuisine comes out of this kitchen. Southern fare like flavorful pork chops, cornmeal-dusted local trout, and house-made pimento cheese also make appearances on the menu. The contemporary and elegant space once housed a bank, providing a variety of seating areas from mezzanine to high-top tables and bar, or a private dining room next to the vault.

SEASON'S AT HIGHLAND LAKE INN, 86 Lillypad Ln., Flat Rock, NC; (828) 693-6812; hliresort.com; $$$–$$$$. With much of the food grown right on the premises in organic gardens and greenhouses, which you're welcome to tour, you can be assured that the food here is some of the freshest you'll find anywhere and in a very picturesque setting. Besides a seasonally changing a la carte menu, Season's is known for excellent themed buffet meals. Reservations are recommended.

UMI, 633 North Main St., Hendersonville, NC; (828) 698-8048; umisushi nc.com; $–$$$. Still a perennial favorite for great sushi in Western North Carolina, Umi offers an array of gorgeous and tasty sushi platters, all in a sleek two-dining room space. Belly right up to the sushi bar itself to see the magic happen.

WEST FIRST WOOD-FIRED, 101B 1st Ave. W., Hendersonville, NC; (828) 693-1080; flatrockwoodfired.com; $–$$. A vast contemporary space with a beautiful wood-fired oven as its centerpiece, West First has created a huge following of crisp-crust pizza lovers. Goat cheese, Gorgonzola, pesto, and artichokes are only a few of the toppings that up the ante here from a regular tomato-pie joint. European-style bread is also baked here; sandwiches and house-made desserts are also spot-on.

Polk County

THE ORCHARD INN, 100 Orchard Inn Ln., Saluda, NC; (828) 749-5471; orchardinn.com; $$$$. This lovely, plantation-type inn with its beautiful view of the Warrior Mountains has an elegant glassed-in dining area that stretches across the back of the main building. Newman's, as the restaurant is called, features a prix-fix four-course dinner prepared according to the seasonal offerings from local producers. Inn guests dine here as well as locals, so a reservation is a must.

PINE CREST INN, 200 Pine Crest Ln., Tryon, NC; (800) 633-3001; pinecrestinn.com; $$$$. The dining room at Pine Crest, called Carter's Tavern, with its hunter green, burgundy, and deep blue decor, is indeed reminiscent of an elegant English tavern. Both breakfast and dinner are served to the public here by reservation only and the menu changes every day. All entrees are perfectly matched with fresh vegetable and various starches that have been sourced from local purveyors. The Pine Crest Inn's dining room is open Mon through Sat.

Rutherford County

LAKE LURE INN VERANDA RESTAURANT, 2771 Memorial Hwy., Lake Lure, NC; (888) 434-4970; lakelure.com; $–$$$. This stately inn overlooking beautiful Lake Lure has been a tradition in Hickory Nut Gorge since 1927. The dining room is an elegant setting for such classics as chicken cordon blue and rosemary lamb lollipops. Look for the prime rib Sunday brunch buffet and Bloody Mary bar!

LARKIN'S ON THE LAKE, 1020 Memorial Hwy., Lake Lure, NC; (828) 625-4075; larkinsonthelake.com; $$–$$$$. Gorgeous views of Lake Lure only add to the atmosphere of a relaxing place that offers fresh mountain trout, hand-cut steaks, and tender ribs, in addition to elegant dishes and a good wine list. For a casual take on some of the dishes, plus sandwiches, burgers, and peel-and-eat shrimp, try the Bayfront Bar and Grill downstairs, under the same venue's tutelage.

MEDINA'S VILLAGE BISTRO, 430 Main St., Chimney Rock, NC; (828) 989-4529; medinasvillagebistro.com; $. A quick stop here while sightseeing brings you great diner-style breakfasts; there's a kids' menu, takeout, and dinner offerings that won't break the bank, but will satisfy with Mediterranean-influenced favorites, as well as pizzas and calzones from the wood-fired oven.

Transylvania County

THE FALLS LANDING RESTAURANT; 18 East Main St., Brevard, NC; (828) 884-2835; thefallslanding.com; $$. When it comes to fresh seafood with a Caribbean touch, the owners of the Falls Landing, former longtime residents of the Virgin Islands, know how to do it right! Their Cajun mahi-mahi is done to a turn, too. When you come here, it's essential that you try the famous conch fritters. Fresh nightly specials include lots of fresh seafood, steaks, pasta, and chicken. Friday night is lobster night. If you're lucky, you might be there when superb cheese soup is on the menu. The bar also mixes some excellent drinks. Serves lunch and dinner.

MAGPIE MEAT AND THREE, 170 King St., Brevard Lumberyard, Brevard, NC; (828) 877-3773; magpiemeatandthree.com; $. Wood-smoked BBQ and Southern specialties made from fresh seasonal produce. The simple menu allows you to pick a meat and add three sides, like mac and cheese, sweet potato home fries, and red rice. Desserts are on-point. Grapefruit pie? Butter & Blooms salted caramel? Sounds exciting! Hours change seasonally.

THE SQUARE ROOT, 33 Times Arcade Alley, Brevard, NC; (828) 884-6171; squarerootrestaurant.com; $–$$$. Set off the main street in a small alley, The Square Root's outdoor terrace leads to the sublime bar area. A polished slab of oak that still resembles the tree comprises the counter. More interesting woodwork on the floor, brick walls, and artwork make for a delightfully warm interior. Time here slows down on an outdoor patio with mountain breezes. Lunch, dinner, and brunch serve up a variety of salads,sandwiches, and burgers, but also some twists like rabbit gumbo, scallop saltimbocca, peach-glazed pork, and flat iron steak make for quite a variety.

Southern Mountains

Cherokee County

BISTRO 29, 29 Tennessee St., Murphy, NC; (828) 837-9022; mybistro29 .com; $$–$$$. This is a lovely new lunch and dinner venue for casual dining. European and American fare (maybe a hint of Asian, too), with plenty of vegetarian and gluten-free options that are still redolent with flavor. Lots of fresh items here, but also indulgences like oven-fried brie, stuffed dates, and spicy wontons. A good wine menu and creative drinks invite sitting. Convivial brunch served first Sun of every month.

THE PARSON'S PUB, 19 Tennessee St., Murphy, NC; (828) 837-4151; theparsonspub.com; $. A jovial Irish pub with hearty pub food such as shepherd's pie, corned beef and cabbage, Irish pasties, bangers and mash, plus Reubens, fish sandwiches, and great plates for sharing and noshing. And all the great beers from the isle, and local.

SHOEBOOTIES, 25 Peachtree St., Murphy, NC; (828) 837-4589; shoe booties.com; $–$$. A longtime local favorite, Shoebooties maintains a hometown feel with plenty of booth seating and hearty appetizers, good soups, and pleasant entrees with vegetable sides. Nightly specials, live music on the weekends, and Shoetini's Lounge upstairs keep the crowds coming back.

Haywood County

CATALOOCHEE RANCH, 119 Ranch Dr., Maggie Valley, NC; (828) 926-1401; cataloocheeranch.com; $$. Cataloochee Ranch has endured and prospered in the same family for more than a half-century for many reasons, including its lovely location high on a mountain overlooking Maggie Valley.

DINING

The food it serves has also played a big part in its popularity. These are family-style meals to which the public is invited by reservations only. The Cataloochee Ranch is open year-round, but meals are served in the winter by special arrangement only (for more information, see our **Accommodations** chapter).

THE SWAG, 2300 Swag Rd., Waynesville, NC; (828) 926-0430, (800) 789-7672; theswag.com; $$$$. The Swag, an exclusive inn 5,000 feet up in the Smoky Mountains with 50-mile views, takes a limited number of outside guests by reservation only for its lunches Mon through Sat, its sensational dinners seven days a week, and its unforgettable Sunday brunches. The chef-chosen dinners feature four-course meals. The Swag is open from mid-May through Oct (see our **Accommodations** chapter for more information). Reservations required.

Jackson County

GUADALUPE CAFE, 606 W. Main St., Sylva, NC; (828) 586-9877; guadalupecafe.com; $–$$. Self-described as "deliciously quirky," this art-filled space with the eclectic look of an old diner, serves Latin-American inspired and island-kissed cuisine like mango pork tacos, red curry shrimp, curried goat, and blackened plantains. Desserts, baked in-house, are incredible—tres leches cake, lavender lime almond tart, you get the idea.

HIGH HAMPTON RESORT, 1525 Hwy. 107 S, Cashiers, NC; (828) 743-2411, (800) 334-2551; highhamptonresort.com; $$–$$$$. The High Hampton Inn believes in tradition, right down to the food it serves. Many dishes you'll eat—served buffet style at the inn—are the same favorites you'd have found here 50 years ago: fried chicken, fresh local trout, and prime rib; a memorable cream of peanut soup; a cranberry Waldorf salad; Southern-style vegetables such as stewed corn; homemade bread, including sausage cornbread; and peppermint ice cream with chocolate syrup. (For more information, see our **Accommodations** chapter.)

LULU'S ON MAIN, 678 West Main St., Sylva, NC; (828) 586-8989; lulusonmain.com; $$. Lunch, dinner, and lively libations accompany a menu rich in experimentation and vegetarian dishes, since 1989. Trained in the classic French style of cookery, Chef McCardle also offers Greek, Italian, Caribbean, Indonesian, and American dishes. It's a great gathering place, especially with its own martini bar. Lulu's is open for lunch and dinner.

Macon County

THE GAZEBO CREEKSIDE CAFE, 44 Heritage Hollow Dr., Franklin, NC; (828) 524-8783; gazebocreeksidecafe.com; $. This award-winning cafe is the perfect place to relax and unwind. Built around an old gazebo, the beautiful outdoor setting allows for creekside seating while you enjoy the abundant North Carolina bird life. Open for lunch only, the homemade fare includes soups, salads, deli sandwiches, desserts, gourmet coffees, and ice-cream delights. Open year-round, lunch only.

ON THE VERANDAH, 1536 Franklin Rd., Highlands, NC; (828) 526-2338; ontheverandah.com; $$$. The scenic dining setting overlooking Lake Sequoyah sets the tone for the exquisite menu at this restaurant, to which *Wine Spectator* magazine has given its Award of Excellence yearly since 1987. The food is prepared with fresh ingredients and is cooked to order. Maine lobster piccata, spicy Thai coconut shrimp, and coq au vin (braised natural chicken) give you an idea of but a few options. Daily fresh fish and seafood specials are paired with complementary wines. In addition to dinner, On the Verandah offers a Sunday champagne brunch with soup, a salad bar, Mimosa cocktails or Kir Royale, and such entrees as poached eggs on crab cakes topped with fresh lime Hollandaise sauce.

RISTORANTE PAOLETTI, 440 Main St., Highlands, NC; (828) 526-4906; paolettis.com; $$$. Celebrating 35 years in 2019, this Highlands favorite specializes in the freshest seafood dishes, but also serves the full Italian multi-course meal, with homemade pastas, breads, salads, and desserts. Veal chops with champagne cream, roasted rack of lamb, and dry-aged Angus sirloin strip steak are just a few of the extensive offerings on the menu. The 20-page wine list is a veritable trip around the world without leaving the table. The wine cellar has been designated by the *Wine Spectator* for an Award of Excellence. Open seasonally.

WOLFGANG'S ON MAIN, 474 Main St., Highlands, NC; (828) 526-3807; wolfgangs.net; $$$. Built in 1880, Wolfgang's is located in one of the oldest houses in Highlands. Whether dining inside by a fireplace on a handmade rhododendron table, outside on the awning-covered deck, or in the garden pavilion, you're in for a dining treat. Chef Wolfgang, former executive chef for the Brennan's Family Commander's Palace in New Orleans, is internationally acclaimed, having won numerous awards, including chef of the year in both Jamaica and Texas. His background brings a freshness and variety to a menu that's so attractive, it's really difficult to decide what to order. New Orleans specialties include Wolfgang's Signature Soup, a shrimp and lobster bisque; crawfish étouffée; Maryland blue crab cakes served on a lobster cream sauce with pecan-crusted shrimp; Veal Medallions Wolfgang on a cabernet sauce topped with crawfish and béarnaise sauce; as well as many other selections. This is a true classic in fine dining.

DINING

Swain County

THE BISTRO AT THE EVERETT HOTEL, 24 Everett St., Bryson City, NC; (828) 488-1934; theeveretthotel.com/bistro.html; $–$$$. Located inside a quaint hotel, this bistro serves elevated mountain comfort foods like cornmeal-crusted trout with red quinoa and toasted garlic. Open for breakfast and dinner, it also serves brunch (Sat and Sun only) listed in delectable detail on two pages.

HEMLOCK INN, 911 Galbraith Creek Rd., Bryson City, NC; (828) 488-2885; hemlockinn.com; $–$$. The food at the Hemlock Inn, set on 65 wooded acres, 3 miles from the Great Smoky Mountains National Park, is so good that, at their guests' insistence, the inn put many of its recipes into a cookbook called *Recipes from Our Front Porch*. If you are not a guest here (see our **Accommodations** chapter), you can still make a reservation for dinner Mon through Sat. You'll be seated at a lazy-Susan table laden with native foods, including fruits and vegetables provided by the Hemlock's neighbors' gardens (in the summer, you may be offered corn on the cob picked just a few minutes before it's cooked and served). Entrees might include country ham and fried chicken, accompanied by homemade yeast rolls and biscuits with mountain honey. The delicious desserts are all made from scratch, too.

RIVER'S END RESTAURANT, Nantahala Outdoor Center, 13077 US 19, Bryson City, NC; (828) 488-7172; noc.com; $–$$. Open since 1972 and feeding hungry hikers, paddlers, and other nature enthusiasts, this sweet spot on the river with indoor and outdoor deck seating above the rushing river serve fresh, flavorful fare. Try the sherpa rice—a hearty mix of fragrant basmati rice, lentils, barley, and topped with veggies and beans, with choice of proteins and cheese to fill ya belly and soul. Wraps, tacos, pork chops, grilled salmon, and pizza, too.

SPECIALTY VENUES, CAFES & BARS

In many of our mountain communities, outside of the busy hub of Asheville, the appeal of life is the love of the land and the opportunity to control the pace of life. In smaller towns you won't find too many dusk-to-dawn party venues. Instead, the emphasis is on dining and music—traditional, old-time, alternative, folk, singer-songwriter, jazz, and the like. Many restaurants will have nice bars, and will often feature live music.

Additionally, our urban centers have an excellent reputation for post-theater or concert cocktails and dessert. Asheville, for one, is a beacon for sophisticated diners, theatergoers, and art aficionados. Live music is so popular here, you'll find a variety any night of the week in several different venues, such as the nationally known Orange Peel and its new private club, Pulp. There is a thriving downtown, both day and night. The people who live downtown, in the vast lofts with wooden floors and beamed garrets, grab their morning coffee and newspaper at the corner coffee shop, walk to Sunday brunch at several cafes with such offerings, and spend their summer evenings chatting over a glass of wine at the outdoor Italian trattoria. Beer is big in the mountains these days—microbreweries, tap-rooms, and brew pubs have multiplied in the past decade, with more opening every month, it seems.

In this chapter we recommend a number of the more eclectic venues for weekend or evening entertainment, featuring adult beverages and sometimes food, as well as cafes and tea rooms.

> **i** Be aware that some counties in North Carolina are dry. That means you won't get a drink there. Some restaurants will allow "brown bagging" and might charge a small corkage fee.

Northern Mountains

Bars

LOUISIANA PURCHASE, Hwy. 184, 397 Shawneehaw Ave., Banner Elk, NC; (828) 898-5656; louisianapurchasefoodandspirits.com. The Purchase draws young and old alike to live jazz and their wine bar on Fri and Sat nights. Local jazz duo Culpepper and Dulin are often featured Thurs night. The wine list has been recognized by *Wine Spectator* as one of the best in the country.

RANSOM, 747 West King St., Boone, NC; (828) 264-5117; ransomeboone .com. The pub now called Ransom has been a landmark in Boone for more than two decades. The drawing card at this busy place is the straight forward pub menu. Two bars offer a friendly place for a quick bite to eat, a little liquid refreshment, and a gander at a favorite sports game, plus a lively live music scene here on the weekends.

WOODLANDS BARBECUE AND PICKIN' PARLOR, 8304 Valley Blvd., Blowing Rock, NC; (828) 295-3651; woodlandsbbq.com. Woodlands features live entertainment nightly with no cover in a down-home casual atmosphere. Woodlands holds all ABC permits, so you can enjoy your favorite cocktail or beer while enjoying some of the best music our region has to offer.

Central Mountains

Bars, Pubs, and Winebars

ANTIDOTE BAR, 151 Coxe Ave., Asheville, NC; (828) 505-2882; antidote .bar. Calling itself the "cure for the common cocktail," this spectacular new space also houses a gin distillery next door called The Chemist. A new structure set to look like the 1900s with true antique ephemera displayed throughout, this members-only bar serves craft cocktails on three floors, including a cozy mezzanine and outdoor terrace with fireplace one floor up. No food served as of this writing, so eat before you try the heady spirits.

BATTERY PARK BOOK EXCHANGE CHAMPAGNE BAR, 1 Page Ave., Asheville, NC; (828) 252-0020; batteryparkbookexchange.com. Spectacular used- and rare-book store, divided up into a warren of cozy nooks with soft leather chairs and marble-topped tables for sipping on champagne, luscious wines, or coffee drinks. Massive wine menu. Gracious servers will ply you with charcuterie boards and warm sandwiches. There's something delightfully European about this magical place. Soft, light guitar music on weekend nights.

THE BRANDY BAR, 504 Seventh Ave., Hendersonville, NC; (828) 513-1336; thebrandybar.com. Open Wed through Sat, this private bar provides small noshes like nuts and cheese plates to accompany the array of brandies, noted on a multipage menu. Seating is at small tables, the atmosphere sleek and Nordic, with live music at times and special evenings focusing on various regions and styles of this beverage.

DISTRICT WINE BAR, 37 Paynes Way, Asheville, NC; (828) 505-8606; districtwinebar.com. This bar is a fantastic addition to the River Arts District, behind the Wedge Studios, with a large patio and roll-up garage door to allow light and breezes off the French Broad River. Owners Lauri and Barrett Nichols have transformed this warehouse-turned-studio (of legendary sculptor John Payne) into a convivial space for tasting varietals from small family-owned vineyards. Bio-dynamic wines, bubbly, and international bottled beers. Charcuterie, locally-made hummus, dips and cheeses, and only the best house-made pimento cheese ever, make this a great hang-out. Many nights feature bands, DJs for impromptu dance parties. Rotating art exhibitions and outdoor fire feature, too.

JACK OF THE WOOD, 95 Patton Ave., Asheville, NC; (828) 252-5445; jackofthewood.com. This English-style pub, which features darts, long wooden tables and benches, and a small raised stage, is a great drop-by nightspot for any season. Celtic music jams have people bringing their own instruments on certain nights of the week, while regular groups, ranging from folk to Celtic, to balladeers, to bluegrass and alterna-grass take the stage on the weekends. Bring your Greenman Ale (founded by Jack of the Wood's own brewers) outside to the benches, and you'll be sure to hear the tales of all

District Wine Bar, Asheville. DISTRICT WINE BAR (ASHEVILLE)

sorts of interesting folks. Mon night is Quizzo game night. Quality pub grub, including a tasty shepherd's pie, Guinness stew, bangers and mash, and other tasty bits.

LITTLE JUMBO, 241 Broadway St., Asheville, NC; (828) 417-4783; littlejumbobar.com. A lovely spacious, yet cozy, neighborhood bar with a Prohibition-era speakeasy vibe. Well-crafted cocktails plus salads and dips. Good cake! Members only, but fee is nominal. Art installations, antiques-market finds on the walls, jazz combo on Mon. Try the Cocktails for Two, served on silver trays with decanters and crystal.

THE POE HOUSE, 105 1st Ave. W., Hendersonville, NC; (828) 696-1838; facebook.com/the-poe-house. The Poe House is a slightly irreverent, small, dark bar on a side street that packs in a crowd. There's a small space for live music. Classic and experimental cocktails plus wine and beer.

SOVEREIGN REMEDIES, 29 N. Market St., Asheville, NC; (828) 919-9518; sovereignremedies.com. A small multi-level bar serving beautiful locally-sourced, plant-forward dishes from an award-winning chef, but all in a bar setting. Inventive cocktails and a European outdoor cafe vibe make a winning combination.

DINING

Cafes

DOBRA TEA, 78 N. Lexington Ave., Asheville, NC; (828) 575-2424; dobra teanc.com. A three-in-one tea room celebrating all things tea, featuring the garden-like English tea patio, a Moroccan tea room, and the Asian-style back room with silk cushion seats on the floor. The massive tea menu features many styles you've never even heard of, all served in authentic pots with utensils. Wonderful and unique locally-made sweets are served; the West Asheville location provides wholesome vegetarian wraps, harmony bowls, soups, and other toothsome items.

DONATELLI BAKERY AND CAFE, 7 Haywood St., Asheville, NC; (828) 225-5751; donatellicakedesigns.com. Beautifully designed cakes, pastries, and tarts are the allure at this lovely cafe. Classically trained, Karen Donatelli produces stunningly beautiful baked goods for celebrations and every day. A great lunch place as well for croissant sandwiches, soups, and salads. But the pastries and cakes are key.

LIBERTY HOUSE CAFE, 221 S. Liberty St., Asheville, NC; (828) 412-3225; libertyhousecafe.com. Located in a charming little house on a quiet street near yoga studios, offices, and homes, this cafe serves rustic and delightful breakfast and lunch, like avocado toast with egg; ricotta toast with jam; BLTs on the best bread ever with applewood smoked bacon; baked muffins and brioche; home-made granola; great tea and coffee beverages, hot and cold. Also offers a garden seating space and patio overlooking its herb and veg garden.

OLD EUROPE, 13 Broadway St., Asheville, NC; (828) 255-5999; old europepastries.com. A longtime Asheville favorite—serving delectable pastries, cakes, colorful macaroons, shortbreads, and gluten-free also, baked by the Hungarian owner Melinda and her protégés with heart and soul. Also serves savories like flaky ham and cheese croissants. Authentically European and located in a sweet, cozy space in the downtown area. Open late. Fine coffee beverages,wine, and bubbles, too.

WELL-BRED BAKERY CAFE, 25 N. Main St., Weaverville, NC; (828) 645-9300; wellbredbakery.com. In a former grand old pharmacy with arched windows and travertine floors, this cafe makes all its own baked goods and lunches. Fine lattes and caffeine drinks are served. Weaverville is the original spot for Well-Bred, but another bustling version is opening in Asheville's Biltmore Village.

Music Venues

ASHEVILLE GUITAR BAR, 125 Riverside Dr., Asheville, NC; (407) 616-4917; facebook.com/ashevilleguitarbar. Housed in the corner of the Cotton

Mill Studios, this intimate listening room hosts local and regional veteran performers as well as themed evenings like gypsy jazz. Velvet sofas, musically-themed, hand-crafted decor, and a bar and an outdoor deck make this a special stop.

ASHEVILLE MUSIC HALL, 31 Patton Ave., Asheville, NC; (828) 255-7777; ashevillemusichall.com. The music hall catches some great bands. The dance floor is spacious, though you practically have to walk through it to reach the bar on entering the club. It only holds 360, so be sure to line up early if your fave band is playing. Downstairs, the One-Stop is smaller with lesser-known artists, but cheap drinks.

BARLEY'S TAPROOM, 42 Biltmore Ave., Asheville, NC; (828) 255-0504; barleystaproom.com. The original Barley's that has branched out to other towns. Billiards upstairs, great pub grub, and popular pizzas on the main floor with endless taps of local beers. A great family place, as well as roomy gathering place with long farm tables for teams and larger groups. Live music on a small stage almost nightly.

> **i** Bars in North Carolina have a 2 a.m. last call, so night owls, start early!

GREY EAGLE, 185 Clingman Ave., Asheville, NC; (828) 232-5800; greyeaglemusic.com. Located in the artsy River District, with working studios just a stone's throw away, Grey Eagle has a devoted audience. The club highlights singer-songwriters, regional bands, and top national acts like Arlo Guthrie, Doc Watson, Leo Kottke, and others. The bar serves local brews, and a Cajun kitchen satisfies the hungry. It's the ultimate laid-back, quality music scene. If you're lucky, you can catch one of the occasional Latin dance evenings.

> **i** A summer secret in Asheville is the adorable Mayfel's Courtyard. The College Street eatery filters into the courtyard on summer nights with a tiki bar, refreshing "Mayfelaide" cocktails (like lemonade but with ginger and alcohol!), twinkle lights, little gurgling fountains, and a magical atmosphere all on cobblestones with cafe chairs and tables. Mayfel's, 22 College St., Asheville, (828) 252-8840, mayfels.com.

DINING

From Triple X to Extraordinary

An ode to resplendent movie houses of the past, the Fine Arts Theater maintains a grand hall with Art Deco sconces, stucco walls, and plush seats in the high-ceilinged main theater. Upstairs, another more intimate theater runs an alternate film offering. Fine foreign films, independents, and less-commercial American films are featured here. Besides the usual sweets and popcorn, beer, wine, hard ciders, coffee, and biscotti are also sold. This cinema, a drama theater at its inception and later an X-rated movie theater during a period of downtown Asheville decay, has been fully reconstructed and restored to lavish splendor. Go for the quality films, go for the atmosphere, go for the history! Fine Arts Theater, 36 Biltmore Ave., Asheville; (828) 232-1536; fineartstheater.com.

ISIS MUSIC HALL; 743 Haywood Rd., Asheville, NC; (828) 575-2737; isisasheville.com. Dinner and a show defines this great space, a 1937 single-screen movie theater that had several incarnations before being fully renovated by the family now running it. Excellent farm-to-fork casual restaurant in front, with a long bar that leads into the modern concert venue in back. Up to 450 people can dance to touring and local bands here, also viewable from the mezzanine balcony. Some concerts begin with dinner served at linen-covered tables by the stage, which are then removed for boogying down.

THE ORANGE PEEL, 101 Biltmore Ave., Asheville, NC; (828) 398-1837; theorangepeel.net. A premier music hall that can hold up to 1,000 people, pulls in national and international acts, but also has a steady stream of famed local and regional performers on any given day of the week. A grand stage,

> **i** Due to the erratic nature of nightclubs and bars, and their often quick turnover, we have listed the mainstays of various towns. Be sure to check the local listings for the most up-to-date info. In Asheville the Mountain Xpress newspaper runs an excellent listing of concerts, locales, and movies; look for The Scene, the daily newspaper's weekend section on Fri.

plenty of dancing room, and a long chrome bar are home to benefits, parties, and concerts alike. Pulp, the venue's smaller club downstairs (where you can sit at tables and lounge a bit), hosts separate events. It usually requires a small entrance fee and serves cocktails as opposed to beer, cider, and wine (which is only poured upstairs).

> **i** Because of North Carolina State liquor laws, a certain percentage of an establishment's profit has to be food sales; therefore, many bars serving liquor choose to be "private clubs." Generally a member can sign you in as a guest, or you might be charged a nominal fee for "membership" at the door.

DINING

Southern Mountains

Bars

INNOVATION BREWING, 414 W. Main St., Sylva, NC; (828) 586-9678; innovation-brewing.com. Great little brewpub with over 30 house-made beers. Pint night, trivia night, and fun locals events.

ROOT AND BARREL, 77 E. Main St., Franklin, NC; (828) 369-3663; rootandbarrel.com. Truly a fine restaurant, but we love their bright bar. Also outdoor seating for Tini Tuesdays and Wine Wednesdays.

Close-up

Beer City USA

In an unofficial internet poll in 2009 Asheville was named "Beer City USA," beating out larger and more established beer-brewing cities like Portland, Oregon, and Denver, Colorado. Asheville topped the list an additional three times. While the poll has since been retired, the moniker stuck, and could be applied to the entire region. With small breweries popping up on the regular in almost every midsize mountain town, there's no stopping this tide of quality suds.

The granddaddy of Asheville's beer boom is retired engineer Oscar Wong, who began brewing beer in the basement of a downtown bistro in the early '90s. That venture eventually turned into Highland Brewing, the first brewery in Asheville since Prohibition. Western North Carolina boasts over 50 breweries, and growing. Given the good mountain water, the penchant for beer tourism, and the embracing of beer culture by locals and visitors, it's no wonder that two national heavy-weights in the beer industry, Sierra Nevada and New Belgium, opened their East Coast outposts in WNC. These both have large facilities for touring and tasting. Most craft breweries here have tasting rooms—ranging from cozy and atmospheric to bare-bones. Some serve

David Huff

food or host food trucks on a rotating basis. And there's more than just beer! Entrepreneurs have opened operations for making hard cider, ginger beer, and even mead. Below is a list of the most accessible and better-known breweries and cideries in the Asheville "Beer City" area, plus larger notable operations elsewhere. Have fun exploring and compiling your own list of favorite discoveries, too!

Archetype Brewing, 265 Haywood Rd., Asheville; (828) 505-4177; archetypebrewing.com. A newish West Asheville space with patio; hosts bands. Also opening a branch in downtown Asheville.

Asheville Pizza and Brewing Company, 77 Coxe Ave., Asheville; (828) 255-4077; ashevillebrewing.com. Underrated long-time brewers with fantastic pizza and other eats. Large covered outdoor patio for showing movies in the summer.

Burial Beer, 40 Collier Ave., Asheville; (828) 475-2739; burialbeer.com. In the new South Slope downtown. Charming without outdoor space and a monthly "moonlight art market" in the warmer months. Innovative snacks as well.

Bhramari Brewing Co., 101 South Lexington Ave., Asheville; (828) 214-7981; bhramaribrewing.com. Beautiful tasting room and restaurant with outdoor patio right downtown.

Catawba Brewing Company, 32 Banks Ave., Asheville; (828) 552-3934; catawbabrewing.com. In Asheville's South Slope area. Always has a food truck out back with outdoor seating. Spacious with TV screens for sports.

Ginger's Revenge, 829 Riverside Dr., Asheville; (828) 505-2462; gingers revenge.com. Warehouse-like tasting room, yet charming, with live music and food truck in evenings. Fantastic incarnations of ginger beer, but also local ale on tap.

Green Man Brewery, 27 Buxton Ave., Asheville; (828) 252-5502; greenmanbrewery.com. An old Asheville favorite, but now housed in a gorgeous stone structure with outdoor balcony and street-side seating. Dirty Jack's is the older, grittier beer bar next door.

Highland Brewing Company, 12 Old Charlotte Hwy., Asheville; (828) 299-3370; highlandbrewing.com. Oldest in Asheville, large facility east of the city with a massive tasting room, tours, and outdoor meadow with stage for concerts. Food trucks always at hand.

Hillman Beer, 25 Sweeten Creek Rd., Asheville; (828) 505-1312; hill manbeer.com. Newer space off a busy thoroughfare south of downtown with wooden picnic tables out front and back; live music and excellent deli-style food.

DINING

Interior of Green Man Brewery. ExploreAsheville.com

New Belgium Brewing, 21 Craven St., Asheville; (828) 333-6900; newbelgium.com/brewery/asheville. The large East Coast outpost for this national company. Right on the French Broad River with a state-of-the-art tasting room, tours, and balcony overlooking the river.

Noble Hard Cider, 356 New Leicester Hwy., Asheville; (828) 575-9622; noblecider.com. A no-nonsense taproom for tasting a dizzying array of ciders at the production facility.

One World Brewing, 10 Patton Ave. and 520 Haywood Rd., Asheville; (828) 785-5580; oneworldbrewing.com. Sweet and cozy barrel basement space with a new overground West Asheville location.

Oskar Blues Brewery, 342 Mountain Industrial Dr.; Brevard; (828) 883-2337; oskarblues.com. With an outdoor patio bar, the Tasty Weasel taproom also hosts tours; there's food and live music five nights a week. Pisgah National Forest is a 10-minute bike ride away.

Oyster House Brewing Company, 625 Haywood Rd., Asheville; (828) 575-9370; oysterhousebeers.com. Restaurant and small production facility utilizing oyster shells for brewing some of the beer!

Pisgah Brewing Company, 150 Eastside Dr., Black Mountain, (828) 669-0190; pisgahbrewing.com. Large space with a gorgeous outdoor stage with popular concerts.

Sierra Nevada Brewing Company, 100 Sierra Nevada Way, Fletcher; (828) 708-6242; sierranevada.com. A bit like an amusement park for beer lovers, featuring a state-of-the-art brewery with tours, big amphitheater, and meadow in back with herb garden and bocce ball courts; large restaurant and bar. Huge crowds, but fun.

Twin Leaf Brewery, 144 Coxe Ave., Asheville; (828) 774-5000; twinleaf brewery.com. A shiny, new space of blond wood and gleaming vessels, with outdoor seating, in South Slope.

Urban Orchard Cider, 210 Haywood Rd., Asheville; (828) 774-515; urbanorchardcider.com. A cidery making delectable hard ciders with local apples, often paired with other fruits. This lovely space in West Asheville also has a great menu of charcuterie boards and other noshes. Sun-filled outdoor patio, too.

Wedge at Foundation, 5 Foundry St., Asheville; (828) 253-7152; wedge brewing.com. A long-time favorite and hyper local, Wedge Brewing just opened this second fabulous large space in the midst of a growing section of the famed River Arts District, with large outdoor area, food truck, a private events room, mezzanine, and great beer!

DINING

Wicked Weed Brewing, 91 Biltmore Ave., Asheville; (828) 575-9599; wickedweedbrewing.com. Opened by locals and sold to the beer giant AB InBev in 2017, this downtown space has a restaurant, huge patio with fire bowls, stone-lined basement space, and more outdoor seating. There are usually lines. They also specialize in sour beers in their Funkatorium in the South Slope area of downtown Asheville.

THE UGLY DOG PUBLIC HOUSE, 294 S. 4th St., Highlands, NC; (828) 526-8364; theuglydogpub.com. Inventive pub grub, small to large bites here, and plenty of beer, wine, and stronger beverages. Nice hang out in this small town. Also has a Cashiers satellite bar.

Cafes

BUCKS COFFEE CAFE, 384 Main St., Highlands, NC; (828) 526-0020. Fantastic blends of coffee in a cozy space on Main Street. Also serving sandwiches, cookies, and yeasty danishes. Delish. A great stop when doing your Highlands shopping.

MOUNTAIN FRESH GROCERY, 521 E. Main St., Highlands, NC; (828) 526-2400; mfgro.com. A true gem in this small town—sausage, biscuits, pancakes, and the like for breakfast; pizzas, and much more for lunch. But there's also a grocery store for picking fun things to take to your cabin or hotel. Somewhat deli-esque, with specialty olive oils and infused vinegars. The Espresso Bar will get your day going here, but there's beer and wine by the glass, too, and a wine shop in back as well. Bustling place.

PANACEA COFFEE HOUSE, 66 Commerce St., Waynesville, NC; (828) 452-6200; panaceacoffee.com. A favorite locals' haunt in the cute Frog Level neighborhood. It is also a roastery so the coffee is top notch. Also serving breakfast, sweets, and light lunch like wraps and salads. Super comfortable for hanging out, also out back on the terrace over the stream.

Music Venues

BOGART'S RESTAURANT AND TAVERN, 222 South Main St., Waynesville, NC; (828) 452-1313; bogartswaynesville.com. No matter what type of music you like, you'll eventually hear it if you drop into Bogart's for a couple of Fri or Sat nights. A little bit of everything—folk, country, rock, and blues—is played here, though not every week. It's a fun watering hole, with a cozy upstairs loft area.

HARRAH'S CHEROKEE CASINO RESORT; 777 Casino Dr., Chero-kee, NC; (828) 497-7777; ceasars.com/harrahs-cherokee. Open seven days a week, 24 hours a day, this popular casino—three football fields big—has 2,300 video gaming machines, three restaurants, a gift shop, a child-care facility, and a 1,500-seat theater with big-name, live entertainment. Tribal Bingo is also available in Cherokee.

JOHN C. CAMPBELL SCHOOL DANCE EVENTS, 1 Folk School Rd., Brasstown, NC; (828) 837-2775, (800) FOLK-SCH; folkschool.org. Square and contra dances, clogging, and circle dances with live musicians and callers are held here both on weekends and during the week. You also can learn English country dances and Balkan and other folk dances. Free concerts are held most Fri nights.

THE STOMPIN' GROUND, 3113 Soco Rd., US Hwy. 19, Maggie Val-ley, NC; (828) 926-1288; stompingroundpresents.com. From spring through fall every Fri and Sat from 8 to 11 p.m., the Stompin' Ground, going strong since 1982, offers music and dancing in "the mountain clogging capital of the world." No alcohol is served at this 100-seat music hall, so it's fun for the whole family. Just come in and stomp!

DINING

Arts, Culture, and Mountain Crafts

Long known for a rich craft heritage, (borne of necessity, then honed into beauty—the eternal question of "form versus function"), North Carolina's mountains flourish in both the traditional and innovative arts and crafts. Home-grown talent—beginning with native Cherokee—as well as an influx of professional artists, is generating an exciting mix of creativity and commerce.

Artists' studios can be found in remote hollows, back roads, industrial wastelands, and suburban neighborhoods in Western North Carolina. Contemporary crafts with novel material or new techniques have made their mark on the area.

Theater, music, and dance abound to varying degrees in our communities. Museums document the history of these mountains. Some are more academic in nature, devoted to departmental disciplines and regional displays of traditional mountain life, while others are restored farmhouses, grand old homes, and vast estates that stand as tributes to the virtues and careers of pioneering citizens. Best of all, these museums are not of the stodgy, cement-building stock. These home museums transport you into the past with the scent of aged wood, slightly musty attics, and wildflower-filled surroundings. They welcome you to step onto the back porch and drink in the deep valley views just as the mountain settlers of yore did. This chapter gives you a glimpse into the melting pot of artistic interests that mirrors the quality of life here—and helps define it. The abundance of arts and crafts in this region and their many similarities often make it hard to characterize what is "art" and what is "craft." So why try? It's *all* a part of the culture and enjoyment of this area.

ART GALLERIES

Northern Mountains

Ashe County

ASHE ARTS CENTER, 303 School Ave., West Jefferson, NC; (336) 846-2787; ashecountyarts.org. Housing a gallery and year-round exhibition space that showcases works of art by local and regional artists, the Arts Center is in a restored stone building constructed in 1938, built by the Works Progress Administration as a gathering place for the community.

Close-up

Mountain Craft Origins

Many of these crafts flourished in the isolation caused by the lack of good transportation to and from the remote mountain regions. With the advent of good roads in the middle of the 20th century, the crafts of "makin' do" were transformed into beautiful art forms. The Cherokee Indians who occupied the area for countless generations influenced handcrafts, as did the Old World settlers, passing down skills that eventually evolved into the region's style. And there's no doubt that many crafts were inspired by the wealth of natural resources. There were honeysuckle, river cane, and white oak for baskets; willows for furniture; silver bell and rhododendron for making canes; and the country's largest variety of wood for carving bowls, spoons, and statues.

Natural dyes were derived from wild pokeberries, blueberries, black walnuts, yellow root, and any number of other plants. Skilled hands transformed pinecones and weeds of the fields and roadsides into wreaths and stunning dried-flower arrangements. Corn shucks became dolls, flowers, and fans. Handmade toys that amused our great-grandparents still delight our children today. Clay for pottery was there for the digging, and some of this malleable earth was of such high quality that it ended up as table settings for royalty.

To fend off cold mountain winters, craftswomen turned scraps of old clothing into quilts; many of these works of art can be found in national museums. While spinners and weavers kept old skills alive out of necessity, today's fabric artists delight in introducing new and beautiful creations for the sheer joy of it.

The abundance of hardwoods and the need to create entertainment spawned some of the finest instrument makers around. Their delicate fiddles and sturdy dulcimers have inspired a wealth of accomplished musicians, unique songs, and joyous dances.

CATCHLIGHT GALLERY, 118 N. Jefferson Ave., West Jefferson, NC; (336) 846-1551; catchlightgallery.net. Co-op style gallery concentrating on photography with rotating exhibitions and themes, photo contests, workshops, and a visiting artists series.

CHER SHAFFER ART, 19 E. Ashe St., Ste. B, West Jefferson, NC; chershaffer.com. Housing the works of Cher Shaffer's renowned vibrant folk art (collected by the likes of Oprah Winfrey, Jane Fonda, and Henry Winkler, among others) this gallery also acts as a studio space in addition to the artist's private studio on her farm.

ORIGINALS ONLY, 3-B N. Jefferson Ave., West Jefferson, NC; (336) 846-1636; originalsonlygallery.com. Beautiful space with hand-crafted pottery, large-scale landscapes, and figurative paintings, as well as wood furniture, all by local artists.

Avery County

THE ART CELLAR, 920 Shawneehaw Ave., Banner Elk, NC; (828) 898-5175; theartcellaronline.com. Along with a wonderful selection of fine art representing the work of local artists, the Art Cellar in Banner Elk features animation art and "outsider art." It's folk art created by those outside the art world's mainstream.

CARLTON GALLERY, 10360 NC Hwy. 105 S., Banner Elk, NC; (828) 963-4288; carltonartgallery.com. Carlton Gallery celebrates close to four decades as the largest, most established gallery in the High Country. Fine art and upscale handmade crafts from over 300 artisans are showcased here. The gallery is situated under the gaze of Grandfather Mountain between Boone and Banner Elk on Hwy. 105.

i If old cemeteries fascinate you, check out the large one at Old Mother Church on Fort Hill, overlooking the town of Robbinsville in Graham County. Its exact founding date is unknown, but it probably dates back to the 1840s. The present building at the site, constructed around 1875, has served as a one-room school, a court of justice, and a place of worship.

CLARK GALLERY, 393 Shawneehaw Ave., Banner Elk, NC; (828) 898-2095; chrisclarkgallery.com. The owner of this gallery is a master of painting the landscapes and seascapes of the American continent and the islands of the Caribbean. His paintings of the entertainment world of New Orleans are especially favored by those who collect his works. James Kerr's paintings are exhibited in many prominent galleries throughout the country and are in hundreds of private and corporate collections throughout the United States, Canada, Europe, and the West Indies. Hours vary, so call for an appointment.

Madison County

MARSHALL HIGH STUDIOS, 115 Blannahassett Island Rd., Marshall, NC; (828) 649-0177; marshallhighstudios.com. These studios are open to the public only a few times a year, but bear discussing. Their home is a historic brick schoolhouse, built in 1925 as home to the high school in this small town. Nestled on a 10-acre island in the French Broad River, the restored building houses around 30 studios with plenty of paintings, textiles, jewelry making, sound recording, yoga/movement, ceramics, photography, design, writing, massage, print making, music, and fiber.

WEIZENBLATT GALLERY, 79 Cascade St., Mars Hill, NC; (828) 689-1209; mhu.edu. Fine art gallery of the Mars Hill University campus. The variety of exhibitions showcases many styles and mediums by artists of local and national prominence. An annual faculty show is always popular. The gallery also hosts art talks.

Mitchell County

PENLAND SCHOOL OF CRAFTS, 67 Doras Trail, Bakersville, NC; (828) 765-2359; penland.org. Resting on the crest of a remote mountaintop in Mitchell County, the Penland School is one of the country's finest institutions devoted entirely to the study of crafts. It was founded by Miss Lucy Morgan in 1929 after an inspirational sojourn to the craft haven of Berea, Kentucky, where she spent a summer learning to weave. On her return Miss Lucy set forth with a twofold purpose: to revive the mountain tradition of weaving here at home and to help the economically distressed women add to their livelihood. Word spread; students wanted to learn to weave. Soon new crafts were added, and suddenly Miss Lucy found her project becoming a school. Today the school has a 450-acre campus and boasts a broad curriculum that includes book arts, glass, photography, printmaking, wood, surface design, metals, iron, drawing, clay, and fibers. The Penland community includes staff, resident artists, and students, who are composed of a mix of college students, graduates, professionals looking for a different career, and those who seek the arts as an avocation. This diversity of life experience only adds to the flow of creativity and the quality of Penland.

Watauga County

ALTA VISTA GALLERY, 2839 Broadstone Rd., Valle Crucis, NC; (828) 693-5247; altavistagallery.com. This gallery features mostly two-dimensional art of the surrounding mountain scenery from area artists. Some jewelry and woodwork are also represented.

DOE RIDGE POTTERY, 585 West King St., Boone, NC; (828) 264-1127; doeridgepottery.homestead.com. Doe Ridge showcases pottery in all its forms in downtown Boone. You can find both functional stoneware like French butter jars and vegetable steamers, as well as decorative works and handmade Christmas ornaments. Commissions for promotional logos are also a great feature here.

HANDS GALLERY, 543 W. King St., Boone, NC; (828) 262-1970; hands gallery.org. This gallery has been a part of the Boone arts scene for more than 40 years. A consistently fine selection of wearable fiber art, wood sculpture, and imaginative, functional, and decorative pottery is featured here.

MAIN STREET GALLERY , 960 Main St., Blowing Rock, NC; (828) 295-7839; mainstreetgallery.com. This cooperative gallery features a variety of glass, prints, photography, stained glass, functional and decorative pottery, woven pieces, leather work, and wearable art. Special exhibits are on display each season.

MORNING STAR GALLERY, 915 Main St., Blowing Rock, NC; (828) 295-6991; morningstartgalleryusa.com. Established in 1985, Morning Star Gallery shows primarily handcrafted treasures: paintings and sculptures, pottery and jewelry, glass, wood, etchings, and garden accessories and small whimsies.

MOUNTAIN BLUE GALLERY, 151 Shawneehaw Ave. S., Banner Elk, NC; (828) 898-4477; mountainbluegallery.com. Showcasing some 25 artists in this bright, airy space, Mountain Blue offers a diverse selection of original encaustics, oils, acrylics, mixed media, kiln-formed glass, stoneware, pottery, silk, fabrics, and jewelry.

PARKWAY CRAFT CENTER at Moses Cone Manor, Mile 294, Blue Ridge Pkwy., Blowing Rock, NC; (828) 295-7938, southernhighlandguild.org. Every May through Oct with demonstrations and displays by members of the prestigious Southern Highland Craft Guild of works in clay, fiber, wood, fabric, metal, and materials native to the mountains. Be sure to save some time to sit on a rocking chair on the expansive front porch and take in one of the most inspiring views in the mountains.

Yancey County

TOE RIVER ARTS, 102 W. Main St., Burnsville, NC; (828) 682-7215; toeriverarts.org. One-of-a-kind works are showcased at the gallery at the Toe River Arts Council space in Burnsville, from prints to metals, fiber arts, paper, wood works, photography, pottery, and watercolor. These are the offices of this organization that work with the diverse mix of the over 400 artists who call this area home, especially with the annual Toe River Studio Tours spread throughout the rural area.

Central Mountains

Buncombe County

AMERICAN FOLK ART & FRAMING, 64 Biltmore Ave., Asheville, NC; (828) 281-2134, amerifolk.com. This shop features cheerful and intriguing outsider art, as well as contemporary crafts such as pottery and wood sculpture. Also a frame shop, American Folk Art features a vast array of frames from elegant to barnwood styles.

APPALACHIAN CRAFT CENTER, 10 N. Spruce St., Asheville, NC; (828) 253-8499. This nondescript storefront on a side street houses an array of mountain crafts, from handmade brooms to turned wood bowls, pottery, quilts, ornaments, and much more. It is located in downtown Asheville between the Renaissance Hotel and College Street. Their pricing of these crafts is customer-favorable.

ARIEL GALLERY, 19 Biltmore Ave., Asheville, NC; (828) 236-2660; arielcraftgallery.com. This cooperative arts and craft gallery features the crème-de-la-crème of local artisans. With everything from modern textiles to pottery, jewelry, furniture in wood, glass and metal, numerous decorative items, and wearable art, this is a treasure trove of the region's handcrafted works. The artists themselves man the store, so you may be striking up a conversation with the person who created your find.

ASHEVILLE GALLERY OF ART, 82 Patton Ave., Asheville, NC; (828) 251-5796; ashevillegallery-of-art.com. One of Asheville's oldest galleries, this downtown co-op art space represents a fine assortment of area artists.

THE BENDER GALLERY, 29 Biltmore Ave., Asheville, NC; (828) 225-6625, thebendergallery.com. Beautiful glass art in every form, from vessels to stained glass, wall hangings, and sculptures by leading national glass artists, grace this airy space.

BLUE SPIRAL 1, 38 Biltmore Ave., Asheville, NC; (828) 251-0202, bluespiral1.com. The elegant and luminous gallery space of Blue Spiral 1 in downtown Asheville is a masterfully planned multilevel showcase for painting, sculpture, and fine crafts. Changing exhibits cover the expansive 15,000-square-foot space. A separate wing includes pull-out display "walls" on wheels for more exhibition space. This is a true state-of-the-art gallery. The Blue Spiral 1 is

Close-up

The North Carolina Fresco Trail

Remote Ashe County, in the far northwest corner of North Carolina's mountains, seems an unlikely place for a collection of religious frescoes, but this is where the trail starts . . . or ends, depending on which way you're approaching.

Noted American artist Ben Long, born in Statesville, found his niche as an artist who keeps alive the ancient art of the fresco. Fresco painting is a tenuous art, based as it is on the immediate application of pigment to wet plaster. So quickly does the bonding of the two take place that great skill and meticulous planning must be maintained in order to achieve beautiful results.

In 2005 a Benjamin F. Long Fresco Trail Consortium, which included representatives from Burke, Buncombe, Iredell, and Wilkes Counties, created the Fresco Trail, growing into Ashe, Mecklenburg, and most recently, Avery Counties.

A grant from the Blue Ridge National Heritage Area (covering 25 counties in Western North Carolina) has provided the consortium to create a website, print brochures with trail locations, and create educational materials to be used in schools, colleges, and universities.

In two picturesque Episcopal churches, St. Mary's in West Jefferson, on Highway 194, off US Highway 221, and Holy Trinity, just off Highway 16 at Glendale Springs, are housed a collection of wonderful religious frescoes created by Long and his students, spanning a period of years from the mid-1970s to the mid-1980s. The marvelous beauty of the work and the powerful

also home to the largest collection of paintings by Will Henry Stevens (1881–1949). Stevens was a renowned regionalist and modernist who worked in oils, watercolor, pastels, and mixed media.

GRAND BOHEMIAN GALLERY, 11 Boston Way, Asheville, NC; (828) 398-5555; grandbohemiangallery.com. Inside the Grand Bohemian Hotel this European-art-salon-style gallery features international, national, and local artists, with monthly receptions that spill out into the grand lobby. The exhibition continues on each floor of the hotel with artwork on every available wall space. A private viewing room in the gallery allows collectors to consider artwork under different lighting conditions. Unique, one-of-a-kind artisan-made jewelry, also.

subjects have drawn thousands of visitors from all over the country to witness firsthand the evocative frescoes that decorate the walls of these tiny churches.

Over the last 30 years Benjamin Franklin Long IV has established an international reputation as a portrait painter and rare contemporary master of the ancient art of "true fresco," painting directly on wet plaster walls. Born in Texas, Long is the grandson of McKendree Robbins Long (1888–1976), a revivalist preacher and visionary painter whose early art training had grounded him firmly in the Western classical tradition. Long grew up in Statesville, North Carolina, and studied at the University of North Carolina at Chapel Hill and the Art Students League in New York. Traveling to New York City, Long became a member of the Art Students League and began studying with Robert Beverly Hale and Frank Mason. In 1967 he interrupted his art studies to enlist in the Marine Corps, serving two years in Vietnam, initially as an infantry officer and later as a combat artist.

Upon leaving Vietnam, Long traveled to Italy to apprentice himself to Pietro Annigoni. Long committed himself to Annigoni for almost eight years, working beside him in fresco work and teaching himself to paint in oil.

After completing several frescoes in Italy, including the only painting by a non-Italian at the Abbey of Montecassino, Long brought his fresco talent to America. Since 1978, Long has completed 13 frescoes in North Carolina, including a dome at the TransAmerica building in Charlotte.

Besides his major fresco work, Long has had works in the Royal Academy as well as the Royal Portrait Society. He has exhibited in Florence, London, Paris, Atlanta, San Francisco, and North Carolina, and is represented in major collections in Europe and North and South America. He has lived and worked in Europe for over 30 years and now divides his time between Europe, Asheville, and Brevard, North Carolina.

THE HAEN GALLERY, 52 Biltmore Ave., Asheville, NC; (828) 254-8577; thehaengallery.com. A spacious gallery with a minimalist atmosphere—artwork is not crowded in here—Haen showcases landscape painting, graphic art, and sleek sculpture from a variety of local, regional, and southeastern artists.

MOMENTUM GALLERY, 24 N. Lexington Ave. and 52 Broadway St., Asheville, NC; (828) 505-8550; momentumgallery.com. A contemporary and modern art gallery with an emphasis on emerging and mid-career artists. Set in two spaces, two blocks apart, each venue creates compelling, museum-quality art exhibitions.

NEW MORNING GALLERY, 7 Boston Way, Biltmore Village, Asheville, NC; (828) 274-2831; newmorninggallerync.com. Founded in 1972 as a modest crafts gallery, the New Morning Gallery is one of the best showcases of fine handcrafts in the region. Owner John Cram describes New Morning Gallery as "art for living." You can enjoy browsing the newly expanded shop filled with sculptural pottery, handmade jewelry, fine art glass, and unusual furniture.

ODYSSEY CENTER FOR THE CERAMIC ARTS, 236 Clingman Ave., Asheville, NC; (828) 285-0210; odysseyclayworks.com. In Asheville's Historic River District, close to the train tracks and the banks of the French Broad River, this large pottery center offers courses in clay crafts for beginners and advanced students. Nine-week classes are offered in pottery, hand building, and figurative sculpture, as well as kids' classes for after school and homeschoolers. Weekend and weeklong workshops, along with frequent lectures, feature nationally and internationally known ceramic artists. An independent study program gives returning students the opportunity to use the facility during open studio hours and work independently. The Odyssey Gallery markets and exhibits ceramic works from local and national artists and serves as an educational tool for students as well as the public. Call for a detailed course brochure and workshop schedule.

SEVEN SISTERS GALLERY, 117 Cherry St., Black Mountain, NC; (828) 669-5107; sevensistersgallery.com. The wonderfully rustic brick interior, original pressed-tin ceiling, hardwood floors, and antique furniture—all serving as display space for gallery work—set the mood for this relaxed gallery that is an integral part of Black Mountain. Seven Sisters Gallery is an anchor for the Cherry Street Historic District in this quaint old resort town.

WOOLWORTH WALK, 25 Haywood St., Asheville, NC; (828) 254-9234; woolworthwalk.com. An egalitarian juried art bazaar, the Walk maintains individual artisans' booths that feature everything from jewelry to photography, clothing, pottery, and much more.

Henderson County

ART MOB STUDIOS AND MARKETPLACE, 124 4th Ave. E., Hendersonville, NC; (828) 693-4545; artmobstudios.com. With over 5,000 square feet of space, this art space hosts studios with resident artists, classes, and the work of over 90 local artists.

SILVER FOX GALLERY, 508 Main St., Hendersonville, NC; (828) 698-0601; silverfoxonline.com. The Silver Fox maintains an interesting collection of utilitarian works like collectible salt-shakers, artisan lighting, indoor and outdoor furniture, as well as paintings, and sculpture. A collection of Judaic arts and jewelry is also unique here.

Polk County

HEARTWOOD CONTEMPORARY CRAFTS GALLERY, 21 Main St., Saluda, NC; (828) 749-9365; heartwoodsaluda.com. With a focus on a more contemporary collection, this gallery is the perfect place for anyone who not only enjoys fine crafts, but also likes to bask in the small-town atmosphere that makes Saluda special. Regional and national craftspeople of the highest caliber display their wares here, such as delicate porcelain sculpture, pottery (one of the finest collections in the region), jewelry in all its forms, wood items, garden sculpture, and original prints and paintings.

TRYON PAINTERS AND SCULPTORS, TRYON FINE ARTS CENTER, 78 N. Trade St., Tryon, NC; (828) 859-0141; tryonpaintersandsculptors.com. Tryon Painters and Sculptors is a membership-based nonprofit visual arts organization founded in 1968 to provide members with opportunities and resources for artistic growth, through gallery exhibitions, a retail sales venue, and workshops. Regular art and sculpture classes are held in the studio. The retail store features members' creations.

UPSTAIRS ARTSPACE, 49 N. Trade St., Tryon, NC; (828) 859-2828; upstairsartspace.org. The Upstairs Artspace got its name from former upper-floor locations, the first being an artist's upstairs bedroom when the gallery was founded in 1978. This well-known contemporary art gallery features fine arts, crafts, thought-provoking installations, literary readings, musical performances, art education, and other events in its spaces totaling some 3,000 square feet. Art exhibitions selected by committee and independent curators rotate every six weeks.

Transylvania County

BREVARD COLLEGE VISUAL ARTS, 1 Brevard College Dr., Brevard, NC; (828) 883-8292; brevard.edu. Exhibitions of visual art at the college can be found in two locations: the Mezzazine Gallery in the Paul Porter Center for Performing Arts and the Spiers Gallery in Sims Art Center. In addition to displays of art produced by the faculty and students, visitors may enjoy the talents of regionally and nationally known artists. Exhibitions include work that spans the spectrum of the visual arts, including ceramics, painting, sculpture, photography, and installations.

RED WOLF GALLERY, 8 E. Main St., Brevard, NC; (828) 862-8620; redwolfgallerync.com. This is a small and astute space with vibrant landscapes, woodwork, and copper sculptures that is owned by the Dergara family. It displays works of the family artistans as well as local and regional artists. The building in which the gallery is housed underwent restorations to recreate a marvelous facade.

TRANSYLVANIA COMMUNITY ARTS CENTER AND GALLERY, 349 S. Caldwell St., Brevard, NC; (828) 884-2787; tcarts.com. This gallery highlights local and regional artists with 10 themed exhibitions a year. Nov brings the annual Art Mart, a sale of fine arts and crafts at significantly discounted prices.

Southern Mountains

Haywood County

BLUE OWL STUDIO AND GALLERY, INC., 11 N. Main St., Waynesville, NC; (828) 456-9596. If you wonder how the cities and landscapes of the mountains appeared in yesteryear, you can relive some of those days in this gallery. Filled with antique graphics of the past, the artists at Blue Owl bring them to life in brilliant hand-painted colors. Animal paintings on wood are predominant here—particularly black bears, wolves, raccoons, and other creatures indigenous to this area.

> i Many arts councils in various towns hold "gallery hops" or "gallery crawls" every few months. During these events galleries and studios throw their doors open wide to the public, sometimes offering light hors d'oeuvres and wine, while visitors stroll from gallery to gallery for some art appreciation and a bit of socializing. Often the artists are on hand to discuss their works. Check local newspaper listings or consult individual art councils.

T. PENNINGTON ART GALLERY, 15 N. Main St., Waynesville, NC; (828) 452-9482; tpennington.com. You'll be amazed by the intricate colored-pencil drawings of Western North Carolina created by Teresa Pennington. In addition to original works, the gallery also carries limited-edition prints of local mountain scenes.

TWIGS & LEAVES, 98 N. Main St., Waynesville, NC; (828) 456-1940; twigsandleaves.com. A downtown gallery with ceramics, paintings, intriguing hand-made decorative pieces, and jewelry is a big draw on Main Street. The gallery is packed full, but be sure to peruse the cases of jewelry for one-of-a-kind hand-wrought works by both professionals and emerging artists.

Jackson County

CITY LIGHTS BOOKSTORE, 3 E. Jackson St., Sylva, NC; (828) 587-2233; citylightsnc.com. In addition to offering new and used books, City Lights has a small gallery of rotating exhibitions from local artisans, and sells book accessories such as place-holders and reading pillows.

> **i** Waynesville's Mast General Store (63 North Main St.) makes for interesting browsing anytime (see our Shopping chapter). Now its Mast Store Crafter Series demonstrations make it the home of a real learning experience. Several times a month, talented craftspeople show off their skills in such things as doll making, jewelry design, raku masks, and stenciling. Call (828) 452-2101 for more information about the series.

OAKS GALLERY, 29 Craft Circle, Dillsboro, NC; (828) 586-6542; oaks gallery.com. The talents that flower in these mountains are beautifully expressed in this gallery with the works of over 100 local artisans. Located at the Riverwood Shops, the Oaks Gallery maintains ceramics, wood arts, jewelry, glass, and other gifts from area artists.

TREE HOUSE POTTERY, 148 Front St., Dillsboro, NC; (828) 631-5100; treehousepotterync.com. At Tree House Pottery you can see pottery being made in an open studio by artisans Travis Berning and Joe Frank McGee. Other artists' ceramic works are carried here also.

Macon County

THE BASCOM, 323 Franklin Rd., Highlands, NC; (828) 526-4949; thebascom.org. The Bascom is a nonprofit center for the visual arts in Highlands, and has a beautiful new home as of May 2009: a 6-acre, "green," architect-designed pastoral campus where it serves people through high-quality rotating exhibitions, classes, and educational presentations. The campus features historic buildings, a covered bridge, a nature trail, a 27,500-square-foot main building for two-dimensional adult and children's art, a separate reconstructed Studio Barn for three-dimensional art, a cafe, a shop, and a terrace for venue rentals.

SUMMERHOUSE GALLERY, 2089 Dillard Rd., Highlands, NC; (828) 526-5577; summerhousehighlands.com. Tiger Mountain Summerhouse Gallery is the showroom for woodworks. This shop sells handcrafted furnishings, including custom lodge furniture and country reproductions of beds, tables, dressers, and other items for the entire house.

THE UPTOWN GALLERY, 30 E. Main St., Franklin, NC; (828) 349-4607; franklinuptowngallery.com. Members of the Macon County Art Association (see Art Organizations) display their oils, pastels, watercolors, acrylics, mixed media, and sculpture here on a year-round basis.

ART ORGANIZATIONS

Northern Mountains

Alleghany County

ALLEGHANY COUNTY ARTS COUNCIL, PO Box 962, Sparta, NC; (336) 372-2578; alleghanyartscouncil.org. The Alleghany County Arts Council, housed in a charming historic house in Crouse Park in downtown Sparta, is a young organization that sponsors local artists in yearly exhibits held in the local public library. The council also puts on the annual Blue Ridge Mountain Craft Fair on the last Sat in June at the Justin Higgins Agricultural Center and Fairgrounds on US Hwy. 21 in Sparta.

Ashe County

ASHE COUNTY ARTS COUNCIL, 303 School Ave., West Jefferson, NC; (336) 246-2787; ashecountyarts.org. This organization is headquartered in a lovely old stone building known as the Ashe Arts Center. This structure, constructed as a community center during the Great Depression, was a Works Progress Administration project. The Ashe County Arts Council is an active organization that sponsors 32 in-school arts programs, numerous arts residencies in the school system, and eight community concerts. The group also sponsors continuously changing exhibits of the work of local artists in its Ashe Arts Center gallery.

Avery County

AVERY COUNTY ARTS COUNCIL, PO Box 2505, Banner Elk, NC; (828) 898-8755; averyartscouncil.org. The Avery County Arts Council coordinates myriad cultural activities for county residents. The group sponsors numerous arts festivals during the year, such as a Christmas Craft Show and the Very Special Arts Festival in the spring. It also creates opportunities for arts through education and programming.

Watauga County

WATAUGA COUNTY ARTS COUNCIL, 604 W. King St., Boone, NC; (828) 264-1789; wataugaart.org. This county arts council is housed in the Jones Community Center in downtown Boone, a building that's also home to two art exhibition galleries. The council is a vital part of the community, sponsoring a number of events during the year and promoting education in the arts with fund raising for the support of art scholarships. The council office is open Wed through Sat.

Yancey County

TOE RIVER ARTS COUNCIL, 102 W. Main St., Burnsville, NC; (828) 682-7215; toeriverarts.org. This incredibly busy arts council serves two counties (Yancey and neighboring Mitchell) with an inordinate number of artists and craftspeople—in part due to the presence of the revered Penland School of Crafts in Mitchell County. Services provided by the Toe River Arts Council include a winter arts program and a symphony program. The group also sponsors art and music festivals each summer, along with summer art workshops. The group has developed a map outlining the location of the numerous studios of Yancey County artists and craftspeople and a free directory listing all the cultural offerings in the two-county area served by the council.

Central Mountains

Buncombe County

ASHEVILLE AREA ARTS COUNCIL, 207 Coxe Ave., Asheville, NC; (828) 258-0710; ashevillearts.com. This nonprofit organization has been dedicated to the support and perpetuation of the cultural arts in the Asheville/Buncombe County area for more than 50 years. The group provides technical support, management assistance, and allocation of grants and other funding to emerging artists and area cultural activities and organizations. The Arts in Education program brings art into the schools. The arts council works closely with the community in an effort to identify these needs. Regular exhibitions are displayed in the gallery space, and working studios are hosted in this large space.

Henderson County

ART LEAGUE OF HENDERSON COUNTY, PO Box 514, Hendersonville, NC; (828) 692-0575; artleague.net. The Art League was established in 1958 and is a tax-exempt, not-for-profit corporation. Its purpose is the promotion, development, and enjoyment of the visual arts. They hold monthly meetings at the Opportunity House in Hendersonville. Members get to exhibit their work and attend demos of techniques or methods by qualified artists. All of these events are open to the public. The Sidewalk Art Show has been held on Main Street in downtown Hendersonville for over 50 years.

HENDERSON COUNTY ARTS COUNCIL, INC., 2700A Greenville Hwy., Flat Rock, NC; (828) 693-8504; acofhc.org. Henderson County Arts Council, an active organization, sponsors special art events throughout the year, including the spring Jubilee Arts Festival and a performance of Folkmoot, the International Dance Festival. In cooperation with the North Carolina Museum of Art, the council promotes art education through its Art Appreciation School Slide Program in Henderson County schools. It's also responsible for the Mountain Arts Program, the Regional Arts Project Grant Program, and the distribution of public and grant monies for the arts in the county.

Polk County

TRYON FINE ARTS CENTER, 34 Melrose Ave., Tryon, NC; (828) 859-8322; tryonarts.org. A nonprofit organization, Tryon Crafts, located in the Tryon Fine Arts Center, sponsors classes that include weaving, silversmithing, enameling on copper, rug hooking, crewel and needlepoint, macramé, wood carving, knitting, chair caning, stained glass, lampshade making, and oshibana. Tryon Crafts also has a weaving cottage on the property called the Cate-Hall Weaving Center. Member shows are held each year at Christmas and in spring, and a shop is open next to the Tryon Crafts office on the lower level of the TFAC building. The arts center for the town is 100 percent privately funded. Built in 1969, the center contains a 345-seat theater with a hearing-impaired system, an exhibition room called Gallery I, a Mural Room for meetings and receptions, art studios, a crafts room for classes, and an outdoor garden. In addition to all the activities of its affiliates, TFAC offers musical performances by local and professional artists, recounting of personal travel experiences, benefits, lectures, slide shows, Christmas song fests, summer socials, North Carolina Shakespeare Festival performances, jazz bands, contemporary subject seminars, and more.

Transylvania County

TRANSYLVANIA COUNTY ARTS COUNCIL, 349 S. Caldwell St., Brevard, NC; (828) 884-2787; tcarts.org. This center provides inspiration and support to local artists, art groups, and school children. TC Arts oversees 30 art programs and services, including Grassroots Arts and Regional Artist Project grant programs. TC Arts also joins Brevard College in presenting the Performing Arts Series for the community. The council holds a gala fund-raising event each year. TC Arts also sponsors a juried show of regional artists from six Western North Carolina counties at the Transylvania Fine Arts and Crafts showcase. Art classes, Arts in Schools, and the TC Arts Center Gallery are but a few of the dynamic activities run by the council.

Southern Mountains

Haywood County

HAYWOOD COUNTY ARTS COUNCIL, 86 N. Main St., Waynesville, NC; (828) 452-0593; haywoodarts.org. Ensconced in a new office on Waynesville's charming Main Street, the HCAC sponsors International Festival Day—a day of dance, music, food, and a juried crafts show—each July in association with Folkmoot, the International Dance Festival. HCAC also is involved in Haywood's own production of *The Nutcracker* and the annual Holiday Tour of Homes. The council brings the Atlanta Ballet to Waynesville for its two-week annual residency in late summer. In addition to open rehearsals, the ballet holds workshops for area youth.

Jackson County

JACKSON COUNTY ARTS COUNCIL, 310 Keener St., Sylva, NC; (828) 293-5458; jacksoncountyarts.org. Whether it's dance, literature, drama, or the visual arts, this council lends its support to dozens of activities and performances each year, including lectures, concerts, and exhibitions. The Rotunda Gallery in the Historic Jackson County Courthouse serves as one of the great spaces for the council's art shows.

Macon County

ARTS COUNCIL OF MACON COUNTY, 33 E. Main St., Franklin, NC; (828) 524-7683; artscouncilofmacon.org. Macon County's Arts Council is dedicated to getting people actively involved in the arts, particularly with grass roots grants assistance and scholarships. Typically hosts a biannual artists' showcase.

ART LEAGUE OF HIGHLANDS-CASHIERS, PO Box 2133, Highlands, NC; (828) 787-1538; artleaguehighlands-cashiers.com. The Arts League of Highlands-Cashiers, founded in 1980, is a nonprofit association of artists and supporters of visual arts and serves the Western Carolina/North Georgia mountain areas. With over 100 members, the league sponsors several shows a year, supports and helps publicize visual arts in the area, and takes field trips to galleries, art shows, and other places of interest.

MACON COUNTY ART ASSOCIATION, 30 E. Main St., Franklin, NC; (828) 349-4607; franklinuptowngallery.com. One of the oldest art associations in Franklin (1962) continues to grow and flourish. Members are artists of oil, pastel, watercolor, acrylics, mixed media, and sculpture. These members run the Uptown Gallery for displaying and selling their artwork. Many of these originals depict the surrounding Appalachian Mountains, in addition to works of all subjects. The league also holds a children's art camp at the rec park in the summer.

Reel to Reel:
Films Made in the Mountains

The mountains of North Carolina form a dynamic backdrop for the big screen. While exploring this area, make note of sites for some of the films listed below.

This first listing is of those made at Biltmore Estate. Grace Kelly graced *The Swan* along with Louis Jordan and Alec Guinness. Peter Sellers emulated a gardener rescued by Shirley MacLaine in *Being There*. Tim Conway and Don Knotts survived the mystery of *Private Eyes*. Forrest Gump's run across America included the roadways of Biltmore Estate. The little wealthy kid, *Richie Rich*, luxuriated in Biltmore House. Hannibal, in the film *Hannibal*, dined in his own inimitable style with Biltmore sharing billing with scenes in Italy. *Patch Adams* was shot on the back 40 at the Princess Anne Hotel in Asheville, and in the mountains of Madison County, while the King's courier in *The Last of the Mohicans* drove an ornate carriage across the brick bridge at the Bass Pond on Biltmore Estate. *Thunder Road*, starring Robert Mitchum, had some scenes at Biltmore and along the rivers and mountains of Western North Carolina. Gracing Biltmore in *Mr. Destiny* were Michael Caine and Sir Laurence Olivier.

Meanwhile, Harrison Ford was escaping his pursuers in *The Fugitive* in Dillsboro and along the Tuckasegee and Oconaluftee Rivers. This featured the expenditure of an engine from the Smoky Mountains Railroad crashing into the Illinois State Prison Bus. Also down in the southern mountains, Jodie Foster, as Nell, portrayed a taste of mountain living of years ago. *Song Catcher* depicted another portrayal of mountain living and mountain music of an earlier century. That was filmed around the hamlet of Dillingham.

Swain County

SWAIN COUNTY CENTER FOR THE ARTS, 1415 Fontana Rd., Bryson City, NC; (828) 488-7843; swainartscenter.com. This center holds performance events and hosts gallery events showcasing Cherokee art, as well as student art and work from local artists. Classes and workshops are also held in this multi-functional venue.

Filmdom presidents Jack Lemmon and James Garner in *My Fellow Americans* were on the run through Marshall, marched in a parade in Asheville, rode the Great Smoky Mountains train, landed a helicopter at Lake Lure, and continued their adventure to the Lagoon at Biltmore, where the White House was standing in an adjacent field. Some years earlier Patrick Swayze and Jennifer Grey did their famous lifts from Lake Lure in *Dirty Dancing*.

Baseball reigned at Asheville's McCormick Field with the filming of *Bull Durham*. Meanwhile just up Biltmore Avenue at Pack Square, many of the scenes were shot for the early silent film *Conquest of Canaan*. Some of the old-timers of Asheville were extras in the Civil War film *Tap Roots* featuring Susan Hayward and Van Heflin. According to these fellows, it was such a low-budget film that they donned Yankee blues, proceeding to fire across the French Broad River at the Rebels. Cameras stopped rolling as they changed into Confederate grey and crossed the river to return fire.

Daniel Day-Lewis and company were all over these mountains in *The Last of the Mohicans*. The film company had offices on Pack Square. They rented a warehouse for costuming across from the Ritz restaurant in "The Block" on South Market Street, taking many of their meals there. The Red Coats marched from Grove Park Inn to the English Manor Inn on Charlotte Street. Waterfalls at Linville were featured as a hiding place, but to no avail. Lake James was the scene of the fallen Fort William Henry. And Chingachgook made his stand as the last Mohican at Chimney Rock as Hawkeye raced up the mountain firing his muskets, dispersing the enemy, in a desperate run to assist his adopted father.

Here for a drying-out period in *28 Days* was Sandra Bullock with the main scenes taking place at the Blue Ridge YMCA Conference Center, standing in as the Sanatorium, and the Black Walnut Bed and Breakfast in Historic Montford providing the domestic ambience for the kitchen scene of ranting, raving, and smashing dishes. And most recently Robert Redford used the former grounds of old Camp Sequoya up Reems Creek just past the Zebulon Vance birthplace outside Weaverville for the film *The Clearing*.

DANCE

Central Mountains

THE ACADEMY AT TERPSICORPS, 1501 Patton Ave., Asheville, NC; (828) 761-1277; terpsicorpsacademy.org. Terpsicorps brings in professional dancers from various troupes around the country to perform at Diana Wortham

Close-up

The Asheville Urban Trail

The Urban Trail in downtown Asheville, a meandering 1.7-mile walk through Asheville's history via plaques and sculptures, was created by volunteers and community donors over a period of 10 years. It initially began as a way to attract people to a sparsely populated downtown and ended up as a contributor to one of the largest collections of public art in the state.

Thirty "stations," in the form of sculptures or sidewalk plaques, take you through numerous eras, starting with the pioneering age when the mountains were first developed by settlers (on what was Cherokee land), through the industrial era, to the period of blossoming art deco architecture in the city, and onwards. Locally-based and national artists were commissioned to create sculptures and bas-reliefs that would echo this history.

A bronze sow and her piglets, turkeys, and other creatures' footprints in concrete symbolize the drovers taking their livestock to market over these very crossroads in the station of the same name, for example. A little bronze girl bending over for a drink from a fountain symbolizes the innocence of childhood. A giant iron in front of the Flat Iron Building recalls an old Asheville laundry that was once part of the neighborhood.

The trail has, in fact, become such a success that other cities in North Carolina and elsewhere are trying to emulate it. Now, of course, the downtown is abuzz with activity, thanks, in part, to the Urban Trail. The Asheville Area Arts Council offers maps of the Urban Trail and conducts walking tours. *Artful Asheville—Along the Urban Trail*, by one of the authors of this book, supplies a more in-depth examination of each aspect of the trail, along with walking maps, history, and a guide to art venues in the city. The trail falls under the auspices of the City of Asheville's Public Art Program. To learn more, visit exploreasheville.com/urban-trail.

Theatre in modern dance pieces choreographed by the young founder of this troupe. Often the works are narrative in nature, in addition to minimalist modern dance.

ASHEVILLE BALLET/FLETCHER SCHOOL OF DANCE, 4 Weaverville Rd., Asheville, NC; (828) 252-4761; ashevilleballet.com. This distinguished school of dance, started more than 50 years ago by the late Beale Fletcher, is an institution in Asheville. The school's performing arm, the Asheville Ballet, annually produces a polished, well-received version of *The Nutcracker* for holiday audiences and regularly trains dancers who enter major troupes around the country. Performances typically held in downtown Asheville.

ASHEVILLE CONTEMPORARY DANCE THEATRE AND THE NEW STUDIO OF DANCE, 20 Commerce St., Asheville, NC; (828) 254-2621; acdt.org. This fascinating, experimental dance/theater company presents lavishly produced original works adapted from ancient legends of different world cultures—particularly the richly imaginative Aztec and Mayan legends—such as the story of the feathered serpent Quetzalcoatl. Meticulous research, typically taking as long as eight months, incorporates experimental movement, puppets, sword play, mime, traditional music, and interpretive costuming (including some interesting ones of sculpted foam) for each production. The 6- to 15-member company has performed across the Southeast, in France, and in Cuba, and offers artistic exchanges with international dance theater companies.

> **i** Many mountain crafters who don't have other outlets for their wares sell them exclusively at the numerous annual street fairs and celebrations held throughout the year. (See our Festivals and Annual Events chapter for detailed descriptions.)

MOUNTAIN CRAFTS

Northern Mountains

CROSSNORE WEAVERS & GALLERY/CROSSNORE SCHOOL, 205 Johnson Ln., Hwy. 221, Crossnore, NC; (828) 733-4660; crossnore.org. The Weaving Room is a self-help project of Crossnore School. All proceeds benefit the boys and girls of Crossnore School, children from the Carolina mountains and foothills. These children from families in crisis find a stable environment on the school's 72-acre campus. At the Crossnore School watch weavers at their looms, creating traditional patterns and contemporary wares. Since 1920 the school has kept alive the almost forgotten art of producing handwoven clothing and home furnishings in patterns used by the early settlers of the Appalachians. In the Weaving Room, you will find throw rugs in the Lee's Surrender pattern, capes and stoles in a Honeysuckle pattern, and table runners and baby blankets in the Bronson Lace pattern. The weavers use all natural cotton, wool, and linen, as well as some easy-care materials like rayon, orlon, and synthetics.

Kaolin

In 1767 an English tableware manufacturer, Josiah Wedgwood, sent a South Carolina planter, Thomas Griffith, to make an arrangement with the Cherokee to export the high-quality clay known as "kaolin" that was found in the region. Huge amounts of kaolin were shipped to Wedgwood and transformed into the famous Queensware. A Wedgwood dinner service of Macon County clay graced the table of Catherine the Great.

Central Mountains

THE CENTER FOR ART AND INSPIRATION, 125 S. Main St., Hendersonville, NC; (828) 697-8647; thecenterai.com. A community arts gathering place for art and inspiration, featuring coffee, books, and art for sale.

FOLK ART CENTER, Mile 382 Blue Ridge Pkwy., Asheville, NC; (828) 298-7928; southernhighlandguild.org. The Folk Art Center is the grand showcase for the work of the more than 700 members of the Southern Highland Craft Guild. The guild was founded in 1930 as an educational, nonprofit organization to provide economic support to the many fine craftspeople of the southern Appalachian region. Guild members come from a nine-state region and produce some of the finest traditional mountain crafts as well as outstanding contemporary craft work being done today. The Folk Art Center, Asheville's gateway to the Blue Ridge Parkway off US Hwy. 70, welcomes 350,000 visitors annually from all over the country and the world. They come to see the fine traditional mountain heritage on display in the permanent collection and the traditional and contemporary crafts in the ever-changing exhibitions. Allanstand Craft Shop, America's oldest craft shop, is a feast for the eyes with its displays of glassware, blankets, dishware, wooden toys, exquisitely crafted jewelry, prints, brooms, and baskets. The main level houses a 250-seat auditorium that serves the guild's educational purposes and is also used by the National Park Service. Here, as well as in the foyer, demonstrations are produced throughout Apr through Dec. Special events, such as Clay Day and Fiber Day, involve the public with hands-on participation projects and provide fun for the entire family. (See our **Attractions** chapter.)

The Folk Art Center is open Apr through Dec from 9 a.m. to 6 p.m. daily except Thanksgiving, Christmas, and New Year's; 9 a.m. to 5 p.m. Jan through Mar. Admission is free.

GROVEWOOD GALLERY, 111 Grovewood Rd., Asheville, NC; (828) 253-7651; grovewood.com. This fine gallery is in the former home of the Biltmore Industries woolen homespun operation. The interior of this interesting English-style cottage adjacent to the Grove Park Inn has been wonderfully renovated as gallery and shop space without sacrificing the integrity of its origin. The Grovewood Studios, in the next cottage, houses 11 artists specializing in wood work, blown glass, stone carving, jewelry, and furniture. Their work, along with the work of other area craftspeople, is represented by the Grovewood Gallery. The furniture gallery upstairs has expanded and features fabulous designs from the Southeast.

Artists in Residence at Asheville's River District Studios

Asheville's River District Studios, located along the French Broad River in the city's old industrial area close to downtown, is home to no less than 100 working studios. Over 200 artists and artisans work here. Some buildings include galleries, and many studios have regular hours to welcome visitors. Ceramics, printmaking, painting, woodworking, sculpting, garden art, photography, welding, candle making, and many other crafts can be found here.

Twice a year the River District Studios host a studio stroll, where artists host guests while doing demos, sometimes offering refreshments. Feel free to wander and watch and make a purchase or two. You'll be sure to run into a bevy of local supporters. Strolls take place on a weekend once in the fall and once in summer. The Cotton Mill Studios offer tours of certain studios year-round. The River District Studios are concentrated on Riverside Drive, Clingman Avenue, and Lyman and Roberts Streets. Check the website for a complete listing of artists and studios, broken down into genres; (828) 552-4723; riverartsdistrict.com.

Southern Mountains

DOGWOOD CRAFTERS, 90 Webster St., Dillsboro, NC; (828) 586-2248; dogwoodcrafters.com. Housed in a large, renovated log building around the corner from Front Street, this is one of Dillsboro's most charming stores. We are particularly taken with the lovely, artistic cornhusk dolls here, but there also

The Swannanoa Gathering

In the heart of the summer, about the time the katydids crank up, folks from all over the country converge upon the Asheville area for the Swannanoa Gathering at Warren Wilson College. These five weeks of music workshops run through July and into mid-Aug. The schedule is full of special weeks that focus on specific styles and disciplines, including Celtic Week, Performance Lab, Dulcimer Week, Dance Week, Old-Time Music & Dance Week, Contemporary Folk Week, Guitar Week, and Fiddle Week. Some years include Blues Week as well. With an advisory board that reads like a Who's Who in Folk Music—David Holt, John McCutcheon, Fiona Ritchie, Billy Edd Wheeler, and Asheville's own David Wilcox—it's no wonder the programming and attendance are stellar every year.

The workshops convene at various sites around the Warren Wilson campus. Classes are open to everyone, and many are structured for beginners. Students are free to create their own curriculum for each week (with the exception of some restrictions by individual teachers), although participants are urged to concentrate on one or two classes.

Certain weeks include programs for children ages 6 to 12. Classes in crafts, field trips to local attractions such as Pack Place and the Nature Center, and swimming activities are scheduled during the daytime class sessions.

A typical week begins with supper, an orientation session, and socializing on the Sunday before the courses begin in earnest. Most classes meet for morning or afternoon sessions Mon through Fri. Some may meet in the evenings for performance critiques, rehearsals, or jam sessions. Other evening activities include concerts by staff instructors, dances, song swaps, and impromptu happenings, such as picking sessions and slow jams (tune-learning sessions).

For sports and recreation, the college's facilities include a gymnasium, weight room, aquatic center, and tennis courts, as well as a pond, nature trails, a working farm, and a kayak run on the nearby Swannanoa River.

are hundreds of contemporary and traditional handicrafts on display, including pottery, pillows, art, and toys.

JOHN C. CAMPBELL FOLK SCHOOL, 1 Folk School Rd., Brasstown, NC; (828) 837-2775, (800) FOLK-SCH; folkschool.org. The John C. Campbell Folk School has been a mountain institution for more than 80 years, and

The musical traditions of Scotland and Ireland, possessing separate and distinctive personalities, nonetheless share a common heritage. **Celtic Week** acknowledges this dual heritage with a program featuring the best from each tradition. Irish flute, Irish step dancing, uilleann pipes, Celtic harp, tin whistle, Scottish fiddle, hammered dulcimer, bodhran (traditional Irish frame drum), Celtic guitar, and bouzouki (like a large, long-necked mandolin) are just some of the courses offered.

Performance Lab Week is designed for those who have a serious interest in moving to a higher level in their performing activities. The first three class days are spent on the campus, working on performance skills in a lab setting. Then the acts hit the road to perform three concerts in the region, presented as a revue, with each act doing a short set as a part of each show.

Old-Time Music & Dance Week explores the rich music, dance, singing, and storytelling traditions of the southern Appalachian region. Old-time fiddle is a popular course, as are old-time banjo, old-time guitar, and autoharp. Shape-note singing, a fascinating musical tradition stretching back to the 16th century, is also offered.

Dulcimer Week includes instruction in both the mountain dulcimer and one of the most appealing and accessible of folk instruments, the hammered dulcimer.

Contemporary Folk Week is a unique program of workshops covering a variety of related topics: songwriting, performance, sound reinforcement and recording, and vocal coaching.

Guitar Week features contemporary fingerstyle guitar, flatpicking, blues, and guitar accompaniment.

Fiddle Week offers instruction in swing, Irish, old-time, and bluegrass fiddle.

Whether you are a musician or not, there's a magic in the air at the Swannanoa Gathering. A series of concerts showcasing workshop staff is scheduled at the end of each week and is open to the public.

For more information contact the Swannanoa Gathering at (828) 298-3434 or swangathering.org.

there's really no other place like it. Though Brasstown is only two hours from Atlanta, Chattanooga, and Asheville, the school—set in a mountain-rimmed farming valley—seems to be from another century. Actually it began in the 20th, when Indiana-born educator John C. Campbell took his new bride, Olive Dame, on a fact-finding survey throughout the Appalachian Mountains. While he investigated the agricultural practices, she studied the music and handicrafts.

After John's death in 1919, Olive Campbell and friend Marguerite Butler went to Scandinavia to study hands-on schools without credits, degrees, grades, or competition. They returned to the mountains to see if such a school would be welcomed in the region. More than 200 enthusiastic people showed up at an organizational meeting at a Brasstown church. Fred O. Scroggs, the local storekeeper, donated 75 acres of land, and the people pledged labor, building materials, and most importantly, their heartfelt support.

Today the 372-acre campus contains 27 buildings, some designed by Belgian architect Leon Deschamps in a romantic European style, while others are more typical of Appalachian farm houses. It has fully equipped craft studios, a sawmill, meeting rooms, a covered outdoor dance pavilion, a nature trail, a craft shop, a vegetable garden, rustic lodgings, and the Community Room, which has one of the best dance floors in America. The National Register of Historic Places has declared the campus a Historical District.

Over the years the school's role in the community has changed as many of the needs it served (such as health care and job training) have been taken over by public programs. It continues, however, to enrich and serve the local community. Its craft shop, for example, sells the work of more than 200 mountain craftspeople, including the famous Brasstown Carvers, whose delicately carved animals are all-time favorites.

Most of today's 3,000 annual Folk School students come from all over the United States for a week or two to learn a craft, pick up an instrument, or learn to dance.

Regularly scheduled concerts of traditional music, along with dances, are open to the public. For those who want to learn a new skill or improve an old one, there are hundreds of weekend and one- or two-week-long courses offered year-round in basketry, beadwork, blacksmithing, book arts, broom making, calligraphy, chair seats, clay, crochet, dance, dolls, drawing, dyeing, embroidery, enameling, felting, food, genealogy, glass, jewelry, kaleidoscopes, knitting, lace, leather, marbling, metalwork, music, nature studies, painting, paper art, photography, printmaking, quilting, recreation, rugs, spinning, stone carving, storytelling, thread art, tinsmithing, weaving, wood carving, wood turning, woodworking, and writing.

Three family-style meals are included with tuition. Lodging (meals included) is provided in a number of on-campus buildings. Costs vary. Call to receive a catalog.

There are 12 campsites with full hookups and modest bathroom facilities on campus. Campsites are available for a cost.

THE MUSEUM OF NORTH CAROLINA HANDICRAFTS, 49 Shelton St., Waynesville, NC; (828) 452-1551; sheltonhouse.org. The white-framed Shelton House, built in 1875 and listed on the National Register of Historic

If you are planning to attend one of John C. Campbell's regular concerts, why not enjoy a meal at the school's table beforehand? Make reservations at least one day in advance by calling (800) FOLK-SCH or (828) 837-2775. Then prepare yourself for a tasty repast!

Places, is as interesting as the museum and offers a perfect setting for the comprehensive exhibits of 19th-century crafts.

Just a short walk from Waynesville's charming Main Street, the museum contains examples of furniture from the 19th century, a Victorian bed and shaving stand, a dining table, handcrafted cupboard, toys (including a handmade miniature farmstead), and a working pioneer village.

It also features an exhibit of handicrafts made by artisans who have participated in the educational demonstration of heritage crafts in the North Carolina State Fair's Village of Yesteryear since 1951. You'll see such once-necessary tools as Saxony spinning wheels and walking spinning wheels. There is also a fine collection of Cherokee Indian artifacts, as well as the Will Shelton collection of Navajo rugs, pottery, jewelry, and baskets.

A small gift shop carries pottery, braided rugs, hand-carved birds, and other handcrafted items and a selection of regional craft books. The museum is open from 10 a.m. to 4 p.m. Tues through Fri, May through Oct. There is an admission charge.

Potters of the Roan

Potters of the Roan is a guild of professional potters living and working in the Bakersville area of the mountains of Western North Carolina in Mitchell County. Roan Mountain dominates the views of the area with extensive balds and huge natural rhododendron gardens. Potters of the Roan can be recognized throughout Mitchell County by red signs with white interior ovals. Inside the ovals are the individual names of their studios. (For information contact Fork Mountain Pottery, 1782 Fork Mountain Rd., Bakersville; 828-688-9297; forkmountainpottery.com.)

MUSEUMS

Northern Mountains

HICKORY RIDGE HOMESTEAD, 591 Horn in the West Dr., Boone, NC; (828) 264-2120; horninthewest.com. This living history museum, sponsored by the Southern Appalachian Historical Association, is composed of a series of log structures, a main log cabin, a weaving room, and a smokehouse, all depicting the period of the late 18th century in the Appalachian Mountains. The homestead reflects the same period covered by the outdoor drama *Horn in the West*, also on the site. The Olde Christmas Celebration and the Hickory Ridge Homestead Apple Festival in Oct are two special events celebrated here.

TURCHIN CENTER FOR THE VISUAL ARTS, 423 W. King St., Boone, NC; (828) 262-3017; tcva.appstate.edu. This state-of-the-art museum presents exhibitions, workshops, and visual arts activities throughout the year, as well as educational workshops for children and adults in the university setting. An annual juried sculpture competition showcases contemporary American sculpture in outdoor settings across the campus, and traveling exhibitions of note are shown in the galleries throughout the year.

Central Mountains

ALLISON-DEAVER HISTORICAL HOUSE, 2753 Asheville Hwy., Pisgah Forest, NC; (828) 884-5137; tchistoricalsociety.com. Just two days before it was scheduled to be demolished, Western North Carolina's oldest frame house west of the Blue Ridge Mountains was saved by the Transylvania County Historical Society. Built in Quaker or Federal architectural style in the early 1800s by Benjamin Allison, it housed his family of 11 children. In 1830 he sold the house and its 420 acres to William Deaver, who, in the early 1840s, remodeled the six-room, 1,100-square-foot structure into a Greek Revival house and expanded it. Then in the 1860s, the roof was raised to make room for second- and third-floor Charleston-, or Low Country-style porches. This "house-restoration museum" is open for tours from Apr through Oct from 10 a.m. to 4 p.m. on Fri and Sat, and on Sun from 1 to 4 p.m. There is no admission charge, but donations for this ongoing project are appreciated.

APPLE VALLEY MODEL RAILROAD MUSEUM, 650 Maple St., Hendersonville, NC; (828) 890-8246; avmrc.com. Hendersonville got its first train depot in 1879, which was replaced in 1902 by the present structure. Now the quaint building has undergone restoration. Dressed up in its original colors, it houses an operating 420-square-foot model railroad in its old baggage room. The model features the Hendersonville, Asheville, Brevard, and Saluda stations, including the Saluda Grade (the steepest grade in the country), plus mountains, waterfalls, lakes, towns, and industries. The train runs over 500 feet of track and has more than 100 switches. The Depot features historical artifacts, a Southern Railway caboose, and a special children's exhibit where they can operate a Thomas the Tank train in a scenic layout. It's open to the public free of charge year-round (donations are appreciated) from noon to 3 p.m. on Wed and 9 a.m. until noon on Sat.

THE ASHEVILLE ART MUSEUM, 2 S. Pack Square, Asheville, NC; (828) 253-3227; ashevilleart.org. Founded in 1948, this first-rate museum maintains a fine permanent collection of 20th-century American art, including the work of such renowned artists as Romare Bearden, Jacob Lawrence, and George Inness; the sculpture of Louise Nevelson; and contemporary abstracts of Asheville natives Kenneth Noland and Donald Sultan. Permanent works are rotated every few months to bring new interest to the museum's collection, and significant traveling exhibitions are curated several times a year. After extensive renovations the museum's state-of-the-art glass and steel facade and new interior anchors downtown's Pack Square in the center of downtown. It reopened in 2019 to much fanfare, with many more galleries to house its impressive permanent collection, a rooftop cafe, national touring exhibitions, regional scholastic awards, classroom space, a contemporary gift shop, and so much more.

BILTMORE HOMESPUN MUSEUM, 111 Grovewood Rd., Asheville, NC; (828) 253-7651; grovewood.com. Built in 1917, the English-style pebble-dash cottage housing the museum was one of the original Biltmore Homespun Shop buildings. Photos and artifacts preserve the old weaving operation begun a century ago under the auspices of Edith Stuyvesant Vanderbilt, wife of railroad heir George Vanderbilt of Biltmore Estate. Artifacts such as bolts of cloth, antique handmade looms, and an original, old-time clock bring back the flavor of the Biltmore Industries and Biltmore Homespun Shops of days gone by. During the week there are weaving demonstrations throughout the day. There's no entrance fee.

BLACK MOUNTAIN COLLEGE MUSEUM + ART CENTER, 120 College St., Asheville, NC; (828) 350-8484; blackmountaincollege.org. This exhibition and resource space pays tribute to Black Mountain College, a progressive school founded in 1933 in Black Mountain that became an intellectual learning space for many avant-garde thinkers, artists, and educators, particularly a number escaping Nazi-occupied Europe. The actual college closed in 1957, but the legacy of teachers and alumni like Willem and Elaine de Kooning, Robert Rauschenberg, Josef and Anni Albers, Merce Cunningham, John Cage, Cy Twombly, Kenneth Noland, and Buckminster Fuller, is explored and expanded upon here.

CARL SANDBURG HOME, 1928 Little River Rd., Flat Rock, NC; (828) 693-4178; nps.gov/carl. Carl Sandburg—poet, author, lecturer, musician, onetime political activist, social thinker, and winner of two Pulitzer Prizes for his four-volume Abraham Lincoln: The War Years and his Complete Poems—spent the last 22 years of his life at Connemara, a 240-acre farm 3 miles south of Hendersonville. The main house was built in 1838 as a summer home for Charleston's Christopher Gustave Memminger, who served as secretary of the treasury for the Confederacy from 1861 to 1864. Like many mountain residents today, Memminger wanted to escape the heat and humidity of the coast, while Sandburg sought relief from cold northern winters. Sandburg moved here in 1945 with his wife, three daughters, grandchildren, and his wife's prize-winning Chikaming goats—a herd that grew as large as 200; the milk was turned into a successful dairy operation. The Sandburgs spent happy and productive years in a lovely setting of rolling pastures, ponds, lakes, and wooded mountains. Sandburg died in 1967, and Connemara became a National Historic Site the following year. It's open daily except on Dec 25.

CRADLE OF FORESTRY, US 276, Pisgah National Forest; (828) 877-3130; cradleofforestry.com. In the late 1800s George Vanderbilt hired Gifford Pinchot to restore and manage the forest on the 8,000 acres surrounding his famous estate. His holdings were later expanded to 125,000 acres that, after his death, became part of Pisgah National Forest. In 1895, Dr. Carl Schenck, a brilliant German forester, succeeded Pinchot and was a magnet for young men wishing to learn the new sustainable forest methods. As a result, in 1898 Schenck started the Biltmore Forest School, the first forestry school in America. For his campus he utilized an old schoolhouse and abandoned farm buildings in a 3,200-foot-high valley that was named the Pink Beds, after its lush bloom of flowers. In 1964, 6,500 acres in this area were established as a National Historic Site and became known as the Cradle of Forestry. Special interpretive programs and guided tours are offered here. There are two beautiful, mile-long paved trails, each with guided tours that will tell you of the Cradle's history and teach you a lot about the plants and trees along the way.

ESTES-WINN ANTIQUE AUTOMOBILE MUSEUM, 111 Grovewood Rd., Asheville, NC; (828) 253-7651; grovewood.com. Next door to Grovewood Gallery, in the massive original weaving shed that once housed 40 looms for the old Biltmore Industries, is the Estes-Winn Antique Automobile Museum. This delightful collection is a veritable history of how America took to the highway, from the first Model T to shiny post–World War II roadsters. You can fantasize about grand old autos such as a 1926 Cadillac and a 1927 La Salle convertible. There's even a 1922 La France fire engine on display that once was used by the Asheville Fire Department. They just don't make 'em like they used to!

THE HISTORIC JOHNSON FARM, 3346 Haywood Rd., Hendersonville, NC; (828) 891-6585; historicjohnsonfarm.org. Located 4 miles north of Hendersonville on Highway 191, this late-19th-century, 15-acre tobacco farm became a popular summer tourist retreat in the 1920s. Today, owned by the Henderson County Public Schools, an 1870s brick farmhouse, 1920 boarding house, barn-loft museum, 10 historic buildings, and two nature trails are operated as a heritage education center and farm museum. Guided tours are available at 10:30 a.m. and 1:30 p.m. Tues through Sat from May through Oct, and Wed through Sat from Nov through Apr. A small admission is charged for guided tours.

JIM BOB TINSLEY MUSEUM AND RESEARCH CENTER, 20 W. Jordan St., Brevard, NC; (828) 884-2347; jimbobtinsleymuseum.org. Transylvania County may seem an unlikely place to find a cowboy museum, but this is a great one. It houses the extensive collection of art, memorabilia, and research records of Jim Bob Tinsley, a Brevard native and famous author, educator, and musicologist. He performed with Gene Autry in the late 1940s and has received many awards for his work, including one from the National Cowboy Hall of Fame for his book (one of 10) He Was Singing This Song, a compilation of traditional American cowboy songs. Here you'll find original art, lithographs, photographs, and bronze statues by famous sculptors of the caliber of Frederick Remington. There is also, as you might expect, a lot about country-and-western music, including a large collection of records, tapes, and CDs. There are reels and TV tapes of western movies and old television programs played during office hours. And there are all those other things connected to cowboys: saddles, spurs, branding irons from famous ranches, Florida Cracker cowboy whips, and an original Zane Grey 30-foot riata, to name a few items.

But Tinsley's interests go far beyond cowboys. The museum contains his historic Transylvania County memorabilia, including one of only six known Gillespie rifles. The gun dates from the early 1880s and was manufactured at the Gillespie rifle factory in nearby South Mills River. You'll also find art and literature concerning two of his other passions: pumas and sailfish.

POLK COUNTY HISTORICAL ASSOCIATION & MUSEUM, 1 Depot St., Tryon, NC; (828) 859-2287; polkcountyhistoricalsociety.com. Housed in the old but charmingly renovated Tryon railroad depot, the association exhibits household, agricultural, and historical artifacts used by the early settlers and Indians in this area. There is also a collection of folklore, old maps, records, and pictures, including important items in American history such as "the cannonball that started the Civil War," said to have been picked up at Fort Sumter by a young Union officer, Abner Doubleday. Monthly historical meetings are held, and the public is invited. The museum is open on Tues and Thurs from 10 a.m. until noon and by appointment. Admission is free, but donations are appreciated.

SILVERMONT MANSION, 364 E. Main St., Brevard, NC; (828) 884-3156.; silvermont.org. John Silversteen and his wife, Elizabeth, moved to Transylvania County in 1902. He opened the Toxaway Tanning Company, around which the town of Rosman grew, and later established the Gloucester Lumber

Company. His enterprises, the largest in the county, provided work for several hundred people until the 1950s. He was active in and generous to the community, building the first brick elementary school in Rosman and donating the land for that town's high school. But he's most remembered for Silvermont, the 1917, 33-room, Colonial Revival house that still stands on its spacious grounds on East Main Street. Silvermont was willed to the county when the last daughter died in 1972. It was placed on the National Register of Historic Places in 1981. Full of interesting furniture and Silversteen memorabilia, its first floor is used for community club meetings, by private groups, and as a senior meal and recreation center. The 8-acre grounds have tennis and shuffleboard courts, a basketball court, a playground, and a picnic area.

On summer evenings square dancing takes place on Tues, ballroom dancing on Wed, and mountain music "on the porch" on Thurs. Christmas at Silvermont features decorations by the Transylvania Council of Garden Clubs, usually involving musical performances. The mansion is available for weddings, receptions, family reunions, class reunions, and other special events, but is closed when not in use.

SMITH-MCDOWELL HOUSE, 283 Victoria Rd., Asheville, NC; (828) 253-9231; wnchistory.org. This fine old Asheville residence is on the campus of Asheville-Buncombe Technical Community College. The stately, early Victorian-era home, built around 1840, is Asheville's oldest brick residence, furnished with period antiques. You'll enjoy the marvelous architectural details and appointments of this palatial beauty. Personalized tours are available. There is a nominal admission fee.

SWANNANOA VALLEY MUSEUM, 223 W. State St., Black Mountain, NC; (828) 669-9566; swannanoavalleymuseum.org. The Swannanoa Valley Museum, open seasonally from Apr through Oct, is the guardian of a remarkable collection of artifacts of everyday life in Western North Carolina, from pioneer times to recent years. Local residents donated many of the items here. This unique museum is also home to an exhibit honoring Rafael Guastavino, architect and designer of the century-old Basilica of St. Lawrence in Asheville; displays spotlighting Billy Graham's crusades; the US Navy artifacts of Rear Adm. G. C. Crawford; and an extensive collection of wildflower photography. The museum is open Tues through Sat 10 a.m. to 5 p.m. and Sun 2 to 5 p.m.

THOMAS WOLFE MEMORIAL, 52 N. Market St., Asheville, NC; (828) 253-8304; wolfememorial.com. Asheville's native son, noted author of the classic coming-of-age novel *Look Homeward, Angel*, spent his boyhood here in his mother's rambling old boardinghouse on Spruce Street, just off legendary Pack Square. This old house figured prominently in Wolfe's work and is important for its ability to convey the forces that helped shape this remarkable

American writer. The Thomas Wolfe Welcome Center adjacent to the house offers information about the house and the author.

WCU FINE ART MUSEUM, BARDO ARTS CENTER, Western Carolina University, 199 Centennial Dr., Cullowhee, NC; (828) 227-3591; wcu.edu. On the university's campus in the new Fine and Performing Arts Center, the museum offers art exhibits by local, regional, and national artists on a year-round basis. The Fine Art Museum includes nearly 10,000 feet of exhibit space in four galleries, featuring a growing permanent collection and interdisciplinary programs.

WESTERN NORTH CAROLINA AIR MUSEUM, 1340 Gilbert St., Hendersonville, NC; (828) 693-9708, (800) 828-4244; westernnorthcarolinaair museum.com. It's appropriate that this air museum, in the state where flight was born, is located at the Hendersonville Airport. That also enables it to feature spring and fall air shows. Award-winning, beautifully restored airplanes as well as restored replica antique and vintage planes are on display here. They range from a 1917 Nieuport 11 (Bebe) replica to a 1950s Ercoup and a Corbin Ace. You can even view a 1510 ornithopter designed by Leonardo da Vinci. The museum is open each Wed, Sat, and Sun from noon until 6 p.m. Admission is free, but donations are welcomed. Gifts and souvenirs are available. Museum memberships and lifetime memberships are also available.

ZEBULON B. VANCE BIRTHPLACE, 911 Reems Creek Rd. off Old US Hwys. 19/23, Weaverville, NC; (828) 645-6706; historicsites.nc.gov/all-sites/zebulon-b-vance-birthplace. This charming mountain homestead was home to one of North Carolina's most prominent political figures. Zeb Vance

A Hillside in Highland Park

A bright star among the Montgomery, Alabama, Southern belles, Zelda Fitzgerald left a path of broken hearts behind her. An accomplished painter, she also wrote. The dark shadows of her mind eventually brought her to Highland Psychiatric Hospital in Asheville, founded in 1904 by Dr. Robert Carroll. In 1939 Dr. Carroll gave 100 percent interest in the hospital to Duke University. Zelda, who earlier had been diagnosed in Europe with schizophrenia, frequented the sanitarium from the 1930s until her death in an all-consuming hospital fire in 1948. Meanwhile, her husband, author F. Scott, resided at the Grove Park Inn during his visits with her.

The former hospital grounds are now known as Highland Park. Amid this landscape Zelda once painted; you will find a plaque dedicated to her.

began his career as a lawyer, assuming public office by the young age of 24. He was elected governor of North Carolina three times, most notably during the Civil War. He also served three terms as a US senator. At his death in 1894, this most capable public servant was admired by colleagues and beloved by his constituency. His life and career are profiled in an exhibit in the adjoining visitor center.

The two-story cabin and outbuildings are reconstructions, built from hewn yellow pine logs around the original chimney with its two massive fireplaces. The furnishings and household items depict the period from 1790 to 1840 and include a few pieces original to the Vance family.

Gift of the Magi

William Sidney Porter claimed to his final day that it was only a coincidence that both he and a large sum of money were missing from the Texas bank where he was a teller in 1894. Eventually Porter found his way to Asheville and as both a widower and as the noted author, O. Henry, married a local girl, Sara Lindsey Coleman. He obviously became familiar with many of the mountain folks, as he used mountain names and the circumstances of folks from this region in "The Gift of the Magi." To commemorate this tale, the Urban Trail of Asheville displays a plaque with items from the story (cast in bronze) surrounding it. It is located on Patton Avenue close to Pack Square. Meanwhile, in death, O. Henry remains in our area noted by a simple grave marker in Riverside Cemetery, William Sidney Porter.

Southern Mountains

CANTON AREA HISTORICAL MUSEUM AND VISITOR CENTER, 36 Park St., Canton, NC; (828) 646-3412; blueridgeheritage.com/destinations/canton-area-historical-museum. With its library of old family histories and historical documents, this city-run museum, housed in the town's old library building, is an excellent place to research local history. Displays include artifacts, records, heritage handicrafts, and pictures from the past, all of which combine to tell the story of the settling of Canton and the Pigeon River area, Haywood County, and Western North Carolina (in that order of importance). The artifacts include everything from Indian arrowheads and tools to butter molds, quilts, glassware, and pottery.

CHEROKEE COUNTY HISTORICAL MUSEUM, 87 Peachtree St., Murphy, NC; (828) 837-6792; blueridgeheritage.com/destinations/cherokee-county-historical-museum. This museum is housed in the former Carnegie Library building, right next to the even grander county courthouse. Its largest collection is devoted to the life of the Cherokee during their many centuries in the mountains and their removal to Oklahoma. There are over 2,000 Cherokee artifacts collected. Murphy itself was established near the site of the ancient Cherokee village of Guasili (pronounced "gau-ax-u-le"), visited by de Soto in 1540, and was also the site of Fort Butler, the largest of the forts built in the area for the Cherokee removal via "The Trail of Tears." In the museum are leftover weapons from Spanish explorers and another large collection of tools, housewares, and other items from the early pioneer days in the region. Some of the most interesting things among the mineral and rock collections are "fairy crosses" (see our Close-up, "**Little People and Fairy Crosses**"). The museum also houses a collection of more than 700 priceless dolls donated by Louise S. Kilgore. They include, among other things, representations of famous personalities (including Elvis and Princess Diana) and unique older dolls made in pre-factory days. The collection takes up about one-fourth of the space on the museum's top floor. The museum is open Mon through Fri from 9 a.m. until 5 p.m. Admission is free.

HISTORICAL ARTS MUSEUM, 21 Davis Loop, Hayesville, NC; (828) 389-6814; clayhistoryarts.org. The museum, housed in the town's old jail, is devoted to local history and is sponsored by the Clay County Historical and Art Council. Here you'll see a cross-section of memorabilia—the first telephone switchboard and a kitchen from the 19th century—from earlier times. Receptions and showings of local artists are also held here. It is open from June through Sept.

MACON COUNTY HISTORICAL SOCIETY MUSEUM, 36 W. Main St., Franklin, NC; (828) 524-9758; maconhistorical.org. This museum, supported by the Macon County Historical Society, preserves the area's heritage through displays of artifacts, documents, and photographs that illustrate the social, cultural, and historical background of the county.

MOUNTAIN HERITAGE CENTER, Western Carolina University, Administration Building, NCHwy. 107, Cullowhee, NC; (828) 227-7129; wcu.edu. If you're of Scotch-Irish ancestry, this museum is a must! Even if you're not, it's a very special place for learning about the land, culture, and people of the Appalachian region. A large permanent exhibit, "Migration of the Scotch-Irish People," relates the saga of this group's departure from their native Scotland to settle in Northern Ireland, and in a later generation, its journey from Ulster to the New World. It also highlights the homes and culture that developed here in the coves and hollows of Western North Carolina. Murals and a life-size 18th-century Irish cottage make the story come alive.

Other exhibits illustrate the mountains' natural history and society, both past and present. This section also preserves objects of historical significance,

Close-up

Little People and Fairy Crosses

Those of us steeped in Western culture know all about the Old World's fairies, elves, gnomes, trolls, and the like, but few of us are acquainted with the Little People who reside in these mountains, though some folks of European descent have encountered them over the years. James Mooney, in his classic work, *History, Myths, and Sacred Formulas of the Cherokees*, first published in 1900 by the Bureau of American Ethnology, identifies a whole pantheon of spirit folk, some of whom are mentioned in other legends in our book.

The Cherokee's name for Little People is *yunwi tsunsdi*. They usually live in rock caves on mountainsides, though one group, called *yunwi amaiyinehi*, lives in water (they are the ones fishing enthusiasts should try to please). When full grown, *yunwi tsunsdi* are only as tall as a man's knee, but they are well-formed and handsome, with long hair down to their heels. They love music and spend a lot of time singing and dancing.

They are also powerful workers of wonders. Generally speaking, they are kind and helpful (particularly to children or people lost in the woods) but not always. If you hear their drumming in the distance, don't follow the sound: If disturbed in their homes, Little People will cast a spell that will make you lose

including the heirlooms of hundreds of families who lived here. There are exhibits on cornshuck handcrafts and the traditions of milling, tilling, and stilling corn. A good place to start your tour is in the museum movie theater, where nine-projector, multi-image shows complement the thematic exhibits. The center also publishes books and other materials on mountain culture. All these—the exhibits, the shows, and the literature—are based on thorough and extensive research. The Mountain Heritage Center is also the focus for Mountain Heritage Day, held in Sept, which attracts more than 35,000 visitors (see our **Festivals and Annual Events** chapter). There is no admission charge.

MUSEUM OF THE CHEROKEE INDIAN, 589 Tsali Blvd., Cherokee, NC; (828) 497-3481, (888) 665-7249; cherokeemuseum.org. Outside the building is a 20-foot wooden sculpture of Sequoyah (the Cherokee genius who is—as far as we know—the only human to create a written form of language all alone). Inside, walk through Cherokee history with interactive displays and multi-sensory exhibits. You can listen to storytellers, play the ancient butter

your way. Even if you are found, you may spend the rest of your life in a daze. If you find an object, such as a knife or other item in the woods, you must say, "Little People, I want to take this," because if you don't and it belongs to them, they will throw stones at you on your way home.

Like the busy elves in Western lore, they will sometimes come near a human house at night and, before morning, finish a great task like clearing a field that would require the efforts of a huge workforce. However, if you hear them at work, don't go out to see them, or you'll die.

Many little footprints were seen, and a number of encounters with these little folk were described in accounts by both Indians and whites (mainly hunters) at the end of the 19th century. Some of these took place near or at the head of the Oconaluftee River, which flows through the present-day Cherokee Indian Reservation. There is also a certain spot in what is now the Great Smoky Mountains National Park where *yunsi tsunsdi* came to the Cherokee during summer solstices to tell them, among other things, tales of the Cherokee nation's history.

One day, the Little People were near Brasstown, doing their favorite things—singing and dancing—when a foreign "messenger" arrived and told them the sad tale of Christ's death on a cross. They were so moved, they cried. As their tears fell, they turned into little stone crosses that can still be found today. A wonderful collection of these Fairy Crosses can be seen in Murphy's Cherokee County Historical Museum (which is described in this chapter).

bean game, travel the infamous Trail of Tears, and much more. The fine gift shop is loaded with a large selection of books, crafts, artwork, and other Cherokee or Native American items. The museum is open year-round except on Thanksgiving, Christmas, and New Year's Day. Hours are 9 a.m. to 5 p.m. Sept through May and 9 a.m. to 8 p.m. June through Aug. Admission is under $10.

SHELTON HOUSE, MUSEUM OF NORTH CAROLINA HANDI-CRAFTS, 307 Shelton St., Waynesville, NC; (828) 452-1551; sheltonhouse .org. The Shelton House, built in 1875 and listed on the National Register of Historic Places, is the setting for these comprehensive exhibits of 19th-century crafts. It also has an interesting exhibit of handicrafts made by artisans who have participated in the educational demonstration of heritage crafts in the North Carolina State Fair's Village of Yesteryear since 1951 (see our **Mountain Crafts** chapter for more information). Exhibits include a working Pioneer Village and a collection of railroad memorabilia. The museum is open from 10 a.m. to 4 p.m. Tues through Fri, May through Oct. There is an admission charge.

SCOTTISH TARTANS MUSEUM AND HERITAGE CENTER, 86 E. Main St., Franklin, NC; (828) 524-7472; scottishtartans.org. If you can't get to Scotland this year, this museum, recognized and authorized by the Scottish Tartans Society (the official registry of all publicly known tartans), is the next best thing. Opened in 1994, the 3,200-square-foot facility includes exhibits of tartan and Highland dress from 1700 to the present and shows the evolution of the kilt and the weaving of tartan. It also traces the influence of the Scots and other settlers on Appalachian and Cherokee culture and the history of North Carolina. Those of Scottish ancestry can investigate the tartan research library and find their family's tartan in the Tartan Room.

There is also a great gift shop full of Celtic and Scottish treasures. All tartan items are imported from Scotland and come in 100 percent new wool. You'll also find scarves, shawls, sashes, tams, men's ties, caps, and children's items. Immediate delivery can be had on books, music, clan videos, jewelry, Highland dress items, dirks, skean dubbs, and Scottish weaponry.

THEATER

Northern Mountains

ASHE COUNTY LITTLE THEATER, 962 Mt. Jefferson Rd., West Jefferson, NC; (336) 246-ARTS; ashecivic.com. Ashe County is well represented by this amateur theatrical group, which features local actors of all ages in an energetic annual program of popular Broadway productions. Past productions have included *Oliver!*, *The King and I*, and *The Sound of Music*.

APPALACHIAN STATE UNIVERSITY, 287 Rivers St., Boone, NC; (828) 262-3063; theatreanddance.appstate.edu. Boone's community-minded university offers a series of cultural events throughout the year. The Department of Theater and Dance at ASU presents a wide array of one-act plays, full dramatic productions, and dance performances, all of which are open to the public. The ASU Forum Series is the university's formal lecture series that has featured national speakers addressing topics of national and international importance. During the summer the community is treated to An Appalachian Summer Festival, offering the best in music, dance, theater, visual arts, and symposia. The Performing Arts Series also brings national and international performers to the campus. These events are also open to the public.

ENSEMBLE STAGE COMPANY, 166-185 Azalea Circle SE, Banner Elk, NC; (828) 414-1844; ensemblestage.com. This High Country's resident professional theater, drawing the services of professional Actors' Equity players every summer. Now located in a permanent space in Banner Elk the theater also has a summer theater camp for kids.

PARKWAY PLAYHOUSE, 202 Green Mountain Dr., Burnsville, NC; (828) 682-4285; parkwayplayhouse.com. The Parkway Playhouse opened its doors in 1947 as the Burnsville Playhouse. Eventually it was housed in a former school gymnasium, which was moved up the South Toe River to its present location. As the oldest continuously producing summer stock theater in North Carolina, The Parkway Playhouse is a "teaching theater" that utilizes a small corps of professional actors, pre-professional college students, as well as people from the WNC community who have a passion for theater. Performances begin in June and end in Sept, with a typical variety of three musicals and two to three plays per year.

Central Mountains

ASHEVILLE COMMUNITY THEATRE, 35 Walnut St., Asheville, NC; (828) 254-1320; ashevilletheatre.org. This award-winning theater is ranked one of the best in the Southeast, consistently providing the Asheville area with the best in live theater since its inception in 1946. This long tradition of excellence has a colorful heritage that includes an association with the late motion picture actor Charlton Heston. Heston was co-director of ACT in the 1947 season, making it his springboard to stardom the following year when he returned to New York. The Asheville Community Theatre produces a six-show season that includes the best of Broadway musicals, comedies, and classics. An edgier program of plays is held at the blackbox theater within ACT, called 35 Below. During intermission visitors can enjoy rotating exhibitions in the lobby gallery space.

DIANA WORTHAM THEATRE, 18 Biltmore Ave., Asheville, NC; (828) 257-4530; dwtheatre.com. The Diana Wortham Theatre is a gem of a performance space for audiences, performers, and technicians. The 500-seat theater is an intimate, sophisticated setting with a full-size stage, exquisitely detailed woodwork, impeccable acoustics, and accessibility for people with disabilities. Diana Wortham Theatre presents, produces, and hosts performing arts events that range from Shakespeare to Mamet, classical ballet to modern dance, lectures to performance poetry, symphonies to Brubeck, and world-renowned storytellers to local school pageants.

MONTFORD PARK PLAYERS, Montford Park Recreational Facility, 92 Gay St., Asheville, NC; (828) 254-5146; montfordparkplayers.org. This legendary Asheville theater company grew out of one woman's fascination with the English Bard. Founder Hazel Robinson created the Montford Park Players on a financial shoestring back in 1973, bringing the works of Shakespeare to the public. The plays in those days were performed in the natural, grassy amphitheater of old Montford Park, with costumes and props scavenged by Ms. Robinson and her loyal thespian followers. As the Great Man said, "The play's the thing." And so it was. The performances are free, but in the true tradition of early Shakespearean troupes, a hat is passed at intermission. You can find the Montford Park Players at the outdoor amphitheater of Montford Recreation Center, one block off Montford Avenue at the intersection of Montford Avenue and Pearson Drive. A highlight of the Christmas season is the Montford Park Players' production of *A Christmas Carol*. This and other winter performances take place at the old Masonic Temple space downtown

NORTH CAROLINA STAGE COMPANY, 15 Stage Ln., Asheville, NC; (828) 239-0262; ncstage.org. One of the most energetic and interesting professional theater companies to set up shop in the mountains, NC Stage Company consistently pushes the envelope with bold directing and contemporary pieces by both national and local playwrights. The intimate blackbox theater also adjoins an art gallery/reception hall.

Henderson County

FLAT ROCK PLAYHOUSE, 2661 Greenville Hwy., Flat Rock, NC; (828) 693-0731; flatrockplayhouse.com. Flat Rock Playhouse, the State Theatre of North Carolina, is a professional theater operating under a contract with the Actors' Equity Association, the national union of professional actors and stage managers. Founded in 1937, the playhouse entertains more than 65,000 guests each season. Eight productions are offered between late May and mid-Oct annually. A variety of comedies, musicals, and dramas, which range from world premieres to the latest from Broadway and London to the classics, compose the summer/fall series. The Playhouse's dual mission of producing and providing education in the performing arts includes a 10-show professional series; a summer and fall college apprentice and intern program; performances and cabaret series by the YouTheatre; and year-round classes and workshops for students from kindergarten to adults.

HENDERSONVILLE LITTLE THEATRE, The Barn on State Street, 229 S. Washington St., Hendersonville, NC; (828) 692-1082; hendersonville littletheatre.org. This all-volunteer group of players has entertained the town since 1966, putting on four shows in a refurbished barn from Sept to May. These shows usually include a couple of comedies, a mystery, and sometimes a serious drama. There are more than 400 members in this organization, and a large number of them actively work on each production.

TRYON LITTLE THEATER, Tryon Fine Arts Center, 516 S. Trade St., Tryon, NC; (828) 859-2466, (828) 859-3545 (info. line); tltinfo.org. Since 1969 this organization has produced more than 100 plays and musicals. The nearly 800 members create six productions a year at the Tryon Fine Arts Center, including at least one musical each season. There are more than 150 individuals participating in some facet of every production. Tryon Little Theater also holds acting workshops and play-reading groups. It has sponsored various theatrical events, premiered original productions, and won a North Carolina Theater Award.

Southern Mountains

HAYWOOD ARTS REPERTORY THEATRE, 250 Pigeon St., Waynesville, NC; (828) 456-6322; harttheatre.com. HART is the region's most active theater company, producing seven main stage productions each year and up to six "studio" shows, including major musicals, classics, and new plays. In recent years the theater has hosted a production direct from off-Broadway, sent a production to New York, and staged a new play in its studio that won honors at the John F. Kennedy Center. The Performing Arts Center, where HART is at home in a summer stock barn-style facility, sits in the middle of an 8-acre National Historic Site shared with the Museum of North Carolina Handicrafts. It includes a 250-seat auditorium, a visual arts gallery, and a 75-seat studio theater.

HIGHLANDS PLAYHOUSE, 362 Oak St., Highlands, NC; (828) 526-2695 (tickets), (828) 526-9443 (information); highlandsplayhouse.org. This community theater has been operating since 1938. The playhouse stages four productions in a season that runs from June into Aug. It combines professional talent with outside equity guest stars. The theater also hosts film evenings here.

SMOKY MOUNTAIN COMMUNITY THEATRE, 134 Main St., Bryson City, NC; (828) 488-3030; .smctheatre.com. The Smoky Mountain Community Theater presents four plays a year in an old movie theater on Main Street. The group itself refurbished the more-than-50-year-old structure, installing a sophisticated lighting system, building dressing rooms, and more than doubling the size of the stage. Members are undaunted by large-scale productions.

THE VALLEYTOWN ARTS CENTER, 125 Chestnut St., Andrews, NC; (828) 321-3453; vcahs.com. This center, originally the First Baptist Church, has been renovated with the purpose of providing a facility for the community to stage performing and visual arts. It houses both the Community Youth Players, an ensemble of young local talent that has been active since 1986 and that performs a Christmas play in early Dec and another performance in the spring, and the Andrews Community Theater, which offers plays throughout the year. Concerts and other events are also staged here. Call for information.

Shopping

Shop 'til you drop! Each of the three geographical regions identified in this book is anchored by a larger city that has fine shopping opportunities: Boone and Blowing Rock in the Northern Mountains; Asheville, Hendersonville, and Brevard in the Central Mountains; and Waynesville, Highlands, and Dillsboro in the Southern Mountains. Fanning out from these cities are smaller towns and country crossroads that add to unique shopping opportunities. You'll find quite a bit of sophisticated shopping in many of these areas—from art and antiques to jewelry and unique home decor, but also bohemian treasures, vintage finds, traditional crafts, and much more. Don't miss the buys waiting for you out in the countryside, where a turn down a back road can put you at the door of a charming country store. Once the backbone of our rural economy, these simple shops are often treasure troves of Americana. If you are an antiques-lover, you'll be amazed at the great buys you can find in the middle of nowhere. What looks like an old farmhouse with junk out on the front porch may actually be an "antique barn," where you can find fascinating old farm tools, cupboards, tables, dishes, and the like. Because shops do tend to open and close so quickly, we highlight notable merchants who continue to make their mark.

BOOKSTORES

Northern Mountains

DANCING MOON EARTHWAY BOOKSTORE, 553 W. King St., Boone, NC; (828) 264-7242. This tiny shop offers those unique books, cards, and posters you can't find at a chain store. It also carries incense, candles, and other items.

FOGGY PINE BOOKS, 471 W. King St, Boone, NC; (828) 386-1219; foggy pinebooks.com. Newer bookstore in downtown Boone, specializing in fiction and science fiction, as well as young adult literature.

Central Mountains

BATTERY PARK BOOK EXCHANGE, 1 Battle Sq., Asheville, NC; (828) 252-0020; batteryparkbookexchange.com. Visit this unique venue where gently-used tomes, crisp new art books, and leather-bound classics share space with petite syrahs and cavas by the glass or bottle. These are served at the marble bar or in cozy reading corners with elegant sofas and easy chairs.

ExploreAsheville.com

BLUE RIDGE PARKWAY BOOKSTORE, FOLK ART CENTER; Mile 382, Blue Ridge Parkway, Asheville, NC; (828) 298-0495; nps.gov/blri/learn/bookstore.htm. Small but well stocked, this bookstore offers the best selection in nature books, trail maps, books on regional culture, and beautiful wildlife cards.

DOWNTOWN BOOKS AND NEWS, 67 Lexington Ave., Asheville, NC; (828) 253-8654; dbnbooks.com. You can usually buy hard-to-find newspapers, periodicals, and obscure books at this excellent and interesting combination newsstand/used-book store. Subjects include foreign, obscure fashion, computers, food, art, photography, and alternative living.

HIGHLAND BOOKS, 36 W. Main St.; Brevard, NC; (828) 884-2424; highlandbooksonline.com. Highland carries the latest in new paperbacks and hardbacks in fiction and nonfiction and a wonderful, large selection of greeting cards and gifts. It has extensive gardening and children's sections and travel and regional books, including nature books, field guides, and maps. Moved downtown in 2019.

JOY OF BOOKS, 242 Main St., Hendersonville, NC; (828) 551-7321; joyofbooks.net. Good selection of used books. Right on Main Street in Hendersonville, but odd hours, so call first or check website.

MALAPROP'S BOOKSTORE/CAFÉ, 55 Haywood St., Asheville, NC; (828) 254-6734; malaprops.com. Malaprop's is an Asheville institution. Founder Emoke Bracz, a writer, poet, and translator of Hungarian poetry and literature, fine-tuned the art of the book trade in the more-than-30-year life span of this once-small bookstore and cafe. Malaprop's boasts shelves of fascinating fiction, alternative nonfiction, prose, and poetry, as well as a large section with works of local authors and books on the region. Coffee table gift books, stationery, cards, journals, and artistic calendars make this one-stop shopping for all your literary gift needs. And then there's the cafe! Author signings, prose readings, poetry readings, and singer-songwriter evenings gather hoards of literati of all types into the spacious adjoining cafe.

Southern Mountains

BLUE RIDGE BOOKS, 428 Hazelwood Ave., Waynesville, NC; (828) 456-6000; blueridgebooksnc.com. Blue Ridge Books and former Osondu Booksellers merged into this modern bookstore and cafe that features international magazines, sundry genres of books, and accessories. The cafe has Wi-Fi, a pleasant seating area, and a counter for muffins, cookies, scones, and coffee and tea beverages.

CITY LIGHTS BOOKSTORE & CAFE, 3 East Jackson St., Sylva, NC; (828) 586-9499; citylightsnc.com. City Lights offers new and used books, including great regional and children's sections, as well as cards and calendars. Enjoy your book purchase with a specialty coffee, soup, sandwich, salad, and/or dessert either in the store or at the outside seating area. On Fri and Sat evenings, acoustic and folk musicians provide live entertainment.

WALL STREET BOOKS, 181 Wall St., Waynesville, NC; (828) 456-5000; wallstreetbooksnc.com. Small and cozy shop for new and used books, also for trade.

CLOTHING & ACCESSORIES

Northern Mountains

TANGER SHOPPES ON THE PARKWAY, 279 US 321, Blowing Rock, NC; (828) 295-4444, (800) 720-6728; tangeroutlet.com/blowingrock. This outlet center features over 30 name brand outlets—some the best known in the industry—such as Gap, Nautica, Polo Ralph Lauren, Coach, Bass, and Izod. Cooks will especially enjoy Corning Revere and Kitchen Collection, which feature every gadget a cook needs. The center also features a full-service restaurant, Parkway Cafe, and well-known Kilwins, serving locally made gourmet ice cream, candy, and fudge. Relax in the courtyard and enjoy a meal or a treat.

CELESTE'S, 1132 Main St., Blowing Rock, NC; (828) 295-3481; celestes interiors.com. Versatile boutique for women's wear and children's clothing. Also offers monogramming and embroidery.

FINLEY HOUSE COUTURE, 1121 Main St., Blowing Rock, NC; (828) 295-6373; finleyhousecouture.com. Fab jewelry (including an array of tasteful clip earrings,) elegant perfumes, candles, Lilly Pulitzer, Caspari, Thomas Madden and other designer brands for the discerning dresser. Hand-bags, select silver pieces and crystal for the home, Nest fragrances, Julie Vos jewelry and trunk shows are make this a hotbed of shopping activity.

LUCKY PENNY, 693 W. King St., Boone, NC; (828) 264-0302; lucky pennyboone.com. Beautifully-appointed clothing and accessories store with "free-spirited" forward-fashion, sporting fashion and trunk shows, part of the Boone downtown art walk and hosting other community events whilst dressing local fashionistas.

100 WEST UNION, 1179 Main St., Blowing Rock, NC; 100westunion .com. Let's not forget the men. This fab boutique features an array of menswear from preppy to chic, hipster and high-fashion. It's been a stable of the South-marke Shoppes since 1993.

TAZMARAZ, 1107 Main St., Blowing Rock, NC; (828) 295-3737; tazmaraz .com. Women's apparel from Bohemian cotton dresses and skirts, stacks of colorful jeans and a small selection of eclectic shoes, to cocktail dresses, satin jackets and knitwear. Fun jewelry that lets you express yourself as well as smart hats, make this a fun and funky shopping staple.

Central Mountains

AD-LIB, 23 Haywood St., Asheville, NC; (828) 285-8838; adlibclothing .com. This store features women's clothing that emphasizes natural fabrics and colors. Comfort and quality are of the utmost importance here. Sweaters, jumpers, dresses, shirts, skirts, and pants in silks, linens, cottons, and wools in an array of magnificent natural colors set this clothing store apart from others.

BANANA MOON, 338 N. Main St., Hendersonville, NC; (828) 697-1941; moononmain.com. This is by far our favorite clothing store on Main St., and one of our favorite sections is the selection of outfits made of flax. In addition

Close-up

Grovewood Studios and Gardens

Directly across from the Grove Park Inn is the Grovewood Gallery, Gardens, Homespun Museum, Car Museum, Artist Studios, and Grovewood Café. These pebble-dash buildings take one back to the days when Fred Seely, Grove Park Inn manager and son-in-law of the inn owner E.W. Grove, bought the Biltmore Estate Homespun Industries from Edith Stuyvesant Dresser Vanderbilt, the widow of George Vanderbilt. He moved the business from Biltmore Village and into these buildings. Eventually, local philanthropist Harry Bloomberg would purchase the buildings and the Biltmore Homespun Industries from Fred Seely Jr. He continued the homespun clothing industry over the next several years, but eventually closed it.

The late Bloomberg, once a leader in the automotive industry in Asheville, replaced 45 looms with historic antique motor cars, trucks, and a fire engine. There is no admission fee to view these beauties of an earlier era; however, donations can be placed in a wishing well, which supports the American Cancer Society.

In addition to fine dining at the Golden Fleece, or visiting the museums, observing artisans plying their trade, or shopping in the gallery, one can enjoy a picnic among the outdoor sculptures with the majestic Grove Park Inn at one shoulder and a glorious panorama of the mountains once owned by George Washington Vanderbilt.

to all the dresses, sweaters, hats, and handbags, there's everything wonderful for the bath and oodles of charming jewelry. Be prepared to buy.

BELLAGIO, 5 Biltmore Plaza, Asheville, NC; (828) 277-8100; bellagioarttowear.com. This is a most unusual shop devoted to wearable art. Richly colored, sensually textured fabrics are transformed into exquisite garments and then complemented by handcrafted jewelry. Unique handbags, shoes, and jewelry make this spot well worth a stop.

BELLAGIO EVERYDAY, 40 Biltmore Ave., Asheville, NC; (828) 255-0221; bellagioarttowear.com. Quality contemporary clothing that is artistic in nature. Wonderful fabrics, as well as sculptural jewelry.

BETTE, 2 All Souls Crescent, Asheville, NC; betteboutique.com. Designer clothing, jewelry, shoes, plus a variety of local goods like essential oil candles, artisan jewelry all in the charming setting of an old pebble-dash cottage in Biltmore Village.

> ℹ Souvenirs for friends, family, or the house sitter back home can be as simple and delightful as a jar of local jam or honey. Check out the Western Carolina Farmer's Market in Asheville or any number of small tailgate markets on Saturday mornings.

DUNCAN AND YORK MODERN MARKET, 33 N. Lexington Ave., Asheville, NC; (828) 575-2441; duncanandyork.com. A gift shop with unique items including many local Asheville designers. Cool T-shirts, jewelry, cards and paper goods, perfumes—not all local items, but a carefully curated, fun collection of small treasures.

HAZEL TWENTY, 16 Patton Ave., Asheville, NC; (828) 575-9720; hazel twenty.com. This centrally-located boutique started as a mobile fashion truck, creating pop-up shopping events at street festivals. Hip clothing, shoes, jewelry, bags in a bright setting. Some local designers, too, and a great source of inspiration.

HIP REPLACEMENTS CLOTHING, 72 N. Lexington Ave., Asheville, NC; (828) 255-7573; hipreplacementsclothing.com. Super cool vintage clothing shop that is jammed full of retro hats, clothing, bags, silk scarves, and shoes.

> ℹ Wait until dark, when the lights of Asheville begin to twinkle, and drive along Town Mountain Road up the crest of the mountain. Start at Old Toll Road, which winds along behind Grove Park Inn and through residential areas and runs into Town Mountain Road. As you climb higher, you'll be able to see the lights of Asheville below, the view widening as you ascend the ridge.

MINX BOUTIQUE, 64 N. Lexington Ave., Asheville, NC; (828) 225-5680; minxboutique.wordpress.com. Stylish and eclectic clothing designs. Some by local designers. Also accessories, jewelry, and gifts for the hip young dresser.

ROYAL PEASANTRY, 80 N. Lexington St., Asheville, NC; (828) 559-1835; royalpeasantry.com. Stunning space filled with unique hand-made jewelry and locally-designed leather-, fiber-, and feather-based clothing and accessories. All of high quality and very unique.

SCOUT, 10 All Souls Crescent, Asheville, NC; (828) 505-1984; www.scout avl.com. The fashionista's treasure chest—with frequent convivial trunk shows from fine designers—Scout carries carefully curated quality clothing, shoes, jewelry and accessories from international names.

SERENITY AND SCOTT APOTHECARY, 1 Page Ave., Asheville, NC; (828) 505-4075; serenityandscott.com. Locally-owned retail shop for Asheville-made cosmetics, fragrance, men's grooming essentials, such as beard oils and shaving soaps, as well as other unique brands. Expert in-shop makeup services, as well.

TOPS FOR SHOES, 27 N. Lexington Ave., Asheville, NC; (828) 254-6721; topsforshoes.com. This is another of those gutsy establishments that survived the decay of downtown and persistently worked to make the area a viable business district again. Since the 1970s, Tops has been known for quality footwear for the whole family, and the shop has a reputation for its service and large inventory.

2 ON CRESCENT, 4 All Souls Crescent, Asheville, NC; (828) 274-1276; 2oncrescent.com. An elegant boutique for women's clothing and accessories, including colorful leather bags, scarves, wraps, and jewelry.

VAVAVOOOM, 57 Broadway St., Asheville, NC; (828) 254-6329; vavavooom.com. A beautifully-appointed lingerie store and more (think corsets, garter-belts, stockings, body-safe adult toys, sex-positive books) with national brands as well as local designer's apparel aimed at comfort and beauty, with heavy emphasis on education and body-positive philosophy. Knowledgeable, kind sales associates who make everyone feel comfortable shopping for intimate items.

Southern Mountains

C. ORRICO, 343A Main St., Highlands, NC; (828) 526-9122; corrico.com. Stylish fashions for women, from casual designer-wear to resort-wear and elegant shoes and dresses for holidays.

MCCULLEY'S CASHMERE, 242 S. 4th St., Highlands, NC; (828) 526-4407; mucculleys.com. McCulley's, with another shop in Aspen, Colorado, specializes in Scottish cashmere knitwear for women and men. Also jewelry and accessories, including high-quality outerwear.

THE SOUTHERN WAY, 342 Main St., Highlands, NC; (828) 526-4777. Emphasizing goods made in the southeast, this retailer has fashionable items, but also casual work wear and sportswear.

> **i** Many towns around the mountains show their hospitality by providing visitors with centrally located public restrooms. In Hendersonville, you'll find them in Iron Gate Marketplace at 318 North Main St. between Third and Fourth Streets and at Henderson County Travel & Tourism, 20 South Main St. located between Barnwell Street and Allen Street.

HOME DECOR

Northern Mountains

CABIN FEVER, 915 Main St., Blowing Rock, NC; (828) 295-0520; nccabinfever.com. Cabin Fever offers a complete collection of log cabin and vacation home furnishings. Choose from unique and distinctive furniture, lighting, kitchen items, bed-and-bath decor, hardware, gifts, and more. Cabin Fever is a family-owned business with its largest store located in downtown Blowing Rock.

DE PROVENCE ET D'AILLEURS, 131 Morris St., Blowing Rock, NC; (828) 295-9989. This elegant shop features gifts and accessories imported directly from France, particularly from the area of Provence. Collectibles include Quimper Faience, blown and bubbled glasswork from Biot, and many one-of-a-kind items straight from the French markets. Household accessories include Provence linens, pottery, olive oil soaps, lamps, and other fine casual tabletop items. You'll also find hand-crafted furniture and original French artwork, lovely perfumes not easily found in this country, and other gifts.

DEWOOLFSON DOWN, 9452 Hwy. 105, Banner Elk, NC; (828) 963-4144; dewoolfsondown.com. Did you ever wonder where innkeepers get those sumptuous down comforters for your nightly lodging at some of the Boone area's best bed-and-breakfast inns? Well, the secret's out . . . it's DeWoolfson Down, 9 miles south of Boone on Hwy. 105. But there is so much more here: down pillows hand-stuffed to your order, silk comforters from China, Egyptian cotton sheets designed in France, crisp damasks from Germany, and silky Jacquard sheets from Italy—with up to 590 threads per inch. Clear out the trunk of your car before you come because you won't go home empty-handed.

GREENHOUSE CRAFTS, 248 J. W. Luke Rd., Glendale Springs, NC; (336) 982-2618; greenhousecrafts.com. Greenhouse Crafts is located across the road from the Holy Trinity Episcopal Church, where noted North Carolina artist Ben Long completed his fresco "The Lord's Supper" in the early 1980s. (The other of the two Churches of the Frescoes is St. Mary's Episcopal, about 12 miles away near West Jefferson, off US Hwy. 221). Greenhouse Crafts has tastefully complemented the frescoes' religious theme with angel statuary, inspirational art, literature, and an array of music. The shop also has traditional mountain crafts, collectible figurines, and unusual functional and whimsical pottery. Handmade jewelry, including silver rings and bracelets made in the area, can be found here, along with stained-glass lamps, gorgeous wooden dulcimers, and other smaller gift items.

HANNA'S ORIENTAL RUGS & GIFTS, 1123 Main St., Blowing Rock, NC; (828) 295-7073, hannahsofblowingrock.com. Another fine shop on Main Street, Hanna's sells imported items of exceptional quality, including Oriental and Central Asian rugs, exquisite Austrian Swarovski crystal, Lladro porcelain figurines, and cloisonné, jade, and ivory pieces from around the world.

THE LAST STRAW, 978 Main St., Blowing Rock, NC; (828) 295-3030; thelaststrawinc.com. Since 1988 this glorious store (in various incarnations) has brought the outside in—from lanterns and artistic lighting to silk flowers and plants that defy reality, fountains, and kinetic wind spinners for the garden. Check out the autumn and holiday specialties. There's even a clothing boutique and carefully-selected jewelry designs.

MIRROR LAKE ANTIQUES, 215 S. 4th St., Highlands, NC; (828) 526-2080, Highlands; mirrorlakeantiques.com. This full-service antique store has a large selection of estate jewelry. It's the place to look for semiprecious stones, mineral specimens, gold jewelry, jewelry design, and remodeling.

ORIGINALS ONLY GALLERY, 3B N. Jefferson Ave., West Jefferson, NC; (336) 846-1636; originalsonlygallery.com. This comely gallery features paintings of American artists who have spent a great deal of their lives abroad. Lenore Depree, who lived in the Middle East, offers most fascinating lithographs and even a commissioning service of original Persian storybook art.

RUSTIC ON MAIN, 915 Main St., Blowing Rock, NC; (828) 295-9033; rusticnc.com. This shop displays incredible handmade furnishings and objects for home, lodge, camp, and cabins, all made from reclaimed wood. Also hand-crafted accessories like trunks, game boards, and authentic lovely holiday decor.

SALLY MAE'S EMPORIUM, 414 Trading Post Rd., Glendale Springs, NC; (336) 982-2543; sallymaesemporium.com. Think jam jars with sweet preserves and honey, homemade soaps, hand-carved items, especially holiday ephemera, antiques, and other finds. Closed for the winter so catch this place before or after.

TIGER MOUNTAIN WOODWORKS, 2089 Dillard Rd., Highlands, NC; (828) 526-5577; summerhousehighlands.com. Shopping for a rustic look? This shop sells handcrafted furnishings, including custom lodge furniture and country reproductions, such as beds, tables, dressers, and other items for the entire house.

TWIN CREEKS AND SOUTHERN MARKET, 14 N. Jefferson Ave, West Jefferson, NC; (910) 358-3452; twincreeksouthernmarket.com. Filled to the brim with home and garden decor from around the world, with a special emphasis on country chic. Think milk paint on cupboards with lamp-worked glass knobs, ceramic fountains for the garden, teapots, and cake plates.

Village at Banner Elk

The Shoppes of Tynecastle is an attractive grouping of specialty shops at the junction of Highways 105 and 184. Sports shops, galleries, home furnishings stores, nail salons, and kitchen and wine stores are anchored by a distinctive stone tower that makes this destination easy to spot.

Head north on Highway 184 to the town of Banner Elk and its attractive upscale shopping complex called the Village at Banner Elk.

Central Mountains

MOBILIA, 43 Haywood St., Asheville, NC; (828) 252-8322; mobilianc .com. A very groovy furniture and home design store shows design classics as well as rare and hard-to-find pieces by the furniture industry's most visionary manufacturers and upstart designers. Some local contemporary artwork can be found here.

NEW MORNING GALLERY, 7 Boston Way, Asheville, NC; (828) 274-2831; newmorninggallerync.com. This gallery and shop occupies two stories and is surrounded by urban landscaping. This is one of the South's premier arts and crafts shops, displaying the work of some of America's finest artists and craftspeople for more than 30 years. The lavish show space for handcrafted furniture is a place to dream.

Southern Mountains

ACORNS, 212 S. 4th St., Highlands, NC; (828) 787-1877; acornshighlands .com. Luxury shopping featuring European and American antiques, gifts, glass, unique lighting, and elegant accessories. Part of the beautiful Old Edwards Inn complex.

THE KITCHEN SHOP, 5 N. Main St., Waynesville, NC; (828) 452-7672; thekitchenshop.business.site. The items here can make cooking an adventure. This kitchen shop offers all that is necessary to make a cook a chef. In addition to cookbooks, it has fine German-made cookware, small appliances, Burton burners and stove-top grills, gourmet coffees and all the items needed to brew them, handmade cutting boards and butcher-block tables, gift baskets made to order, and much more.

SPECIALITY STORES & MARKETS

Northern Mountains

APPALACHIAN ANTIQUE MALL, 631 W. King St., Boone, NC; (828) 262-0521; appalachianantiquemall.com. This is a storehouse of American and European antiques spread over three floors and 27,000 square feet. Here you'll find antique jewelry, furniture, linens, decorative items, prints, and family china from more than 75 dealers. Take your time browsing. Each vendor has set up almost an entire store within the allotted space.

FOOTSLOGGERS, 139 S. Depot St., Boone, NC; (828) 355-9984; footsloggersnc.com. Footsloggers carries all the stylishly rugged, top-quality clothing and footwear for those who like the outdoors or just the outdoorsy look. This is also the place to go in Boone for all kinds of camping, hiking, and outdoor gear.

FRED'S GENERAL MERCANTILE COMPANY, 501 Beech Mountain Pkwy., Banner Elk, NC; (828) 387-4838; fredsgeneral.com. This store has stepped in to fill the void for the brave few who live here year-round, as well as for the legion of tourists who continually make the pilgrimage to mile-high Beech Mountain. Fred Pfohl and his colorful, old-fashioned store anchor the community. Among Fred's inventory are groceries, ski accessories, warm clothing, crafts, toys, even hardware and toothbrushes. Stay and have lunch at Fred's Backside Deli (828-387-9331) at the rear of the store. And you can't miss, nor would you want to, Wildbird Supply (828-389-4838), also inside Fred's

General Mercantile Company. The company's motto is, "Wildbird's supplies everything but the birds," and that includes seed, feeders, books, and nature guides. In back of this store you can watch birds, squirrels, and chipmunks romp and munch on the feed left in the landscaped forest-garden plot. Fred's motto reads, "If we don't have it, you don't need it."

HAM SHOPPE, 124 Broadstone Rd., Banner Elk, NC; (828) 963-6310; hamshoppe.com. Up Hwy. 105, just as you turn toward scenic Valle Crucis, is the Ham Shoppe. This is a store for jams, jellies, homemade breads, pies, dry pasta, and other staples for your kitchen. Even better, though, are its made-to-order takeouts. Touted as "Ham Sweet Hams," the mouthwatering honey-glazed, spiral-cut baked hams are the obvious house specialty. But there is so much more to feast on here: strawberry-rhubarb pie, ham spread, cinnamon buns, preserves, and fresh-baked sourdough bread. Use the Ham Shoppe as your special corner grocer or as a deli—it serves this dual purpose well.

THE INCREDIBLE TOY COMPANY, 3411 US 321 S., Blowing Rock, NC; (828) 264-1422; incredibletoycompany.com. Toys, toys, toys! The kids will see this one before you do, so you might as well be prepared to stop and enjoy this fun place between Boone and Tweetsie Railroad. It offers a large selection of educational toys, games, books, puzzles, science kits, and the well-known Brio and Playmobil sets.

MAST GENERAL STORE, 630 King St., Boone, NC; (828) 262-0000; mastgeneralstore.com. If you're looking for wool socks and flannel, down-filled outerwear, and general mountain attire, this is the place. Just like its sister stores in Valle Crucis and other spots in this area, Mast General Store in Boone stocks quality leisure clothing, hats, belts, and other leather accessories. We like the seasonal sale bins! The Boone store is a two-story, turn-of-the-20th-century-style department store in the restored 1913 Boone Mercantile at the corner of King and Depot Streets. Boone's Mast Store also carries shoes, housewares, and gifts and has departments for children and maternity needs. The candy shop adjacent to the clothing section is one step over the threshold into sugar heaven. Sold by the pound, the candy is stocked in barrels. Just carry your little basket around and start filling it up with old-fashioned horehound candy, peppermints, taffy, imported hard coffee candies, mints, and other tooth-rotting goodness!

MAST GENERAL STORE, Hwy. 194, Vale Crucis, NC; (828) 963-6511; mastgeneralstore.com. The ultimate shopping destination once you reach Valle Crucis is the historic Mast General Store on Highway 194. Built in 1882 by Henry Taylor, the store was sold around the turn of the 20th century to W. W. Mast. Over the next 70 years, the Mast family business established a tradition in the region for offering "everything from cradles to caskets." The interior of the store remains very much the same as it was a century ago. The old post office, still in service, is at one end, and the store's classic potbellied stove, an asset in these snow-prone hills, is still a central element. You'll delight in a ramble around this old-time mercantile. Sit out on in the porch swings or rockers on the back porch. This is where you should be sipping your ice-cold A & W or hot-and-spicy ginger ale. It certainly revved us up after lunch for more sight-seeing. This place has quality seasonal apparel, camping and fly-fishing gear, as well as sun hats, shoes, hiking boots and sandals. The candy store offers barrels of taffy, jawbreakers, horehound candy, licorice, and about a hundred other sweets sold by weight. Just take your basket around and fill it up.

THE MUSTARD SEED MARKET, 5589 US 321, Boone, NC; (828) 295-4585; themustardseedmarketnc.com. You might miss this little stand if you blink. This unassuming roadside market on US 321 at Aho Road, 2 miles north of Blowing Rock, is open daily and is much more than a produce stand. English garden statuary, unusual perennial flowers, honey, herb vinegars, hand-painted gifts, and custom-made flags share the space with the fresh fruits and vegetables.

NEACO, 1053 Main St., Blowing Rock, NC; (828) 295-0709; neaco.com. This is an eclectic shop that features a variety of "sophisticated-cool" items such as cocktail napkins and linen towels with cleversayings, lounge and jazz CDs, contemporary art-lighting fixtures, artwork, invitations and cards, sassy parlor games, and other chic novelties. It's the place to pick up unusual decorative welcome mats, unique dishes, serving utensils with rhinestones, and other such lovelies.

THE SHOPPES AT FARMERS, 661 W. King St., Boone, NC; (828) 264-8801; shopsatfarmers.com. This decades-old landmark formerly known as the Farmer's Hardware and Supply Company is replete with creaking wood floors, back open stairways, and large picture windows on two floors. Some 35 individual merchants fill the many booths of the 12,000-square-foot space with everything ranging from farm antiques to gems and handmade jewelry, housewares, sweets, artwork and photography, clothing, and much more in the basement.

THE TOY STORE, 364 Main St., Highlands, NC; (828) 526-9415. We never go to Highlands without dropping in at the Toy Store to see the latest in toys and games. Here you'll find old and new favorites, plus stuffed animals, dolls, and so much more.

Central Mountains

ASHEVILLE WINE MARKET, 65 Biltmore Ave., Asheville, NC; (828) 253-0060; ashevillewine.com. You can take home an exquisite sampling of the grape from the Wine Market. The array is staggering, so you might be wise in choosing the Wine Samplers, six international vintage wines specially priced and packaged.

CHEVRON TRADING POST AND BEAD CO., 40 N. Lexington Ave., Asheville, NC; (828) 236-2323. A quintessential Asheville shop marked by the glowing paper lantern stars in the window. Also an array of beads, pendants,

Stars in the window at Chevron Trading Post. CONSTANCE E. RICHARDS

raw gemstones, and every ilk of jewelry-making material to create your own, plus jewelry, fabrics from around the world.

THE CURB MARKET, 221 N. Church St., Hendersonville, NC; (828) 692-8012; curbmarket.com. The Curb Market started out on Main St. in 1924 with eight merchants selling their wares beneath umbrellas. It has mushroomed to 137 selling spaces, many staffed by third- and fourth-generation sellers. Merchants here are required to be Henderson County residents and to make or grow all items they sell. Among these are fresh vegetables, fruits, flowers, dairy products, baked goods, jams, jellies, pickles, relishes, and handmade gifts of all kinds, including afghans, aprons, booties, dolls, folk toys, pillows, quilts, rag rugs, table linens, walking sticks, woodwork items, and wreaths.

DANCING BEAR TOYS, LTD., 418 N. Main St., Hendersonville, NC; (828) 693-4500; dancingbeartoys.com. In addition to almost every toy currently popular with children today, Dancing Bear carries a good selection of delightful puppets, costumes, puzzles, and educational toys and books.

GROVE ARCADE, 1 Page Ave., Asheville, NC; (828) 252 7799; grovearcade.com. One of America's early shopping arcade jewels, the Grove Arcade reopened in 2002 after years of renovation. The arcade houses an open market, individual shops, fashion boutiques, and antiques stores. Cafes, delis, and restaurants also fill the venerable space that was lovingly brought back to its original splendor. You must see the interior as well as the exterior to appreciate all the shops the arcade has to offer. Not all of them are visible from the street. On warm days vendors set up on the south side of the arcade showing unique items.

KRESS EMPORIUM, 19–21 Patton Ave., Asheville, NC; (828) 281-2252; thekressemporium.com. An architectural landmark, the Kress building in downtown Asheville was built in 1918 as a five-and-dime. Constructed of rich ceramic tile, the Kress building is only one of the many brilliant examples of art deco in the city. For years the building fell into disrepair and its first floor was used for various flea markets. Today this restored space is a showcase for over 80 artists, artisans, sculptors, hat makers, jewelry designers, and many others devoted to artistic endeavors. Artists rent booths, decorate the walls, and add their works, so you are essentially strolling through many galleries under one roof. Everything from Turkish kilims, handmade dolls, hand-blown glass vessels, and hand-sewn hats to paintings, hand-carved furniture, antique tools, more is on display in this high-ceilinged bright hall.

LEXINGTON GLASSWORKS, 81 S. Lexington Ave., Asheville, NC; (828) 348-8427; lexingtonglassworks.com. A hot glass studio with a retail space,

EXPLOREASHEVILLE.COM

showcasing vases, vessels, pitchers, glasses, ornaments, bowls and every other piece of stunning glass the artists put out. They also serve beer, so you can sip while you watch the glassblowers at work.

THE L.O.F.T., 53 Broadway, Asheville, NC; (828) 259-9303; loftof asheville.com. "L.O.F.T." stands for Lost Objects, Found Treasures. This eclectically funky shop, filled with a menagerie of distressed furniture, paper lamps, candles, natural soaps, stationery, frames, handmade journals, and other gift and decorative items, is truly a local favorite. Handmade paper, beeswax soaps, picture frames, mirrors, sketchbooks, plush furniture, flowerpots, and so much more grace this home designer's dream of a shop.

O. P. TAYLOR'S, 2 S. Broad St., Brevard, NC; (828) 883-2309; optaylors .com. This store is a world unto itself. The main attractions are the toys that fill its two floors and flow down the stairs, sometimes right out on the sidewalk. One entire room is devoted to toy trains. Handmade wooden toys and educational games are here, too.

THE WHITE SQUIRREL SHOPPE, 2 W. Main St., Brevard, NC; (828) 877-3530; whitesquirrelshoppe.com. This wonderful shop's jam-packed with collectibles; odds and ends of small, wonderful pieces of furniture; lamps; statues; and gifts and crafts. There are also a number of its namesake white squirrels in all sizes and shapes. These make great souvenirs of the area because there really are white squirrels in Brevard.

WOOLWORTH WALK, 25 Haywood St., Asheville, NC; (828) 254-9234; woolworthwalk.com. This former Woolworth's, originally constructed in the 1920s, was brought back to life after renovation and the infusion of booths and wall spaces featuring the work of local and regional artists and crafters. Decorative art, jewelry, glass, pottery, textiles, painting, metal sculpture, photography, and other imaginative art and crafts make this a lively emporium of gifts. Several artists maintain working studios on the lower level.

ZAPOW, 150 Coxe Ave., Asheville, NC; (828) 575-9112; zapow.com. Fantastic collection of small works of illustration, paintings, pop art, and much more. Small bar allows you to purchase a beer from the tap, coffee or tea to sip as you stroll through the exhibitions.

Southern Mountains

DOGWOOD CRAFTERS, 90 Webster St., Dillsboro, NC; (828) 586-2248; dogwoodcrafters.com. Housed in a large, renovated log building around the corner from Front Street, this is one of our favorite stores in Dillsboro. We are particularly taken with the lovely, artistic cornhusk dolls, but there also are hundreds of contemporary and traditional handicrafts on display, including pottery, pillows, art, and toys.

ENLOE MARKET PLACE, 78 Front St., Dillsboro, NC; (828) 586-3603. Housed in a historic old home, Enloe carries fine gifts, prints, and home accessories and offers a children's corner full of items to delight the kids. Want to impress your friends? Pick up a few bars of monogrammed soap.

FRONT STREET COMPANY/YARN CORNER, 64 Front St., Dillsboro, NC; (828) 586-0089. Needleworkers will love the variety they'll find at this shop. Gifts, fine yarns, hand-painted needlepoint, and cross-stitch supplies are sold here. You can also take a class or receive assistance on your latest project. And for a respite before more shopping, you can dine at the Front Street Cafe or out in the courtyard. Front Street Company is a great place to purchase delectable gourmet items like teas and coffees, plus jams and jellies, which make great gifts or personal indulgences.

TWIGS & LEAVES, 98 N. Main St., Waynesville, NC; (828) 456-1940; twigsandleaves.com. David Erickson and his wife, potter Kaaren Stoner, whose studio is in this craft gallery, call their shop "an adventure into the art of Nature," and it certainly is! Kaaren's leaf-enhanced pottery, arches, and outdoor seating made of twigs and branches, nature photos and handmade fountains, meditation pools and organic plant vessels, whimsical lizards, and many, many other artists' nature-related items, plus reasonable prices, make it nearly impossible to leave this shop without making a purchase.

Attractions

It doesn't matter if rain is pouring through the treetops or sunshine is bursting over the rugged terrain, you'll always find something to do in North Carolina's mountains. We've included a variety of attractions in this chapter that can keep a whole family busy without costing a bundle—some are even free.

NORTHERN MOUNTAINS

Ashe County

ASHE COUNTY CHEESE FACTORY, 106 East Main St., West Jefferson, NC; (336) 246-2501, (800) 445-1378; ashecountycheese.com. Did you know that it takes 10 gallons of milk to make one pound of cheese? That's one of the facts you'll learn as you watch cheese being made in this factory founded in 1930. The factory's varieties include cheddar, Colby, and Monterey Jack. Guides escort groups through a viewing room, explain the process, and answer questions. Sample your favorites and take a few home from the company cheese shop across the street from the factory. The plant is open 8:30 a.m. to 5 p.m. Mon through Sat. Admission is free.

CHURCHES OF THE FRESCOES, ST. MARY'S, 400 Beaver Creek Rd., West Jefferson, NC; (other location: Holy Trinity, 120 Glendale School Rd., Glendale Springs); (336) 982-3076. Ben Long painted three frescoes at St. Mary's: "Mary Great with Child" in 1974; "John the Baptist" in 1975; and "The Mystery of Faith" in 1977. In the summer of 1980 he painted the frescoes of "The Lord's Supper" at Holy Trinity. Visitors are welcome.

Avery County

GRANDFATHER MOUNTAIN STATE PARK, 9872 Hwy. 105 S., Banner Elk, NC; (877) 722-6762; grandfather.com. The rugged outline of this ridge that takes on the appearance of a bearded face—the "grandfather"—gives this mountain its name. Grandfather Mountain is the highest in the Blue Ridge chain. It is part of the International Network of Biosphere Reserves, "a special place where man and nature thrive in harmony." Of the 324 existing Biosphere Reserves, Grandfather is the only one privately owned. This wonderful oasis allows you to come close to the natural wildlife habitats of black bears, cougars, deer, eagles, and river otter. The nature museum offers valuable information.

If you have no fear of heights, you might attempt the exhilaration of the famous Mile High Swinging Bridge (keep remembering to look at the view).

Work off those wobbly knees with 12 miles of hiking trails. The Grandfather Trail is a favorite, a rugged but beautiful trail traversing 2.3 miles. The mountain also offers meandering footpaths and scenic walks for novice hikers. Once you've relaxed, spread a picnic and enjoy this majestic place, a reminder of the fragility of our relationship with this earth. The site is open daily except Thanksgiving and Christmas from 8 a.m. to 5 p.m. in winter, 8 a.m. to 6 p.m. in spring and fall, and 8 a.m. to 7 p.m. in summer. Ticket sales stop at 6 p.m. A gift shop and restaurant are on the site. Children younger than four are admitted free.

i To see how Grandfather Mountain got its name, head south on Highway 105 from Boone. In the heart of Foscoe, look toward the mountain on your left, and lo and behold, there he is, sleeping on his back. You can almost hear him snore!

Madison County

HOT SPRINGS SPA, 315 Bridge St., Hot Springs, NC; (828) 622-7676; nchotsprings.com. Historically the mineral springs of Hot Springs, North Carolina, maintaining a natural 100-degree temperature year-round, have provided relief for visitors as early as the turn of the 20th century. That was the heyday of this once-fashionable health resort. With the passage of time and a changing world, the springs fell into disuse, and the population dwindled away. But in 1990 the famous hot springs came into new ownership and are now back in business, offering a modern version of "taking the waters." Jacuzzis filled with the curative waters are available for hourly rates, determined by the number of people in your party. Several resident massage therapists are available by appointment. The word *spa* may be a misnomer, though. This is a very casual place—don't expect luxury—but do expect to commune successfully with nature as tubs are set alongside the rushing French Broad River and Spring Creek.

A log fire in the central yard is perfect for lounging and communing with friends. Open year-round. Rates increase for evening sessions (after 7 p.m.). Lodging facilities are available in the RV park and campground, for which options include electric, water, and sewer hookups and tent sites. There is also a facility for hot showers. Primitive camping cabins are also available, as is one fully furnished log cabin with a Jacuzzi on the back porch, fed from the natural spring. When camping, children 6 or younger stay free. Special discounts and group rates are also available for the campground.

McDowell County

LINVILLE CAVERNS, 199929 US 221, Marion, NC; (828) 756-4171, (800) 419-0540; linvillecaverns.com. These limestone caverns with marvelous stalactite and stalagmite formations were first explored in the late 1880s by H. E. Colton and his local guide Dave Franklin. However the Indians had known about the caverns since 1822. Found deep inside Humpback Mountain, these caverns were also hideouts for army deserters from both sides during the Civil War. Today, in the company of experienced guides, you can take a path that leads along an underground stream filled with trout whose life in perpetual darkness has resulted in blindness. The limestone formations, suspended like jewels, have developed over eons into interesting shapes, such as the Frozen Waterfall, Natural Bridge, and Franciscan Monk. Did you ever wonder what absolute darkness looks like? You'll get your chance deep in these caverns. This must be the guides' favorite part—switching off those lights! You literally can't see your hand in front of your face. The temperature underground is a constantly cool 52 degrees, so come prepared with a sweater or jacket. A gift shop is well stocked, and items are reasonably priced. Admission charged.

Mitchell County

THE ORCHARD AT ALTAPASS, 1025 Orchard Rd., Spruce Pine, NC; (828) 765-9531, (888) 765-9531; altapassorchard.org. This historic orchard features fresh apples and peaches from May to Nov and is open only during these months. You can pick your own or just buy the already-picked baskets and brown-paper bags of juicy fruits. Tours of the orchard are free. Come enjoy music, stories, and hayrides on Sat. The Orchard is open seven days a week. The Apple Core Grill has a concise menu of delish comfort-food treats like burgers, wraps, corndogs, BLTs, and such at great prices.

Watauga County

THE BLOWING ROCK, 432 The Rock Rd., Blowing Rock, NC; (828) 295-7111; theblowingrock.com. Fanciful tales about this beautiful spot are

> There are more than 16,000 southern varieties of heirloom apples. The Orchard at Altapass provides hayrides and stories while you ride among some of these heirlooms. You might have the opportunity to taste a Grimes Golden, a Sheepsnose, or a Limbertwig. You might even be able to pick your own.

as interesting as the facts. This rocky granite outcrop is swept by a constant updraft from Johns River Gorge 3,000 feet below. Those are the facts. The most familiar romantic legend of the Blowing Rock is that a beautiful Indian maiden was taken from the plains to Blowing Rock by her father, a Chickasaw chieftain who was fearful of a white man's adoration of his daughter. The daughter met an Indian brave wandering below the Blowing Rock and shot an arrow in his direction to capture his attention. They fell in love, but a reddening of the sky brought them back to the rock. It was a sign of trouble to the brave, commanding his return to his tribe on the plains. With the maiden's entreaties not to leave her, the brave, torn by conflict of duty and heart, leapt from the rock. The maiden prayed to the Great Spirit every day until one evening, a gust of wind blew her lover back onto the rock and into her arms. The Blowing Rock claims a panoramic view of Mount Mitchell, Hawksbill, Grandfather, and Table Rock Mountains in the distance. Blowing Rock is just outside the town of the same name and is open daily from Mar through Nov; it's open weekends in winter months, weather permitting. Hours are 9 a.m. to 5 p.m. Mar, Apr, and Nov; 9 a.m. to 6 p.m. May through Aug; and 8 a.m. to 7 p.m. Sept through Oct. Small admission charged.

DANIEL BOONE NATIVE GARDENS, 651 Horn in the West Dr., Boone, NC; (828) 264-6390; danielboonenativegardens.org. The stone gatehouse bids you welcome as you enter the gardens through the handsome wrought iron gate, a gift made by Daniel Boone VI, a direct descendant of the great pioneer. Adjacent to *Horn in the West*, these beautiful gardens include an extensive collection of native plants covering six acres, informally landscaped with trails, split-rail fences, and a reflection pool at the Squire Boone Cabin. Many plants, such as bloodroot, dogtooth violet, yellow lady slippers, and maidenhair fern, are marked. A spring trickles through the enormous boulders of the Rockery, while a statue of St. Francis stands in the center of the secluded prayer retreat. There's even a meditation sanctuary that lets you pause and give thanks for such beauty. The gardens are open daily May through Aug and weekends in Oct 10 a.m. to 6 p.m. (until 8 p.m. when *Horn in the West* is running). A small admission is charged, but those under 16 are admitted free.

HICKORY RIDGE HOMESTEAD/LIVING HISTORY MUSEUM, 591 Horn in the West Dr., Boone, NC; (828) 264-2120; horninthewest .com. You'll swear you just saw Daniel Boone, but it was one of the costumed

> **i** Jan Karon, author of the best-selling Mitford series of books, based her novels on the village of Blowing Rock.

interpreters at Hickory Ridge Homestead on the grounds of *Horn in the West*. This living museum offers a glimpse into 18th-century mountain life and culture through a variety of activities, including regular demonstrations in weaving and candle making, as well as presentations of other crafts. Try your hand at weaving on a 180-year-old loom, spinning wool, or participating in other hands-on activities. A nominal admission helps support the museum and its projects. Hours vary with the seasons, so call ahead. And while you're at it, ask about the intensive living history weekends and workshops.

HORN IN THE WEST, 591 Horn in the West Dr., Boone, NC; (828) 264-2120; horninthewest.com. This outdoor drama, one of several in this region, depicts the lives of North Carolina's early settlers—Daniel Boone among them—and their struggle for independence from Britain. This production, set in pre-Revolutionary 1771, lasts about two hours and is a one-of-a-kind experience: history and excitement all rolled into one. Remember, this is an outdoor production. Summer evenings can be cool, especially at this elevation, so bring a light jacket just in case. The season is mid-June to mid-Aug, and the drama begins each evening at 8 p.m., with reserved seating. There are no performances on Mon. Admission charged.

> ℹ The movie *The Green Mile* was partially filmed at Moses Cone Manor on the Parkway in Blowing Rock. The manor portrayed the character's retirement home.

CENTRAL MOUNTAINS

Buncombe County

ASHEVILLE TOURISTS BASEBALL, 30 Buchanan Place, McCormick Field, Asheville, NC; (828) 258-0428; milb.com. Professional baseball at McCormick Field has been a fixture in Asheville since 1924. Many of the all-time greats of the game, such as Babe Ruth, Ty Cobb, Jackie Robinson, Pete Rose, and Nolan Ryan, played here en route to the majors. The old McCormick Field, with all its well-worn charm, was actually famous for a bit part as background in some of the final scenes for the popular baseball movie *Bull Durham* with Kevin Costner. The new stadium is grand, with plenty of local beer booths, great food, VIP seating in two places, but it's Asheville's baseball tradition that keeps folks coming to McCormick Field to cheer on the Tourists. Thirsty Thursday is a grand old tradition for locals, $3 beers! Grab some boiled peanuts and a cold one!

The Tourists' baseball season begins in Apr and runs through the first week in Sept. The Asheville team, a member of the South Atlantic League, plays about 72 home games.

THE ASHEVILLE URBAN TRAIL, Downtown Asheville, NC; (828) 259-5800, ext. 4000; exploreasheville.com/urban-trail. Asheville's formative period, the boom time from 1880 to 1930, left an indelible imprint on the character of the city. This series of 30 stations is marked by plaques, sculptures, mosaics, murals, and other interpretative visuals created by world-class artists from Russia, Italy, and the United States that bring the area's history to life. The open-air museum is located 1.7 miles around downtown through five themed paths. The walking benefits of the trail are free, along with the pleasure of the path. Regularly scheduled guided tours of the Urban Trail are run from Apr to Nov, the second Fri of each month at 4 p.m., the third Sun of each month at 3 p.m., and other special group tours as requested. The two-hour tour meets in front of Pack Place at the marquee sign, on the southeast corner of Pack Square in downtown Asheville. Tours will be on schedule except in extreme weather conditions. A $5 donation per person is suggested (no charge for children under 12 accompanied by an adult).

> **i** Touring the Asheville Urban Trail on your own is made easy with the aid of "Artful Asheville—Along the Urban Trail," a comprehensive take-along guide with maps and informative history about each of the 30 stations (sculptures and plaques) around the city. The booklet is available at bookstores, the Asheville Area Arts Council, and the Asheville Convention and Visitors Bureau.

BILTMORE HOUSE & GARDENS, 1 Lodge St., Asheville, NC; (800) 411-3812; biltmore.com. This magnificent 250-room chateau is the largest private home in America, surrounded by 8,000 acres of forested trails and spectacular gardens (the estate was designed by Central Park landscape designer Frederick Law Olmstead). George Vanderbilt built the estate in the 1890s as his grand retreat in the North Carolina mountains, and officially opened it to friends and family on Christmas Eve 1895. (Read the in-depth history in this chapter's **Close-up**.) On the estate today, you'll find the most-visited winery in the country, two hotels, a number of restaurants, gift shops, hiking trails, and much more than can be experienced in just a few hours. Plan an entire day here! The ticket price runs upwards of $60, and you can add on

"Cat Walk" sculpture by Vadim Bora along the Urban Trail. Constance E. Richards

private tours for additional feeds. Many locals and frequent visitors opt for an annual pass.

THE BOTANICAL GARDENS, 151 W. T. Weaver Blvd., Asheville, NC; (828) 252-5190; ashevillebotanicalgardens.org. This wonderful 10-acre garden oasis in the middle of bustling North Asheville is adjacent to the campus of

To the Manor Born

Biltmore attracts more than a million guests each year. George Washington Vanderbilt brought his legendary status of grandson of the Commodore, Cornelius Vanderbilt, to the mountains. This historic family arrived in America in the 17th century, part of the Dutch migration. While still a bachelor, George Vanderbilt arrived in Asheville with his widowed mother. The railroad had just arrived in this small mountain town, as tunnels through Old Fort Mountain had made easy access possible.

The time was ripe for the legend of the Vanderbilts to take root in Western North Carolina. As the 25-year-old millionaire beheld the beauty of the mountains, he claimed that he would build his private residence in this location. His agents began purchasing land until he amassed 125,000 acres. He then brought the best builders to Asheville. In 1890 America's leading architect, Richard Morris Hunt, began the five-year project that would become known as the country's largest privately owned home. English architect Richard Sharp Smith supervised the building project. Raphael Gustavino came from Barcelona, Spain, to grace the walls and ceilings with his magnificent tile work. Frederick Law Olmsted, who was most renowned for developing Central Park in New York City, came to Biltmore to begin work on the 250 acres of gardens and roadways throughout the estate.

On Christmas Eve 1895, George Vanderbilt and his mother opened their magnificent home, which was inspired by the 16th-century chateaux of the Loire Valley in France. Family members gathered to celebrate the opening of the house and the season. Eighty-five servants provided service to the guests. Also at this time a multitude of farmers began preparing the earth for spring planting. Thus Biltmore House opened as a residence and farm.

The estate boasted outstanding floral gardens; meanwhile the land produced goods for the table and the local markets. A dairy herd, eventually known as the finest in the Southeast, was begun in 1897; and Gifford Pinchot, who would eventually found the US Forestry Service, began a timber industry and "rotation of the tree crops" in the mountains. Dr. Carl Schenck of Darmstadt, Germany, later took over Pinchot's work. Not only would Schenck continue the work for which he was noted in Europe, but he also founded what has become known as the Cradle of Forestry in America. The Biltmore School of Forestry was the first school of its kind in this nation.

Upon George Vanderbilt's death in 1914, his widow, Edith Stuyvesant Dresser Vanderbilt, began deeding his mountain holdings to the US government. They have since become the nucleus of Pisgah National Forest. On March 6, 1924, the Vanderbilts' only child, Cornelia, married the Honorable John Francis Amherst Cecil of England. Together they had two sons.

Eventually the estate was opened to the public in concert with the Asheville Chamber of Commerce offering an added inducement for travelers to visit Asheville. This was during the last days of the Great Depression in 1930.

In due course, the elder grandson of George Vanderbilt, George Henry Vanderbilt Cecil, continued the operation of the Biltmore Farms and Dairy and allowed public access to Biltmore Estate. In 1960 his younger brother, William Amherst Vanderbilt Cecil, returned to Biltmore and began expanding its enterprise. In the early 1980s the two grandsons of George Vanderbilt divided their inheritance, with William assuming operation and ownership of the Biltmore Company, of which Biltmore Estate is the main component.

The legacy moves forward today, with William A. V. Cecil Jr. as chief officer of Biltmore Estate, watching over 8,000 acres of the estate, which include Biltmore House, Biltmore Gardens, Biltmore Winery, Biltmore Equestrian and Outdoor Center, the Inn on Biltmore Estate, the Village Inn, Antler Hill Village, and farming and beef cattle industries. Diana "Dini" Cecil Pickering serves as Vice Chairman of the Board of Directors, is a member of the company's Executive Committee, and acts as the Family Office Director and Chairman of Biltmore's Corporate Philanthropy program. It remains a Cecil family private enterprise.

While you can tour Biltmore at your own pace, we recommend a "tour by tape," which you can rent for a few dollars. Upon entering the Winter Garden, Coco squawks a greeting and the Karl Bitter fountain, "Boy with Geese," begins gurgling. Once inside, only those with the headsets will hear other sounds of the past, such as servants' footsteps echoing through the corridors of this 250-room house or the great organ resounding in the Banquet Hall.

This great hall features a huge Christmas tree from early Nov through the first week in Jan. Candlelight tours during the Christmas season have become a tradition since the 1980s, when for the first time Biltmore remained open beyond the fall color season. Today Biltmore only closes two days a year—Thanksgiving and Christmas.

The treasures at the Biltmore House were collected by George Vanderbilt. Artworks from the Smithsonian were secreted here for protection during World War II, but have all been returned. The mind-boggling collection of the Biltmore includes paintings by Boldini, Whistler, Renoir, Gerhardt, and more. The Pellegrini ceiling dominates the library. Statuary is found throughout the grounds—these friezes are reproductions from the Temple of Athena in Athens. Twenty-five thousand books are in the private collection. The house is a virtual art museum, yet still maintained as George Vanderbilt's palatial residence.

Visiting the four-and-a-half-story house is an adventure in itself. Yet there is even more. Special guided tours are offered at additional fees that provide an "insider's" look at the house. One such tour is Behind the Scenes; another is the Roof Top Tour. The Legacy of the Land tour takes visitors beyond the house and into the gardens and surrounding acres.

the University of North Carolina at Asheville. The gardens were begun in 1960 by the Asheville Garden Club and designed by Doan Ogden, a noted landscape architect, to preserve the heritage of native mountain plants and flowers. Today this mature garden has a wealth of beauty around every bend in the path and within every leafy bower. A bonus is the proliferation of birds and other small wildlife that have made this wonderful garden their home. You may spot a few rabbits at dusk; squirrels and chipmunks abound in the daylight hours. A meadow for sunning, a gazebo for lounging, and a cool creek make this an oasis close to the city, perfect for those after-dinner walks. Many of the trees and other flora are marked with small tags for identification. This site receives support from volunteers, donations, and memberships. A botany center offers nature-related gift items. Admission is free. No pets are allowed.

FOLK ART CENTER, Mile 382, Blue Ridge Parkway, Asheville, NC; (828) 298-7928; southernhighlandguild.org. The Folk Art Center is home to the Southern Highland Craft Guild, an educational nonprofit organization founded in 1930 to give economic support and development to the craftspeople of the Appalachian region. The guild serves nine states and has a membership of more than 700 craftspeople who work to preserve and perpetuate the Appalachian heritage as well as develop the contemporary face of craftsmanship. The center's century-old Allanstand Craft Shop offers for sale the work of guild members throughout the nine-state region. There is also a fine crafts gallery on the upper level and a 250-seat auditorium that is the scene of workshops, programs, and lectures by the guild and National Park Service. Craft demonstrations are held Apr through Dec in the foyer of the center. Clay Day and Fiber Day are two of the special events also sponsored by the guild at the Folk Art Center each year. Admission is free.

NAVITAT CANOPY ADVENTURES, 242 Poverty Branch Rd., Barnards-ville, NC; (828) 626-3700; navitat.com. Awesome tree-top tour of the mountains by zipline! The beautiful drive to get to this valley is fabulous as well. Once there, guides will take you on a high-adventure zipline canopy tour.

NORTH CAROLINA ARBORETUM, 100 Frederick Law Olmsted Way, Asheville, NC; (828) 665-2492; ncarboretum.org. This 426-acre facility boasts a 25,500-square-foot Visitor Education Center, the Horticultural Support Facilities and Greenhouses, the Plants of Promise Garden, and the mile-long Natural Garden Trail, all of which are open to the public. The Core Area Gardens include the Stream Garden, Spring Garden, Outdoor Events Garden, Appalachian Quilt Garden, Blue Ridge Court, and Grand Promenade. Numerous woodland trails lace the forested areas and follow the path of Bent Creek. Guided tours are available for groups if you call ahead. Educational lectures, tours, and workshops are scheduled throughout the year. A cafe and plant retail shop are also on the premises. A per-vehicle car fee is required at the gate. Nominal fees apply for educational programs. The outdoor areas are open seven days a week from 7 a.m. to 7 p.m. The greenhouse is open 8 a.m. to 4 p.m. Mon through Fri. Turn off US Hwy. 191 to the Blue Ridge Parkway. The arboretum entrance is directly before you enter the parkway.

RIVERSIDE CEMETERY, 51 Birch St., Asheville, NC; (828) 350-2066. Sitting high on a hill overlooking part of downtown Asheville is the Riverside Cemetery in the historic Montford district. Among the notables laid to rest here are Sidney Porter (O. Henry); Zebulon Baird Vance, North Carolina's Civil War governor and US congressman; and two detachments of World War I German mariners who had been captured off the coast of the Carolinas. You can trace writer Thomas Wolfe's life to Riverside, from his birthplace on

Woodfin Street to Old Kentucky Home, his mother's boarding house, to First Presbyterian Church on Church Street, where his memorial service was held, and to his final resting place. The cemetery gate is locked during daylight savings by 8 p.m. Thereafter, from fall to spring, it is locked at 6 p.m. It's a lovely place for strolling, but please leave your dogs behind.

WESTERN NORTH CAROLINA FARMERS MARKET, 570 Brevard Rd., Asheville, NC; (828) 253-1691; wncfarmersmarket.org. It's been described as shopping at a 36-acre roadside stand. The WNC Farmers Market, southeast of Asheville, offers a bounty of fresh produce and quality plants, shrubs, trees, and garden supplies. The retail area is reminiscent of an old market square with wooden tables overflowing with goods, fresh vegetables, crafts, and other gifts from the farm. The garden center is operated by several generations of garden specialists, Jesse Israel & Sons, supplying every gardening need.

The restaurant, the Moose Cafe, is on US 191 just south of the main entrance and serves good, basic home cooking. The truck stands are a feast for the eye and food for the soul, too. The conversation from the back of the truck gives as much pleasure as the brown-paper sack of Red Delicious apples you carry home with you. Sections of the market are open 24 hours daily, and the retail buildings are open from 8 a.m. to 6 p.m. daily in summer and 8 a.m. to 5 p.m. in winter.

Moose Cafe

Before shopping at the Farmers Market outside of Asheville, try the Moose Cafe, just above the market's entrance, for a hearty country breakfast. Steaming hot biscuits grace your table before you even order and can be slathered with the honey, molasses, or homemade apple butter already provided. Lunches and dinners are traditional Southern fare; the menu includes a daily special and a four-vegetable plate. Prices are reasonable. Soak in the local atmosphere, try a piece of deep-dish pie, and buy a jar of apple butter to take with you. Moose Cafe, 570 Brevard Rd., Asheville; (828) 255-0920; eatatthemoosecafe.com.

WESTERN NORTH CAROLINA NATURE CENTER, 75 Gashes Creek Rd., Asheville, NC; (828) 298-5600; wcnaturecenter.com. In a word (or two): Red Pandas. These cute critters just arrived as the focal point for this wildlife center. From the moment you step through the door and a three-dimensional, full-size diorama of woodland creatures greets you, you know you are indeed crossing that bridge to the natural world. Exhibits such as weather forecasting, animal identification, a real working beehive, archaeological

Close-up

Fruit of the Tarheel Vine

Prior to passage of Prohibition, North Carolina was legendary for its vineyards and wine production. When America went "dry," only a limited amount of wine could be produced, and for medicinal and religious purposes.

In the case of the Waldensian Winery in Valdese, the huge redwood tankards were sunk—empty—into the mountain lakes. It wasn't until the 1980s that they were retrieved and the Waldensian Vineyards was reactivated.

In 1972 the Fussen family of Rose Hill, North Carolina, in concert with North Carolina State University, explored the idea of making North Carolina a wine-producing state. Using the Muscadine and Scuppernong grapes of eastern North Carolina, they opened the Duplin Winery. Their wine was as sweet as the fresh pressed grapes, and the industry reemerged. Their first fermentation tanks were bought from a dairy; thus milk was turned into wine . . . in a sense.

Other experimental wineries opened, and in the 1970s Biltmore Estate planted its first grapes. By 1982, third-generation wine maker Philippe Jourdain of Carcasson, France, had arrived in North Carolina and applied his techniques in developing the Biltmore Estate Winery. In 1985 the owner of Biltmore Estate, William Amhurst Vanderbilt Cecil, renovated the dairy barn of 1890s vintage, reopening it as the home of Biltmore Estate Winery.

Other wineries followed and are continuing to open, particularly in the northern mountains, where the soil is rich and the climate just right. Of the 400 vineyards and 200 wineries currently operating in North Carolina, nine are found in the western mountains. The remainder stretch out across the state all the way to Knotts Island, accessible only by ferry. As you tour the Tar Heel state, you have many options to "taste the wine where the grape was grown."

displays, and zoological collections of live reptiles and amphibians make this a special stop.

ZEBULON B. VANCE BIRTHPLACE, 911 Reems Creek Rd., off Old US Hwys. 19/23, Weaverville, NC; (828) 645-6706. This charming mountain homestead was home to one of North Carolina's most prominent political figures. Zeb Vance began his career as a lawyer, assuming public office by the young age of 24. He was elected governor of North Carolina three times, most notably during the Civil War. He served three terms as senator from North Carolina, before his death in 1894. His life and career are profiled in an exhibit in the adjoining visitor center. But better yet is the opportunity to see a period mountain home replete with old utensils, kitchenry, rope-spring beds, and other objects whose uses are explained in the informative and free guided tours. The two-story cabin and outbuildings are reconstructions, built from hewn yellow pine logs around the original chimney with its two massive fireplaces. The furnishings and household items depict the period from 1790 to 1840 and include a few pieces original to the Vance family. Pioneer Living Days are celebrated here each spring and fall. Costumed staff members demonstrate skills and occupations of earlier days. Military encampments and battle reenactments are frequently part of the events. The homestead is open Mon through Sat 9 a.m. to 5 p.m., Sun 1 to 5 p.m., and admission is free.

Henderson County

ST. JOHN IN THE WILDERNESS, 1895 Greenville Hwy., US Hwy. 25 South, Flat Rock, NC; (828) 693-9783; stjohnflatrock.org. This charming chapel has an interesting background. In 1837 English-born Charles Baring, in search of a healthier summer climate, brought his beloved wife, Susan, the former widow of a wealthy Charleston rice planter, to an area between the Watauga settlements in what is now Watauga County and Greenville, South Carolina, known simply as "the Wilderness." Thus began a migration of wealthy families from the coast that turned Flat Rock into "the little Charleston of the mountains." Baring bought hundreds of acres in the area and built a grand home called Mountain Lodge, developed on the order of an English country estate, complete with a gatekeeper's cottage, a billiard house, and a deer park. The hilltop private residence, hidden by tall pines on Rutledge Drive, is one of many grand old homes from this period still in the area.

WOLFE'S ANGEL, OAKDALE CEMETERY, US Hwy. 64 W.; Hendersonville, NC. Just a short distance from downtown Hendersonville on US 64 West, the cemetery plot of a local family, the Johnsons, is marked by an angel. She holds a stone lily in her left hand and extends her right hand upward. This statue, imported from Italy and sold to the Johnson family by novelist Thomas Wolfe's father, W.O. Wolfe, is prominently featured in the author's first novel, *Look Homeward, Angel*. Today an iron fence protects the famous angel, and a historical marker on the highway next to the cemetery notes its importance. You can enter the cemetery for a close-up look.

Polk County

FOOTHILLS EQUESTRIAN NATURE CENTER (FENCE), 3381 Hunting Country Rd., Tryon, NC; (828) 859-9021; fence.org. Foothills Equestrian

Nature Center—FENCE, as it is commonly called—is a 300-acre nature sanctuary dedicated to education, recreation, and preservation. The state-of-the-art equestrian facility hosts more than 18 events each season, including two steeplechases, hunter/jumper and dressage shows, and driving rallies. The facility is home to the Carolina Carriage Club. It also has bridle trails. Even if you aren't a horse person, FENCE has great hiking trails that are open to the public free of charge from dawn until dusk all year long. It also offers on- and off-site programs for school classes as well as adult classes in wildflowers and other nature subjects. Its Bird Center activities are outstanding. In addition to lectures and slide shows, there are frequent bird-watching outings. These include regular Thurs morning bird walks at FENCE or at nearby good birding sites in the spring and fall, as well as local, regional, and international birding "ventures" throughout the year.

Rutherford County

CHIMNEY ROCK STATE PARK, 431 Main St., Chimney Rock, NC; (828) 625-9611; chimneyrockpark.com. Chimney Rock Park, in Hickory Nut Gorge, has been a favorite in the Southeast. Its unusual rock formations, spectacular Hickory Nut Falls dropping 404 feet to the gorge below, winding mountainside trails, and delicate wildflowers draw a steady stream of visitors annually. From the parking area, take a 26-story elevator ride to the Sky Lounge, the park's snack and gift shop area. From the deck just outside, you have a wonderful view of the park's landmark and namesake, Chimney Rock. Or try the steps to the Chimney—the rock formations and spectacular views along the way are well worth it. This prominent rocky pedestal gives visitors a spectacular 180-degree view of the Hickory Nut Gorge area and beautiful Lake Lure. Make your way down a stairway from the chimney and choose one of several beautiful trails threading through the rocky outcrops, cliffs, and mountainside. The Skyline Trail winds upward through the woods, leveling out after about a quarter-mile and proceeding along a flat path to the top of beautiful Hickory Nut Falls. A children's trail has playful wildlife sculptures.

The park is full of fascinating rocks, ledges, and natural wildlife. You can squeeze through the crevice known as the Needle's Eye; visit the Grotto, the Rock Pile, and the Moon-Shiner's Cave (with a replica of an old moonshine still); and journey up to the magnificent heights of Inspiration Point. If you get a little weak in the knees at the thought of high places, don't worry. Chimney Rock Park's Forest Stroll Trail, leading from the parking area, is a leisurely 0.75-mile walk to the base of Hickory Nut Falls. There is a viewing deck with a few picnic tables for your convenience. The park closes at 7 p.m. in the summer and one hour and a half after the ticket office closes in the winter.

LAKE LURE TOURS, Lake Lure Marina; 2930 Memorial Hwy., Lake Lure, NC; (828) 625-1373; lakelure.com. Tour the lake *National Geographic* called

Close-up

The Bride and Groom of Pisgah

Many years ago 17-year-old Jim Stratton fell in love with Mary Robinson, the 15-year-old daughter of "Old Man" Robinson. Mary lived with her father at Frying Pan Gap, while Jim Stratton lived across the ridge at Bald Mountain.

Old Man Robinson told Jim to leave his daughter alone and not to come around Frying Pan Gap. Jim, however, didn't pay much attention to the warning, because he and Mary were in love. Just about everyone had a still in the mountains in those days, and Old Man Robinson knew that one sure way to get Jim Stratton's attention was to do something grandiose to let Jim know that he meant business.

One late fall day Jim Stratton was stirring the mash at his still, which was hidden high above a clearing of an old trail on the face of Bald Mountain. Suddenly all the animals and insects of the forest fell silent. Jim took up his long rifle and hid amongst the trees as he watched his mash boiling and bubbling. Soon he saw a fellow appear, cautiously at first, then stepping confidently over to the mash bucket. He was a "federal man," one of many, and Jim knew right away that Old Man Robinson had told them where to find his still.

More than a half-dozen federal officers stepped into the clearing. They proceeded to smash the catching bucket and spill all the good "squeezins" onto the ground. With large axes they crushed the mash vat. It was only when the first federal agent held the still's copper worm in the air like some trophy that Jim was seized by anger and lost all control. With a squeeze of the trigger, the bullet entered the left eye of the federal officer, exiting the back of his skull. The other officers ran back into the woods and down the mountain.

Jim leaped into the clearing and scooped up the brass worm and took off up the mountain. He knew that he had a great deal to do before the feds came looking for him for what he had just done. He headed to Frying Pan Gap, planning to even the score with Old Man Robinson. Crossing the Pisgahs he stopped off at the Widow Peggy Higgins's cabin. He had helped her when she lost her husband. He told her he did wrong, and he had to go higher in the mountains. But there were two things he had yet to do: The first was to even the score, and the second was to get Mary to go away with him. The widow said she'd fetch Preacher Ball and that Jim should return with Mary so they could be properly joined.

Jim got to Frying Pan Gap, and he looked for Old Man Robinson. He was actually relieved when Mary said that her daddy left for town that morning and would be gone into the late evening. Mary said that she'd go anywhere with Jim and that she'd be with him forever.

When the two of them got back to the Widow Higgins's cabin, Preacher Ball was there and ready to perform the wedding ceremony. However, the bride didn't have a proper wedding gown, and they didn't have a wedding ring. Peggy Higgins resolved that right away. She pulled an old trunk from the foot of the bed, and digging down deep, she pulled out a dusty bridal veil, yellowed from age. It was the one she had worn more than 40 years ago. She shook out the dust and smoothed out the wrinkles. Next Peggy Higgins worked the old wedding band off her hand and offered it to the new bride.

When all the right things had been said, the "I dos" and the "I promise," Preacher Ball called down a blessing on them—and it was then they could hear, off in the distance, the braying of the bloodhounds.

The couple went out the back of the cabin and followed the trails that led high up in the Pisgahs. They could hear the hounds coming closer. They climbed higher and ran faster. Soon they could hear the shouts and calling of the men.

Now it's not unusual to see snowfall in the higher elevations in late fall. The snow melts by day and refreezes by night forming rime ice. And that very night a soft snow did begin to fall. As their feet carried them higher and higher, the snow fell faster and faster. The little flakes turned into big flakes. Soon their footprints began to be covered by more snow, and the dogs couldn't follow their scent any longer. The snow got up to their ankles. As they went higher and deeper into the woods the snow reached up to their knees, and when they broke into the clearing on the east face of Pisgah, they were waist deep in the snow.

It was then that winter really set in to the mountains, and it wasn't until the next spring that the federal officers resumed their search. The couple was never found. What was found was a rusted out old long rifle and an old copper worm from a still.

Some say that they got away on that snowy night, over many ridges and through many mountain ranges until they found a place where no one knew them, and where no one ever questioned strangers.

Others know that they are still up on the east face of Pisgah. In fact whenever there is a very hard snowfall, and when it melts and refreezes, you can see Mary standing with her bridal veil down her back, Jim Stratton kneeling beside her with his head bowed. Just stand in Asheville on such a day facing Pisgah, and you'll see them, too.

"one of the 10 most spectacular man-made lakes in the world." A fleet of modern boats offers deluxe seats, full-length canopies, and clear enclosures to keep you comfortable whatever the weather. Tours take 60 minutes, departing every hour from the Town Marina. Be sure to arrive early enough to enjoy the surroundings. Before hopping on board, stroll the wooden boardwalk along the lake or the mile-long walking trail to the gazebo and picnic area with swings for the kids. Even parking your car is a delight here—the rocky-faced mountains are exquisite (especially when the dogwoods are in blossom in the spring). Tickets cost around $6 for children 4 to 12 and $12 for adults. Tours operate Mar through Nov from 10 a.m. to 8 p.m. Visit the website for details about various lunch and dinner cruises. Private charters are also available for all occasions.

> **i** Look out! Heading southeast on Highway 74 just as you come into Chimney Rock is a view so beautiful that you might miss a curve on this windy mountain road. Just take it slow and look to your right at the mountains above with shimmering rock faces and the Rocky Broad River with its swift current tumbling and cascading below.

Transylvania County

BREVARD LITTLE THEATRE, 55 East Jordan St., Brevard, NC; (828) 884-2587; thebrevardlittletheatre.org. This theatrical group is the official theater company of the city and county. The BLT established a new home at 55 East Jordan Street in downtown Brevard, where it still resides today. The group produces four plays for a season that runs from Oct through Aug. It also puts on children's plays, including the very popular *The Nutcracker* in Dec. In addition, there's a very active "BLT to Go" group that provides benefit performances for community and charitable organizations. Certain productions are also staged at the larger Dunham Auditorium on the college campus.

BREVARD MUSIC CENTER, 349 Andante Ln., Brevard, NC; (828) 884-2011, (888) 384-8682; brevardmusic.org. Held on 140 beautiful acres just on the outskirts of town, the Brevard Music Festival had its beginning in 1936. Today it presents more than 70 different concert events from mid-June through mid-Aug in the center's 1,800-seat, open-sided auditorium. Lawn tickets are available after all house seats have been sold. Performances include symphony orchestra, opera, jazz, Broadway musicals, pops, and those of internationally acclaimed guest artists. Included in the past seasons' appearances were Kathleen Battle of the Met, composer/entertainer Marvin Hamlisch, harpist Deborah

Henson-Conant, pianist Garrick Ohlsson, Rhythm & Brass, the US Army Orchestra, and staged productions of Gilbert and Sullivan's *The Mikado*, Puccini's *La Bohème*, Massenet's *Manon*, and Herbert's *Naughty Marietta*. More than half of the events are free to the public. Noted Maestro Keith Lockart, who was a student here, is current artistic director of the center. He continues to serve as the conductor of the Boston Pops Orchestra, and is chief guest conductor of the BBC Concert Orchestra in London, having served for eight years as its principal conductor.

ENGLISH CHAPEL, US 276, Pisgah National Forest; transylvaniaheritage .org. This Methodist church just a few miles from the entrance to Pisgah Forest is a simple structure. It is worth a historical exploration and the setting by the Davidson River is lovely. The Rev. A. F. English bought the land for $5 and founded the church in 1860. It was built by local folks and continues to serve the community and forest visitors. It is usually locked except for Sunday 9:30 a.m. services. An exercise trail that borders the river's rushing, clear waters leads from the church to the Davidson River Campground. Unlike many trails in the forest, this one is wide and level, making for a relaxed stroll.

PISGAH CENTER FOR WILDLIFE EDUCATION, 1401 Fish Hatchery Rd., Pisgah National Forest; (828) 877-4423; ncwildlife.org. Situated adjacent to the Pisgah Forest Fish Hatchery, this educational facility, operated by the North Carolina Wildlife Resources Commission, has exhibits and programs that explain how human activities affect and are affected by wildlife and the natural environment. The center includes a paved walkway to outdoor exhibits focusing on wildlife and fish management, law enforcement, and conservation education. Indoor exhibits feature aquariums containing coastal, Piedmont, and mountain aquatic species and an auditorium. Wildlife educational programs are offered at the center throughout the year.

The center is open daily from 8 a.m. until 5 p.m. except Thanksgiving Day, Christmas Day, and New Year's Day. Admission to both the center and its courses is free.

PISGAH FOREST FISH HATCHERY, 1401 Fish Hatchery Rd., Pisgah National Forest; (828) 877-3121; ncwildlife.org. First it was a logging camp, then a camp for the Civilian Conservation Corps during the Great Depression. Today the Pisgah Forest Fish Hatchery, just off US 276 and at the base of John Rock, is operated by the North Carolina Wildlife Resources Commission. It raises thousands of trout that are released in area streams. Children really like this place. They particularly delight in the wild frenzies when the fish, which come in all sizes, are fed. Even more, they like to feed the fish themselves. To get to the hatchery, drive several miles up US 276 from the Brevard entrance to Pisgah Forest and turn off on FR 475, which is well marked and paved. The hatchery is less than a mile down this road. There are also a number of nice hiking trails in the area.

SOUTHERN MOUNTAINS

Cherokee County

FIELDS OF THE WOOD, 10000 US Hwy. 294, Murphy, NC; (828) 494-7855; cogop.prg/fow. Fields of the Wood is unique in the world. Stretched over 200 acres, this Christian theme park is made up of symbols and words taken from the Bible, often presented in a majestic form. One of the most spectacular displays is a 300-foot-wide marker listing the Old Testament's Ten Commandments in letters 5 feet high and 4 feet wide. Another is the representation of a huge open Bible that takes its text from Matthew 22:37–40, with the words painted in bold, black lettering that can be read from a great distance. A 150-foot cross lies atop All Nations Mountain, surrounded by the flags of all the countries where the Church of God of Prophecy, the park's owners, are active. There is a tomb constructed in the likeness of the one in Jerusalem where many believe that Jesus' body was taken after his crucifixion. You'll also find a cafe, gift shop, and Christian bookstore. The cafe is closed on Mon. The park is open year-round from sunrise to sunset. Admission is free.

Graham County

CHIEF JUNALUSKA'S GRAVE, Off Main Street, Robbinsville, NC. In 1814 a Cherokee leader joined the US Army in a fight against the Creek Indians, vowing that he would kill all the Creeks. During the Battle of Horseshoe Bend, he saved Gen. Andrew Jackson's life but had to admit he left some of the enemy alive. It was then that he was given the nickname of Junaluska, which means "he tried repeatedly but failed." Despite his service to Jackson, who became a US president, he also failed to stop the forced removal of his fellow Cherokee and himself to Oklahoma on the infamous Trail of Tears. The chieftain reportedly remarked at the time that had he known what the future would bring, he would have killed Jackson himself at Horseshoe Bend. Later Junaluska walked from Oklahoma all the way back to North Carolina, where he continued to struggle to keep the remaining Cherokee in their mountain home.

On January 2, 1847, the state legislature made him a North Carolina citizen and gave him a tract of land. When he died on November 8, 1858, he was more than 100 years old. His grave and that of Nicie, his wife, are on a hilltop outside Robbinsville. To reach it, drive past the courthouse on Main Street and turn right toward the Stanley Furniture plant. The gravesite is on the left, marked by a sign. A trail leads up to the two boulders that mark the graves, which are surrounded by an iron fence. It's said that it took eight yoke of oxen a half-day to pull Junaluska's gravestone up the hill. There is also a museum near the site devoted to Junaluska.

FONTANA DAM, 71 Fontana Damn Rd., Fontana Dam, NC. You can drive across this 480-foot-high dam, the highest east of the Rockies, but don't be satisfied with that. Stop at the visitor center for a breathtaking view and make use of the picnic tables there. Inside the center you can take in a short video and other exhibits to learn about the dam's construction and history. After that, spend a dollar for a ride in the stainless steel tram to the dam's base for a look inside the plant itself, where you'll get a lesson on hydroelectric power. This 2,365-foot-wide structure began providing power in 1942 to produce goods during World War II, and it closed in 1944. Today it impounds the 10,600 acres of water that form 29-mile-long Fontana Lake. Historic Fontana Village, now a resort community, was built to house the workers who constructed the dam. The visitor center is open from 9 a.m. until 8 p.m. and is staffed by volunteers who are former TVA employees.

Haywood County

STOMPIN' GROUND, 3116 Soco Rd., US 19, Maggie Valley, NC; (828) 926-1288. The folks in Maggie claim that this is the "Clogging Capital of the World." It features some of the area's best mountain clogging teams from May to Oct on Fri and Sat from early evening to late. The opening event for Folkmoot USA is always held at the Stompin' Ground. It takes place the last week in July. (See our **Festivals and Annual Events** chapter.)

Jackson County

GREAT SMOKY MOUNTAINS RAILROAD, 119 Front St., Dillsboro; (828) 586-8811, (800) 872-4681; gsmr.com. There are few attractions more popular in Western North Carolina than this railway, and there's no better way to watch some of our area's great scenery glide by than from one of its passenger cars. When you catch a ride on the Great Smoky Mountains Railroad, you have your choice of diesel, electric, or steam locomotives, with seating in heated and air-conditioned coaches and open-sided cars. Some seating options at a small additional charge are the Club Car (for adults only) and the Crown Coach. Several different excursion options are offered: the Tuckasegee River Excursion, the Nantahala Gorge Excursion, the Red Marble Gap Excursion, Raft 'n' Rail Excursion, Moonshine and Dine, and many more!

HARRAH'S CHEROKEE CASINO, 777 Casino Dr., Cherokee, NC; (828) 497-7777, (800) HARRAHS; ceasars.com/harrahs-cherokee. The casino, three football fields in size, is open 24 hours a day. Here you'll find 2,300 video gaming machines, including video blackjack, video poker, and video craps, plus many other games. When you've gambled up an appetite, you can satisfy it at several restaurants. Tribal Bingo, run by the Eastern Band of Cherokee Indians, takes place at Harrah's also. A 3,000-seat concert hall brings in huge acts.

JUDACULLA ROCK, 552 Judaculla Rock Rd., off Hwy. 107, Judaculla, NC; judacullarock.com. Judaculla (a name corrupted from the Indian *tsulkalu,* meaning "slant eyes") was a fearful giant of Cherokee lore whose farm was on Tanasee Bald at a point where Jackson, Haywood, and Transylvania Counties converge. One day, it's said, he jumped from his mountaintop home to a valley near what is now Caney Fork Creek, leaving the marks of his landing on a large, exposed piece of soapstone. These marks—pictographic writing on the rock—long predate the Cherokee. There are many theories as to their meanings. Is the rock a boundary marker? A battle commemoration? A peace treaty among unknown tribes? Or is it just ancient graffiti? Judaculla Rock, well-marked by signs, is off Highway 107 between Cashiers and Cullowhee on Caney Fork Road (SR 1737). A lovely 3-mile drive through a bucolic valley of scattered two-story, white frame farmhouses will bring you to the rock, which sits under an open-sided shed next to a cow pasture.

> **i** When visiting the Cherokee Indian Reservation, your first stop should be at the Cherokee Visitor Center across US Highway 441, facing the Museum of the Cherokee Indian (828-497-9195 or 800-438-1601). Here you'll find brochures and information on all Cherokee and area attractions, local restaurants, and sight-seeing. It's open daily from 8 a.m. to 9 p.m. from mid-June through late Aug, 8 a.m. to 6 p.m. from late Aug through Oct, and 8 a.m. to 4:30 p.m. from Nov through mid-June.

MUSEUM OF THE CHEROKEE INDIAN, 589 Tsali Blvd., Cherokee, NC; (828) 497-3481, (888) 665-7249; cherokeemuseum.org. Plan to spend at least two hours at this museum, which has been called "a cutting-edge" example of "how all museums should be." Outside the building is a 20-foot wooden sculpture of Sequoyah (the Cherokee genius who is—as far as we know—the only human to create a written form of language all alone), and inside you can literally walk through Cherokee history. Interactive displays and multisensory exhibits allow you to experience the past. You can listen to storytellers, play the ancient butter bean game, travel the infamous Trail of Tears, and much more. The fine gift shop is loaded with a large selection of books, crafts, artwork, and other Cherokee or Native American items. The museum is open year-round except on Thanksgiving, Christmas, and New Year's Day. Hours are 9 a.m. to 5 p.m. Sept through May and 9 a.m. to 8 p.m. June through Aug. Admission is under $10.

> **i** In the early 1800s, Sequoyah (George Gist), an illiterate, non-English-speaking child of a Cherokee mother and an absent white father, invented the Cherokee alphabet, making the Cherokee the first Native Americans to have a written language. In 1828 the first Cherokee-language newspaper came off the press—the Cherokee Phoenix. Sequoyah has been honored, with a spelling change, by having Sequoia National Park and the sequoia tree named for him. Both are in California.

OCONALUFTEE INDIAN VILLAGE, 218 Drama Rd, Cherokee, NC; (828) 497-2111. Step back more than two centuries in time when you visit this re-created 1750s Cherokee village. Indian guides in native costumes will take you through the village, while others demonstrate such life skills as weaving, pottery, beadwork, food preparation, canoe construction, and arrow-making and hunting techniques. You will see Cherokee homes, a sweat lodge, and the important seven-sided council house. Cherokee history, culture, and social customs will be explained, and you'll have ample opportunity to ask questions. Afterward go back to the areas that interested you and spend as much time as you like exploring further. The village is open from 9 a.m. to 5:30 p.m. daily May 15 through Oct 25. Admission is $20.

Cherokee Lands

Historically the land of the Cherokee encompassed parts of the following states: Kentucky, Tennessee, Alabama, Georgia, South Carolina, North Carolina, Virginia, and West Virginia. Today the nation of the Eastern Band of the Cherokee encompasses less than 60,000 acres in Western North Carolina.

The 1838 removal of the Cherokee has become known as "The Trail of Tears" for the thousands who died en route to the Oklahoma Territory. Each Cherokee was allotted 110 acres in the northeast corner at Thalequah, Oklahoma. Unscrupulous "land grabbers" were able to reduce acreage significantly.

Close-up

The Invisible Warriors

The town of Franklin was built where the Cherokee settlement of Nikwasi once stood. Nikwasi was one of the oldest Cherokee towns and an important ceremonial center. In the old days Indians built their town lodges on large manmade mounds, and Nikwasi's was one of the few that possessed the "everlasting fire," or spiritual connection; hence the lodge was used in religious ceremonies.

Once, long ago, a powerful, unknown tribe invaded the land, destroying the villages and killing the people. One morning at dawn the intruders were seen approaching Nikwasi. The villagers rushed to defend their town but were eventually forced to retreat.

Suddenly a stranger appeared. He spoke and dressed like a chief from the Overhills settlements. The villagers thought he had come to their aid with reinforcements. He shouted to the Nikwasi chief to call off his men—he would defeat the enemy. As the Nikwasi villagers fell back toward the lodge, they saw hundreds of warriors, armed and painted for battle, streaming out of an open doorway in the side of the mound where no doorway had existed before. It was then the villagers recognized the warriors as *nunnehi*—"immortals," or the "people who live anywhere."

Theirs was a race of spirit people, fond of music and dancing, who lived in the highlands and had a great many town lodges, especially on mountain balds. As soon as the *nunnehi* got a short distance from the mound, they became invisible. The invaders could see the weapons but could not see who wielded them; frightened, they began to flee. They tried to hide behind large rocks as they retreated, but the *nunnehis'* arrows flew around the boulders and killed them. When only six or so of the invaders were left alive, they were so upset they just sat down and cried. Since that day the Cherokee have called that spot at the head of the Tuckasegee River *dayulsunyi,* "where they cried."

It was Indian custom to spare a few warriors to return home and tell of their defeat. Thus the invaders went home to the north and the *nunnehi* returned to the mound.

There are countless Cherokee stories involving this spirit race who, when they chose to show themselves, looked like ordinary people. They also appeared to whites during the Civil War. It's said that a large troop of Union soldiers came to Franklin to surprise a small number of Confederates posted there but, upon seeing so many soldiers guarding the town, they turned away.

Macon County

HIGHLANDS NATURE CENTER AND BOTANICAL GARDENS, 930 Horse Cove Rd.; Highlands, NC; (828) 526-2623; highlandsbiological.org. The Highlands Biological Station, one of the oldest research facilities in the country, operates both the center and the gardens. The center is a showcase for the animals and plants found on the Highlands Plateau, a unique ecosystem that attracts top researchers from around the world. Here you'll find user-friendly exhibits, American Indian artifacts, mineral and rock specimens, snakes, salamanders, and mounted specimens of area mammals and birds. In the Botanical Gardens, the trails, with their excellently identified plants and trees, will take you around Lake Ravenel, along a creek, and up to a small waterfall. The center is open from 10 a.m. to 5 p.m. Mon through Sat from Memorial Day to Labor Day. Admission is free. The gardens are there for you to enjoy anytime. Even in winter thick growths of rhododendron, Galax, and doghobble make it a deep-green little paradise.

PERRY'S WATER GARDEN, 136 Givson Aquatic Farm Rd., Franklin, NC; (828) 524-3264; perryswatergarden.net. Even if you never intend to have a water garden, this 12-acre aquatic plant nursery—with its hundreds of lotuses, water lilies, blue-flag irises, and other old and new water- and bog-loving plants—might change your mind. Claiming to be the largest such nursery in the country, it offers a tropical greenhouse, exotic koi and goldfish, old-fashioned antique rose beds, picnic tables, and walking trails. Perry's is open from 9 a.m. to noon and 1 to 5 p.m. Mon through Sat and 1 to 5 p.m. on Sun from Mar through Sept.

Swain County

DARNELL FARMS, 2300 Governors Island Rd., Bryson City, NC; (828) 488-2376; darnellfarms.com. Corn maze season runs July to the end of Oct. The Great Smoky Mountain Corn Maze at Darnell Farms has more than five acres of corn that have been carved in the shape of "Teddy Roosevelt and the Rough Riders." It's a real farm with 20 acres of pumpkins, 17 acres of tomatoes, and 20 acres of sweet corn, ornamental gourds, beans, peppers, and squash, with a daily farmer's market, music, hayrides, and a pumpkin picking patch in the fall. There's entertainment on Sat nights, and in Sept, this is the site for the Old-time and Bluegrass Fiddlers' Convention. There is a small admission charge for the maze.

ATTRACTIONS

Recreation

Leisure time reigns supreme here in the mountains. The quality and diversity of recreational opportunities are unparalleled. After you've been swept along in a white-water raft, come close to nature on a scenic hiking trail, and reeled in a trophy trout on a mountain lake, you're still not finished. Whether you prefer the tamer environs of a city park or the wild river adventure just over the ridge, you'll find just what you're looking for in these hills. The suggestions that follow are just a few of the recreation possibilities.

This chapter highlights major parks and accompanying recreation programs. We also give you an overview of the best water sports here, fishing, mountain biking, rock climbing, hiking, camping, skiing, golfing, rock hounding, and other fun endeavors.

OUTDOOR SAFETY

Let's talk safety. The mountains of North Carolina are still plenty rugged. Nature here, as spectacular as it can be, is also a powerful force and should be respected as such. National parks and forests and any other wilderness areas, are primitive environs, where cell-phone signals don't often reach, are given to drastic temperature fluctuations, and are privy to mud and rock slides. Invariably, every year a hiker or two is lost in the mountains, requiring rescue teams to scour the area. Often there will be no shelters, campgrounds, water spigots, or restrooms, and wilderness trails are maintained to the most primitive standard. There will be few blazes or signs, so a compass and topographic map and knowledge of how to use them are essential. NEVER walk around the top of a waterfall or try to climb one. Every, and we mean *every* year, there are tragic deaths from people slipping on the slick rocks and bashing their heads on the rocks below or drowning.

Driving

When traveling by car on the Blue Ridge Parkway or the back roads of the national forests, make sure you observe all traffic regulations and drive a vehicle that's in good working order. Breaking down in some of the remote regions can spell disaster (or at least great inconvenience). Have enough gasoline to take you to your destination and back again, because gas stations are few and far between on the parkway and can seem a world away when you're sitting by the wayside on a dusty back road. Bring along necessary auto tools and a good spare tire, and make sure your brakes and headlights are in good working order. (These mountains often have steep grades to negotiate, and the Blue Ridge

Parkway's 27 tunnels require the use of headlights.) When packing the car for the trip, include the following items: a first-aid kit, flashlight, blanket, light jacket or sweater, and a change of clothing in case the weather changes.

What to Pack

For any extended hiking or camping activity that will be longer than just a stroll to a waterfall, always have these essentials with you: a map, a compass, a flashlight/headlamp with extra batteries and bulbs, extra food, bottled water, extra clothing, sunglasses, first-aid supplies, matches in a waterproof container, and fire starter.

When taking off into the woods, don't forget to take along a respect for the land and your own personal safety. Before you step foot on the trail, study a map of the area. (Maps are often available at visitor centers and ranger stations or posted on a bulletin board near park entrances.) Know where you're going and don't stray from the trails, many of which are clearly marked. It's easy to become disoriented in deep woods, and steep drop-offs covered by foliage can mean sudden disaster. If you get lost, stay put; you're easier to find that way. It's good to have a pocket whistle when hiking. Use three blasts on the whistle to alert those in search of you. If you get lost near a stream or creek, follow the water downstream; it will most likely lead to a community.

Dress properly for the season, and wear sturdy worn-in shoes with thick, absorbent socks to prevent blistering. This helps in terms of comfort as well as navigation of rough terrain. Changes in elevation make for unpredictable weather. Be aware of the potential for change and be prepared. Bring hats and sunscreen. Sun burns are brutal.

When hiking or camping, never go alone. Always tell someone your route (you are required to sign in with a park ranger for overnight hikes in national parks). And always make your whereabouts and intentions known to others.

Carry plenty of water. Streams may look sparkling and your thirst may be great, but, unfortunately, the water can be contaminated.

Carry along a fully charged cell phone, but do be aware that you may not find a signal everywhere in these mountains.

Trails

Trails are rated by difficulty level, steepness, how obvious the trail is to follow, and the roughness of the tread. Markers indicating difficulty are provided by the forest service and are usually at the beginning of the trail. The easiest trails have obvious routes and easy grades, with some pitches up to 20 percent maximum and a relatively smooth tread. They are indicated by a green mark with a slight curve. More difficult trails are marked with a curving blue line and have routes that are usually recognizable but are somewhat challenging with moderate grades, with some pitches up to 30 percent maximum and a smooth to rough tread. A most difficult trail may not be recognizable, requiring a high degree of skill, and may have a steep grade with some pitches greater than 30 percent and rough tread. The hardest trails will have markers with a black zig-zag on them.

Food and Cooking

It's a good idea to bring a camp stove if you have one (or can borrow or rent one). Use existing fire rings when possible, but make sure there are no burn bans out, due to dry weather. Always make sure the fire is dead before leaving, using sand or water to douse the smoldering embers thoroughly. Fires are prohibited in the Shining Rock Wilderness and Middle Prong Wilderness Areas; therefore you must carry a backpack stove if you wish to cook in this area. Bring plenty of energy-rich, protein-packed edibles. You'll be exerting a great deal of energy while hiking, swimming in mountain pools, or rafting and kayaking. Carry plenty of water and drink often, even when not thirsty. You may become dehydrated before you feel the urge to quench your thirst.

What to Do with Waste

"Pack it in, pack it out." Leave no sign of your time in the woods, not only for the sake of future generations but also for the benefit of the true residents of the woods—the wildlife. Use thoughtful methods of sanitation. Bury all human waste and toilet paper in a hole 6 inches deep and at least 100 feet away from any water source. Tampons and pads should be carried back out with you in sealed containers—the scent of blood could attract wild animals. Do use biodegradable soap and a wash pan; scatter your wash water away from creek banks. Obviously you should take all trash back out with you. Carry re-sealable bags that can be shut almost airtight for your food waste.

Wild Animals

Be aware of your intrusion into the animals' woodland home. Leave all wild animals alone. Black bears have been hibernating for shorter periods and visiting suburban neighborhoods. Do not approach bears. They may look cuddly, but they can be dangerous, especially if you get between a mama bear and her cubs. If one approaches your car, stay inside with the windows rolled up. Make noise on the trail or at your campsite—bears won't be interested in investigating foreign clamor. Do not run; do not climb a tree. Make yourself as large as possible (open up an umbrella or parka if you have one; back away slowly. Before you sleep, take all food out of your tent. Seal your edibles as securely as possible in a backpack and hang it from a tree many yards from your sleeping area.

Snakes seldom bite unless disturbed or teased, but be aware of them and be able to identify poisonous snakes. Rattlesnakes and copperheads thrive in these parts. Dry conditions tend to bring snakes to water sources. Take note: Rattlesnakes do not always rattle their tails before striking and can strike from any position, in any direction. If you are struck by a poisonous snake and have no suctioning kit, seek help immediately. Immobilize the limb and keep the wound below heart level at all times. Try to identify the markings (or snap a photo) of the snake, so medical personnel will know which antivenin to administer. Not every bite will require antivenin, but every bite does need medical evaluation.

Rabies can be carried by the common raccoon, another cute, cuddly looking creature you don't want to approach. Rabies affecting even squirrels and domestic kittens has been reported from time to time. A rabid animal will generally foam at the mouth, act aggressively, and have wild eyes, often rolling back into the head. Stay far away from such animals. If bitten, seek medical treatment immediately.

Insects
Ticks can be a problem almost year-round. Infected ticks can cause Lyme disease. (Should a tick bite you, leaving a red spot that takes on the looks of a bull's-eye, itches, and is accompanied by a fever, see a doctor as soon as possible. These are the indications of Lyme.) Check yourself after being in the woods and follow these tips: Wear light-colored clothing so you can quickly spot ticks on you, tuck pant legs into socks; use insect repellent with DEET, and do not remove ticks with your fingers. Use pointed tweezers or splinter pickers. Lightly grasping the body of the insect, gently and slowly pull the body straight out, so as not to leave the head behind. Do not squeeze the tick, as this could push its bacteria directly into your bloodstream. You should save the tick and take it with you when you seek medical help, enabling the physician to analyze it and prescribe prophylactic antibiotics if necessary.

Mosquitoes can flourish in the damp woods, so bring plenty of repellent. West Nile virus has arrived in the mountains and has claimed its first human victim. So be particularly vigilant about protecting yourself from mosquitoes: Use insect repellent even over clothing, and wear long pants, socks, and long sleeves in heavily infested areas. Mosquitoes are most active from dusk to dawn, so consider avoiding outdoor activities during the early morning or evening hours.

Plant Life
Foliage is abundant on the trails. One of these plants, poison ivy, a common bush, causes an itchy rash and more severe reactions in those allergic to it. It grows as a vine or short shrub with three glossy light-green leaves per stalk. Avoid it. If you feel you have been in poison ivy, wash your skin thoroughly with soap and warm water after contact. The oily sap this plant emits, known as urushiol, can cling to pets' fur, clothing, shoelaces, and even gardening tools for an extended period and plague you months afterward. Wash everything that may have come into contact with the plant.

RECREATION

Hunting

Two words: hunting season. If you hike trails during hunting season, always wear bright "hunter orange" for your protection. Deer season runs from early to mid-Oct and again from late Nov to mid-Dec. Bear season runs from mid-Oct to early Nov and again from mid-Dec to early Jan. These are very general time frames. Be sure to call for specific dates each year.

You can call the 24-hour phone line at the North Carolina Wildlife Resources Commission (919-662-4381 or 800-662-7137), for information on hunting and fishing seasons and regulations in this region of North Carolina.

Waterfalls

Waterfalls are another deceptively beautiful lure of nature here in the mountains. They have a magnetic quality, but they can be deadly. Each year someone thinks the view must be better from the top of the falls—a fatal mistake. There have been deaths every year due to slipping and falling from the tops or even sides of waterfalls. The rocks in any of our mountain streams are moss-covered and slippery, and the water rushing over the falls is swift and cold. One misstep can be the last. View these wonderful waterfalls at the proper distance and from the bottom, looking up. Do not attempt to climb them.

Hypothermia

Hypothermia, the condition that causes a potentially fatal drop in body temperature, is a term you need to know. And contrary to popular belief, you don't have to be stranded in a snowstorm to experience this life-threatening condition. Whenever cold, moisture, and fatigue persist, it takes only a few hours to bring on the fatal results of hypothermia. Poor food intake, improper clothing, and alcohol can contribute to the problem.

Symptoms of hypothermia include exhaustion, uncontrolled shivering, confusion, loss of motor coordination, slurred speech, irrational behavior (like trying to disrobe in the cold), and unconsciousness. A victim of severe hypothermia, which occurs when the body core temperature falls below 92 degrees Fahrenheit, shivers in waves, cannot walk, curls into a fetal position to find the last remnants of warmth in the body, and has rigid muscles. All forms of hypothermia must be treated immediately by drying and warming the victim. For severe hypothermia create a shell of total insulation around the victim and surround the victim with dry clothing, blankets, and multiple sleeping bags. Wrap all of the above in plastic to prevent heat loss as the core temperature rises and pushes warmer blood toward the extremities. Remember that even a 50-degree day can bring on hypothermia if conditions are wet and windy. Keep your head covered in this kind of weather. Body heat may quickly be lost without a hat. All victims of hypothermia should get medical attention.

RECREATION

Heat Exhaustion and Heat Stroke

In warm weather the sun can be intense at these higher elevations. And it's getting hotter. Bring along enough sunblock for all exposed skin. We also recommend sunglasses to cut the glare, and a sun hat. Bring plenty of fluids along and drink them, whether you're thirsty or not. You may become dehydrated even before you feel the urge to quench your thirst. Heat exhaustion, which can lead to heat stroke, must be taken care of immediately. A major increase in the body core temperature can kill a victim within minutes.

Signs to watch out for are sweating, increased pulse, weakness, dizziness, nausea, and thirst. Signs of heat stroke are hot skin, either very pale skin or very flushed skin, decreased urine output, increased temperature, and a change in mental status—disorientation and incapacity to reason or make judgments. Try to help relieve these symptoms immediately. For heat exhaustion, rest in the shade, replace fluid loss with a water-and-salt solution (a teaspoon of salt per quart of water), remove all but the most necessary articles of clothing, and refrain from further physical activity for the day. For heat stroke move the victim to a cool spot. Remove the victim's clothing and pour water on the extremities. Then fan him or her, increasing air circulation and evaporation, or cover the victim with cool, wet cloths and fan him or her. You can also immerse the victim in cool (but not cold) water. Do not allow the heat-stroke sufferer to become cold or the body will begin shivering to produce more heat. Also make sure the person refrains from all physical activity; then seek medical help.

Final Thoughts

Don't be afraid of challenging yourself, but do enter into your outdoor endeavors armed with knowledge, preparation, and training. If you're a wilderness novice, start with the light stuff and work your way up. If we remember to respect the natural environment, our visits to these wood and park lands will be memorable for all the right reasons.

CANOEING

Mountain lakes, including most of those mentioned earlier, are excellent places to go canoeing. Experienced canoeists also like to paddle "white-water rafting and kayaking" rivers. (No canoeing is allowed, however, on the Chattooga River until it crosses the Georgia–South Carolina line.) The New, Davidson, and Green Rivers are also popular, but the French Broad, along with its many tributaries, is probably the favorite and has been designated as a canoe trail by the state. This river forms near Rosman, where the North, West, Middle, and East Forks of the French Broad meet; then it gathers force and below Asheville becomes a wide, sweeping waterway that at times can demand some solid canoeing experience.

If you are inexperienced or simply want assistance with your trip, several companies in the area are outfitters specifically for canoeing.

French Broad River Access Areas

BLANTYRE RIVER PARK, Old Blantyre Rd. This 4-acre park on the western boundary of Henderson and Transylvania Counties off US 64 has river access and a canoe landing ramp.

BUNCOMBE COUNTY RIVER PARKS. There are several river parks in Buncombe County. South of Asheville, three parks—Hominy Creek River Park, Bent Creek River Park, and Glen Bridge River Park—hug the French Broad River along Hwy. 191 and offer easy access. The Ledge River Park is north of town off Hwy. 251. Water picks up speed here.

CHAMPION PARK, US 64. You can put your canoe in at this park or access the river just west of Rosman, where US 64 W. crosses the North Fork of the French Broad. These accesses put you in the quieter stretch of the French Broad as it meanders through woods and farms.

HAP SIMPSON PARK, US Hwy. 276. From Island Ford, it's 13 miles to this park, just south of Brevard. It's a small, pleasant park with picnic tables and river access. A 15-mile paddle from here will take you to the Blantyre River Park, mentioned earlier.

ISLAND FORD ACCESS AREA, off US 64 W. To reach this area 13 miles downstream from Champion Park, turn off US 64 W. onto Island Ford Road just a short distance outside Brevard. There's a large sign marking the site at the bridge across the river on Island Ford.

TRACKING STATION, off Hwy. 215. During the spring and after a rain, sections of the North Fork of the French Broad are runnable, but only by the very experienced canoeist. Cutting through a gorge on the eastern edge of the Nantahala National Forest, the trip is 7.2 miles from the access point by the bridge at the old tracking station just off Hwy. 215 (SR 1326) to the access point on US 64 at Island Ford Road near Brevard mentioned in the Island Ford description earlier. In that distance the river drops 390 feet with a difficulty factor generally of 4 to 5 (two areas rate a 6). Before you attempt this run, make sure that the river gauge on the south side of the bridge at US 64 is at least 3 inches above 0. You need that much water for a reasonably safe journey on the North Fork.

WESTFIELD RIVER PARK, Fanning Bridge Rd. This 19-acre park has river access, a canoe landing camp, and a recreation area. Fanning Bridge Road is off Hwy. 280 at the northern boundary of Henderson and Buncombe Counties.

FISHING

No matter where you are in the Western North Carolina mountains, you're never more than a few miles from a fishing lake, a trout pond, or one of our hundreds of miles of trout streams. However, with the exceptions noted below, North Carolina State fishing licenses and permits are required for all residents and nonresidents older than 16 who want to fish. Anyone younger than 16 may use a parent's or guardian's license. Licenses and permits are available at most discount stores, such as Wal-Mart and Kmart. The cost will range from $20 to $40 depending on the duration of the license and whether or not you are a state resident.

Fishing in National Forests

Fishing in national forest lakes is allowed year-round, but fishing in the forests' rivers and streams is regulated and sometimes restricted. To fish in state-designated trout waters, anglers will need a North Carolina fishing license and trout permit. Streams located on game lands require a special-use permit as well.

Brook, brown, and rainbow are the dominant species of freshwater trout in the area, and for management purposes public mountain trout streams are designated as Wild Trout Waters (high-quality waters that sustain trout populations by natural reproduction) and Hatchery Supported Waters (waters that must be stocked periodically to sustain fishing and are usually closed in Mar). These are further classified as Catch and Release/Artificial Lures Only, Catch and Release/Artificial Flies Only, and Delayed Harvest Waters. These designations are marked with specifically colored signs along the watercourses, but these colors can vary from area to area, so acquaint yourself with them.

Because regulations, including catch limits, change according to where you're fishing, it's up to you to know the rules. So before baiting a hook, contact the North Carolina Wildlife Resources Commission (919-662-4373) for full information or pick up a copy of *N.C. Inland Fishing, Hunting, and Trapping Digest* where licenses are sold.

The Cherokee Indian Reservation

The Cherokee Indian Reservation has 30 miles of regularly stocked streams. State records for a brown trout (15 pounds, 8 ounces) and a brook trout (7 pounds, 7 ounces) were caught in these waters. To fish in tribal water, you need no state license, North Carolina or otherwise. All you need is a Tribal Fishing Permit, available at nearly two dozen reservation businesses.

The permit sells for a nominal fee and is valid for one day, with a creel limit of 10 fish. Permits for longer periods, such as three or five days, are also available. Children younger than 12 don't need a permit as long as they are with someone with the proper permit. Fishing is permitted on the reservation from a half-hour before sunrise to a half-hour after sunset. Most of Mar is closed to fishing, with the annual season opening the last Sat of Mar and continuing until the last day of Feb the following year.

Over 400,000 rainbow, brook, and brown trout are added to the existing fish population each year, so some streams are closed on Tues and Wed for stocking. The reservation's "Fish and Game Management" brochure, which is readily available almost everywhere, gives the schedule for which streams are closed for stocking. If you'd prefer pond fishing, you'll find three well-stocked trout ponds on Big Cove Road in front of the KOA campground. A tribal permit is required to fish in ponds and streams.

The Great Smoky Mountains National Park

The Great Smoky Mountains National Park has more than 600 miles of streams full of rainbow and brown trout. Some of the more popular ones include Deep Creek, Noland Creek, and the Oconaluftee River and its tributaries. Remote Forney, Hazel, and Eagle Creeks, all very good fly-fishing streams, can only be reached by boat over Lake Fontana, by horseback, or by long treks through the park. In the park you must have either a valid North Carolina or Tennessee fishing license; fishing stamps are unnecessary. Make sure you check park regulations at a ranger station or visitor center before you fish.

Possession of any native brook trout is prohibited. That's because that fish's range in the Smokies has declined by 70 percent since 1900 due to unsound logging practices before the park was established and from competition with the rainbow and brown trout that were introduced into the waters.

Trout Ponds

Other places where you don't need a state fishing license are the more than 35 trout farms scattered throughout the region. You can contact the North Carolina Agricultural Department (919-733-0635) or a local North Carolina Cooperative Extension Service for a trout farm brochure that lists the names, addresses, and phone numbers of members of the North Carolina Trout Growers Association and includes a map to help you find the farms. Recreational trout fishing in these ponds requires no elaborate equipment, and there are no limits to the catch. Many places will clean your fish free of charge.

Rates at trout farms vary. You might pay $2 or $3 per pound or perhaps $10 per day with a catch limit.

GOLF

Cool summers and mild winters divided by long rejuvenating springs and lingering, colorful autumns make "mountain golf," as it's commonly called here, a year-round pleasure. During the dog days of summer, you can head for one of the higher-altitude courses—up at 3,000 feet or more—for a decided drop in degrees. Or later in the year, if a particular day seems too chilly for a game, you can play one of the courses in the warmer "thermal belt" down around Tryon in Polk County, where the elevation is only 1,100 feet.

Wherever you play, you'll be surrounded by beauty and challenged by courses sculpted around undulating hills, deep mountain valleys, rivers, lakes, waterfalls, and majestic rock formations, all kept lusciously green by some 50 inches of rainfall spread relatively evenly throughout the year. Because of the hilly nature of many of the courses, golf carts are popular. Some courses require them.

There are dozens of public, semipublic, resort, and private courses scattered around the region. Some resort courses are open only to guests, but many offer reasonably priced golf packages that include accommodations and, often, meals. Others are open to the general public, but most require advance reservations. Here we give you a taste of the variety offered at our favorite courses that allow some public play.

Northern Mountains

Alleghany County

NEW RIVER GOLF AND COUNTRY CLUB, 611 Golf Course Rd., Sparta, NC; (336) 372-4869; sparta-nc.com/newrivergolf. New River Golf and Country Club is an 18-hole, par 71 rolling terrain course featuring front and back nines as different as night and day. The front nine is like a flatland course, whereas the back nine is a true mountain course, with many hills. Yardages are 5,601 and 5,741 (women's and men's tees). The club is open to the public daily. To get here, turn at the sign after Twin Oaks General Store on US Hwy. 221 S.

Ashe County

MOUNTAIN AIRE GOLF CLUB, 1104 Golf Course Rd., West Jefferson, NC; (336) 877-4716; mountainaire.com. This well-established public course offers 18 holes on well-maintained fairways complemented by the natural, rugged beauty of the Appalachian Mountains. Greens fees are under $40 per person including cart. Amenities include carts, club rentals, and a driving range. Lessons and seasonal memberships are available, as are group rates. The club pro is Mark Hagel. The developers here also offer home sites in an adjacent golf course community called Fairway Ridge.

Avery County

BLUE RIDGE COUNTRY CLUB, US 221 N., Linville Falls, NC; (828) 756-7001; blueridgecc.com. This relatively new semiprivate championship golf course sits in a beautiful valley with wonderful mountain views. Four tee boxes allow for various skill levels and playing options. Yardage for this challenging mountain course ranges from 4,800 to 6,900. The course features subtle elevation changes, gentle terrain, and mountain vistas. Ongoing development is enhancing the course's lovely North Cove Valley location. Fees include carts.

Memberships are available. The Lodge at Blue Ridge operates as a 12-suite facility with all rooms including a private riverfront deck and a stone fireplace. Conference rooms are also available.

HAWKSNEST GOLF AND SKI RESORT, 2058 Skyland Dr., Banner Elk, NC; (828) 963-6561 or (888) 429-5763; hawksnest-resort.com. Located off Hwy. 105, Hawksnest Golf Course is nestled high in the Blue Ridge Mountains. This par 72 course with large bentgrass greens offers the challenge of a true mountain course to golfers of all abilities. The thrill of playing this championship course is surpassed only by the majestic views from every hole (and the cool High Country weather). Facilities also include a well-stocked golf shop and full-service snack bar. Yardage is 4,799 and 5,953.

Mitchell County

GRASSY CREEK GOLF CLUB, 2360 Swiss Pine Lake Dr., Spruce Pine, NC; (828) 765-7436; grassycreek.com. This public championship 18-hole, par 72 course is just 4 miles from the Blue Ridge Parkway. An 8,000-square-foot clubhouse includes a restaurant, meeting space, and pro shop. There is also a driving range on site. Greens fees are $35 weekdays and $42 weekends and include carts. Yardage is 6,277 and 5,744.

Watauga County

BOONE GOLF CLUB, 433 Fairway Dr., Boone, NC; (828) 264-8760; boonegolfclub.com. This 18-hole course designed by Ellis Maples is a par 71. Level and gently rolling fairways and large bentgrass greens are features. Yardage is 6,400. The club is open daily to the public and features electric carts and a restaurant.

WILLOW CREEK GOLF COURSE, 354 Bairds Creek Rd., Vilas, NC; (828) 963-6865; willowvalley-resort.com. This challenging nine-hole, par 27 course is set in a valley. The course features a great deal of variety and offers senior citizens and student discounts during weekdays. Yardage is 1,351 and

1,574. The golf course is 3 miles outside Boone, coming from Banner Elk on Hwy. 105.

Yancey County

MOUNT MITCHELL GOLF CLUB, 11484 Hwy. 80 S., Burnsville, NC; (828) 675-5454; mountmitchellgolf.com. This perfect vacation course is cradled in the valley below Mount Mitchell, the highest peak east of the Mississippi. Vacation rentals—privately owned houses and town houses—are available around the perimeter of the course. It is a lovely, scenic location. Yardage ranges from 5,500 to 6,500.

Central Mountains

Buncombe County

ASHEVILLE MUNICIPAL GOLF COURSE, 226 Fairway Dr., Asheville, NC; (828) 298-1867; ashevillegc.com. An 18-hole golf course designed by Donald Ross to be challenging and fun for golfers of all skill levels. The front nine holes are flat with a wide-open layout allowing the use of a driver on most holes. The back nine holes of the course are wooded with several elevation changes. The Swannanoa River runs along the course with beautiful views of the Blue Ridge Mountains. Be sure to visit the putting green, chipping green, and practice bunker before heading out onto the golf course.

BLACK MOUNTAIN GOLF COURSE, 17 Ross Dr., Black Mountain, NC; (828) 669-2710; blackmountaingolf.org. This public par 72 course, operated by the town of Black Mountain, about 20 minutes east of Asheville, boasts one of the country's longest par 6 holes at 747 yards. The course offers not only challenging fairways but marvelous views of the surrounding mountains. The quaint town of Black Mountain, noted for its antiques shops, restaurants, and musical tradition, is nearby. This friendly, community golf course offers a multitude of discounts for senior citizens, Black Mountain residents, junior golfers (18 and younger whose parents are not members), and families. A pro shop and snack bar are also available.

Henderson County

CROOKED CREEK GOLF COURSE, 764 Crooked Creek Rd., Hendersonville, NC; (828) 692-2011; crookedcreekhendersonville.com. This 18-hole, 6,636-yard, par 72 championship course, situated just 1.5 miles from Hendersonville, is close enough for residents to take off for a quick game on a long lunch hour. Open to the public year-round, the course has a wide-open feel with Bermuda grass fairways and bentgrass greens. There's a practice green, range, snack bar, and pro shop. Crooked Creek provides both riding and push carts as well as lessons from a pro.

CUMMINGS COVE GOLF AND COUNTRY CLUB, 3000 Cummings Rd., Hendersonville, NC; (828) 891-9412; cummingscove.com. Designed by Robert E. Cupp, former on-site golf architect of Nicklaus Design Company, this Scottish-style course has been rated as one of the top 50 in North Carolina by *Golf Week* magazine. Embankments flank many of the greens of this challenging 5,288-yard, par 71 course, and woods border the entire course. Amenities include a modern clubhouse, pro shop, tennis courts, and pool. The golf shop is in the clubhouse adjacent to the Cummings Road entrance gate at 925 Lakeledge Court, Hendersonville. Cummings Cove is 8 miles from Hendersonville off US Hwy. 64 W. and is semiprivate. Tee times are required.

> **i** Due to frequent Carolina showers, it's wise to get a covered cart and stick an umbrella in your golf bag

ETOWAH VALLEY COUNTRY CLUB AND GOLF LODGE, 470 Brickyard Rd., Etowah, NC; (828) 891-7141 or (800) 451-8174; etowahvalley .com. Conveniently situated halfway between Hendersonville and Brevard in the small community of Etowah, this semiprivate, 18-hole championship course, designed by Edmund Ault and beautified by horticulturist Jean-Claude Linossi, has bentgrass greens measuring up to 9,000 square feet. Its three nine-hole courses and four tee positions allow for a variety of 18-hole combinations. For example, the rather flat south course plays from 2,822 to 3,507 yards (par 36); the west course, with its large greens and bunkers, from 2,800 to 3,601 yards (par 36); and the open, rolling north course from 2,615 to 3,404 yards (par 37). Other amenities include modern lodges, lighted putting greens, a driving range, heated swimming pool, clubhouse, bathhouse, fitness center, pro shop, restaurant, lounge, and meeting and banquet facilities for groups of up to 200.

ORCHARD TRACE GOLF CLUB, 3389 Sugarloaf Rd., Hendersonville, NC; (828) 685-1006. Night doesn't bring an end to golfing at this 18-hole, par 54, 2,139-yard public course nestled in the heart of Henderson County's apple country. Seventy-two floodlights illuminate its entire 34 acres, making it the first fully lighted links in Western North Carolina. The course is made up of bluegrass fairways and bentgrass greens meandering around a small pond and two winding creeks. Hole distances vary from 81 to 212 yards. The clubhouse features a snack bar and a pro shop.

Rutherford County

CLEGHORN PLANTATION GOLF & COUNTRY CLUB, 183 Golf Circle, Rutherfordton, NC; (828) 286-9117; cleghornplantation.com. This 18-hole George Cobb–designed course is in the foothills of the mountains. The course tips out at 6,762 yards with a course rating of 73.3 and slope of 136. There are large putting greens for short game practice as well as a grass driving range for warming up before your round. The pro shop is fully stocked with balls, gloves, shoes, and shirts and there's a full service restaurant with full bar.

MEADOWBROOK GOLF CLUB, 1211 Meadowbrook Rd., Rutherfordton, NC; (828) 863-2690 or (866) 863-2690. This 6,400-yard course was built on the historic Deck family farm. It continues to be family owned. The 18-hole course runs up hills and down, through meadows, and along two creeks, creating challenges on both nines. All rates include carts.

RUMBLING BALD ON LAKE LURE, 112 Mountains Blvd., Lake Lure, NC; (828) 625-3016 or (800) 260-1040; rumblingbald.com. Two golf courses here provide ample diversion. Apple Valley Golf Course will challenge and delight pros and novices alike with an 18-hole, 72 par course at 6,756 yards and 74.4 USGA rating, designed by Dan Maples. It was named one of the most beautiful mountain courses by *Golf Digest*'s "Places to Play." Bald Mountain Golf Course, at 6,283 yards, 18 holes and a 71.3 USGA rating, designed by William B. Lewis in 1968, has stunning mountain views to boot.

Transylvania County

SHERWOOD FOREST GOLF CLUB, 29 Cardinal Rd., Brevard, NC; (828) 884-7825; sherwoodforestncgolf.com. Sherwood Forest Golf Course is an 18-hole, par 3 course in an Audubon Sanctuary development. The course has received the first stage of certification from the Audubon Sanctuary Golf Course Certification Program. A fully stocked pro shop, custom club repair shop, and a club room with snack bar are good amenities.

> **i** Does your golf game improve in the mountains? Some players swear their shots travel higher and farther here due to the thinner atmosphere.

Southern Mountains

Clay County

CHATUGE SHORES GOLF COURSE, 260 Golf Course Rd., Hayesville, NC; (828) 389-8940; chatugeshoresgolf.com. This very attractive 18-hole, par

72 course serves the residents of several surrounding counties including Clay, Cherokee, and Graham. Yardage is 6,687. There's a pro-shop and golf instruction available, too. The Greenside Grill is open for lunch and dinner seven days a week during the summer months.

Haywood County

LAKE JUNALUSKA GOLF COURSE, 756 Golf Course Rd., Waynesville, NC; (828) 456-5777. This attractive golf course is directly across the highway from the Lake Junaluska Conference Center. Several holes provide panoramic views of the 200-acre lake and surrounding mountains. This is an 18-hole, 5,034-yard par 68 course. Wireless internet access is available in the cafe area.

MAGGIE VALLEY CLUB AND RESORT, 1819 Country Club Dr., Maggie Valley, NC; (828) 926-1616 or (800) 438-3861; maggievalleyclub.com. This nationally acclaimed, 18-hole, par 72 course has been the site of four North Carolina Open Golf Tournaments and numerous other tournaments. *Golf Week* rates Maggie Valley as one of America's best, and its bentgrass greens have been ranked among the top 15 in the nation. It's diverse and challenging: The first nine holes run through the rolling terrain of the valley, while the back nine wind through the mountains. Accommodations include cozy guest rooms and mountainside villas surrounded by more than 35,000 square feet of well-tended gardens. There is a heated pool, a restaurant, and a pub that offers resort-style nightlife. Call for special package rates.

SPRINGDALE COUNTRY CLUB AND RESORT, 200 Golfwatch Rd., Canton, NC; (828) 235-8451 or (800) 553-3027; springdalegolf.com. Springdale is another community resort centered around its excellent golf course. Eleven miles from Canton, not far from its entrance to the Blue Ridge Parkway, and surrounded by the grandeur of the Great Smoky Mountains, the course measures a challenging 6,812 yards from the championship tees. The 429-yard, par 4 no. 4, for example, has you punching your second shot through a narrow opening up to a trap-protected green. On the flatter and shorter back nine, the 417-yard, par 4 no. 15 doglegs left and calls for a second shot across a pond. Family owned and operated since 1968, and now under new ownership, the roots of Springdale are firmly planted in a mix of golf, food, and good old Southern hospitality. Golf packages include unlimited golf, your personal golf cart for two, full country breakfast buffet, and family-style dinners each evening.

WAYNESVILLE COUNTRY CLUB INN, 176 Country Club Dr., Waynesville, NC; (828) 456-3551 or (800) 627-6250; twigolfresort.com. Here 27 holes of golf blend with mountain streams, ponds, and the ever-present

RECREATION

mountain views. The links, made up of lush fairways and picture-perfect bent-grass greens, consist of three separate and distinct par 35, nine-hole courses that start and finish at the clubhouse. Each hole offers four sets of tees, thus ensuring a pleasurable experience for golfers at all levels of play. Guests can choose from lodge rooms, cottages, or villas, and several restaurants. You'll also find tennis courts, a pool, and a pro shop. Be sure to ask about Waynesville's special Getaway Holiday Packages as well as daily golf packages that start as low as $35 per person, double occupancy, during the uncrowded winter season.

Jackson County

HIGH HAMPTON RESORT, Hwy. 107 S., Cashiers, NC; (828) 743-2450 or (800) 334-2551; highhamptonresort.com. Sitting at 3,600 feet, this 1,400-acre estate with its private 35-acre lake surrounds a historic country inn and its nearby cottages. Lined by towering pines, hemlocks, and mountain laurel, the stunning High Hampton Resort golf course created by eminent golf course architect, George W. Cobb, ASGCA, is currently being redesigned as a Fazio course to take full advantage of its magnificent mountain setting. The inn is also undergoing renovation until 2020.

SAPPHIRE NATIONAL GOLF CLUB, 50 Slicer's Ave., Sapphire, NC; (828) 743-1174 or (800) 533-8268; sapphirenational.com. This challenging 6,147-yard golf course, with water hazards on nine holes, plus a waterfall hole, is a part of the 5,000-acre, all-season Sapphire Valley resort that grew around the old Fairfield Inn, built in the late 1890s. National offers a memorable experience for all avid golfers, from its dramatic par 4, 13th hole that is nestled beside a majestic waterfall, to the postcard par 3, 15th hole that hosts an island green. Military, fire, and police receive special discount rates. Also discounts for junior golfers and students and twilight rates.

> i The top of Whiteside Mountain in Jackson County offers a fantastic view of Cashiers Valley, the upper Chattooga River watershed, and the surrounding Blue Ridge Mountain peaks. A fairly easy 1.5-mile loop circles the summit with a 0.5-mile side trail to Devil's Courthouse. From Cashiers, take US Highway 64 West for 5 miles to Whiteside Mountain Road (SR 1690). Turn left onto this road and continue for about a mile until you reach the Whiteside Mountain parking area on your left. There is a $2 per vehicle parking fee (see our Forests, Parks, and Waterfalls chapter).

Macon County

GOLF CLUB AT MILL CREEK, 341 Country Club Dr., Franklin, NC; (828) 524-4653; thegolfclubatmillcreek.com. Bordered on three sides by the incredible natural beauty of the Nantahala National Forest, the main attraction at this 380-acre community resort is still the 18-hole championship golf course. Rolling terrain, rippling creeks, and thick stands of pine and willow trees interweave with the lush fairways and carefully manicured greens. As interesting as it is beautiful, this course can challenge players of any skill level. Half- and three-quarter-acre home sites and single-family homes are for sale. Two-day, weekly, and monthly rentals of deluxe villas also are available. Prices vary with the season. Golf packages are available.

Swain County

SMOKY MOUNTAIN COUNTRY CLUB, 1300 Conley Creek Rd., Whittier, NC; (828) 497-2772; carolinamountaingolf.com. This course features impeccably maintained bentgrass greens and Bermuda tees and fairways. The course plays just over 6,100 yards (par 71), with almost 400 feet of elevation change. Brace yourself for arresting views at significant elevations to target areas below. For golf package guests, Smoky Mountain Country Club offers a full destination resort with on-site luxury condominium lodging, heated pool and whirlpool spa, lighted tennis courts, fitness room, and dining (with a full bar) at The Persimmon Grille.

> **i** For a stunning view of the town of Highlands in Macon County, drive to the nature center on Horse Cove Road just outside town. It's a 20-minute, moderate hike from there to the Sunset Rocks Overlook. In addition to Highlands, you'll be able to see the whole of historic Horse Cove. A sign, ravenel park, marks the trailhead.

HIKING

Here in the North Carolina mountains, we are blessed with an amazing array of beautiful places to explore on foot. There's the spectacular Blue Ridge Parkway that runs almost the entire length of Western North Carolina, and our proximity to major national forests such as Pisgah and the Great Smokies brings hiking possibilities virtually to our back doors. The Appalachian Trail runs right through our mountains. Numerous state and memorial parks in the region also have marked hiking trails. But be alert: The blazes on some trails are becoming faded and more difficult to see.

Be prepared with appropriate clothing and walking shoes or boots suited to the terrain and take water and food along if you'll be traveling any distance into a remote area. Be aware of the sudden weather changes that can occur in these mountains. It's a good idea to carry a small flashlight and a whistle in case you get lost. If you do get lost, stay put. Three periodic short bursts on your whistle will help alert others to your location (see our section on Outdoor Safety in this chapter).

In this section we point out just a few of the top hiking destinations, but you can find your own favorites by just heading toward the horizon or along a dusty country road that runs through a forgotten wood. Numerous excellent books on the subject are available, including: *Hiking North Carolina*, *Hiking the Blue Ridge Parkway*, and *Best Easy Day Hikes Blue Ridge Parkway*, all by Randy Johnson; *Scavenger Hike Adventures: Great Smoky Mountains National Park* by Kat and John LaFevre; and *Walking the Blue Ridge* by Leonard M. Adkins. And be sure and take advantage of another valuable resource: ranger stations in your area. (See our **Forests, Parks, and Waterfalls** chapter for a listing.)

> ℹ If you're hiking alone, let friends know where you are going, which trails you might be taking, and how long you will be gone. A cell phone is often a lifesaver in unusual circumstances, but be aware that reception can be weak or nonexistent in many areas.

RECREATION

Northern Mountains

Hiking in the northern mountains is centered around the Blue Ridge Parkway and the popular trails of Cumberland Knob, the 30-mile trail system of Doughton Park, the mist-shrouded trails of Mount Mitchell (see our chapter on **Forests, Parks, and Waterfalls**), or the family-outing trails of Moses Cone and Julian Price Memorial Parks (see our chapter on the **Blue Ridge Parkway**).

Grandfather Mountain, near Linville, is another popular hiking area; a permit and fee are required (see our **Attractions** chapter). The 3,000-acre preserve is laced with nine trails designated by the National Park Service as National Recreation Trails that vary in length and levels of endurance.

Glen Burney Trail skirts the cascading New Year's Creek in Blowing Rock, as the stream falls into the John's River Gorge south of town. The 1.5-mile foot trail is steep—it descends some 800 feet below Blowing Rock—and provides breathtaking vistas of two substantial waterfalls: the 45-foot Glen Burney and the 55-foot Glen Mary. Take Laurel Lane off Main Street to the Annie Cannon Park parking area where a wooden trail map marks the trailhead.

Close-up

Three Famous Trails

The Appalachian National Scenic Trail

This legendary trail runs through 14 eastern states from Mount Katahdin in Maine to Springer Mountain in Georgia and takes an average of four to five months to hike. More than 9,000 people have made this journey, but thousands of others have enjoyed shorter sections of it.

Almost 302 miles of the Appalachian Trail pass through our mountains. The trail crosses the Georgia–North Carolina line near Bly Gap in Georgia, runs through the Nantahala National Forest, crosses into the Great Smoky Mountains National Park at the Fontana Dam, cuts diagonally across the length of the park, and weaves its way along the North Carolina–Tennessee border, exiting our state near Elk Park. It is blazed with white rectangles and a chain of shelters are spaced 8 to 12 miles apart throughout the entire trail.

You can access this famous trail at many points throughout its journey through North Carolina. Any good trail map of the region will show you where. You can also get detailed guidebooks at district offices or from the Appalachian Trail Conference, PO Box 807, Harpers Ferry, WV 25425-0807. For more information, call toll-free (888) 287-8673 or visit appalachiantrail.org.

The Mountains-to-the-Sea Trail

The trail, which was begun in 1985, will eventually run from Clingmans Dome, the highest point in the Great Smoky Mountains National Park, to the state's lowest elevation on the Outer Banks at Nags Head. This will be a travelway with various sections open to hiking, mountain biking, horseback riding, and/or canoeing. It will cover more than 900 miles and is scheduled to be completed in the year 2020. However, 216 miles already cross our mountains from Blowing Rock on the Blue Ridge Parkway south to Balsam Gap, where the parkway crosses US 19 north of Sylva.

Central and Southern Mountains

Even in the more urban central mountain region surrounding Asheville, there are plenty of easy-to-get-to hiking opportunities. Head out on the Blue Ridge Parkway where many trails intersect with parking and overlook areas or stroll along the paths that follow the Swannanoa River on the Warren Wilson College campus just east of Asheville. The North Carolina Arboretum also features many miles of wildflower-rich, wooded trails in its 426-acre park.

This trail will take you through just about every ecosystem found in the Southern Appalachian Mountains, from high-elevation grass balds to cove hardwood forests and from mountain ridges to thickets of rhododendrons. It is generally blazed with three-inch white dots, except in areas such as the Middle Prong Wilderness, where routed wood signs point the way.

The Bartram Trail

From 1773 until 1777, William Bartram, a Philadelphia naturalist, traveled throughout the Southeast, writing exact and vivid descriptions of the plants and animals he saw and of the Native Americans he encountered. He published the writings in 1791 as *The Travels of William Bartram*, and they are still wonderful to read today.

Now a memorial trail follows as closely as possible his original route across South Carolina, Georgia, and the Nantahala National Forest of North Carolina. The trail enters the state just south of Highlands, near Rabun Bald, curves in a north-to-west direction through Western North Carolina, and will eventually link up with the John Muir Trail in Tennessee. Currently it climbs from the Georgia line to the crest of the Blue Ridge Mountains before descending to the Little Tennessee River Valley south of Franklin. Here a canoe trail down the Little Tennessee River to Franklin is under consideration. At Franklin it turns west and ascends the Nantahala Mountains to Wayah Bald, which at 5,385 feet is the highest point on the trail. It joins the Appalachian Trail briefly and descends to Nantahala Lake. Continuing mainly on private lands, it reaches Appletree Campground in the upper Nantahala Gorge then climbs up and over Rattlesnake Knob before reaching the "put in" on the Nantahala River. From the river it ascends Tulula Gap and continues along the crests of the Snowbird Mountains. The trail has been constructed as far as Porterfield Gap, south of the Joyce Kilmer Memorial Forest.

To learn more about this trail, order maps, or to become a member of the society that is establishing the trail, write to the North Carolina Bartram Trail Society, Route 3, PO Box 406, Sylva. Maps are also available from the NFS.

US 276 from the Blue Ridge Parkway down to Pisgah National Forest is a hiker's paradise. Some of the favorite trails originating off this highway include North Cove, Pilot Mountain, Art Loeb, Coon Tree, Looking Glass Rock, Cedar Rock, and Black Mountain Trails. Stop by the ranger station/visitor center just a mile inside the forest's boundary for maps and information. There is also a 0.6-mile Pisgah Ecology Trail behind the center. (For other great hiking trails, see "**Three Famous Trails**" Close-up in the chapter.)

HORSEBACK RIDING

This is true "horse country." Beautiful horse farms—many specializing in Arabians, Appaloosas, Tennessee Walkers, or other breeds—beautify our mountain landscapes. Riding stables and riding schools are scattered throughout. Many children have horses for pets instead of dogs or cats, and two horses in a pasture seem almost as common as two cars in a garage. WATCH FOR HORSES signs dot the secondary roads, and somewhere in the region nearly every weekend, a horse show takes place.

Where to Ride

Part of the reason for the popularity of horses here is that there are so many places to ride. In addition to private trails, fields, and pastures, there are many quiet dirt and paved roads that are used for horseback riding. There are also designated riding trails in the Pisgah and Nantahala National Forests and in the Great Smoky Mountains National Park. These are clearly marked with a horse sign, and you're not allowed on any other trails, though horses are permitted on many Forest Service roads.

The Tsali Recreation Area in the Nantahala National Forest (see our earlier Fontana Lake entry) is one of the premier riding areas in the Southeast. There is a trail fee charged. There is access to more than 18 miles of bridle trails, but be forewarned: Mountain bikes are also allowed here, and although hikers and bikers should yield to horses, riders should always yield to motorized vehicles. Meandering through pine and hardwood forests, the trails cover terrain as varied as wide-packed dirt paths and rocky ones that overlook the lake.

In the Pisgah Forest two of the longer trails are the 12-mile South Mills River Trail in the Pisgah District and the rugged 18.4-mile Buncombe Horse Range Trail in the Appalachian Toecane District. The latter trail is suitable for overnight rides; on Community Hill, at 5,782 feet, you'll find a trail shelter with 10 wire bunks, a picnic shed, a horse corral, and a nearby spring.

Although most horse trails in the Pisgah District are for day rides or for primitive camping along the trails only, there is more developed camping at the South White Pines group campsite and the Harmon Den Horse Camp (tents only, open year-round). For more information contact the Pisgah District office at (877) 444-6777 or see National Forest Camping in the Accommodations chapter.

Rider Etiquette

To lessen the impact on trails, the park service staff asks that horseback riders travel in groups of six or fewer and that they stay on designated pathways, because cutting across switchbacks tramples plants and can cause severe erosion. Try to avoid tying your horse to a tree, but if this becomes necessary, use a rope or a tree-saver hitch to avoid damage. It's better to picket or hobble your horse and move stock periodically to reduce trampling and prevent overgrazing.

Off-Road Vehicle Trails

The late 1980s locked the Forest Service in conflict with the owners of off-road vehicles. Jeeps, four-wheelers, motorcycles, and other all-terrain gadabouts were racing through the forests, creating erosion that polluted streams and endangered some trophy-trout waters, including the Lower Tellico.

Today, the Forest Service, off-road vehicle (ORV) owners, environmentalists, and landowners whose property was being harmed have worked out a plan that sanctions areas for the sport and establishes rules and regulations to govern it. At this time an individual does not need a permit to use an area set aside for ORVs (or ATVs, all-terrain vehicles), but that could change. A fee is charged for groups or commercial events. You don't even have to have a valid driver's license, but minors who operate these vehicles must be under the direct supervision of adults.

Trails in these areas range from a 15 percent pitch to a 50 percent pitch. You must know your vehicle and have good driving skills, and you should wear a sturdy helmet to lessen your chance of head injuries. Other tips for riders: Protect against erosion and stay on the road or trail, don't cut across switchbacks, and avoid wheel spin and wet trails. The following ORV areas are marked with symbols that show what kinds of vehicles are allowed. Some old routes are badly eroded and have been closed to heal—don't ride on them.

Brown Mountain

Brown Mountain has one four-wheel-drive trail in this area west of Lenoir. The other trails are open to ATVs and dirt bikes. There is no user fee.

Roy A. Taylor ATV Trail System

This trail, in the Wayhutta section, east of Sylva, is open only to ATVs and dirt bikes. Trucks and jeeps are not allowed. User fee is $3; a season pass costs $20.

Upper Tellico

North of Murphy, Upper Tellico is open to all ATVs, dirt bikes, and four-wheel-drive vehicles.

To protect water quality keep horses at least 200 feet from water sources and carry a water bucket and weed-free feed with you. Scatter manure and fill in pawed holes, especially when breaking camp. Horseback riders are required to yield to motorized vehicles, but bikers and hikers are supposed to yield to horses. Because trails are often narrow and some horses are skittish, it helps if you tell hikers where to wait while you pass.

> **i** When horseback riding, always wear long pants and boots with a separation between shoe sole and heel. Wearing shorts on a leather saddle will chap and blister your thighs in no time. Shoes without any type of heel may cause your entire foot to slip through the stirrup, and you could be dragged under the horse if thrown.

Riding Stables

Perhaps your involvement with horses only goes as far as wanting to take a trail ride. You can do that easily enough. There are many places in the mountains that rent horses and most also provide a guide. Most riding stables are open from mid-Apr until the end of Oct. Most have age requirements for children.

Northern Mountains

BANNER ELK STABLES, 796 Showmaker Rd., Banner Elk, NC; (828) 898-5424; bannerelkstables.com. Beech Mountain is your backdrop here. Also a great stable for novices.

BROYHILL EQUESTRIAN PRESERVE, 1500 Laurel Ln., Blowing Rock, NC; (828) 295-4700; blowingrockhorses.com. Blowing Rock Stables and Blowing Rock Equestrian Preserve is almost a mile outside the town of Blowing Rock. Guided trail rides pass near Bass Lake and around the Manor House at beautiful Moses Cone Memorial Park. You can ride daily from Apr through Dec for an hourly fee. Boarding is offered at $300 per month seasonally and $250 a month yearly. Prices are subject to change.

DUTCH CREEK TRAILS, 793 Rubin Walker Rd., Vilas, NC; (828) 297-7117; dutchcreektrails.com. Wooded trails, open fields, and fantastic views greet you at this riding venue.

Central Mountains

BILTMORE STABLES HORSE RIDING, Deer Park Rd., Asheville, NC; (800) 411-3812; biltmore.com. Various riding trails and guided tours available, even with picnic lunches, but all with purchase of a ticket to Biltmore Estate.

PISGAH FOREST STABLES, 476 Pisgah Dr., Brevard, NC; (828) 883-8258; pisgahstables.com. Explore the forest on half-day or full-day trail rides or excursions that last three days and two nights (four-person minimum). For rides of more than an hour, there is a two-person minimum. Reservations are required two days in advance. Children must be 6 years old to ride alone. Pisgah Forest Stables offers a three-hour waterfall ride.

PISGAH VIEW RANCH, 70 Pisgah Ranch Rd., Candler, NC; (828) 667-9100; pisgahviewranch.net. Set in the shadow of Mount Pisgah, this ranch offers breathtaking views and 2,000 acres of fields and forests. As of this writing, horseback riding across this picturesque acreage is under $30, with one low rate for ranch guests. The ranch is open May 1 through Nov 1 and features delicious home-cooked meals in a large old-fashioned dining room. Reservations are required. But this is all changing due to the ranch becoming a state park over the next few years.

QUEEN'S FARM STABLES, 23 Queens Farm Ln., Waynesville, NC; (828) 926-0718. Usually one- to two- hour rides, climbing 1,000 feet in altitude. Stables can handle groups up to 12. Open year-round.

SANDY BOTTOM TRAIL RIDES, 1459 Caney Fork Rd., Marshall, NC; (828) 649-3464 or (800), 959-3513. Here you can get hourly or day rides, including trips into the Great Smoky Mountains National Park. There are also pony rides for children.

Southern Mountains

CATALOOCHEE RANCH, 11 Ranch Dr., Maggie Valley, NC; (828) 926-1401; cataloochee-ranch.com. Two-hour and all-day accompanied rides are available on the 1,000-acre "mountain-top paradise" for adults and children older than 6. Reservations are required.

CHUNKY GAL STABLES, 1306 Hot House Rd., Hayesville, NC; (828) 389-4175; chunkygalstables.com. This stable offers horseback riding, horse training, riding instruction, and long- and short-term boarding. You can choose between one-, two-, and four-hour rides. Arena riding is also offered for children and beginners. Chunky Gal is located 11 miles east of Hayesville. Trail rides are also available.

SMOKEMONT RIDING STABLE CHEROKEE, 135 Smokemont Riding Stable Rd., Cherokee, NC; (828) 497-2373; smokemontridingstable.com. Family fun within the Smoky Mountain National Park, with a choice of hourly rides, waterfall rides, and a half-day ride. Wagon rides available, too.

Clubs, Sites, and Events
Although horses are a part of the lifestyle in all areas of Western North Carolina, the heart of horse country is in the Central Mountains, particularly in

Polk County around Tryon. In fact it's the top area in the state for steeplechases and other equestrian activities. Below are just a few horse-lover activities.

BILTMORE ESTATE EQUESTRIAN CENTER, Biltmore Estate, Asheville, NC; (828) 225-1454; biltmore.com. Guests can expect to find guided trail rides on some 100 miles of trail throughout the Biltmore Estate. The Equestrian Center offers riding for children and adults as well.

FOOTHILLS EQUESTRIAN NATURE CENTER, 3381 Hunting Country Rd., Tryon, NC; (828) 859-9021; fence.org. The Foothills Equestrian Nature Center, or FENCE, presents more than 18 various equestrian events during the year and provides interpretive nature study for adults and children (see the FENCE listing in our **Attractions** chapter). The 330-acre preserve has equestrian facilities with stabling, a steeplechase course, three show rings, a cross-country course, and access to the Foothills Equestrian Trails Association (FETA) trail system.

TRYON RIDING AND HUNT CLUB, PO Box 1095, Tryon, NC; (828) 859-6109, or (800) 438-3681; trhcevents.com. For more than 70 years the Tryon Riding and Hunt Club has hosted the Spring Block House Steeplechase held on the next-to-last Sat in Apr, and the Tryon Horse Trials, where horses perform dressage, stadium jumping, and cross-country, held in Oct.

THE WESTERN NORTH CAROLINA AGRICULTURAL CENTER, 1301 Fanning Bridge Rd., Fletcher, NC; (828) 687-1414; wncagcenter.org. There's a horse show here nearly every weekend, and most are free. The free shows start at 8 or 9 a.m. and finish around 9 p.m. There is a charge for the occasional rodeo and gaited horse shows, which start at 6 or 7 p.m.

HUNTING

Among the species of game available to hunters in North Carolina's mountains are deer, turkey, bear, squirrel, grouse, raccoon, wild boar, red and gray fox, rabbit, dove, and waterfowl. The North Carolina Wildlife Resources Commission (919-733-0635) schedules such seasons as deer (bow and arrow), deer (gun), deer (muzzle loading), black bear, squirrel, grouse, quail, wild boar, and wild turkey.

To hunt in national forest game lands, you must have a hunting license and a game-lands use permit. A big-game license is required for hunting deer, turkey, bear, and wild boar. Hunters entering game lands from the Blue Ridge Parkway must have a hunter parking and crossing permit, which is good for a one-year period and obtained in person from a park ranger (see the list of ranger stations in the **Forests, Parks, and Waterfalls** chapter). However, you must have a hunting license to get a parking and crossing permit.

Licenses and permits can be purchased at most discount stores, such as Wal-Mart, and at other sports-oriented places, such as gun shops or camping supply stores. To help you with regulations, pick up a copy of *N.C. Inland Fishing, Hunting, and Trapping Digest* where licenses are sold.

Beware: Deer Hunting Season

The Sierra Club reminds its members that deer gun season (which usually runs from Nov to Dec) is the most dangerous part of the hunting season. Therefore it's wise to stay out of both public and private game lands during such times. The game lands include the Pisgah and Nantahala National Forests and the Shining Rock, Middle Prong, Linville Gorge, and Southern Nantahala Wilderness Areas. The club's advice: "Go to the Great Smoky Mountains National Park, where there is no legal hunting allowed. If you must go into the woods, wear blaze orange that is visible from all directions."

MOUNTAIN BIKING

Rugged root-covered forest floors, gradual but devastating hillside climbs, lush trails near rushing creek beds—this is the biking environment you will encounter in this region. Mountain biking is one of the fastest-growing sports in the mountains, and while the Nantahala National Forest and the Great Smoky Mountains National Park have their share of great riding trails, Pisgah Forest is gaining a reputation as the place to go for this sport. There are more than 400 miles of marked trails in Pisgah Forest alone, and the rugged and often difficult terrain on many of these paths makes them a sporting challenge even for the experienced biker. Not all trails, however, are that bad (or good, depending on how tough a biker you are!).

Some of the trails on our public lands are gated forest service roads that are closed to motor traffic and have good riding surfaces. Some are single-track forest trails with a great variety of rigorous turf. However, because such trails are shared with hikers, some of the more popular hiking trails, such as the Pink Beds Loop in Pisgah Forest, are only open to bikers from Oct 16 to Apr 14, when there are fewer hikers.

Ski resorts are taking advantage of their slopes in the warmer months by opening them up to mountain bikers. Check out the **Recreation** chapter for websites of ski areas that potentially offer summer recreation, too.

OUTFITTERS

The North Carolina Mountains are home to many outstanding recreation outfitters who provide services for outdoor enthusiasts. These services can be as comprehensive or specialized as you want, depending on the outfitter and what you want to do. Recreational clothing, customized adventures, specialty bike parts, and canoeing supplies—these are some of the stock in trade at the region's outfitters, which are divided into two basic types: retail and full-service.

In most North Carolina mountain counties, you'll find retail outdoor outfitters that supply the fundamentals for fun but not guide services. The shops can clothe you in sturdy foot gear, jackets, pants, and vests to protect you from the elements, and they carry packs, from overnight frame backpacks to roomy day packs. Retail outfitters can provide hiking and camping food supplies, including a dehydrated five-course meal and the packable Sterno stove on which to cook it. And they have maps—detailed USGS topographical maps or basic day-hike trail maps—plus compasses and safety gear to get you there and back. Don't hesitate to ask questions. These people make a business of supplying recreation needs and can put you in touch with professional guides or just recommend a local day hike, fishing spot, or swimming hole.

Other Recreation

Hot-Air Ballooning

Asheville Hot Air Balloons, 1572 Sand Hill Rd., Candler, NC; (828) 667-9943; ashevillehotairballoons.com. Hot air balloon rides for special occasions or take the family up, up, and away.

Bowling

AMF Starlanes, 491 Kenilworth Rd., Asheville, NC; (828) 254-6161; amf.com. Such an Asheville place, with craft beer and cocktails, billiards, an arcade, and sports bar.

Skylanes, 1477 Patton Ave., Asheville, NC; (828) 252-7566; skylanesasheville.com. Great old-school bowling here. There's a grill; serves local brews and ciders also.

Tarheel Lanes, 3275 Asheville Hwy., Hendersonville, NC; (828) 692-5039; tarheellanes.com. Western North Carolina's largest bowling center, featuring 32 lanes, is 2 miles north of downtown Hendersonville. It's a modern facility that also has a billiard and video game room, a pro shop, and a snack bar. Tarheel Lanes hosts local, state, and regional bowling tournaments.

The popularity of mountain biking and river canoeing has created a demand for superior service and products for these two sports, and specialty shops have sprung up in some mountain counties to fill the void. These places concentrate on service and repair, but the owners, more often than not, know their merchandise from longtime experience. Rentals are usually also available, as are tours. A full-service outfitter does it all, supplying everything from gear to guided treks.

The primary focus with adventure services is group adventure, often including the entire family in the white-knuckle thrills of white-water rafting, canoeing, caving, or rock climbing, depending on the outfitter. Safety is given paramount consideration and detail. Gear is available as a sideline, or you can rent it for the trip.

Below, we've listed some of the well-known outfitters and adventure services here in North Carolina's mountains.

Northern Mountains

BOONE BIKE AND TOURING, 774 E. King St., Boone, NC; (828) 262-5750; boonenike.com. This full-service bike shop near Appalachian State University offers high-quality models, accessories, repair service, and rentals.

EDGE OF THE WORLD SNOWBOARD SHOP AND WHITEWATER RAFTING, 394 Shawneehaw Ave. S., Banner Elk, NC; (828) 214-7256; edgeoworldnc.com. Edge of the World guides rafting and canoeing tours on a portion of the Watauga River in the northwest part of the county. They also supply caving and rock-climbing equipment. But here in the High Country of Watauga County, where skiing is king, no other outfitter covers the snowboarding scene as well as Edge of the World. The best quality equipment and advice are at your disposal here. You can also shop online from their website.

FOOTSLOGGERS, 139 S. Depot St., Boone, NC; (828) 262-5111; footsloggers.com. This upscale outdoor retailer in downtown Boone is popular with both students and tourists in the High Country of the northern mountains. It carries a full array of high-quality outdoor clothing, hiking boots, rock-climbing and hiking equipment, and camping gear (see our **Shopping** chapter for more details).

HIGH MOUNTAIN EXPEDITIONS, 915 Main St., Blowing Rock, NC; (828) 295-4200 or (800) 262-9036; highmountainexpeditions.com. For information and guide service for overnight camping, caving, trips, family float trips, and white-water rafting on the Nolichuckey and Watauga Rivers and Wilson Creek Gorge, High Mountain Expeditions is one of the best places to go. When you stop for lunch, you will enjoy a gourmet feast by the river. All meals are prepared fresh daily by the Speckled Trout Cafe in Blowing Rock. They also outfit other popular mountain sports and offer kayak clinics, packages, and specialty trips.

MAGIC CYCLES, 140 S. Depot St. #2, Boone, NC; (828) 265-2211; magic cycles.com. Magic Cycles is a specialty bicycle shop that also carries a large line of accessories. The staff repairs all types of bikes; rentals are also available.

NEW RIVER OUTFITTERS & GENERAL STORE, 10725 US 221 N., Scottsville, NC; (336) 982-9192; canoethenew.com. The historic New River General Store in Ashe County is the site of this well-known river outfitter, a seasonal adventure operation focusing on family tubing and canoeing along the New River. Camping and fishing areas are nearby.

RIVERSIDE CANOE AND TUBE RENTALS, 2966 Garvey Bridge Rd., Chestnut Hill, NC; (336) 982-9439; riversidecanoeing.com. Riverside offers canoe trips by the hour, day, or weekend. Prices include paddles, life jackets, and shuttle service. Inner tubes of all sizes are also available. At the facility itself, enjoy other recreation, including basketball, volleyball, and horseshoes.

WAHOO'S OUTDOOR ADVENTURES AND CANOE OUTFITTERS, 3385 US 321, Boone, NC; (828) 262-5774 or (800) 444-RAFT; wahoos adventures.com. Wahoo's—you can almost feel the white-water spray in your face—is an apt name for this adventure-trek outfitter that emphasizes white-water rafting. During the summertime Wahoo's conducts rafting adventures down the Nolichucky River in nearby eastern Tennessee, several sections of the Watauga River, the French Broad and Pigeon Rivers near Asheville, and the Ocoee in southeastern Tennessee, which was the site of the '96 Olympic Games canoe and kayak competition.

ZALOO'S CANOES, 3874 Hwy. 16 S., West Jefferson, NC; (336) 246-3066 or (800) 535-4027; zaloos.com. Zaloo's is one of the oldest adventure operations in the High Country, guiding canoeists along the pastoral turns of the New River, one of the world's oldest and one of the few north-flowing rivers in America. These people know the New River like the back of their hand. Canoe season runs from mid-Mar to late Oct. Individual canoes and tubing rentals are also available.

Central Mountains

BLACK DOME MOUNTAIN SPORTS, 140 Tunnel Rd., Asheville, NC; (828) 251-2001; blackdome.com. Black Dome is one of those shops that does it all. In operation since 1993, this outfitter store has an expert staff and nationally known brands of gear and outdoor clothing for mountain sports as well as bikes and kayaks. You can also make your purchases through the shop's mail-order service. Black Dome's local mountaineering guide service offers an array of adventure trips throughout Western North Carolina. Rock climbing

RECREATION

is a specialty here, and the company's special-use permits allow excursions into Pisgah National Forest, not only for climbing, but also for caving, backpacking, and day hiking. Linville Gorge, Table Rock, and Wiseman's View are featured destinations. Also offered are guided flatwater trips for those who want to canoe.

CLIMBMAX MOUNTAIN GUIDES, 43 Wall St., Asheville, NC; (828) 252-9996; climbmaxnc.com. Obviously this outfitter's specialty is climbing. Experienced guides offer craggy rockface climbs to chilly ice cliffs. Climbing is taught in an indoor facility at the downtown Asheville location. Educational clinics and classes are continued in the field for those who want to move beyond bouldering. ClimbMax offers customized guided backpacking, hiking, and rock-climbing trips to various destinations around Western North Carolina. This outfitter reaches even beyond our borders, with trips to the American Northwest and volcano climbing in Mexico.

DAVIDSON RIVER OUTFITTERS, 49 Pisgah Hwy., Pisgah Forest, NC; (828) 877-4181; davidsonflyfishing.com. Specializing in fly-fishing, this outfitter can supply all the clothing and equipment you'll want for this sport. They also have fly-tying material, rent fly rods and reels, and offer fly-fishing lessons and instructional trips.

HEADWATERS OUTFITTERS INC., 25 Parkway Rd., Rosman, NC; (828) 877-3106; headwatersoutfitters.com. Headwaters provides canoeing, kayaking, and tubing adventures. It specializes in trips on the French Broad River but will also provide canoeing on other rivers by appointment. Trips range from 10 to 20 miles. Expect a 10-mile trip to take three to four hours and a 20-mile trip to last six or seven hours. A favorite place to go tubing is on the North Fork of the French Broad. Headwaters provides a drop-off, and the lively mountain waters will take you right back to their shop. The company also offers a full-day "sea" kayak adventure on Lake Jocassee with an instructor/guide, transportation, and a very nice lunch as another option. It can also arrange fishing trips, waterfall tours, and other outdoor excursions. Headwaters is open from Apr through Oct.

HEARN'S CYCLING & FITNESS, 28 Ashland Ave., Asheville, NC; (828) 253-4800; hearnsasheville.com. Hearn's is a tradition in downtown Asheville. Since 1896 the name Hearn has been synonymous here with bicycles. From the turn-of-the-20th-century elegance of bicycle touring to the mad dash and rugged individualism of mountain biking of 100 years later, Hearn's has seen it all. This versatile shop has a wide variety of bikes, parts, and accessories. They offer custom design and complete repair.

Southern Mountains

NANTAHALA OUTDOOR CENTER, 13077 US 19, Bryson City, NC; (828) 488-2175 or (800) 232-7238; noc.com. NOC, a long-established, employee-owned company, deserves its good reputation. The center can arrange food and lodging, and provide canoe and kayak instruction, white-water rafting, custom-designed programs, bicycle tours and rentals, and foreign and domestic adventure travel. It also has an outfitters store.

SLICKROCK EXPEDITIONS INC., PO Box 1214, Cullowhee, NC; (828) 293-3999; slickrockexpeditions.com. Slickrock specializes in recreational and educational backpacking, camping, and canoeing trips in the southern wilds. The company's trips in the southern Appalachians include North Carolina's Joyce Kilmer/Slickrock Wilderness, Big Snowbird Wilderness, Bonas Defeat Gorge, and Panthertown Valley. Slickrock also runs a number of themed canoeing trips throughout the United States, including on the Big South Fork National River in Tennessee. The latest offerings are canoe trips on the Rio Grande Wild and Scenic River in Texas. Trips are completely outfitted and led by a professional wilderness guide.

ROCK CLIMBING

Rock climbing is not for the faint of heart, but for those intrepid few who have taken to this sport, the rewards can be exhilarating. North Carolina's mountains offer some spectacular granite outcrops, sheer cliffs, and steep gorges that make for rock-climbers' heaven. Some of the experts even practice ice climbing in the region.

This high-risk sport requires knowledge, practice, and focus. Bouldering, a good first start, allows you to apply climbing moves just a few feet off the ground. Anything more advanced should be done in the company of an expert rock climber.

The staff at a number of outdoor outfitters will lead rock-climbing expeditions to favorite climbing spots here in the North Carolina mountains (see the **Outfitters** section at the end of this chapter). Below we have listed several rock climbing spots favored for their ease (or difficulty, depending upon your experience). Obviously there will be many more throughout the mountain region, so ask around, especially at the outfitter shops.

Northern Mountains

Shiprock Mountain
Just outside Blowing Rock and behind Grandfather Mountain, Shiprock Mountain can be accessed off the Blue Ridge Parkway at milepost 303, Rough Ridge parking area (do not park along the side of the parkway). It offers a range

of climbing for all levels and is a more traditional crack climbing area that does not require bolts.

Table Rock

There are four access sites at Table Rock. To get there from Asheville, take US Hwy. 221 N. to Linville Falls. At the Rock House Restaurant, turn right onto Highway 183, which turns into Highway 181. Follow the signs to Table Rock parking and picnic area. Paths will lead you down to the rock area. Another path from the parking/picnic area leads to three popular climbing faces: North Carolina Wall, the Amphitheater, and the Chimneys. Don't try to climb around the waterfall, though; it's forbidden and dangerous.

Central Mountains

Snake Den

Snake Den is north of Asheville in Barnardsville. Take US Hwys. 19/23 N. to the Barnardsville exit. Drive several more miles to town, where you take the Dillingham Road to the right. At the end of Dillingham Road, take a left. The pavement ends within 2 miles. Continue on a twisting, winding road that is a Forest Service road. Go about 5 more miles on this Forest Service road until you reach the rock face on your left, within 2 feet of the road. You can't miss it.

ROCKHOUNDING

We've all heard of fantasy cities with streets paved with gold and the Emerald City of Oz, but what about real highways paved with rubies? That's occasionally the case in Western North Carolina, where, if you look closely enough, you can see ruby-flecked gravel along the roadsides. That should give some idea of the copious amounts of gemstones in many sections of these mountains.

Important gems you might find are beryl (aquamarine, blue, golden, and green), corundum (bronze sapphire, pink, ruby, and sapphire), feldspar (moonstone), garnet (general, almandite, and rhodolite), olivine, opal, quartz (agate, amethyst, chrysoprase, jasper, and others), spinel, tourmaline, turquoise, and zircon. Rock hounds collect at least 37 other minerals, some of which can occasionally be classified as gem quality. In the late 1800s even a few diamonds supposedly turned up, but we know of none that have been found for more than 100 years.

It's rather ironic that in 1540 Hernando de Soto visited the Cherokee village of Nikwasi (now known as Franklin, the county seat of Macon County) in search of gold, never realizing he was passing through an area awash in precious and semiprecious stones. Admittedly most of the gems and semiprecious stones found in the mountains have no great commercial value, but many are attractive enough to be custom set and taken home as special souvenirs of an exciting and rewarding afternoon of sluicing through buckets of rock and dirt.

Gem mining can be wet and messy, so make sure you approach this exciting search in old clothes. Because you'll be standing at the flumes for a considerable length of time, a comfortable pair of shoes is a must. So is sunscreen. Although many mines offer some shade in the form of shelters, tents, or big, beach-type umbrellas, the sun reflecting off the water can give you an unexpected burn.

Gem Mines

Although the heaviest concentration of gem mines by far is in the jewel-rich Cowee Valley of Macon County, there are other places scattered throughout the mountains where you can try your luck at finding a jewel or two.

The following list includes several gem-mining operations that are open to the public.

Northern Mountains

Mitchell County

EMERALD VILLAGE, 331 McKinney Mine Rd., Spruce Pine, NC; (828) 765-6463; emeraldvillage.com. This mining attraction just 2.5 miles off the Blue Ridge Parkway in Mitchell County not only provides a guaranteed gem find at the Gemstone Mine but also has a mining museum underground in a genuine mine. The unusual antique displays are worth a look. A gift shop is filled with lapidary supplies and souvenirs, and attendants in the shop will answer your gemstone questions. This was the site of the Bon Ami Mine, developed by a French company that produced a soap product used in home cleaning.

GEM MOUNTAIN, 13780 Hwy 226 S., Spruce Pine, NC; (828) 765-6130; gemmountain.com. Open 9 a.m. to 5 p.m. Mar through Dec, except Sun, this gemstone mine maintains modern gem-washing facilities and covered flumes. They will clean and cut your stones there, if you wish. A picnic area by a nearby stream completes the outdoor hounding experience that is just a mile off the Blue Ridge Parkway. In the General Store that's open year-round, you'll find finished jewelry with the gemstones found in the area, as well as quilts, handbags, home decor, toys, knives, and a Christmas shop. There are ice-cream cones for the kids, too. Gem Mountain will cater birthday parties

RECREATION

or special events celebrations and offers discounts on mining and lunches for these catered affairs.

RIO DOCE GEM MINE, 14622 Hwy. 226, Little Switzerland, NC; (828) 765-2099; riodoce.com. Open mid-Apr (or May 1, depending on the weather) to Halloween from 9 a.m. to 5 p.m., seven days a week, the Rio Doce mine is owned by the Jerry Call family. Jerry Call, a gemologist who worked in Brazil's Vale Rio Doce (Sweet River Valley) for over 20 years, is currently involved in large-scale mining in the Brazilian valley. Some of the fine gem exports from the Brazilian valley end up in Spruce Pine's Rio Doce flumes. Rock hounds may be unearthing Mitchell County gems or Brazilian stones! Jerry Call and his family are master gem cutters and offer a complete gemological laboratory and appraisal services. The adjacent gem and gift shop offers 14k gold, sterling silver, and mineral specimens and provides gem cutting, and rough and cut gems. There is also a picnic area. Rio Doce offers group rates. The mine is located a half-mile north of the Blue Ridge Parkway and the Museum of North Carolina Minerals.

Central Mountains

ELIJAH MOUNTAIN GEM MINE, 2120 Brevard Rd., Hendersonville, NC; (828) 692-6560; elijahmountain.com. Buckets of gems to go through here, priced from a gallon of mine dirt for $13 to a tub of six gallons of mine dirt rich with ruby, sapphire, and emerald. Fossil buckets, too! There's a big rock shop and goats on property to pet.

> **i** In 1989 a Cherokee rock hound found a 10.5 pound (18,000-carat) sapphire—9,719-carat star sapphire worth several million dollars once cut and polished. Other sizable gems of value have been found in Macon and Haywood Counties.

Southern Mountains

Macon County

This is the heart of gem mining in Western North Carolina. In Macon County's famous Cowee Valley, you can go to more than a dozen gem mines where the entrance fees are usually under $10. There is an additional charge for buckets or bags of gem-bearing gravel that you can sluice in search of that "find of the century," but it's not much. However prices vary with the size of the buckets from mine to mine. Some in Macon County, as well as those in other counties, offer ore "enriched" or "seeded" with minerals not native to this locale; others offer strictly North Carolina stones.

Most gem mines, especially during the busy midsummer season, are open seven days a week from Apr 1 until Oct 31, and many are open from 8 a.m. until sunset, but times can vary. It's always a good idea to call before heading out to the mines; some closing times may vary according to the numbers of visitors and the weather during the season that you visit. Contact the Franklin Area Chamber of Commerce, 180 Porter St., Franklin, (828) 524-3161 for a listing of the county's many gem mines.

Big Find

In 1999 Jamie Hill of Hiddenite discovered what is now called the Empress Carolina 858-carat emerald. Hill has found 3,000 carats of emeralds in his backyard, which is now known as the North American Emerald Mines. It is located in the Brushy Mountains 50 miles northwest of Charlotte. Local papers note the Empress Carolina weighing in at about three pounds. The emerald is in two pieces, with one a 558-carat crown. The other is a 300-carat base. A consortium of jewelers, six of them from North Carolina, now owns the precious stone.

Swain County

NANTAHALA RIVER GEM MINE, 12121 US Hwy. 19 W., Bryson City, NC; (828) 488-4739. This Swain County mine, which uses enriched and native ore, has been known to produce rubies of good color and clarity. It's open from mid-Mar or mid-Apr through the end of Oct or into Nov, depending on the weather. Ruby, emerald, and sapphire ore are sold by the bag. More heavily enriched bags of ore (called "super-ruby," "super-emerald," and "super-sapphire" bags) cost a bit more. There is no entrance fee.

> **i** Gem mining on your own can be wet and messy—dress appropriately for that venture. No need to worry if sluicing at a commercial dig. Pay for your bucket of fortune, sit on a bench, pick up your sieve, let the water rush down the trough, and let the good times roll.

SMOKY MOUNTAIN GOLD AND RUBY MINE, US Hwy. 441 N., Cherokee, NC; (828) 497-6574. In addition to all the other attractions on the Qualla Boundary or Cherokee Indian Reservation, you can come here to search for such gems as amethysts, garnets, sapphires, rubies, citrine, topaz, and smoky quartz. Fifty dollars will get a mixed gem bucket with a cut gem

RECREATION

somewhere in the mix. Other buckets cost between $4 and $10. Next to the shaded and covered water flumes is a gem shop that will also cut and mount your finds. The mine opens at 9 a.m. seven days a week year round.

GEM MUSEUMS

Aside from small museums associated with some gem mines, there are some outstanding gem museums in the region. At these you can get the scoop on the history of rockhounding in North Carolina and a general education on gems and geology.

Northern Mountains

MUSEUM OF NORTH CAROLINA MINERALS, 214 Parkway Maintenance Rd., Spruce Pine, NC; (828) 765-2761; blueridgeheritage.com. This museum is a great side trip off the parkway. It displays a fascinating collection of minerals in various forms, from raw materials to the cut and polished items we know best. Spruce Pine, just down the road, and Little Switzerland, nearby, are both well known as sources of one of the highest and most varied concentrations of minerals in the United States. A gift shop offers a good variety of rock collections for any young rock hounds and enough material to keep them occupied quite a few miles down the road. The museum is open seven days a week in the summer season. Admission is free. The Mitchell County Chamber of Commerce (828-765-9483) is in the same building.

Central Mountains

ASHEVILLE MUSEUM OF SCIENCE (AMOS), 43 Patton Ave., Asheville, NC; (828) 254-7162; ashevillescience.org. The Colburn Hall of Minerals dazzles the eyes. The museum was founded in 1960 and highlights gems and minerals of all shapes and sizes from around the world. North Carolina–specific garnets, rubies, emeralds, and gold deposits also feature heavily. The Colburn Museum was folded into the new AMOS center and has plenty of activities for kids of all ages.

> **i** The annual Original North Carolina Mineral and Gem Festival at Spruce Pine takes place during the first weekend in Aug. Demonstrations, loose stone and mineral fossil displays, and the sale of lapidary supplies make this an entertaining event for everyone. Call the Mitchell Area Chamber of Commerce for more information at (865) 765-9033.

Southern Mountains

FRANKLIN GEM AND MINERAL MUSEUM, 25 Phillips St., Franklin, NC; (828) 369-7831; fgmm.org. The museum building, with its barred windows, is interesting in itself. It's the old county jail, located between Palmer and Main Streets, which was built in the 1850s and used as a jail until 1972. Now converted to displays, the North Carolina Room contains a huge sapphire, a 49-pound corundum crystal, and a baseball-size ruby crystal, all found at Corundum Hill Mine in Macon County, along with a rock collection, cut and faceted gems, an exhibit of mica types, and so on. The Fluorescent Room, a one-time solitary confinement cell, displays the phenomenon of fluorescence and phosphorescence—what the narrative tape calls "nature's hidden rainbows." The States Room contains specimens from each of the 50 states, including large specimens of fluorite that you can touch. A former high-security lockup known as the Slammer holds a display of rocks used in the manufacturing of glass. The museum also has a nice collection of fossils and corals as well as beautiful minerals from more than 30 nations. The small gift shop helps support the museum. Admission is free.

> **i** Franklin's gem mines are so numerous that it could have its own chapter (or book!). So make a stop at the Franklin County Chamber of Commerce and Visitor Center at 425 Porter St. or call (866) 372-5546 to get maps and brochures of the many mines and shops in this area. The website franklin-chamber.com also has several pages about gem mining.

RUBY CITY GEMS AND MINERALS, 130 East Main St., Franklin, NC; (828) 524-3967; rubycity.com. There are several "rock shops" in and around the Franklin area, but this establishment also has a great museum section, the result of more than 50 years of collecting specimens, artifacts, ivory carvings, and rare gems. Here you'll find a 385-pound sapphire and a 162-carat gem-quality ruby. The shop carries jewelry, lapidary equipment, and many rough stones. Other treasures found here include arrowheads and old tools, plus pre-Columbian Aztec and Inca vases and statues.

SKIING

Western North Carolina's first ski resort began at Cataloochee around 1961 in the Maggie Valley area of Haywood County when a farmer wanted to use his high-altitude land in the winter. Cataloochee is the oldest of the ski resorts in North Carolina and it adjoins the Great Smoky Mountains National

Park. Beech Mountain Ski Resort (now Ski Beech) opened in 1969, creating a new type of larger ski operation that would incorporate an Alpine village atmosphere. Skiing in the mountains had finally arrived. Thanks to the latest advances in snowmaking technology and some cold winters, ski season, which generally runs from late Nov through Mar, can be enjoyed this far south, too. Recent warm winters, however, have shortened the season. Resorts offer a wide variety of package deals, attractions, discounts, and one-stop vacation planning. They also cater to snowboarding. Some resorts have incorporated snowboard parks to accommodate these slope surfers. Tubing, or sliding down a hill on a large inner tube, akin to sledding, has also been introduced by several resorts. This is a great activity for the kids and folks who want to come along for the trip but don't necessarily want to ski this time.

Northern Mountains

Avery County

HAWKSNEST GOLF AND SKI RESORT, 1800 Skyland Dr., Banner Elk, NC; (828) 963-6561 or (888) HAWKSNEST, (828) 963-6563 (snow report); hawksnest-resort.com. This resort maintains 12 slopes: three beginner, six intermediate, and three advanced, with a peak elevation of 4,819 feet. The vertical drop is 619 feet. Their newest slope, Top Gun, aka. Ski Challenge of the South, is reported to be the best new slope in the Southeast. Two double-chair lifts and two surface lifts get you to the top. The facility offers a restaurant and lounge, cafeteria, lockers, equipment and clothing rentals, ski lessons, and a snowboard park. Kiddy Hawk is a great program available for children ages 5 to 12. Nighthawk, however, is way past their bedtime; this program gives avid skiers the opportunity to ski under the stars on Fri and Sat until 2 a.m. On these evenings live music entertains guests in the Nest's lounge. Discount rates are available for groups of 20 or more.

SUGAR MOUNTAIN SKI RESORT, 1009 Sugar Mountain Dr., Banner Elk, NC; (828) 898-4521, (800) SUGARMT (after Nov); skisugar.com. Sugar Mountain Ski Resort sits at 5,300 feet above sea level. Among the 20 slopes at Sugar are 7 beginner, 10 intermediate, and 3 expert runs. The vertical drop is 1,200 feet. The mountain is serviced by five chairlifts and three surface lifts. Sugar Bears is Sugar Mountain's ski program for children. The resort also offers equipment rentals, ski lessons, a tubing run, lockers, a nursery, game room, two cafeterias, restaurant, deck grill, and club called the Last Run Lounge. The resort offers discounts for groups of 15 or more.

Madison County

WOLF RIDGE RESORT, 578 Valley View Circle, Mars Hill, NC; (828) 689-4111, (800) 817-4111 (after Nov 1); skiwolfridgenc.com. Wolf Ridge is just north of Asheville, a drive of about 40 minutes via US Highways 19/23. The highways split about 20 miles from Asheville; follow US 23 north and watch for signs that lead to the Route 3 (Wolf Laurel) turn-off. This resort is the newest of Western North Carolina's ski areas. Students from nearby Mars Hill College find it a convenient alternative to the resorts farther north, as do a number of Asheville's city dwellers. The Wolf offers 54 acres of skiable terrain, in the form of 20 slopes for beginners as well as more advanced skiers. Elevation is 4,600 feet, with a vertical drop of 650 feet. Four lifts and one high-speed quad chairlift service the mountain. Ski lessons are offered hourly every day until 7 p.m. The lodge provides a ski shop, clothing and equipment rentals, and a grill. Snow-tubing has taken the Wolf by storm, and its new Snow-Tubing Park allows for all-day and evening tubing. Even better, tubers don't have to hike back up the hill, but rather they can hook their tubes up to a lift and ride their tubes back to the top, while enjoying the view. Lessons, season passes, discount packages, night skiing, and a children's Wolf Cub program (for children 5 to 7) are also offered at Wolf Ridge.

Watauga County

APPALACHIAN SKI MOUNTAIN, 940 Ski Mountain Rd., Blowing Rock, NC; (828) 295-7828 or (800) 322-2373 (snow report); appskimtn.com. This family-owned ski resort, begun in 1962, continues to be a popular destination for vacationers. Appalachian Ski Mountain offers 10 slopes—two beginner, three intermediate, three advanced, and two freestyle terrain—with a peak elevation of 4,000 feet. The vertical drop is 365 feet. You can get up the hill on two quad chairlifts, one double chairlift, one rope tow, and one handle-pull tow. A Bavarian-style 45,000-square-foot lodge with a giant fireplace overlooks the slopes, housing a cafeteria, ski shop, and gift shop. A 200-foot observation deck allows for generous views.

SKI BEECH, 1007 Beech Mountain Pkwy., Beech Mountain, NC; (828) 387-2011 or (800) 438-2093; skibeech.com. At 5,505 feet above sea level, Ski Beech is the highest ski area in eastern North America. Established in 1969, the ski resort provides the complete winter sport experience from A to Z. Central to the resort is Beech Tree Village, a complex of facilities designed to anticipate the skier's every need. Its shops and services include equipment and clothing rentals, several gift shops, ski schools, a variety of restaurants, a nursery, video game facility, ski lessons, ski patrol, and even an outdoor ice-skating rink. Ski Beech has 15 slopes, offering terrain for the beginner all the way to the seasoned expert. The vertical drop measures 830 feet. The mountain is serviced by a total of 10 lifts. A half-pipe run is available for snowboarders, along with snowboard rentals for those who just want to try it out. Ski Beech also features a skating rink.

Southern Mountains

Haywood County

CATALOOCHEE SKI AREA, 1080 Ski Lodge Rd., Maggie Valley, NC; (828) 926-0285, (800) 768-0285, (800) 768-3588 (snow report); cataloochee .com. Cataloochee, North Carolina's first ski resort, has long been one of the region's favorites. Its mile-high location provides fine conditions for making and keeping snow. Omigosh, the area's longest advanced slope, plummets 2,200 feet from the very top of 5,400-foot-tall Moody Top Mountain and joins up with the 1,800-foot Lower Omigosh, an intermediate slope. These along with seven other advanced, intermediate, and beginner runs offer skiers plenty of options to match their skills. There are two double chairlifts and one surface lift, and night skiing is offered from Tues through Sat. Snowboading began at Cataloochee in 1984. There are now nine trails, and snowboard clinics are offered seven days a week, five times a day. You can contact Cataloochee for discounted stay-and-ski packages with accommodations in the Maggie Valley area. After you work up an appetite on the slopes, the lodge provides hot, home-cooked meals, or you can enjoy a toddy around the circular fireplace or on the deck.

Jackson County

SAPPHIRE VALLEY SKI AREA, 4350 Hwy. 64 W., Cashiers, NC; (828) 743-1164; skisapphire.com. Sapphire Valley Resort, which bills itself as "a resort for all seasons," has its own ski area for its property owners and resort guests, in addition to such outdoor sports as golf (see our **Recreation** chapter), tennis, horseback riding, canoeing, fishing, swimming, and hiking. The ski area is composed of a novice hill with a rope tow and intermediate and advanced slopes served by a chairlift. There's a base lodge that contains a ski shop and rental shop; a ski school is housed in a separate building. Night skiing is available but cross-country skiing is not. Snowboarding came to Sapphire in 1995 with two trails and clinics available. After a workout on the slopes, skiers can relax at the resort's health club with its indoor pool, Jacuzzi, and sauna.

SCALY MOUNTAIN OUTDOOR CENTER, 7420 Dillard Rd., Scaly Mountain, NC; (828) 526-3737; scalymountain.com. From winter to summer, this center is fun for the whole family. Snowtubing and ice-skating, trout fishing and summer tubing on artificial turf— there's never a dull moment at Scaly Mountain. Parents can relax on the terrace while the kids are busy playing, then all gather at the Lodge BBQ and Trout House for a well-deserved lunch.

SWIMMING

Most of our mountain lakes are found in the central and southern mountains. Some of the smaller ones are private or in residential resort communities. Here we've listed some of the more popular lakes that have public access areas.

Central Mountains

Buncombe County

LAKE JULIAN, 406 Overlook Rd. Ext., Asheville, NC; (828) 684-0376; buncombecounty.org. Lake Julian is a thermal lake used as a cooling agent for Carolina Power and Light. Therefore the lake is deliciously warm, often reaching a scorching 95 degrees in summer! You might find the power plant that looms over one side of the lake a bit disconcerting, but the water never goes below 50 degrees in winter—the best time for fishing here is between Oct and Mar.

Several covered picnic areas make this a favorite spot for family reunions and company gatherings. Picnic shelters range in size from 4 to 10 picnic tables and can be rented for about $20 and $35 for Buncombe County residents. Nonresidents pay roughly $35 and $45. A children's playground, volleyball court, and horseshoe pit provide some free landlubber entertainment. Paddleboats, fishing boats, or canoes can be rented for under $10 an hour if you are a county resident. If not, then expect to pay about double. If you bring your own boat, there is a launch fee of under $5 per day. When there's room, a boathouse and dock can hold your sailboat for approximately $120 (residents) and $180 (nonresidents) per year. The lake is well stocked with bass, crappie, catfish, brim, and tilapia, and the price for fishing is nominal.

Lake Julian Park is open from 8 a.m. to 9 p.m. Apr through Aug, 8 a.m. to 8 p.m. in Sept, and 8 a.m. to 6 p.m. Oct through Mar. It is closed on Thanksgiving, Christmas, and New Year's Day.

LAKE POWHATAN RECREATION AREA, 375 Wesley Branch Rd., Asheville, NC; (828) 670-5627; www.recreation.gov. Lake Powhatan is a popular destination with a lot to offer besides the pretty little lake for fishing (it also has a swimming beach and a lifeguard on duty). There are 96 sites for tents and trailers (no hookups), a trailer dump station, picnic tables with grills, restrooms with flush toilets, hiking trails, information hosts, and a central supply of drinking water. The campground is open from mid-Apr through Oct, and the Forest Service provides numerous activities during the summer season. (See the Camping section in this chapter.)

Powhatan is in the Bent Creek Experimental Forest with a system of hiking trails that can get confusing, so pick up a map from the campground office at the entrance to the area. The Western North Carolina Arboretum with its 10 state-champion big trees is near Lake Powhatan.

Rutherford County

LAKE LURE BEACH AND WATER PARK, 2724 Memorial Hwy./US Hwy. 64, Lake Lure, NC; (828) 625-0077; townoflakelure.com. This sparkling jewel is one of the most picturesque lakes you'll find anywhere—Chimney Rock Park and other spectacular mountains tower over it, and its 1,500 acres include 27 miles of shoreline. You'll find a number of marinas here, but before you haul your boat to the lake, you should be aware that launch fees have been set high to lessen lake congestion. Also, because of its beauty, the shoreline here is quite developed. Still, you'll find a protected, sandy beach area for public use. It is in the center of the Lake Lure Recreation Area, across from Lake Lure Inn.

Lake Lure Water Park is located directly on the public beach. There is an admission charge that provides access to the swimming area. Within the park are climbing areas for kids, slides into the lake, and many other activities. You can bike or hike and explore the roads of Lake Lure/Chimney Rock area.

A water shuttle service operates between the Resort Marina and the Lake Lure Marina. From the Lake Lure Marina, you can easily walk to the water park and the beach. Exploratory boat excursions of Lake Lure are available through Lake Lure Tours. Their toll free number is (877) FUN-4ALL.

Southern Mountains

Cherokee County

CHEROKEE LAKE RECREATION AREA, access off Hwy. 294, Murphy, NC; (828) 837-6617; cherokeecounty-nc.gov. Operated by the Tennessee Valley Authority, this small lake, about a mile in circumference, is fed by the backwaters of Lake Hiwassee. Its pier is a great place to take children fishing, and the pier is designed for easy access for individuals with disabilities.

LAKE HIWASSEE, access off US 64; cherokeecountychamber.com. Built in 1935, the TVA's 307-foot-high, 1,376-foot-long Hiwassee Dam is the highest overspill dam in the United States. It blocks the Hiwassee River to form the center of recreation and fishing in Cherokee County—the 22-mile-long, 6,090-acre Lake Hiwassee. Its 163-mile shoreline is almost completely surrounded by the Nantahala National Forest. In 1955 a second generating unit was added to the dam, along with the world's largest electric motor and reversible pump-turbine, which enable water from the dam to be used to generate electricity during peak hours. During off-hours, the water is then pumped 205 feet back into the Hiwassee reservoir for reuse.

The lake is known for its smallmouth bass and walleyes, but fishermen will also find largemouth bass, bluegill, and crappie here.

Clay County

CHATUGE LAKE, access off US 64. Stretching from Clay County into Georgia, Chatuge Lake, with its gradual 132-mile shoreline, backed up by high mountain peaks, reminds us of a Swiss alpine lake. It provides endless hours of water sports and fishing and presents some of the most beautiful views in the county. Thirty-two species of fish have been caught here; smallmouth and large-mouth bass, spotted bass, and sunfish are the important sport catches. Striped/white bass hybrids are also stocked annually to control the gizzard shad population, and threadfin shad are stocked periodically to augment the prey bass.

Built in 1941 by the Tennessee Valley Authority, Chatuge has been called the crown jewel of the TVA system because of its picturesque setting. It is also one of the most developed of those lakes, with more than 76 miles of shoreline in private hands. There are three commercial marinas in the area.

The popular Clay County Recreation Park, not far from the 144-foot-high Chatuge Dam, sits on the reservoir 6.2 miles from Hayesville on US 64 (turn right onto Highway 175). Here you'll find 25 campsites, picnic shelters, a ballfield, a swimming area, and a boat launch ramp.

Another good facility on the lake, this one in the Tusquitee Ranger District of the Nantahala Forest, is the Jackrabbit Mountain Recreation Area. It is on a pine-wooded peninsula that has three camping loops with 103 campsites, a swimming beach with shower facilities, hiking trails, two picnic areas, and a boat launch ramp. To get to the Jackrabbit Mountain Recreation Area, drive 2.5 miles down Highway 175 from US 64; turn right on SR 1155.

Graham County

CHEOAH LAKE, access along Hwy. 28. This long and narrow Graham County lake is just a few miles west of Fontana Lake. Lying tranquilly between steep green hills, it is reminiscent of a Scandinavian fjord. The water is so clear you can usually see right down to the bottom. A turn onto US Highway 129 from Highway 28 will bring you to the 225-foot Cheoah Dam, which was built between 1917 and 1919 on the Little Tennessee River. In 1930 the Calderwood Dam farther downriver in Tennessee formed Calderwood Lake, which is contiguous to its twin, Cheoah.

LAKE SANTEETLAH, access off US 129 N. This emerald-green lake in the center of Graham County is popular with both motorboaters and canoeists. Santeetlah has a reputation as one of the best bass-fishing lakes in the area, and pike and crappie are also plentiful. Three public boat ramps are located along its shores. A popular one is at Cheoah Point off US 129 North, just outside Robbinsville near the ranger station (see the list of ranger stations in our **Forests, Parks, and Waterfalls** chapter). Cheoah Point also has a campground with 26 campsites, water, flush toilets, a picnic area, and a boat ramp. It is open from

RECREATION

Close-up

Iron Foot Island

Iron Foot Island, Bryson City's 7-acre island park, is just downstream from the Cherokee's Old Mother Town of Kituhawa. Several Cherokee battles with other tribes and whites were fought in the island's immediate vicinity.

The most famous battle occurred in the 1700s and involved the Shawano, a tribe the Cherokee had fought for many years. A noted Shawano leader, Tawa-li-ukwanun, led a raid on the town of Tikwalitsi, near the present site of Bryson City. A Cherokee conjurer named Dead-wood-lighter forecast that the raiders would set an ambush on the island. Some of the Cherokee warriors took his advice and forded the river above the island, entering the site from the rear. But some didn't listen and went straight up the north bank of the river, where they were taken "like fish in a trap." After several bloody encounters, the Shawano were driven up Deep Creek and over the Smokies at Clingmans Dome.

The island was named for Ralph Clark, alias "Iron Foot." While riding with Jesse James, tradition has it, one foot had been shot off during a train robbery. To equalize his gait an iron stirrup was attached to the limb with the missing foot. Clark lived on the island as a hermit.

Apr 15 until Oct 31. To get to Cheoah Point, take US 129 North for 7 miles, turn left at the sign, and go 0.8 mile.

Jackson County

LAKE GLENVILLE, access off Hwy. 107. Lake Glenville Dam, four miles north of Cashiers, was built on the Tuckasegee River in Jackson County in 1941. It was renamed Lake Thorpe in 1951 after Nantahala Power's first president, J. E. S. Thorpe. Today it's marked as Lake Thorpe on many, but not all, maps, but it's still Lake Glenville to most people in this area. The 6-mile-long lake covers 1,462 acres and offers 26 miles of shoreline. At an elevation of nearly 3,500 feet, it's the highest major lake in the eastern United States. Lake Glenville is a great place to cruise, canoe, swim, ski, and fish. Mountain trout, walleye, brim, pike, and largemouth and smallmouth bass are the fish you can expect to catch here.

Three marinas in the Glenville community rent pontoon, fishing, and ski boats. These are well marked by signs on Hwy. 107. The RJ Andrews

Campground also provides boat access to the lake. This reservoir is the source of water for a hydroelectric plant at the 1,200-foot level, said to be one of the highest facilities in the east. To visit it, turn off of Hwy. 107 onto Pine Creek Road and drive about 2 miles past the RJ Andrews Campground to the power plant. The beach area near the dam is a favorite spot for swimming and sunbathing.

Macon County

CLIFFSIDE LAKE RECREATION AREA & VAN HOOK GLADE CAMPGROUND, 14014 Highlands Rd., Highlands, NC; (828) 526-5912. West Cliffside—a pretty and popular little lake in the Nantahala National Forest—is a great place to picnic, swim (the water is cold!), boat, hike, and fish (mostly for rainbow and brook trout). Here you'll find 17 picnic tables, two picnic shelters, a bathhouse with cold-water showers and flush toilets, and the Clifftop Vista Shelter.

There are numerous hiking trails in the area, including an interpretive loop around the lake. Cliffside Vista trail climbs 3 miles to an overlook of the lake. Tent camping used to be allowed here, but all camping has now been moved to the nearby Van Hook Glade Campground, though campers may use Cliffside Lake and showers. (See our Camping section in this chapter for more information on the Van Hook Glade campground.) There is a day-use parking fee at Cliffside from May 1 through Oct 31.

NANTAHALA LAKE, access off Wayah Rd. This large lake, which provides electricity for the Nantahala Power and Light Company, is in a remote area of Macon County, reached by the paved-but-very-windswept, two-lane Wayah Road (SR 1310). The regular releases of water that supply the fast rides for rafters and kayakers on the Nantahala River cause the lake's water level to vary widely. Nevertheless fishing is good here. In fact Nantahala Lake is the only lake in the state that contains Kokanee salmon, a freshwater hybrid of the sockeye salmon. There are two public access sites: Rocky Branch, on the east side of the lake just off Wayah Road, and in the Choga area on the lake's western arm, off FR 440. There's a school and a volunteer fire department in the nearby Nantahala community but no stores to speak of, so stock up ahead of time with what you need for an outing here.

Swain County

FONTANA LAKE, access from Hwys. 129 and 28 (Indian Lakes Scenic Bwy.). At an elevation of 1,710 feet, this deepwater lake reaches 30 beautiful miles into the mountains, covering 10,530 acres when full. Much longer than it is wide (it has a 240-mile shoreline), Fontana runs east and west with the Great Smoky Mountains National Park on the north and the Nantahala National Forest on the south.

The lake was created in the 1940s by the Tennessee Valley Authority's Fontana Dam (see the Fontana Dam listing in our **Attractions** chapter). You'll find public boat launches on Fontana's south shore. There are also boat docks at the Fontana Village Resort (see our **Accommodations** chapter), along with sightseeing cruises and boat rentals, including Wave Runners, bass boats, houseboats, pontoon boats, and ski boats. The lake is home to abundant smallmouth and largemouth bass, native trout, and walleye. You'll also find white bass, muskie (some 4 feet or more in length), and a number of panfish.

WHITE-WATER RAFTING AND KAYAKING

Western North Carolina and its adjoining states have some of the country's most thrilling white water. We've described some of the most popular rivers for rafting and kayaking in this section, listing them in alphabetical order.

Trips on all these rivers can be booked through any number of white-water rafting companies that provide guides and instruction. Children must weigh at least 60 pounds before being permitted to raft (because that's how big they've got to be to fit into a life jacket safely). Some companies also rent rafts, canoes, and kayaks, and offer canoe and kayak clinics. The following are just a few of the white-water runners in the region. Some run trips in other states and other countries.

CAROLINA OUTFITTERS RAFTING, 12121 US Hwy. 19 W., Bryson City, NC; (828) 488-6345, (800) 468-7238, carolinaoutfitters.com

ExploreAsheville.com

NANTAHALA OUTDOOR CENTER, 1044 US 19 W., Bryson City, NC; (828) 488-2175, (800) 232-7238; noc.com

WAHOO'S ADVENTURES, 3385 US Hwy. 321, Boone, NC; (828) 262-5774, (800) 444-RAFT; wahoosadventures.com

> ℹ White-water rafting, canoeing, mountain biking, or horseback riding can all be so much fun that you keep at it a little too long. When aching muscles or sunburns act up, check out the Health Care chapter for medical facilities to help you get back to normal. First aid can often be obtained from your outfitter or guide, but don't count on them having much more than the basics.

The Chattooga River

The Chattooga, made famous by the movie *Deliverance,* can produce some of the best white water in the Southeast and is one of our personal rafting favorites. Designated as a Wild and Scenic River by Congress in 1974, the Chattooga has its headwaters in the North Carolina mountains and flows south to form the boundary between South Carolina's Sumter National Forest and Georgia's Chattahoochee National Forest. There is a 6-mile "floating section" from an access point on South Carolina Highway 28 about 1.5 miles from its border with Georgia. This stretch is also open to canoers and tubers, and while it can be a real challenge, it's great for family rafting trips with children or for youth groups.

One section of the Chattooga has been designated as Section IV. It provides a really exciting raft ride. You'll get great wilderness scenery, steep and technical rapids, and frequent ledges and waterfalls, such as the super-rush of Five Falls. Check with the guide companies for more information. Enjoy the outdoors, but don't venture beyond your capabilities.

> ℹ When white-water rafting for the first time, pay attention to everything your guide says. Always remember the most important thing—if you fall in, keep your feet up and float. Do not try to stand—you may get caught in the rocks and drown in as little as three feet of water, under the rushing force of the current.

The French Broad River

The French Broad is one of the world's oldest rivers, and you seem to keep running into it or one of its many forks—including the North Fork, the East Fork, the West Fork, and the Middle Fork—almost anywhere you travel in the valleys of the central mountains. It was not named, as some think, after a Parisian lady. The French Broad got its name in the 17th century when explorers realized that unlike the area's other rivers, this one flowed to the west toward the land claimed by the French. To the Cherokee, it was the "Long Man," and its many forks were called "Chattering Children."

Longer, warmer, and wider than many mountain rivers, the French Broad offers rapids that range from class II to class V. Class II offers slow moving waters good for floating and drifting. The river becomes more active as the nomenclature increases. Class V rapids, therefore, require more expertise in the fast moving water. How challenging the river is depends on the amount of rainfall and the season. High water and big waves occur most often in the spring and early summer; in midsummer and fall it's usually a gentler river that's better for canoeing and family outings.

The Nantahala River

Because the Nantahala River is a controlled-release river from the Nantahala Dam upstream, it has usually consistent white water from spring until fall. It's clear and quite cold waters rush the rider for 9 miles through the spectacular Nantahala Gorge in the Nantahala Forest. This is one of the most heavily used white-water rivers in the region, with a constant flow of rafters and kayakers who are fun to watch even if you don't care to join in the sport. Typical raft trips include class III rapids at Nantahala Falls.

The New River

The New River is one of the few north-flowing rivers in America. This river runs through the geographically remote Alleghany and Ashe Counties. Though one of the oldest rivers in the world, the New River was named by surveyor Peter Jefferson (Thomas's father), who was surprised to find this "new" river behind the mountains. The North and South Forks of the river flow over 100 miles through forested mountains and valleys. They join just south of the Virginia state line, and the river continues through Virginia. Because of its scenic beauty and recreational value, a 26-mile stretch of the South Fork has been designated a National Scenic River.

The headwaters are shallow with a few mild rapids, allowing for easy paddling. This river is ideal for family fun—for large groups and less-experienced canoers and kayakers. Tubing is great on this river; it allows you to meander downstream at a relaxed pace. Children love tubing, and many outfitters can supply you with dual tubes, allowing Mom or Dad to share the tube with a smaller child. Fishing and swimming are also excellent in this river.

The Nolichucky River

The Nolichucky River that runs through a gorge in the Pisgah National Forest in North Carolina and the Cherokee National Forest in Tennessee has few rivals in the East during the high waters of early spring. Calm pools along the way allow you to catch your breath from some of the adrenaline-pumping rapids you'll have come through. The rafting season here is from Mar through Oct.

The Pigeon River

The Pigeon River in the heart of the Smokies near Gatlinburg and Pigeon Forge, Tennessee, has been considered a "dead" river for nearly 40 years, due to pollution and electric power generation. Now new regulations are restoring its health and requiring the power company to pump 1,200 cubic feet of water per second through the gorge. The upper part of the Pigeon offers exciting class III and class IV rapids; the lower section is better suited to the inexperienced and to families with children.

Kidstuff

North Carolina's mountains are even more fun with kids in hand. Try to view the world the way they do. They can see Daniel Boone behind every log cabin and wood nymphs playing in the shelter of rhododendron thickets. See Santa Claus in the summertime (although there's a logical explanation for that one . . . read on). Organizations throughout the region offer exciting programs for little ones. Parks and attractions in the mountains welcome pint-size visitors and throughout this guide, most places welcome kids, even our breweries! This chapter notes kid-specific "stuff" to do.

Northern Mountains

MAGIC MOUNTAIN MINI GOLF & GEM MINE, 1675 Hwy. 105, Boone, NC; (828) 265-GEMS, (828) 265-GOLF. The kids simply won't get bored here. Open Mon, Tues, and Wed 10 a.m. to 6 p.m.; Thurs, Fri, and Sat 9 a.m. to 9 p.m., spring through fall, Magic Mountain is a kiddie paradise. Adults probably won't mind sifting through the enriched ore either, because there's a chance of finding a ruby, citrine, garnet, amethyst, aquamarine, sapphire, emerald, or other such rocks.

MYSTERY HILL, 129 Mystery Hill Ln., Blowing Rock, NC; (828) 264-2792; mysteryhill.com. This is the place to go for interactive fun with your family or group of friends. Celebrating more than 70 years in business, Mystery Hill explores the relationships of science, optical illusion, and natural phenomena in a hands-on entertainment center. Defy gravity in the Mystery House, where the ball rolls uphill, or leave your shadow on the wall. (Just try getting the kids out of this one.) The Appalachian Heritage Museum and the Native American Artifacts Museum are included in the tour for one low price. There is an admission charge.

TWEETSIE RAILROAD, 300 Tweetsie Railroad Ln., Blowing Rock, NC; (828) 264-9061, (800) 526-5740; tweetsie.com. A charming theme park, now more than 40 years old, Tweetsie brings out the little kid in all of us. This park maintains a 1914 Tweetsie locomotive that still runs, a petting farm with deer, homemade fudge, caramel apples, a Ferris wheel, and other country fair games. The amusement park also holds special events for certain holidays, such as Halloween, July 4, and others. A great place for kids, but parents will have fun, too. Group rates and discounts are available, and check out the Golden Rail Season Pass.

Central Mountains

THE ADVENTURE CENTER OF ASHEVILLE, 85 Expo Dr., Asheville, NC; (877) 247-5539; ashevilletreetopsadventurepark.com. This center is your connection to mountain biking, rafting, and so much more, but it's the only place withe KidZip—a designed-for-kids zipline adventure for kiddos 10 and under (as young as 4).

ASHEVILLE'S FUN DEPOT, 7 Roberts Rd., Asheville, NC; (828) 277-2386; ashevillesfundepot.com. This family entertainment center has all the fun stuff, including indoor mini golf, multi-level laser tag, batting cages, a climbing wall, soft play area, arcade, mini-bowling, indoor and outdoor go-carts, bumper cars, the Depot Diner, and such.

ASHEVILLE MUSEUM OF SCIENCE (AMOS), 43 Patton Ave., Asheville, NC; (828) 254-7162; ashevillescience.org. Rocks and weather—that's the fun stuff here. Three main exhibition spaces let kids explore gemstones and minerals in the Colburn Hall of Minerals. There's the AMOS Mars Rover, a Teratophoneus dinosaur skeleton, Terrabox elevation simulator, "Toddler Nest," Hurricane Simulator, and gift shop.

ODYSSEY CENTER FOR THE CERAMIC ARTS, 236 Clingman Ave., Asheville, NC; (828) 285-0210; odysseyclayworks.com. This recreational craft center offers some very special programs for children. Odyssey's kids' classes have been filling up quickly with eager faces and curious hands. Nine-week classes are offered for after-school kids and homeschoolers. Kids of all ages learn basic skills in wheel throwing and hand building, making anything from animals and castles to cups and bowls. Call for a detailed course schedule.

SLIDING ROCK, 7851 Pisgah Hwy., Pisgah Forest. Sliding Rock is just 7.6 miles from the junction of US 276 and US 64 outside Brevard. Here you're invited to "take the plunge" down a 60-foot slippery cascade into the 55- to 60-degree, 6-foot-deep pool below. If you don't care to make the slide, it's fun to watch the action from paved viewing areas at the top or bottom of this natural, exhilarating ride that's fueled by 11,000 gallons of water a minute. There's a large parking lot adjacent to Sliding Rock (with a per-person parking fee) as well as a bathhouse. Lifeguards are on duty from 10 a.m. to 6 p.m. from Memorial Day through Labor Day.

The rock, while slick, can take the bottom out of an ordinary bathing suit, so old jeans or cutoffs are best for this fast ride. Also, be careful while getting in and out of the water. The surface of the rock, even where the water isn't flowing, can be slick and accounts for some hard tumbles.

WESTERN NORTH CAROLINA NATURE CENTER, 75 Gashes Creek Rd., Asheville, NC; (828) 298-5600; wildwnc.org. The Western North Carolina Nature Center offers a remarkable blend of services to the area. Officially it's "an environmental educational resource, exhibiting and interpreting plants and animals native to the Southern Appalachian Mountains." But it is much more than that. From the moment you step through the door and a three-dimensional, full-size diorama of woodland creatures greets you, you know you are crossing that bridge to the natural world. Well-planned exhibits in the educational facility offer a hands-on approach to everything from weather forecasting and animal identification to a real working beehive!

In the next building are archaeological displays and zoological exhibits of live reptiles and amphibians. In another area a special darkened room allows visitors to observe owls, bats, and other nocturnal creatures. Outside there's more: bobcats, raccoons, cougars, otters, foxes, bears, hawks, eagles, sheep, goats, chickens, peacocks, wolves and as of 2019, red pandas! Make sure you walk along the boardwalk in the treetops; it takes you back to those days of childhood tree houses. The Nature Center is open 10 a.m. to 5 p.m. seven days a week.

Southern Mountains

SANTA'S LAND FUN PARK AND ZOO, 571 Wolfetown Rd., Cherokee, NC; (828) 497-9191; santaslandnc.net. Christmas comes alive in the summertime in this theme park. We expect that young children will refuse to miss its Rudi-Coaster ride, Santa's Overland Express train and, of course, Santa. The family can also paddle boats around Monkey Islands in the lake, view Cherokee from the top of a Ferris wheel, and visit a wealth of shops. In the zoo kids will enjoy petting baby bears and feeding deer and trout. A visit to the gristmill will show them how cornmeal is made, and they can watch pork rinds being cooked. You'll also find a picnic and playground area in the park. It's open from early May until the first weekend in Nov. Admission is under $25. Children younger than 2 are free. Season passes run $50.

SUMMER CAMPS

For generations children and young people have delighted in the many summer camps that thrive in the Western North Carolina mountains. They often attend the same camps that their grandparents enjoyed. Although summer camps can vary in size, price, duration, and age ranges of the campers, most include such activities as hiking, camping, canoeing, swimming, archery, mountain biking, horseback riding, tennis, golf, team sports, and nature studies—thanks in part to the vast recreational opportunities offered by the nearby public lands (see our **Forests, Parks, and Waterfalls** chapter). As the late Frank "Chief" Bell

KIDSTUFF

Sr., founder of Mondamin Camp, put it, "The wilderness can be a magnificent playground and a great university." The cultural heritage of the area's arts and crafts, such as drama, blacksmithing, and pottery, plays a big role in summer activities. Although most camps draw the majority of their participants from the Southeast, many come from as far away as Alaska, Hawaii, and South America for this mountain experience. Campers have been known to spend every summer for 5 to 15 years at the same camp. Many have come back as camp counselors.

Central Mountains

CAMP ARROWHEAD FOR BOYS, 1415 Cabin Creek Rd., Zirconia, NC; (828) 692-1123; camparrowhead.org. Arrowhead is a Christian camp for boys 7 to 15 years old. Set along sparkling Rock Creek, a tributary of the Green River, it has more than 1,000 acres of woodland, streams, meadows, and trails that offer endless opportunities for playing, exploring, camping, and riding. J. O. Bell Jr. started the camp in 1937, and it's been owned and directed by the Bell family ever since.

CAMP CAROLINA FOR BOYS, 1 Lamb's Creek Rd., Brevard, NC; (828) 884-2414; campcarolina.com. Though Camp Carolina is only 2.5 miles from Brevard, its 22 acres feel far from town life. It's bordered by mountain ridges and on two sides by the Pisgah National Forest, and it's only a half-mile from the forest's entrance. The camp, established in 1924, has three streams and a 4-acre lake for swimming, canoeing, kayaking, and fishing for mountain trout. Both group and individual tennis instruction is provided on six tennis courts. Other activities include riflery, archery, soccer, table tennis, basketball, football, baseball, lacrosse, hang gliding, mountain biking, skateboarding, weightlifting, and arts and crafts. Horseback riding in Western and English saddles, forward seat, and jumping are taught, and campers take day and overnight rides in Pisgah Forest. Wilderness classes are also beginning. Carolina's nature program involves collecting and identifying area plants and animals; pioneering projects include using hand tools to build tree houses, forts, dams, bridges, and cabins. The camp, which is open to boys ages 7 to 17, has a capacity of 200.

CAMP GLEN ARDEN FOR GIRLS, 1261 Cabin Creek Rd, Zirconia, NC; (828) 692-8362; campglenarden.com. The vast grounds of this camp contain two lakes, a swimming pool, archery fields, tennis courts, a gym, stables, a woodworking shop, a blacksmith shop, and a great variety of other facilities and cabins. Just inside the Glen Arden gate, a towering 300-foot waterfall greets campers.

CAMP GREEN COVE FOR GIRLS, 617 Green Cove Rd., Zirconia, NC; (828) 692-6355; greencove.com. Camp Green Cove, for girls ages 8 to 17, was founded by the Bells in 1945 at Rockbrook Camp in Brevard. In 1949 the Bells moved the camp to the upper end of Lake Summit. The buildings surround a beautiful cove where a dammed-off stream forms a smaller, private lake for swimming and canoeing. The main building houses the dining room, lounges, offices, and craft shops where such subjects as weaving, pottery, macramé, copper enameling, silk-screen printing, and drawing are taught. This building and the camp cabins are on one side of the lake. On the other side are four tennis courts, an archery field, a ball field, a barn, and five riding rings, including a jumping course. Each of these adjoining camps has its own infirmary with two nurses on staff; one physician in residence serves both camps. Each camp has a combined capacity of 180. The camper-to-counselor ratio is 4 to 1.

CAMP GWYNN VALLEY, 301 Gwynn Valley Trail, Brevard, NC; (828) 885-2900; gwynnvalley.com. Camp Gwynn Valley provides a special, sheltered environment for younger children, ages 5 to 12. Mary Gwynn established the camp in 1935, and it has been in continuous operation ever since, attaining an international reputation for dealing with the needs and interests of the younger child. Camp Gwynn Valley, altitude 2,240 feet, sits in a secluded cove that opens onto a sunlit valley with a view of the Pisgah Range. The camp's 300 acres comprise 250 acres of woods and a 50-acre working farm, where children can take turns feeding the animals, weeding and hoeing the garden, and milking the cow and goats. Cabin cookouts often begin with a trip to the farm to gather fresh eggs and pick vegetables in season. Baby animals—lambs, rabbits, calves, piglets, and kittens—are favorite members of the camp's "family."

CAMP HOLLYMONT FOR GIRLS, 475 Lake Eden Rd., Black Mountain, NC; (828) 686-5343 (winter), (828) 252-2123 (summer); hollymont.com. Founded by George W. Pickering, who has served in this Christian camp's ministry since 1946, Camp Hollymont's tradition is continued by the McKibbens family. Located on the 300-acre campus of the private Asheville School, Camp Hollymont provides for a fun-filled summer for girls from age 6 to 15 in refined living conditions. Acres of rolling hills and lush green forests provide the perfect summer setting for sports, fun and games, and learning crafts and skills. Girls live in the lodges, in clusters divided by age and grade. A cluster consists of four rooms, with one of the four for the counselor. There are 120 campers per session. As a Christian camp, Hollymont closes each day with evening devotions—quiet, sharing moments, inspirational stories, and prayer.

CAMP ILLAHEE, 500 Illahee Rd., Brevard, NC; (828) 883-2181; camp illahee.com. Illahee means "heavenly world" in the Cherokee language, and this camp for girls ages 6 to 16, which was established in 1921, abounds with natural beauty and high spirits. The grounds are beautifully landscaped. They contain 30 cabins, a dining hall, a new recreation lodge that includes a stage and gymnastics area, an infirmary, a crafts shop, a barn, a canoe lake, tennis courts, an open-air woodland chapel, riding rings, rifle range, two climbing walls, and many other facilities. Each camper sets her own schedule, which can include such activities as riflery, team sports, archery, dance, drama, gymnastics, aerobics, painting, drawing, weaving, stitchery, ceramics, printing, woodworking, synchronized swimming and diving, tennis, horseback riding, hiking, white-water canoeing, rappelling, backpacking, and kayaking.

CAMP JOY, BONCLARKEN CONFERENCE CENTER, 500 Pine Dr., Flat Rock, NC; (828) 692-2223; bonclarken.com. This is a special camp for exceptional children. An opportunity is provided for youngsters who are mentally and physically challenged to experience a wonderful life adventure.

CAMP MERRI-MAC FOR GIRLS, 1123 Montreat Rd., Black Mountain, NC; (828) 669-8766; merri-mac.com. Set in the lush Black Mountain area, Camp Merri-Mac offers two four-week sessions for girls ages 6 to 16. The camp is located on a 150-acre tract of land in the Blue Ridge Mountains, at an elevation of 2,800 feet. Campers are divided by age groups into Junior, Intermediate, and Senior camps and are housed in 13 screened and shuttered cabins with adjoining baths. The front porches make for great gatherings at dusk. The dining hall, infirmary, laundry, and camp offices are located in the Big House, a former private home. Between mealtimes, campers may purchase a limited amount of snacks and drinks. The Mike, or the gym, is a central place for recreation, including indoor volleyball and basketball, as well as musical and drama productions. Three tennis courts, volleyball courts, and sports fields assure physical fitness is a large part of the program.

CAMP MONDAMIN FOR BOYS, 413 Mondamin Rd., Zirconia, NC; (828) 693-7446; mondamin.com. In 1922 Camp Mondamin, for boys ages 7 to 17, was established by the late Frank "Chief" Bell Sr. on the then-new 350-acre Lake Summit. It has been owned and operated by the Bell family ever since. The lake and surrounding 800 acres of private woodlands make sailing and nature studies a large part of the curriculum. The camp also includes five tennis courts, a crafts shop, an indoor rifle range, a gymnasium, a barn, and three riding rings.

CAMP ROCKMONT FOR BOYS, 375 Lake Eden Rd., Black Mountain, NC; (828) 686-3885; rockmont.com. Only 15 miles east of Asheville, Camp Rockmont welcomes boys ages 6 to 17. Under Christian leadership, the camp carries a prestigious reputation with it, serving more than 1,200 boys in the Blue Ridge Mountains each summer. Ranging from 13-day to 20-day sessions, the camp is divided into Junior Camp, Intermediate Camp, and Senior Camp; campers range in age from 7 to 16. Rockmont places a spiritual emphasis on the whole camp experience. Counselors enjoy devotional times with their cabins, and a Morning Watch and Sunday services are times set aside for worship through singing, learning, and sharing. Every Sun evening each camp gathers at a Council Ring site on the mountainside to reflect on the prior week. Boys are recognized according to personal performance as it applies to attitude, enthusiasm, and cooperation.

CAMP TIMBERLAKE FOR BOYS, 1229 Montreat Rd., Black Mountain, NC; (828) 669-8766; camptimberlake.com. Due to the popularity of Camp Merri-Mac for Girls, the Boyd family founded Camp Timberlake for Boys in 1983. Providing a challenging adventure for boys ages 6 through 16, Timberlake operates on the same campground as Merri-Mac but has a separate program run by its own staff of skilled young men. The two four-week sessions and a smaller two-week session allow boys to familiarize themselves with the outdoors and with a variety of sports they may not have access to in school.

EAGLE'S NEST CAMP, 43 Hart Rd., Pisgah Forest; (828) 877-4349; enf .org. The staff of Eagle's Nest Camp believes that the big missing ingredient for American children is membership in a tribe, a village, and a nature-based homeland. This sense of "belonging" is one of the missing links that they strive to create for their campers. One way they achieve the goal is through the joy children gain in knowing that they are, according to the camp's brochure, "responsible and viable parts of a greater idealized whole." This coed camp, now in business for more than 85 years, is designed for children age 6 through high school and offers three three-week sessions. It has a camper-to-counselor ratio of 4 to 1. Eagle's Nest also offers expanded wilderness adventures to teenagers, such as 100-mile hikes on the Appalachian Trail.

> **i** Provide your children with a variety of fun stationery for letter writing. Should they get homesick, they may feel better writing to you or friends on stationery that you picked out together expressly for this purpose.

FALLING CREEK CAMP, 816 Falling Creek Camp Rd., Tuxedo, NC; (828) 692-0262; fallingcreek.com. Though conveniently close to I-26 and the

Asheville airport, Falling Creek's home in a hidden cove deep in the mountains seems incredibly remote. Its campus spreads over 1,000 acres. The main section surrounds two lakes with many miles of trails and outpost cabins between its mountaintop and the river pastures in the Green River Valley. This camp for boys offers many competitive activities while realizing it's more important for a boy to work and cooperate with others than to consistently try to outrank his peers. The camp also has its own camp doctor and dietitian and is the brother camp to Camp Greystone for Girls, about 7 miles away on Lake Summit.

ROCKBROOK CAMP FOR GIRLS, 3460 Greenville Hwy., Brevard, NC; (828) 884-6151; rockbrookcamp.com. Rockbrook Camp, which serves girls ages 6 to 16, has been in existence since 1921. The 200-acre site, 4 miles from Brevard on the French Broad River, is replete with beautiful forests and waterfalls, all of which are accessible by numerous hiking trails. It is also just minutes away from Pisgah National Forest, which is used for day hikes, overnight backpacking trips, and rock-climbing trips. Rockbrook has excellent in-camp rock-climbing facilities as well. These include a 70-foot climbing tower, an indoor climbing wall, and rock faces.

Southern Mountains

CAMP MERRIE-WOODE, 100 Merrie-Woode Rd., Sapphire, NC; (828) 743-3300; merriewoode.com. Camp Merrie-Woode was founded in 1919 by Mrs. Jonathan C. "Dammie" Day, born of English parents, who founded the camp on "English traditions and Christian principles" as a place where girls could come for adventure and discover the strength in themselves. Since 1978, when former campers bought the operation, Merrie-Woode has been run as a nonprofit foundation. Though only a mile off US 64, the camp, nestled at the foot of Old Bald Mountain and overlooking the headwaters of Lake Fairfield, sits secluded at 3,300 feet among rhododendron, hemlock, and hardwood forests.

Blue Ridge Parkway

In 1935 the first mules and workmen began carving a ribbon of road that would span from Virginia through North Carolina and complete its journey in the Great Smoky Mountains in Tennessee. This scenic highway was born in the 1930s out of a need to provide work for people forced from their jobs by the Great Depression. The parkway was conceived as a link between the Shenandoah National Park in Virginia and the Great Smoky Mountains National Park in North Carolina and Tennessee. After the political wranglings ended and financing was ironed out, the project employed thousands of workers and engineers. The inspiration of a particularly gifted young landscape architect, Stanley Abbott, and northern Italian stonemasons contributed to the parkway's beauty and grace.

The designers' goals were as lofty as the parkway itself: to create for the traveler a sense of connection to the land and its history and to inspire future generations to preserve this connection. They succeeded. As you travel along the 250 miles of the parkway in North Carolina, you pass sights that fill your soul and summon you to be part of this beautiful place. Scores of overlooks, designed for their grand vistas, invite you to pull over and stop. More often than not, a hiking trail will tempt you up the hill where wildflowers with colorful names such as pink lady's slipper, skunk cabbage, and joe-pye weed grow in abundance from

ExploreAsheville.com

Apr through Oct. Several endangered species live on parkway lands, including wildflowers such as Gray's lily, Heller's blazing star, and small-whorled Pogonia and animal species such as bog turtles, flying squirrels, salamanders, and bats. More than 100 bird species can be seen during the spring migration season. Picnic tables scattered along the parkway make the slightest stopover a special occasion. Visitor centers and roadside historical markers bring to life the story of the mountains and regions, their people, and natural beauty.

When the parkway flows into North Carolina from Virginia at milepost 216.9, you find yourself in the rolling pasture land of Alleghany and Ashe Counties. Those cows grazing in the northern meadows, the pioneer cabins just off the road, and the lichen-covered split-rail fences are part of the parkway by design. These farms in the northern stretches of the parkway were welcomed, their owners encouraged to stay and work in harmony with the National Park Service to preserve the look of a simpler time. It's as if you turned down a country road with no particular destination in mind and found yourself in a tranquil yesteryear.

As you get closer to Watauga, Avery, and Mitchell Counties, the mountains grow taller, the mountaintops stretch higher, and the horizon spreads farther. (Elevations on the parkway range from 649 to 6,047 feet.) The section of the parkway known as the Linn Cove Viaduct, near Grandfather Mountain at milepost 304, is an engineering marvel. This section swings 1,243 feet around the curve of the rugged mountain. Borrowing construction techniques developed in Switzerland, the viaduct was designed and built "from the top down" to create the least impact on delicate Grandfather Mountain. The structure was built of 153 precast concrete sections, no two exactly alike, and was completed in the 1980s.

> **i** A display depicting the building of the parkway is located at the Big Ivy Historical Park in Dillingham, North Carolina.

Milepost 355.4 marks the entrance to Mount Mitchell State Park, where the highest peak in the eastern United States rises up to 6,684 feet. The mountainside becomes more rugged, the terrain more imposing, and views even more panoramic. Misty blue mountains in the distance cradle the small towns in the valleys below.

The parkway changes again as it approaches Asheville and Buncombe County from the north. Many overlooks provide the opportunity to scan the communities down below. Asheville, the largest metropolitan area in the mountains, is a thriving small city with a unique mix of cosmopolitan and mountain flavors.

Heading south, panoramas widen into vistas that surely must extend to the edge of the world. Many of the parkway's 27 tunnels are in this section. Above Pisgah National Forest near Transylvania County stands the prominent peak of Mount Pisgah, milepost 408.6, at an elevation of 5,721 feet, taking its name from the Biblical mountain from which Moses first viewed the Promised Land.

Past Pisgah the road winds around more incredible peaks and spectacular sights, such as Looking Glass Rock, elevation 4,493 feet. This massive sculpted mountain of rock sits majestically in the valley near the Pink Beds (pink with flowers in May) of Pisgah National Forest below. As the parkway leads south, the names of the land take on a wilder, more mythical flavor: Graveyard Fields, Devil's Courthouse, Shining Rock, Big Witch. Many were derived from Indian legend and pioneer folklore. The road climbs to its highest point at Richland Balsam, elevation 6,047 feet, milepost 431, before beginning its descent to the terminus at milepost 469.1, near the entrance to the reservation of the Eastern Band of the Cherokee Nation and the gateway to Great Smoky Mountains National Park.

There are so many places to stop, by whim or design, it's no wonder that the parkway, with 25 million visitors annually, is the most visited of all the 367 territories in the National Park System. Visitor centers are equipped with amenities to make your trip easier, and you'll find accommodations, rustic inns, and restaurants off many parkway exits. Most are within easy driving distance from the parkway.

Plan on taking some extra time if you're traveling the parkway—this is far removed from interstate driving. The speed limit on the parkway is always 45 mph, though between the sharp mountain twists and turns and the plodding recreational vehicles, you'll often find yourself driving much slower than that. Just relax and enjoy the scenery of one of the most beautiful drives in the country. As a courtesy of the road use the pull-off areas along the drive so that you can enjoy driving at your own pace without holding up others. You'll be glad you did. Check out blueridgeparkway.org.

STOPS ALONG THE WAY

In the pages that follow, we've described some of our favorite stops along the Blue Ridge Parkway in North Carolina, beginning at the state line at milepost 216.9 in Alleghany County and traveling south to the parkway's southern terminus at milepost 469.1 at the Oconaluftee Visitor Center. Mileposts are markers that stretch the length of the parkway, each posted a mile apart. Overlooks and other sites of merit are also noted by milepost numbers. This list is by no means exhaustive—there are literally hundreds of overlooks and other stops along the parkway, and all have merit. But these are some of our favorites.

CUMBERLAND KNOB, Mile 217.5. Cumberland Knob, elevation 2,885 feet, was the first recreational area completed on the Blue Ridge Parkway back in 1937. The Civilian Conservation Corps, a government-authorized jobs program during the Great Depression, built the structures at this site and many like it along the parkway and in surrounding areas. On the 1,000 acres at Cumberland Knob, you can picnic, hike, listen to lectures by rangers, or simply marvel at the view. A pleasant 20-minute loop trail starts at the visitor center and passes by Cumberland Knob. For the hardier hiker try the two-hour loop trail from the center of the knob into Gulley Creek Gorge. Drinking water, restrooms, a book shop, and a public telephone are also available.

LITTLE GLADE MILL POND, Mile 230.1. This scenic stop overlooks a delightful pond near an old turbine-type mill. The water is smooth as glass, and a picnic area makes this a restful stop.

DOUGHTON PARK, Miles 234.8 to 238.6. This 6,000-acre park has picnic areas (milepost 241), a campground (milepost 239), trailer sites, comfort stations, and drinking water. The park has 30 miles of trails over bluegrass bluffs (see our "**Autumn in the Mountains**" Close-up).

AIR BELLOWS GAP, Mile 237.1. Air Bellows Gap, elevation 3,729 feet, is designated as the Crest of the Blue Ridge. The spectacular vista includes a 180-degree view into the valley below, which is chock-full of Christmas trees. The rich green of the tree farms stands out in a patchwork of patterns. Hawks soar on the updrafts of this windy gap, and rich autumn colors turn this into a leaf looker's paradise!

BRINEGAR CABIN, Mile 238.5. The Brinegar Cabin, an authentic mountain homestead covered in hand-hewn shake shingles, stands as testament to the harsh, isolated, self-sufficient life of mountaineers that lasted even into the

20th century. This tiny cabin was home to Martin (1856–1925) and Caroline (1863–1943) Brinegar. The toll that mountain life takes can be seen in a simple photo portrait of Caroline at her mother's loom inside the cabin. The spring-house is still down a steep rocky path, and the garden patch that once yielded the necessities of life is now overgrown and barely discernible. The couple is buried nearby. (Admission to the cabin is free.) The Cedar Ridge Trail (4.3 miles) and the Bluff Mountain Trail (7.5 miles) take off from points that begin at the end of the parking area.

WILDCAT ROCKS, Mile 241.1. This is the Caudill family homestead, where visitors can get a glimpse into the rugged mountain life.

NORTHWEST TRADING POST, Mile 259; (336) 982-2543. Near Glendale Springs, this delightfully rustic craft shop of knotty pine with a genuine rock fireplace sells all kinds of items made by North Carolina residents in 11 neighboring counties. Home-baked goodies, handmade baskets, bowls, old-time wooden toys, quilts, and jewelry made from antique buttons are just some of the wares offered by this nonprofit group that donates all profits to local charities. The trading post is open from Apr 15 to Oct 31, 9 a.m. to 5:30 p.m. Restrooms (wheelchair accessible) are also available.

> **i** For the busiest tourist season of Oct, Blue Ridge Parkway rangers suggest that you can get maximum enjoyment and avoid the crowds by making your trip here Mon through Fri, when traffic is less heavy. Oct weekends can quickly become a slow bumper-to-bumper drive, especially on Sunday afternoons.

BOONE'S TRACE, Mile 285.1. Daniel Boone passed by this site on his trek westward. An information marker provides details about his blaze to the West.

MOSES H. CONE MEMORIAL AND VISITORS CENTER, Mile 293; (828) 295-3782. Near the town of Blowing Rock, this former 3,600-acre estate of textile giant Moses Cone was donated to the National Park Service in the 1950s. Today the rambling white manor house is home to a craft shop that displays the work of the Southern Highland Craft Guild. The mansion faces a picturesque lake, and the grounds are threaded with miles of hiking trails and include two trout ponds (check at the center for fishing information).

JULIAN PRICE MEMORIAL PARK, Mile 295; (828) 963-5911. This popular park of 4,344 acres includes a lake, campground, hiking trails, picnic area, and limited boating. There's an easy 2.5-mile loop trail around the lakeside.

LINN COVE VIADUCT, Mile 304. Built around environmentally fragile Grandfather Mountain, this incredible bridge is a marvel of engineering and gives you the sense of flying over the valley below—breathtaking! There's a visitor center and trails underneath the viaduct. Walking is not allowed on the bridge.

LINVILLE FALLS AND GORGE, Mile 316.5. An easy-to-moderate lower trail leads to the falls. A spectacular example of nature's power, these waterfalls were carved from massive quartzite rock millions of years ago. An upper trail with a steeper incline gives you quite a different view.

CHESTOA VIEW, Mile 320.7. *Chestoa* is derived from the Cherokee word for rabbit. From this spot you can enjoy a scenic view of granite-faced Table Rock.

MUSEUM OF NORTH CAROLINA MINERALS, Mile 331; (828) 765-9483. Informative geology exhibits, rock and mineral displays, parkway information, a book shop, gifts, and restrooms make the museum a pleasant diversion for children and rock hounds of all ages (see our chapter on **Recreation**).

> ℹ️ The intensity of the color season is determined by a number of weather variables. The more vivid leaf color is preceded by long dry spells in summer and cool, moist days in fall. When this happens, and the sunlight diminishes, the trees are "tricked" into quicker cessation of the process of photosynthesis. No sugar is produced to keep the lush green of the chlorophyll, so the underlying pigments emerge.

CRABTREE MEADOWS RECREATION CENTER, Miles 339.5 to 340.3 (ranger kiosk). This 250-acre site includes a picnic area, numerous hiking trails, and a campground. Primitive camping is available for tent and RV campers for approximately $10 per night for two adults; add about $2 for each additional adult. Children 18 and younger stay free. Comfort stations are also located here. The 40-minute trek to Crabtree Falls rewards you with a beautiful 125-foot waterfall (see our **Forests, Parks, and Waterfalls** chapter). Look for wildflowers in spring.

MOUNT MITCHELL STATE PARK, Mile 355.4; (828) 675-4611. Take Highway 128 to the summit of Mount Mitchell, the highest peak in the eastern United States. Hiking trails, a memorial to Elisha Mitchell (for whom the peak is named), a small natural history museum, comfort stations, a snack shop, and a picnic area make this a pleasant stop. In June 2001 a new museum opened at Mitchell State Park. This is an amazing facility that is user-friendly. A life-size wood carving of Big Tom Wilson, the mountaineer whose legend is connected with the mountain, stands on his front porch—a facade within the museum—and greets the visitor with a touch of a button. His great-great-great grandson, David Boone, world-class carver, was commissioned for this sculpture. Pictorials and stuffed animals of the mountains are showcased. The highest peaks in the Appalachia chain are rendered in a stair-step manner for easy comparison. Interactive displays permit the viewer to cause a miniature movement of the earth to form a mountain. The entire museum is of interest to children and adults. Unfortunately you can see the dramatic evidence of acid rain on Mitchell's slopes from several vantage points. On a brighter note keep your eyes peeled for the deer that dart through these woods. Bring a jacket because the weather is windy and cool up here, even in summer.

The massive stone-and-frame restaurant in the park is about two-thirds of the way up Highway 128 leading to the summit, which makes it the highest restaurant in the eastern United States. Open from May 1 through Oct 31, the restaurant serves lunch and dinner daily and breakfast on weekends and holidays. It closes one hour prior to park closing, which varies seasonally.

CRAGGY GARDENS VISITORS CENTER; Mile 364.4. This popular stop offers nature exhibits, comfort stations, and parkway and national forest information. The center is open from May through Oct. At the rear of the visitor center, a narrative directs your view to the village of Dillingham, which is at the foot of Craggy. It states that the flora from that village at 2,000 feet up to the mountaintop of Craggy contains all the varieties found from Georgia to Maine.

BULL CREEK VALLEY OVERLOOK, Mile 373.8. This scenic stop-off point overlooks what was once the home of the great bull buffalo.

FOLK ART CENTER, Mile 382; (828) 298-7928. Home of the renowned Southern Highland Craft Guild, this 30,000-square-foot contemporary structure of rock, timber, and glass is an attractive complement to the natural woodland surroundings. Visit Allanstand Craft Shop, America's oldest craft shop, on the main level for exquisitely crafted handblown glassware, functional pottery, handmade toys, handcrafted jewelry, and handwoven coverlets and rugs. The Blue Ridge Parkway also maintains a bookstore and staffs an information

Close-up

Autumn in the Mountains

Sometimes gradually, sometimes overnight, the verdant peaks and valleys do a slow burlesque, teasing with a hint of color here, a little more there, each stage more exciting until the grandest week of all when the mix of red and gold, green and yellow present their breathtaking finale. Somehow Mother Nature can wear colors you'd never put together—chartreuse and red, orange and green—and still look stunning. And even when the inevitable happens and the autumn color leaves us, usually no later than mid-Nov, something special is left behind. Like colorful wrapping paper torn away, the fallen foliage exposes a precious gift—the mountains themselves. Breathtaking vistas, obscured much of the year by the lush vegetation that flourishes in our diverse ecosystem, are revealed until spring works its way north again.

The kaleidoscope of colored trees is more than a treat to the eye. It gives those of us who have forgotten our high school botany a break. We can easily identify hickories and poplars glowing their bright yellow against a Carolina-blue sky, or mountain favorites such as dogwood, sourwood, black gum, and maple turning deep red, sassafras a vivid orange. The various oaks turn russet and maroon, while some trees can't decide which color to turn, offering a rainbow mix on the same tree.

It seems no one wants to stay indoors this time of year. In celebration of the fine weather and natural beauty, festivals and craft fairs abound. Harvest dances, apple cider pressings, mountain music and dances, special tours, and steam-driven trains forging through the red and gold are scheduled throughout the season.

A special breed of wildflowers blooms late in the year. Joe-pye weed nods its foot-wide head high above the rest. Purple-blooming blazing star and ironweed, golden sneezeweed, and lilac aster bloom throughout the fall.

As you travel down the highways and byways, you'll pass stands selling jams and relishes, dried apples and apple butter, pumpkin bread, and pies in anticipation of the coming holidays.

center here. Up the sweeping ramp, the second-floor gallery houses the guild's permanent collection as well as changing exhibits by some of its 700-plus members. A library of handcraft and its history is also on the upper level. Craft demonstrations, interpretive talks, and special events keep the Folk Art Center

Every year thousands upon thousands of nature's admirers return to North Carolina's mountains to drink in the beauty. Touring the Blue Ridge Parkway is the most favored way of taking in this long sweep of fall color. From Boone and Blowing Rock to Asheville and Cherokee, each turn of the road offers a new horizon, a new definition of beautiful. The ever-popular Mount Mitchell State Park area, just off the Blue Ridge Parkway, as well as the communities of Spruce Pine, Linville Falls, and Little Switzerland and the North Carolina Minerals Museum, are other popular leaf-looking sites along the parkway.

The fall foliage season generally reaches its peak any time between mid-Oct and early Nov, but the degree and intensity of color and peak for each area are determined by elevation. At 6,684 feet, Mount Mitchell, the highest peak in the eastern United States, enjoys the distinction of having the early jump on fall leaf color. The peaks of the High Country of the Boone area are next, about mid-Oct. And the Asheville area and southern stretches near Cherokee along the parkway peak around the third and fourth weeks in Oct. But if you choose the Blue Ridge Parkway as your vantage point for viewing fall color, you can pick any time in Oct. From parkway overlooks high above, you can scan the valleys below to see autumn's transformation at many different elevations.

Alternative routes include the major connecting highways to the parkway or maybe a less-traveled two-laner just outside the major towns and cities. The state of North Carolina publishes a 90-page guide, *North Carolina Scenic Byways*, featuring 11 mountain roads (31 statewide) that give visitors and residents a chance to experience the diverse beauty and culture of the Tar Heel State. Routes are clearly marked with signs stating NC Scenic Byway surrounded by green-mountain and blue-sea motifs.

US Highway 194 is a good example of a scenic byway. This winding back road passes near Valle Crucis on its way to Boone, then on to picturesque hilltop ridges near Todd in rural Ashe County. Another gorgeous option is US Highway 321 from Boone to the rocky hills of west Watauga County and the charming country crossroad communities of Sugar Grove and Vilas on the way to the Tennessee state line. Schulls Mill Road off Highway 105 at Foscoe, outside Boone, is a locally used shortcut to Blowing Rock along a beautiful but very winding two-lane road. Cruising along US Highway 221 from Boone through Linville and the Christmas tree country of Linville Falls before heading down the mountain to the beautiful fields of the North Cove Valley area near Marion is a lovely way to spend an October afternoon.

a vital and continuously interesting place for area visitors. The center is open daily 9 a.m. to 6 p.m. Apr through Dec and 9 a.m. to 5 p.m. Jan through Mar. It's closed for Thanksgiving, Christmas, and New Year's Day. The bustling city of Asheville is just off the next exit.

BLUE RIDGE PARKWAY VISITOR CENTER, Mile 384.7. The Park Service and the Blue Ridge National Heritage Area opened the Blue Ridge Parkway Visitor Center at the end of 2007. The center's exhibits highlight the natural and cultural diversity, economic traditions, and recreational opportunities found in Western North Carolina and along the Blue Ridge Parkway. The center also houses a 70-seat theater for a 24-minute film about the famous drive, an information desk, and book sales area.

FRENCH BROAD RIVER OVERLOOK, Mile 393.8. One of the few north-flowing rivers in the United States, the French Broad River figures prominently in the history and development of the Asheville/Buncombe County area and all of Western North Carolina. This overlook at milepost 393.8 is an especially good place to get a view of the river. It is from here that you can exit just a few feet to the North Carolina Arboretum. More than a thousand world-class botanists gathered here for their first international conference in the year 2000.

HOMINY VALLEY OVERLOOK, Mile 404.2. This pull-off from the parkway is a scenic view of the pastoral mountain valley farm community west of Asheville.

MOUNT PISGAH, Mile 408.6. At 5,721 feet Mount Pisgah is visible for miles around, holding court over the vast land once owned by George Vanderbilt that is now part of Pisgah National Forest. The summit can be reached by a moderate-to-strenuous winding trail from the parking area below. The junction of US 276 and the Blue Ridge Parkway is just south of Mount Pisgah. Traveling down this winding and scenic road to Brevard in Transylvania County, you'll pass the Cradle of Forestry, the site of the first forestry school in America, once a part of the Biltmore Estate. Following US 276 toward Waynesville, you'll come to Cold Mountain, the site and title of Charles Frazier's award-winning book. The parking area just past this road intersection is Wagon Road Gap. It is here that the monarch butterflies pass in Sept as they migrate to South America. They return in the spring. (See the Close-up "**Finding Cold Mountain**" in the **Forests, Parks, and Waterfalls** chapter.)

LOOKING GLASS ROCK, Mile 417. This spectacularly sculpted monolith in the valley below is one of the largest masses of granite in the eastern United States. Its name comes from the shimmering effects of sunlight on its surface when wet. Elevation is 4,493 feet. Though you can't get to Looking Glass from this stop, the view is fantastic. (A trail that leads to the top is off the road to the Pisgah Fish Hatchery, off US 276, just past Looking Glass Rock.)

GRAVEYARD FIELDS, Mile 418.8. These flats were once overgrown with mounds of moss that inspired the name Graveyard Fields, but a fire destroyed the moss mounds in 1925.

DEVIL'S COURTHOUSE, Mile 422.4. The top of this rocky, rugged cliff can be reached by a steeply ascending, well-worn trail from a parking area below. Legend has it there is a cave inside the mountain where the devil still holds court. Due to the nesting of the peregrine falcon, the rock face is closed to climbers.

HAYWOOD/JACKSON OVERLOOK, Mile 431.0. This self-guided loop trail climbs with moderate difficulty 1.5 miles to the summit of Richland Balsam.

WATERROCK KNOB, Mile 451. Adjoining this parking area is a short trail that leads to an incredible four-state view (North Carolina, Tennessee, South Carolina, and Georgia) with a panorama of the Great Smoky Mountains just ahead. Information and a comfort station are available here.

PLOTT'S BALSAM RANGE OVERLOOK, Mile 457.9. Yet another beautiful overlook, here you'll see the mountain range that's named for the German immigrant who settled here in the early 1800s. The Plott hound, a legendary dog used for bear hunting, and the state dog of North Carolina, was brought from Hannover, Germany, by these settlers.

BIG WITCH OVERLOOK, Mile 461.6. The interesting name honors one of the last of the great Cherokee medicine men. An exhibit tells of the early Cherokee eagle killers.

Close-up

Origins of the Southern Highland Craft Guild

Along the Blue Ridge Parkway and throughout Appalachia you'll find signs of the Southern Highland Craft Guild. This group was one of the earliest of its type in the country. It all began at Penland School of Crafts in North Carolina in 1928, when craftsmen from the mountains of North Carolina, Tennessee, and Kentucky met in the weaving cabin on the Penland campus to discuss ways of marketing their work. The Penland Weavers led the dialog and were soon joined by Allanstand Cottage Industries of Asheville, Berea College Churchill Weavers from Kentucky, Brasstown Handicraft Association from North Carolina, Cedar Creek Community Center from Tennessee, Crossnore School of North Carolina, and the Spinning Wheel of Asheville. As the organization took form, Cherokee crafters also joined.

Today the exquisite craft work is produced by 930 members from Alabama, Georgia, Kentucky, Maryland, North Carolina, South Carolina, Tennessee, Virginia, and West Virginia. Items produced by members of the guild range from simple Gee-haw whimmy diddles to paintings, sculptures, carvings, jewelry, quilts, fiber craft, and more.

OCONALUFTEE VISITOR CENTER, Mile 469.1; (828) 497-1904; visit cherokeenc.com. This milepost marks the terminus of the Blue Ridge Parkway, or its starting point if you are traveling north. The popular visitor center, a half-mile north on US Highway 441, hosts several events during summer, including Women's Day and the Mountain Life Festival, which celebrate the heritage of these mountains. Park information and restrooms are available. The center is open daily year-round (except major holidays). Hours vary with the season.

Be sure to visit Mountain Farm Museum, an open-air museum featuring historic farm buildings brought here from the surrounding area. The old cabin belonged to the John Davis family and was built in 1901. It is a good place for children to see how things used to be. Watch out for the chickens, ducks, and other farm animals strutting around the barns filled with antique farm implements. It feels as though the Davises have just gone down the road for a bit and asked you to set a spell and make yourself at home 'til they return. Just ahead lies the Cherokee Indian Reservation and the Great Smoky Mountains National Park.

Forests, Parks, and Waterfalls

Western North Carolina is home to more than half of the Great Smoky Mountains National Park and two huge national forests. The Pisgah National Forest and the Nantahala National Forest combined cover more than a million acres scattered over several tracts. In addition the National Park Service oversees the large section of the Blue Ridge Parkway that crosses this region of the state (see our **Blue Ridge Parkway** chapter). There are also three very diverse state parks to be enjoyed: New River, Mount Jefferson, and Mount Mitchell, plus two state forests: DuPont State Forest and Holmes Educational State Forest. Ten thousand rugged acres make up the Green River Game Lands. In this chapter you will find a number of hiking and recreational possibilities, but there are many other suggestions in our **Blue Ridge Parkway**, **Recreation**, and **Forests, Parks, and Waterfalls** chapters for getting out and about in our parks and forests. Detailed camping information can be found in our **Recreation** chapter. As a handy reference, we have included here a special section that lists all ranger stations, their locations, and phone numbers. They are a great source of information on forest trails, camping, plant life, wildlife, etc. And before you head out, check out the Outdoor Safety section in the **Recreation** chapter.

THE GREAT SMOKY MOUNTAINS NATIONAL PARK

This national park, with 276,063 acres in North Carolina and 244,345 acres in Tennessee, hosts nine million visitors annually, making it the most heavily used national park in the country. Congress authorized it in 1926, but because the land was difficult to acquire from both individuals and timber companies, it wasn't dedicated by Franklin Roosevelt until 1940—and just in time, too! During the latter part of the 19th century, and even more so in the early part of the 20th, loggers were stripping these mountains bare, taking, at first, the most easily accessible trees from land that was later included in the park.

Lucky for us the loggers hadn't gotten around to some of the steeper and more remote areas. As a result we still have approximately 110,000 acres of old-growth forest within the 520,408-acre park. Some of these trees, such as poplar and spruce, are over 400 years old. However, in the more than half a century since cutting stopped, second-growth trees have made such a good comeback that most of us can't tell which areas are old growth and which are second growth.

As important as the park's trees are—and there are more than 130 species here—they are only one part of the area's unique ecosystems, which contain 1,500 varieties of flowering plants, 300 kinds of mosses, and 2,000 different fungi. Among the wildlife that makes its home here are 200 species of birds, 60 species of fur-bearing animals, 48 different kinds of fish, and 38 species of reptiles. Of the last, the only two poisonous species are the timber rattlesnake and northern copperhead, the venoms of which are seldom lethal. Of the 27 species of salamanders that make the Smokies the salamander capital of the world, two of the most notable include Jordan's salamander, a subspecies found only here, and the hellbender, which can grow up to 2.5 feet long. Reintroduction efforts are bringing back the red wolf and river otter. Eastern elk have been returned to the park as part of a research project and are flourishing. The American bison that once roamed these mountains can only be found on farms today in Western North Carolina.

The most famous inhabitant here is, of course, the black bear. Around 1,700 make these mountains their home, giving it one of the country's highest bear densities. It's likely, therefore, that if you spend much time in the area, you'll come across a bear or two. To help make such an encounter fortunate instead of frightening, read *Bear Aware* by Bill Schneider.

Except for some fishing it's against the park rules to disturb any of the plants and animals in this wildlife sanctuary.

The Great Smoky Mountains National Park has 17 peaks more than 6,000 feet high. The highest in the park is 6,642-foot Clingmans Dome, which is accessible by trail and by car. Some 250 million years ago, these mountains, some of the oldest on earth, stood more than 15,000 feet tall, but time and erosion have worn them down to the beautiful and often-dramatic forms they take today. The park is also enhanced by 700 miles of fishing streams. Many provide rainbow and brown trout all year long, but possession of any brook trout, our native trout, is prohibited. A Tennessee or North Carolina fishing license is required, but trout stamps are not. Check out the regulations at a ranger station or visitor center before you fish (see our **Recreation** chapter for more on fishing regulations).

For general information on the park, call (865) 436-1200; nps.gov/grsm. You can call or write to get a free catalog of books, maps, hiking guides, and videos that you can purchase. Park headquarters is at 107 Park Headquarters Rd., Gatlinburg, TN 37738.

> i Because Great Smoky Mountains National Park is next to Cherokee, Pisgah, and Nantahala National Forests, visitors need to pay attention to where they are. A perfectly legal activity in a forest may get you cited before a court of law if you do the same thing in a park.

completely through the park. There are numerous scenic pullouts all along this route through Newfound Gap, and a 7-mile spur road (closed in winter) goes out to Clingmans Dome. Efforts are made to keep the highway open all year, but always check at the nearest visitor center for winter road conditions. Sometimes the road is closed due to snow or ice, and sometimes only vehicles with chains are allowed. Although snow is fairly uncommon in the valleys, Newfound Gap receives an average of more than 5 feet a year.

Under normal weather and traffic conditions, it should take about an hour to cross the park on US 441 if you don't make any stops, but during the peak visitor season from May until Oct or in bad weather, it can take much longer. There are other spur roads, some of them unpaved and some of which are closed in winter, which lead to special areas of interest or campgrounds in the park. These "back roads" offer access to less visited areas and are often scenic in their own right. Most are one way and can accommodate two-wheel-drive vehicles. Check on the conditions of these roads, however, before attempting them. A flash flood or mudslide sometimes makes them impassable.

Most park roads are open to bicycles. No off-road vehicles of any kind are allowed anywhere in the park.

Getting Around by Foot

The park's vast area is crisscrossed by over 850 miles of hiking trails, more than half of which are in North Carolina. Many of these trails were converted from old logging railroad grades or old logging roads. There are 51 official hiking trails and 11 self-guiding nature trails. You can pick up a leaflet about each nature trail as you enter it. For visitors just passing through, there are several trails right off of US 441 that are marked by signs.

A relatively level trail in this area, the Kephart Prong Trail, is 9 miles north of Cherokee. It begins by crossing the Oconaluftee River on a footbridge and will take you 4 miles to the Kephart Prong shelter and back, passing the remains of a 1930s Civilian Conservation Corps camp along the way. The longest trail in the park is the 69 miles of the Appalachian Trail between Fontana Dam and Davenport Gap. (You must obtain a free backcountry overnight permit to camp at shelters along the Appalachian Trail, but no permits are necessary on those sections of the trail outside the park boundaries.) The second-longest trail is the 43-mile Lakeshore Trail on the north shore of the Fontana Dam.

If US 441 is open, you can cross-country ski on the Clingmans Dome Road as well as on other roads that are closed in winter. Horseback riding is permitted on designated trails. Saddle horses are available from about Apr 1 to Oct 31, near the park's headquarters at the Gatlinburg entrance to the park.

Pets, on leashes or otherwise contained, are permitted in the park but are not permitted on trails or cross-country hikes. There are two exceptions: the Gatlinburg Trail and the Oconaluftee River Trail.

Places to Stay

Aside from the hundreds of motels, inns, cabins, bed-and-breakfasts, RV parks, and campgrounds that offer accommodations just outside the park (some can be found in our **Accommodations** chapter), there are 10 developed campgrounds within the park itself. Five of them are on the North Carolina side. From mid-May through Oct nature walks and evening programs are offered at most developed campgrounds.

To camp in the backcountry, you need a permit. You can pick one up free of charge from any park ranger station, campground, or at the Oconaluftee and Sugarlands Visitor Centers. However some backcountry campsites and shelters are so heavily used that they require reservations. Call the Backcountry Reservation Office (865-436-1231); smokiespermits.nps.gov; open 8 a.m. to 6 p.m. daily, a month in advance if possible. You can only stay one night in a shelter and three nights in a backcountry campground.

LeConte Lodge, on 6,593-foot Mount LeConte, is the only lodge in the park. It's open from mid-Mar to mid-Nov and is accessible only by trail. The shortest trail to the lodge is nearly 5 miles one way, and reservations are required over a year in advance due to its popularity. Call or write LeConte Lodge, Gatlinburg, TN 37738, (865) 429-5704; lecontelodge.com.

> **i** There are over 270 miles of road in the Smokies. Most are paved, and even the gravel roads are maintained in suitable condition for standard two-wheel-drive automobiles. Travel times on most roads will average 30 miles per hour or slower.

Some Points of Interest

Clingmans Dome

At 6,642 feet, this is the park's highest peak, the third highest in eastern America, and the highest point on the Appalachian Trail. It can be reached by a 7-mile-long spur road off US 441 at Newfound Gap. From the parking lot a fairly steep half-mile trail takes you to an observation platform, which offers an incredible panoramic view.

In addition to the Appalachian Trail, there are other nearby trails you can pick up at Clingmans Dome. One easy trail for a family hike is the 2.2-mile (4.4 miles round-trip) Andrews Bald Trail. Look for the marked hiking trail at the west end of the parking lot. After about 1,000 feet the trail will fork. The right fork goes to Silers Bald. The left fork to Andrews Bald will take you downslope through a spruce fir forest to a grassy bald with excellent views to the south toward Fontana Lake. It's especially nice when the flame azaleas bloom in late June or early July. This trailhead is not accessible by car from Dec 1 through Apr 1.

Cades Cove

When these mountains were turned into a park, many of the people on small farms and in the communities had to leave. Restored log cabins and barns in a number of areas remind us of these hardy settlers. Few places, however, are as beautiful and well preserved as Cades Cove, which contains more pioneer structures than any other location in the park. Pastures, old buildings, and open vistas are a photographer's dream. And if you are in Cades Cove very early in the morning, you'll likely see deer and other wildlife feeding in the cove. There's an 11-mile, one-way loop that circles this scenic mountain valley and many of its historic buildings. Numerous ranger-led walks and lectures on a variety of subjects are held in Cades Cove every day of the week during the summer season.

There are also numerous hiking trails in the area, many leading to lovely waterfalls. (Because many of these are in Tennessee, they are not included in our **Forests, Parks, and Waterfalls** chapter.) One, Abrams Trail, begins in the back of Cades Cove loop road and is a moderate 5-mile, round-trip hike. Abrams Falls has the largest water volume of any of the park's falls and is among the most photogenic. The 2-mile Cades Cove Nature Trail is great for families wanting an hour's outing. Pick up a brochure explaining the cove's cultural and natural history before you take this hike. Surprisingly few people use this convenient trail.

To reach Cades Cove take the Little River Road, a winding but relatively flat road that follows the Little River, from the Sugarlands Visitor Center on US 441 near Gatlinburg. (See our listing of ranger stations in this chapter.)

Cataloochee Valley

The most rugged peaks in the southeastern United States surround this 29-square-mile secluded valley, many of which are over 6,000 feet tall. The valley was once the largest and most prosperous settlement in what is now the park with a population of about 1,200 residents. The churches, a school, and several houses and barns remain. Once known for its farms and orchards, today it's famous for its dense wildlife.

Cataloochee Valley is definitely off the beaten track and requires a 10-mile drive on a winding, narrow, mostly gravel, relatively well-maintained road that seems much longer than it is. To reach it take US Highway 276 toward I-40. Just before it dead-ends into the interstate, turn left onto Cove Creek Road and follow the COVE CREEK MISSIONARY BAPTIST CHURCH signs. There is a ranger station in the valley where you can get more information on the area. There is also a campground with 27 sites that is open from Apr to Nov. (See our **Accommodations** chapter for more information on camping.)

Close-up

Reintroducing the Elk

Great elk once roamed the region of the Great Smokies and much of North Carolina's mountains but were rendered nearly extinct by overhunting and loss of habitat. The last elk in North Carolina was believed to have been killed in the late 1700s. In Tennessee, the last elk was killed in the mid-1800s. By 1900, the population of elk in North America had dropped to the point that hunting groups and other conservation organizations became concerned the species was headed for extinction.

An experimental release of elk into Great Smoky Mountains National Park began in February 2001 with the importation of two dozen elk from the Land Between the Lakes National Recreation Area along the Tennessee–Kentucky border. In 2002 and 2003 the Park Service imported more of the animals from Canada to astounding success—so much so, that park rangers found themselves sometimes rounding up elk who had strayed away from the Park and onto farmers' land

All initial elk were radio collared and monitored during the five-year experimental phase of the project. Project partners include the Rocky Mountain Elk Foundation, Parks Canada, Great Smoky Mountains Natural History Association, Friends of the Smokies, the USGS Biological Resources Division, and the University of Tennessee. Numerous elk calves have been born and survived. The majestic elk do appear in the park to graze in the early morning hours and late evening.

Mingus Mill

Mingus Mill is 0.5 mile north of the Mountain Farm Museum on the New-found Gap Road. Built in the early 1800s, it's an excellent example of a water-powered gristmill, and it's still grinding corn. Hours vary, but the mill is usually open daily in the summer and on spring and fall weekends.

Mountain Farm Museum

From May through Oct you can walk through a collection of southern Appalachian farm buildings, located at the park's southern entrance at Cherokee, with park interpreters who explain life as it existed here generations ago. These buildings, including a chestnut-log farmhouse, barn, apple house, springhouse, and blacksmith shop, were built in the 19th century and assembled for various locations throughout the park in the 1950s. Admission is free.

Roaring Fork Motor Nature Trail

Three miles from Gatlinburg, you can take this 5-mile, one-way loop through rich hardwood forests and past historic buildings and rushing mountain streams. To get to it turn onto Airport Road in Gatlinburg. Enter the park and follow the Cherokee Orchard Road to the Roaring Fork Motor Nature Trail. No RVs, trailers, or bicycles are allowed on this route.

Friends of the Smokies

Over 60 years ago a group of people joined together to establish a national park here to preserve and protect the natural wonders of the region. This organization, based at 160 South Main Street in Waynesville, is still dedicated to fund-raising and to restoring, preserving, and enhancing the park. For an extra fee, a special license plate for North Carolina may be purchased to support the Smokies. For more information and an application call (828) 452-0720 or visit their website at friendsofthesmokies.org.

NATIONAL FORESTS

As we mentioned earlier, the Nantahala and Pisgah National Forests cover more than a million acres in the North Carolina mountains, including a number of wilderness areas. These vast forest lands of rivers, lakes, waterfalls, spectacular views, wildlife, and the richest plant life in the country can be accessed by federal and state highways, forest roads, and trails. You'll find that they can easily be explored by car, on foot, by kayak or canoe, and in designated areas, by horseback, mountain bikes, and off-highway vehicles. (See our **Recreation** chapter for more information on some of these outdoor sports.)

> i Driving in the mountains presents new challenges for many drivers. When going downhill, shift to a lower gear to conserve your brakes and avoid brake failure. For cars with automatic transmission, use L or 2. Keep extra distance between you and the vehicle in front of you, and watch for sudden stops or slowdowns.

Nantahala National Forest

This national forest, in the southwestern part of our mountains between Waynesville and Murphy, contains more than 516,000 acres, sometimes taking in huge chunks of land and sometimes consisting of relatively small plots. When you travel in this part of Western North Carolina, you're constantly entering and leaving the forest. Although this might not make managing these public lands easy, it certainly makes for a lot of diversity.

Elevations in the forest range from a high 5,800 feet at Lone Bald in Jackson County to a low 1,200 feet in Cherokee County along the Tusquitee River below the Appalachian Lake Dam.

To get a better handle on this vast area, which is the largest of the four national forests in North Carolina, it's best to break it down into its four districts.

Cheoah Ranger District

The Cheoah Ranger District is made up of 120,000 acres in Graham and Swain Counties that adjoin four large reservoirs (Lake Fontana, Lake Santeetlah, Lake Cheoah, and Calderwood Lake) and offer a network of 225 miles of hiking trails, including a 27-mile section of the Appalachian Trail. The Cheoah Ranger Station, adjacent to Lake Santeetlah on SR 1116 and 2 miles north of Robbinsville, is built on the site of a Civilian Conservation Corps campsite and contains an interpretive trail and a fine overlook of the lake. Here you can get forest information and maps.

Sitting to the southwest of the Great Smoky Mountains National Park, this part of the Nantahala Forest is often overlooked by visitors, but the slightly off-the-beaten-track district provides some incredibly beautiful places. First off, there is the 3,800-acre Joyce Kilmer Memorial Forest, which, maintained in a primitive state, has one of the nation's most impressive remnants of old-growth forest. The Gennott Lumber Company, which started timber operations in the area in 1890, once owned the timber here, but—lucky for us—these trees were never cut. Now this memorial forest is a part of the 14,000-acre Joyce Kilmer–Slickrock Wilderness Area and contains magnificent examples of more than 100 species of trees, including yellow poplar, hemlock, sycamore, basswood, dogwood, beech, and several species of oaks. Many of them are hundreds of years old, and some are more than 20 feet in circumference and more than 100 feet high. The area was set aside in 1936 as a memorial to Joyce Kilmer, the soldier-poet and author of the poem "Trees," who was killed in France during World War I.

The Joyce Kilmer National Recreation Trail is an easy 2-mile loop that takes you past some of these great giants, many felled by age or lightning. In some areas the tree canopy is so thick that sunlight never reaches the ground. You'll also find a picnic area here and an outstanding variety of vines, ferns, and early-spring wildflowers and shrubs, such as mountain laurels, rhododendrons, and flame azaleas. No plants, living or dead, may be removed from this area. Wildlife is abundant in this undisturbed forest. The adjoining Slickrock Wilderness Area, with 13,100 acres in North Carolina, contains 60 miles of hiking trails that meander along streams and climb high ridges. It's home to bears, bobcats, and nonnative, environment-uprooting wild boars and has a number of dispersed, primitive, no-fee campsites.

For those who want more comforts, such as picnic tables, restrooms, and water taps, there are two campgrounds, not very far from the memorial forest. Horse Cove Campground, which charges $8 a night, has 18 units, and is by a rushing mountain stream called Little Santeetlah Creek. Rattler Ford campground nearby is reserved for groups.

To get to the Joyce Kilmer Memorial Forest, take US 129 out of Robbinsville to SR 1127 and follow the signs. Both the Horse Cove and Rattler Ford campgrounds are off SR 1127.

There are two forest recreation areas near Lake Fontana. The Tsali Recreation Area has 41 camping units with showers and flushing toilets, a boat-launching area, and 38 miles of biking and horseback-riding trails. The popular trail network here now charges a nominal fee for horses and bikes. The Cable Cove Recreation Area also offers camping and hiking, with boating access on Fontana Lake. It's 4 miles from Fontana Dam, the Appalachian Trail, and the entrance to the Great Smoky Mountains National Park. The area also has a mile-long nature loop trail marked with placards that will help you identify the plants and trees growing along it as well as some historical features. There is a small camping fee. On Lake Santeetlah, the Cheoah Point Recreation Area has developed camping, picnicking, fishing, and boating facilities. There is an $8 camping fee but no charge for day use. Nearby the Wauchecha Bald Trail provides access to the Appalachian Trail (see our **Recreation** chapter for more information on all these recreation areas).

Of all the outstanding wild places in the Cheoah District, two great favorites with anglers, hunters, and primitive camping enthusiasts are the Big Santeetlah Creek area and the 10,000 or so acres that encompass the headwaters of Big Snowbird Creek. The latter was one of the last areas to be settled by whites in North Carolina, and it was here in 1836 that a number of Cherokee Indians fled to escape exile in Oklahoma. For more information on these two areas, contact the Cheoah Ranger Station. 1070 Massey Branch Rd., Robbinsville, NC; (828) 479-6431.

Highlands Ranger District

The Highlands Ranger District covers more than 105,000 acres in Macon, Jackson, and Transylvania Counties. Within it you'll find the 39,000-acre Roy Taylor Forest, which has some off-road vehicle trails (see our **Recreation** chapter) and Jackson County's rugged Tuckasegee Gorge.

The Highlands District also contains two national and wild scenic rivers, the Chattooga and the Horsepasture. The Chattooga, on which the movie *Deliverance* was filmed, is very popular with white-water rafters, but only after it passes the South Carolina/Georgia border (see our **Recreation** chapter). No canoeing is permitted on either river within the district. The Horsepasture River is noted for its five waterfalls. Other famous waterfalls in this district include Whitewater Falls, Glen Falls, Dry Falls, and Cullasaja Falls.

One of the most famous mountains in the Nantahala Forest is Whiteside Mountain, between Highlands and Cashiers off US Hwy. 64 on the eastern Continental Divide. Said to be one of the oldest mountains on earth, it rises more than 2,100 feet from the valley floor to an elevation of 4,930 feet. Its spectacular north and south faces contain sheer cliffs ranging from 400 to 750 feet in height. They were formed of metamorphic rock commonly called Whiteside granite, gneiss containing a high content of feldspar, quartz, and mica, along with such minerals as pyrite and rare monazite. The white streaks seen on its south face are feldspar and quartz. These don't show up on the north face due to lichens and mosses that cover the stone.

A 2-mile loop trail, designated as a National Recreation Trail, runs on the top of the mountain. It offers unparalleled views of the east, south, and west, where you will see at least 27 other peaks, the Cashiers Valley and the upper Chattooga River watershed. To reach the mountain drive 6.9 miles from the main Highlands intersection on US 64 going toward Cashiers and turn onto Whiteside Mountain Road (SR 1600). From Cashiers the turn is just past the Jackson-Macon county line. After about a mile, you'll arrive at the mountain's parking area and the trail that follows the edge of the cliffs. Use extreme caution here with pets and children. This is a popular place for rock climbing, but it's only suitable for experts. The rock face is closed to climbers from Feb 15 through July 15 to protect nesting peregrine falcons.

Cliffside Lake and the Van Hook Glade Recreation Areas, off US 64 between Highlands and Franklin, form one of the district's most popular camping, swimming, and fishing areas. Camping here is $10 a night, and day use is $3 per car. This popular area fills up quickly, but there are also a number of

Cherohala Skyway

For a beautiful perspective on our lovely mountains, travel the 51-mile Cherohala Skyway that connects the Tellico Plains in southeast Tennessee to Robbinsville, North Carolina. (In Tennessee, take Tennessee Highway 165 and in North Carolina take North Carolina Highway 143.) Called a mini-Blue Ridge Parkway, it travels through some of the best scenery of the Cherokee and Nantahala National Forests, thus the name which is a combination of Cherokee and Nantahala.

Much of the two-lane blacktop in North Carolina looks down on the Snowbird, Slickrock, and Joyce Kilmer Forests. On clear, unhazy days you can see into the Great Smoky Mountains National Park. Restrooms, picnic areas, and scenic overlooks are constructed along the way. Spirit Ridge, a lookout just east of Hooper Bald, is wheelchair accessible and offers one of the most expansive views along the route.

primitive camping areas in the district. You can get information and maps at the district office off US 64 just outside of Highlands or at the Highland Visitor Center in downtown Highlands. The visitor center is open daily from May through Oct; the office is open year-round from Mon through Fri at 2010 Flat Mountain Rd., Highlands, NC; (828) 526-3765.

Tusquitee Ranger District

Elevations in the 158,579-acre Tusquitee Ranger District range from 1,200 feet to 5,499 feet at Standing Indian Mountain. It's most famous for its "chain of lakes"—Appalachia Lake, Hiwassee Lake, and Chatuge Lake—which offer opportunities to boat, water ski, fish, and swim. You can stay right on Hiwassee Lake at the forest's Hanging Dog Recreation Area, which has a large campground, a picnic area, hiking trails, and a boat launching ramp. At Chatuge Lake, the Jackrabbit Mountain Recreation Area has 103 camping sites, a swimming beach with shower facilities, hiking trails, picnic areas, and a boat launching ramp.

Just to the north of Chatuge Lake, you'll find the Fires Creek Bear Sanctuary, a 14,000-acre block of land that's been set aside as a haven for black bears. This area offers excellent trout fishing, picnicking, hiking, and camping. The most famous hiking trail in the area is the 25-mile-long Rim Trail, which follows the ridge around Fires Creek over several high-elevation balds that provide super-scenic vistas. There are several primitive camping areas here that include Huskins Branch, Hunter Camp, and Bristol Fields.

The Leatherwood Falls Picnic Area provides picnic sites near Leatherwood Falls, plus a wheelchair-accessible trail for wheelchair fishing along Fires Creek (see Leatherwood Falls in our **Forests, Parks, and Waterfalls** chapter for more information). Another interesting place to visit in this district is the Beech Creek Seed Orchard west of Murphy off FR 307. This nursery supplies the southern Appalachian forests with genetically improved seeds of white, short-leaf, and Virginia pines for reforestation. The orchard also has extensive hardwood clone banks of black cherry, oak, and yellow poplar. You can get district information and maps at the district office off US 64 east of Murphy, 123 Woodland Dr., Murphy, NC; (828) 837-5152.

Wayah Ranger District

The Wayah District (*wayah* means "wolf" in Cherokee) is centrally located in the Nantahala National Forest. Its 134,000 acres are adjacent to the Cherokee Indian Reservation in the north and extend all the way down to the Georgia border in the south. Within these boundaries you'll find the Nantahala River Gorge, with opportunities for white-water rafting and kayaking; two famous national trails, the Appalachian Trail and the Bartram Trail, which meet on Wayah Bald (see the "*Three Famous Trails*" Close-up in our **Recreation** chapter); the Standing Indian Basin; and the Southern Nantahala Wilderness Area.

The 25,515-acre Southern Nantahala Wilderness Area, created in 1984, is managed by the Nantahala National Forest (10,900 acres are in North Carolina) and by the Chattahoochee National Forest in Georgia (where the remaining acreage is located). Elevations here range from 2,400 feet to 5,499 feet on Standing Indian Mountain, with numerous peaks higher than 4,000 feet. The terrain, cut by streams, is steep and rugged. The forests are often dense, but there are grass-heath balds along many of the high ridges. All of the developed trails within this wilderness are rated "more difficult" to "most difficult." The Georgia portion of the wilderness has no developed trails. However, old roadbeds, which have been closed to vehicles, are suitable for hiking. Many of these old roads connect with trails in North Carolina. Several trails are open to horse travel. These are clearly marked by horse-with-rider signs.

Standing Indian Basin is a horseshoe-shaped drainage basin for the Nantahala and Blue Ridge Mountains. It's rimmed by several peaks that are more than 5,000 feet in elevation: Albert Mountain, Big Butt, Little Bald, and Standing Indian Mountain. There is an abundance of wildlife and recreational opportunities here, particularly hiking. The nicely landscaped Standing Indian Campground, which is open from Mar 31 to Dec 1, has 84 camping sites, picnic areas, water, and sanitary facilities for a fee of $10 a night. The Nantahala River, which flows right through the campground, offers fine trout fishing. No reservations are required.

Hikers and backpackers will find a special parking area at the Backcountry Information Center on FR 67, less than a half-mile from the campground and picnic area gate. The Appalachian Trail curves around the south and east ridge of the basin with various trails ascending off it. Trailheads can also be found all along FR 67, including the John Wasilik Memorial Poplar Trail that takes you to the second-largest yellow poplar in the United States.

The Big Indian Loop is a good horseback-riding trail—also shared with hikers, hunters, and fishers. It begins at a wildlife field off FR 67 about 4 miles beyond the Backcountry Information Station and meanders through extensive rhododendron and birch thickets with good views of Big Indian Creek. Just follow the orange blazes. And while you're here, you'll probably want to climb Standing Indian Mountain. To do so take the Kimsey Creek Trail that begins at the Backcountry Information Center off FR 67, where there's a bulletin board containing information about the area's many trails, then follow the blue blazes to the road bridge in the campground. Immediately after crossing the bridge, take the Park Creek Trail to the first blue-blazed trail leading to the left. This is the Kimsey Creek Trail, a moderately difficult trail that follows Kimsey Creek upstream, crossing it several times. Along the way you'll go through three wildlife fields where you may see deer, grouse, or other wildlife. When it ends at Deep Gap, you can turn left on the Appalachian Trail and continue a little more than 2 miles to Standing Indian Mountain. Backtrack (about a 7.5-mile round-trip) or return downhill on the rather strenuous Lower Ridge Trail, another popular but steeper trail that's also used to get to Standing Indian Mountain (about a 10-mile hike). You can also drive to Deep Gap on FR 71, thereby cutting the hiking distance to the summit to just more than 2 miles—a 4-mile round trip.

Mountains-to-the-Sea Trail

Allen de Hart founded Friends of the Mountains-to-the-Sea Trail in 1997. He and Alan Householder were the first to hike the entire 934 miles from Clingmans Dome in the mountains of Western North Carolina to the Outer Banks at the Atlantic Ocean in that same year. In Oct 2002, 23-year-old Jason Pass of Waynesville, North Carolina, was the third person to complete the entire walk and the first to do it solo. His trek began at Clingmans Dome in the Great Smoky Mountains National Park on Sept 2, ending Oct 20 at Jockey's Ridge State Park on the Outer Banks. Scores of people continue this tradition every season.

For more information, contact the Wayah Ranger District at 90 Sloan Rd., Franklin, NC; (828) 524-6441.

Pisgah National Forest

In 1886 George Vanderbilt came to this area and bought several thousand acres of abused farmland near Asheville. Here he built his famous Biltmore Estate, which still belongs to his family but is open to the public. To reclaim this used-up land, he hired Gifford Pinchot, a young American who had gotten his degree in scientific forestry in France. America had no schools of forestry at that time, so the studies could only be pursued in Europe.

When the opportunity arose, Vanderbilt also began to buy up acreage in what is now Pisgah Forest. His dream, and that of Pinchot, was to create a vast estate where forest resources could be conserved for a continual supply of goods. Eventually he owned 125,000 acres and named this vast tract after Pisgah National Mountain, a prominent peak on his land. (In the Bible, Pisgah was the mountain from which God showed Moses the Promised Land. The Asheville area's 5,721-foot mountain is thought to have been named by Rev. James Hall, a chaplain who accompanied Gen. Griffith Rutherford on his punitive strike against the Cherokee in 1776.)

Pinchot left Biltmore Estate at the request of Theodore Roosevelt to establish what would become the United States Forest Service. Vanderbilt replaced him with a German forester, Dr. Carl A. Schenck, who eventually started America's first school of forestry in the Pink Beds, a 20,000-acre parcel known for its lovely mountain laurels and other flowering plants. The area where the school stood is now a National Historic Site called the Cradle of Forestry. It still retains many of the school's structures, some of which were former buildings of the settlers who lived in the Pink Beds. The Cradle also offers guided trail walks and a great visitor center with a wealth of exhibits.

In 1914 George Vanderbilt died at the age of 52 of complications from appendicitis. Shortly after that, his widow, Edith, wrote a letter to the secretary of agriculture that began, "Sir: I now confront the question of what disposal I shall make of Pisgah Forest, which, under the terms of my late husband's will, has passed to me without qualifications or condition." What she did was pass on 80,000 acres of the land to the Forest Service that her husband's former employee, Gifford Pinchot, now headed.

Over the years other tracts have been added to this glorious forest so that it now contains 495,979 acres, which is more or less split across the middle by the Blue Ridge Parkway. It contains three wilderness areas: Shining Rock, Linville Gorge, and Middle Prong. The Appalachian Trail runs along its border with Tennessee, and the relatively new Mountains-to-the-Sea Trail crosses through the forest (see the "**Three Famous Trails**" Close-up in our **Recreation** chapter). There are many other popular attractions here, such as the Fish Hatchery, the Pisgah Center for Wildlife Education, Roan Mountain Gardens, and Sliding

Rock. (There are small parking fees at both Roan Mountain and Sliding Rock, with season passes also available.)

Pisgah Forest surrounds the East's tallest mountain, 6,684-foot Mount Mitchell, a state park unto itself. Pisgah has some 40 recreational areas that offer fishing, camping, hiking, and so on. Some have developed campgrounds, but some provide only primitive camping in order to protect the environment, because this forest is a botanical wonderland. For example, the whole state has 55 species of orchids, and 39 of them are found in Pisgah. More than 200 species of plants grow on Roan Mountain alone. Pisgah is more of a whole piece than the Nantahala National Forest, but it still has some scattered boundaries and is divided into four districts. The most used, with more than five million visitors a year, is the Pisgah District, heavily composed of the land that was originally owned by the Vanderbilts.

Appalachian Ranger District

French Broad Station
This is an area of Pisgah National Forest that can almost guarantee you solitude. Mostly in Madison County with a little bit of the northeast section of Haywood thrown in, it contains 79,292 acres of some of the Appalachians' most isolated and craggy terrain. Many peaks here are more than 4,000 feet, the highest being Camp Creek Bald at 4,844 feet. This area is rich in botanical surprises, including a number of threatened or endangered species.

The district's only developed campground is the Rocky Bluff Campground and Picnic Area, on a tree-covered ridge a little more than 3 miles south of Hot Springs on Highway 209 South. There is also a primitive campground at Harmon Den, and there are picnic areas at Murray Branch and Big Creek.

The district includes some 25 trails covering 127 miles, including 3 horse trails. Nearly 85 miles of the Appalachian Trail travels the mountain ridge forming the North Carolina–Tennessee state line. The famous trail can be accessed in many places, including on Max Patch Mountain (4,629 feet), where there are extraordinary views from its grassy summit. To reach Max Patch by car, drive south from Hot Springs on Highway 209 South for 7.3 miles. Turn south on SR 1175 and drive 5.3 miles to SR 1181. Three miles on this gravel road will take you within a half-mile of the top. There you can take a 1.4-mile loop trail across its summit or a 2.4-mile trail around the top for great views from all sides.

Tocane Station
The 74,458-acre Tocane Station is full of history. Even the name dates back to the Cherokee, because it comes from the Toe and Cane Rivers that are in this area. According to legend, Toe was the nickname of an Indian princess, Estatoe, who wanted to marry a young brave from another tribe. Her people not only

rejected the marriage proposal, but they killed the young man, after which the princess drowned herself in the river that came to be called Toe.

In 1913 the National Forest Service purchased the first 25,000 acres that make up this district on the slopes of the Black Mountains. More than 55 miles of the Appalachian Trail meander in and out of North Carolina and Tennessee along a ridgeline to the north. The Craggy Mountain Scenic Area (not to be confused with Craggy Gardens on the Blue Ridge Parkway) is in the southwestern section of the district, where you'll find Douglas Falls (listed in our **Forests, Parks, and Waterfalls** chapter).

One of the most renowned spots in this district is Roan Mountain Gardens, or simply "The Roan," as it's called around here. This 6,286-foot bald summit is the highest point of the Unaka Mountains, a range that forms a high barrier between eastern Tennessee and Western North Carolina. Even when it was nearly inaccessible, Roan Mountain was famous for its scenic beauty. In 1877 Gen. Thomas Wilder built a 28-room log inn on its summit and replaced that in 1885 with the 166-room Cloudland Hotel. His ads read: "Come up out of the sultry plains to the 'land of sky,' magnificent view above the clouds where rivers are born, a most extended prospect of 50,000 square miles in six different states, 100 mountain tops over 4,000 feet high in sight."

The hotel was abandoned after 1900 and burned just before World War I. After that the old stands of spruce and balsam fir trees were cut, and the rootstock of the lovely purple rhododendrons that grew here was sold to nurseries, leaving only a few straggling bushes. But nature prevailed, and the flowering shrubs came back in neat clumps rather than in dense thickets, though some of these bushes grow from 15 to 20 feet tall and produce up to 800 blooms each. Today, like the guests of the Cloudland Hotel, you can enjoy the far vistas, stunning sunrises and sunsets, and full-circle rainbows, plus 600 acres of rhododendron gardens and 850 acres of Fraser fir. The deep magenta-pink flowers are usually in full bloom during the last two weeks of June. You can learn much more about these and Roan Mountain's other wonderful plants on a self-guided trail through the gardens.

The name of the mountain is a mystery. Some say it came from a roan horse left on the summit by Daniel Boone. It may be from the red-berried "roan tree" that grows on its crest. Another mystery is the strange "music" heard there from time to time that sounds like the humming of thousands of bees. Scientists think that electrically charged air currents swirling by each other near the peak might cause it.

The gardens are on Highway 261, 13 miles north of Bakersville. The road to the gardens is open from approximately May 1 through Oct 31, depending on the weather. There is a parking fee.

There are two family campgrounds in the Tocane District: the Carolina Hemlocks Recreation Area and the Black Mountain Recreation Area (see our **Recreation** chapter for more information). There are areas for picnicking, fishing, swimming, and hiking. A mile-long Hemlock Nature Trail begins at the swimming beach. Two others, Colbert Ridge Trail and the Buncombe Horse Range Trail, start nearby.

Three miles on up Highway 80, turn right on FR 472 and drive 3 miles to reach the Black Mountain Recreation Area. The Briar Bottom Group Camp (reservation required) is in the same area. From the group camp's gate, the 1-mile Briar Bottom Trail loops the campground, crossing two footbridges in the process. Both hikers and bikers use it. Another short trail goes up Setrock Creek to a waterfall. Both the Mount Mitchell and Lost Cove Ridge Trails are accessible from the campground. (See our **Accommodations** chapter.)

For more information on the Appalachian Ranger District, contact 632 Manor Rd., Mars Hill, NC; (828) 689-9694.

Grandfather Ranger District

This very scenic district's 186,735 acres cover parts of Avery, Burke, Caldwell, and McDowell Counties. Very near its center is the 10,975-acre Linville Gorge Wilderness Area, where you can still find virgin forests in deep coves and four different species of rhododendrons.

There are two campground/picnic areas in the district: the primitive, tents-only Curtis Creek Campground and the Mortimer Campground. The area also has two primitive camps in the Wilson Creek area at Chestnut and Kawana, and there are other picnic sites at Barkhouse on Highway 181 and at Mulberry, north of Lenoir. (See our **Accommodations** chapter for more information.)

The Linville Gorge Wilderness Area offers a well-worth-it challenge to hikers and rock climbers. Here the Linville River drops 2,000 feet in a 14-mile series of cascades between steep escarpments. Camping in the gorge is limited to three days and two nights. To control the numbers, a free camping permit that you can get from the Forest Service (828-257-4203) is required on weekends and holidays from May 1 through Oct 31. You can get permits at the ranger's office at 109 Lawing Dr., Nebo, NC; (828) 652-2144. The office is open from 9 a.m. to 5 p.m. from Apr through Nov.

Famous Linville Falls is not a part of the Linville Gorge Wilderness Area. Just off the Blue Ridge Parkway, it's under the management of the National Park Service (see our **Blue Ridge Parkway** and **Forests, Parks, and Waterfalls** chapters).

i Any time you visit the Cradle of Forestry, take the camera for spectacular views of Looking Glass Falls on US Highway 276; take bathing suits or shorts for riding down Sliding Rock.

The Grandfather District has around 70 hiking trails, but many are not blazed or well maintained, so be sure to get information and good maps of the area before setting out. The one exception is the Mountains-to-the-Sea Trail, 46.5 miles of which run through this forest.

Deep Gap Trail

One of our favorite hikes, which includes places where you pull yourself up by rocks and tree roots, is Mount Mitchell's Deep Gap Trail. This excellent but strenuous 8-mile round-trip hike covers four knobs on Mount Mitchell, the highest peak on the eastern seaboard at 6,684 feet. You'll see incredible wildflowers and coniferous forests, as well as ferns and lush mosses. To reach the trail entrance in this state park on Highway 128, off the Blue Ridge Parkway at milepost 355.4, leave your car in the picnic area parking lot. Walk directly through the picnic area until you reach a gravel trail with marker DEEP GAP TRAIL. This is a rough hike that will bring on a quick sweat with its straight uphill climbs: pack plenty of water and a snack. It gets very chilly (so bring a jacket) in this high elevation, and much of the trail is the solid granite of the mountain. A walking stick and dependable shoes are a good idea. This is one of the most challenging hikes of the area.

Pisgah Ranger District

This district's 156,103 acres take in parts of Buncombe, Haywood, Henderson, and Transylvania Counties. It contains more than 275 miles of hiking trails that range from easy to very strenuous as well as horse trails and trails open to mountain bikes. The most challenging and the longest trails are the 31.7 miles of the Mountains-to-the-Sea Trail that runs through the district and the heavily used 30-mile Art Loeb Trail. The Pisgah District also has four campgrounds, plus three group campgrounds. Among the most popular are the Davidson River Campground right on the beautiful Davidson River, just 1.5 miles from the Brevard entrance to the forest on US 276, and Lake Powhatan (see our **Recreation** chapter) on FR 3884 about 13 miles south of Asheville.

Definitely the most popular and used part of Pisgah National Forest is the 16-mile stretch of US 276 from the Brevard entrance to the Blue Ridge Parkway. This route brings you to the Davidson River Campground, the Pisgah District Ranger Station, the Fish Hatchery, the Pisgah Center for Wildlife Education, famous Looking Glass Falls and Sliding Rock, a natural waterslide (see our **Forests, Parks, and Waterfalls** chapter), and the Cradle of Forestry next door to the Pink Beds picnic area. All along this route, you'll find picnicking spots by the Davidson River and numerous hiking trails. One very popular one is Looking Glass Rock Trail, a strenuous 6.2-mile round-trip hike to the top of a huge granite dome, which dominates the area and is very popular with rock climbers. Also try Moore's Cove, a 1.4-mile easy hike that ends at a lovely waterfall that you can walk behind (see our **Forests, Parks, and Waterfalls** chapter).

Two of Pisgah Forest's three wilderness areas are also in the Pisgah Ranger District: the 18,500-acre Shining Rock Wilderness and the 7,900-acre Middle Prong Wilderness. For more information, contact the Pisgah Ranger District office at 1001 Pisgah Hwy., NC; (828) 877-3265.

STATE PARKS

Gorges State Park

This newest of state parks in North Carolina offers a primeval experience. It can be reached from Sapphire off Highway 281. Bring your own water and sandwiches. There are no facilities. You will find the splendor of plunging waterfalls, rugged river gorges, sheer rock walls, and one of the greatest concentrations of rare and unique species in the eastern United States. The surrounding forest is a virtual rain forest collecting more than 80 inches of rain per year with an elevation that rises some 2,000 feet in only 3 to 5 miles. Put this all together and it spells a bounty of waterfalls.

There are numerous trails that follow the Horsepasture River (National Wild and Scenic River), Toxaway River, Bearwallow Creek, and Windy Falls. Some of the mountains to be hiked are Chestnut, Grindstone, and Misery Mountains.

A Bass of a Fish Tale

Lake Jocassee, just inside South Carolina, is not only one access to North Carolina's newest park, Gorges State Park, but it has also produced the fourth-largest small-mouth bass ever caught in the entire United States. And at nine pounds and seven ounces, it beat the old South Carolina record as the largest ever taken from Lake Jocassee.

It all happened on a dark and calm night when Rosman, North Carolina, resident Terry Dodson took his rod and reel to the lake to gather a supply for the Old Toxaway Baptist church fish fry. He knew that something big had hit when the pole bent and the line started running. Claiming that it wasn't that much of a fight, he landed the big fellow and by the next morning of May 3, 2001, the South Carolina state biologist confirmed that this was a record-breaking catch.

This lake, sitting plumb on the state line, offers canoe and boating opportunities in addition to fishing.

Backpack camping is permitted at traditional sites along the Foothills Trail. Horses and mountain bikes are permitted on Auger Hole Road from Frozen Creek Road to Turkey Pen Gap on the western boundary of the park. Unlicensed ATVs are prohibited by state regulations throughout the state park system. Licensed four-wheel-drive vehicles are permitted on Auger Hole Road for access to WRC gamelands during hunting season.

Located on the NC/SC state line, you can access the park off US 64 just east of Hwy. 281 S. (976 Grassy Ridge Road, Sapphire, NC; 828-966-9099; ncparks.gov/gorges-state-park). A parking area with restrooms and picnic table is planned for Highway 281 South and also in the Frozen Creek Road access area. Boat access to Lake Jocassee is currently available through Devil's Fork State Park in South Carolina.

Mount Jefferson State Park

Mount Jefferson sparked interest as a park area in the 1930s when the Works Progress Administration constructed a rough 2-mile road to the summit of the mountain. It took another 20 years of local interest and persistence to reach state park status, which Mount Jefferson achieved in 1956.

Mount Jefferson is positioned geographically between the north and south forks of the New River and was once part of a broad plateau that formed much of the region. The drainage line formed by these two water sources played an important part in the formation of the mountain itself. Eons of weathering and erosion ultimately created Mount Jefferson, the majestic promontory that rises 1,600 feet from the rolling meadows and valleys below.

The drive up the mountain provides spectacular views, particularly at sunset, and you can see three states from the top (Tennessee is to the west and Virginia to the north). There are overlooks along the way and two moderately difficult trails at the top. The Summit Trail is just a fraction of a mile from the highest point on Mount Jefferson, and the 1.1-miles Rhododendron Trail that begins at the terminus of the Summit Trail is a delightful, self-guided, moderately difficult trek through the forest with stops at numbered stations. The lush beauty of the purple Catawba rhododendron makes this trail a delight in early June. This trail also passes by a rock outcrop called Luther Rock, made up of a volcanic amphibolite rock that gives Mount Jefferson its dark cast. The trail circles back to the picnic area parking lot below the summit.

Visitors to the High Country can still see evidence of the once-abundant American chestnut in the building materials of area homes and rustic lodges that predate the 1920 blight that devastated the species. And on Mount Jefferson you can see American chestnut seedlings that continue to sprout in profusion. Red maple, basswood, tulip trees, and yellow birch also fill these woods, and you can spot a stand of big-toothed aspen below Luther Rock on the northern slopes of Mount Jefferson (only one other North Carolina county, Haywood, in the central mountain region, has these aspen trees).

Picnicking is popular at Mount Jefferson, which has a tree-shaded area with 32 tables and nine grills near the summit. Restrooms and drinking water are available nearby. There is no camping available here. Canoe-in and walk-in camping is available at nearby New River State Park.

Park hours are 9 a.m. to 5 p.m. Nov to Feb; 9 a.m. to 6 p.m. in Mar and Oct; 9 a.m. to 7 p.m. Apr, May, and Sept; and 9 a.m. to 8 p.m. June through Aug. For more information, contact 1481 Mt. Jefferson Rd., West Jefferson, NC; (336) 246-9653; ncparks.gov/mount-jefferson-state-natural-area.

Rangers urge you to call ahead before visiting Mount Jefferson during the winter. The weather in these northern mountains is often unpredictable, and roads can quickly become impassable.

Mount Mitchell State Park

At 6,684 feet Mount Mitchell is the highest peak in the eastern United States, and it also carries the distinction of being the site of North Carolina's first state park. The park covers part of the rugged Black Mountains, which were formed more than a billion years ago and soar higher than the nearby Blue Ridge range or the Great Smokies of Tennessee. This extreme elevation creates a climate more like that of Canada's, and many of the plants and animals found here are also more akin to their northern cousins than their neighbors down the hill.

Mount Mitchell State Park was formed in 1915, a reaction mainly to the effects of overcutting by the logging industry that had come into prominence at the turn of the 20th century in North Carolina. The disappearance of much of the forests in the Black Mountains prompted Gov. Locke Craig, backed by concerned citizens, to preserve the last vestige of natural lands in this range.

Mount Mitchell is named in honor of University of North Carolina science professor Elisha Mitchell who, in 1835, made the rugged trek into the Black Mountain Range to verify his conclusions that peaks here were indeed higher than Grandfather Mountain. Grandfather had long been thought to be the most prominent peak in the region. Mitchell, on a subsequent trip to the Black Mountain Range in 1857 to verify his measurements, which had again come under dispute, unfortunately fell from a cliff above a 40-foot waterfall, where he was knocked unconscious and drowned in the pool below.

This park has a marvelous array of 1,677 acres of woodlands, wildlife habitat, majestic views, trail systems, and public camping and picnic areas. Because of the alpinelike climate, the weather here is always cooler, even in summer, than in other parts of the state. It's a good idea to keep an extra jacket handy. The mists that roll over Mount Mitchell are a constant reminder of the extreme elevation and have historically been a hazard to small aircraft.

Mount Mitchell's summit has great sight-seeing possibilities. On a clear day the stone observation tower at the top of the mountain affords a 70-mile view. Dr. Elisha Mitchell is buried at the base of the tower, and a marker honors his work. A small nature museum that once stood halfway up the trail from

Close-up

The Cradle Keeps Rocking

On a sun-filled day legendary Congressman Roy Taylor spoke at a celebration of the Cradle of Forestry.

With his unique mountain humor, Congressman Taylor chided the organizers for putting him on a shaded stand with the participants standing in the blazing sun. "By now you'd think that reason, mountain logic, and just plain common sense would tell you to put the speaker in the sun and the congregation in the shade if you desire a short oration and to the point." Being acutely aware of his constituency, even though retired, his comments *were* emphatic and to the point. He next introduced the heir to Biltmore Estate and great grandson of George Vanderbilt, Bill Cecil Jr. The crowd applauded both men for the wisdom they shared as both Roy Taylor and William Amherst Vanderbilt Cecil Jr. vowed that the creative forestry program begun at the Cradle, which was the foundation upon which the US Forestry Service began, was a legacy that would endure and continue. The Biltmore Forest School of Dr. Albert Carl Schenck, supported by the wealth of George Vanderbilt, had its "campus" and the beginnings of American forestry here.

A devastating fire had destroyed the building of the Cradle and all that was stored in it during the winter months.

This occasion celebrated both the history and the future of the Cradle with its reopening. Still intact were two trails. One could view the historic buildings of America's first foresters by following one trail. The other trail was lush with forest growth, a historic portable sawmill, and the 1915 Climax logging locomotive, whose bell children love to ring.

The Forestry Discovery Center opened as a new and exciting chapter for the Cradle. In April 1997, 18 new exhibits opened in the center. One lets

the parking area to the tower has been closed. In the spring of 2001 the new museum was opened adjacent to the parking area. It is wheelchair accessible. In this rustic structure dioramas and recordings give you a feel for the mountain's special plants and wildlife, and you can easily imagine the extremes of weather often found on lofty Mount Mitchell. You will also be greeted by Big Tom Wilson, the mountain man who found the body of Dr. Mitchell and then petitioned for his body to be removed from Riverside Cemetery in Asheville where he had been buried to the summit of the peak that bears his name. The life-size statue of Big Tom was carved from a tree trunk by his great-great-great

you climb a replicated hillside, complete with rocks, trees, wildflowers, and animals, through the different levels of a forest. Below the hill you can crawl through a 30-foot underground tunnel with roots for handholds to observe the creatures living there. A "Water in the Forest" exhibit teaches the dynamics of a watershed, from raindrops to faucet. Interactive computers let you manage a forest ecosystem and show you the consequences of your actions. A "Global Connections" exhibit and video focuses on issues facing forest managers throughout the world.

A highlight is the "Fire-Fighting Helicopter Simulator," a sensory journey using visuals, sound, movement, and smells to replicate a flight into the depths of a wildfire to drop retardant to quench the flames. Even the simulated pilots bob about with the buffeting of the helicopter—and you are there with them.

Here, also, you can view an 18-minute movie that recounts the history of the first forestry school, dine at the Forest Bounty Cafe, and browse through an excellent gift shop full of charming toys and a fine selection of regional and outdoor books. Outside two separate trails, which you can take with a guide or on your own, lead to some of the old buildings built by both early settlers and Dr. Schenck for his school and forest rangers. Modern-day craftspeople with 19th-century skills can often be found on the Biltmore Campus Trail: You might see a toy maker crafting a Gee-haw whimmy diddle, or a weaver, a basket maker, and a skilled open-hearth cook.

In addition to all this, there are many special programs and events that take place throughout the Cradle's season, which runs from mid-Apr through the end of Nov. The Cradle is located on US 276, 4 miles south of the Blue Ridge Parkway at milepost 412, or 11 miles from the intersection of US 64 and 276 and Highway 280 at the Brevard entrance to Pisgah National Forest. It's open from 9 a.m. until 5 p.m. and admission is under $10. Gold Age Passports are honored. For more information call (828) 877-3130 or (828) 884-5713; cradleofforestry.com.

grandson, world class wood-carver David Boone of Pensacola, North Carolina. David is also a direct descendant of Daniel Boone. There is also a gift shop in the same building as the museum.

The parking area at the base of the summit is surrounded by a 40-table picnic area with stone grills and drinking water. Two sites have fireplaces under shelter and are often used for group picnics. Hiking trails branch off in several directions from the parking area. Look for the white-tailed deer.

Stop at the ranger station at the entrance to the park for information on hiking, camping, and maps of trail areas both along the ridge and down the mountain. At Mount Mitchell you can camp family style with a rustic ambience at the nine-site campground that's open May 1 through Oct 31. This is tent camping only, no RVs. Restrooms are nearby, but no showers or hot water are available.

For day visitors who crave sustenance at this mile-high peak, try the concession stand at the summit for light snacks. For a more substantial meal and an inspiring view, you can dine at the park's restaurant a half-mile from the ranger's office. The sturdy stone-and-timber, lodgelike restaurant serves breakfast on weekends and holidays and lunch and dinner daily during park hours. Both food service locations have restrooms.

Hours at Mount Mitchell State Park are 8 a.m. to 6 p.m. Nov through Feb; 8 a.m. to 7 p.m. in Mar and Oct; 8 a.m. to 8 p.m. Apr, May, and Sept; and 8 a.m. to 9 p.m. June through Aug. The park is located at 2388 State Hwy. 128, Burnsville, NC (off the Blue Ridge Pkwy.); (828) 675-4611; ncparks.gov/mount-mitchell-state-park.

New River State Park

The New River, around which this state park is framed, is reported to be the oldest river in North America. It cuts a deep, twisting groove from the state boundary with Virginia and flows like a curling satin ribbon through Ashe and Alleghany, the two northernmost counties of Western North Carolina. The beauty of this primeval river was almost lost more than 30 years ago when the Appalachian Power Company applied for a license to dam the New River and build reservoirs along its length. Fortunately citizen opposition gained momentum, and in 1975, after extensive hearings and litigation, the North Carolina General Assembly acted to preserve a 26.5-mile stretch of this historic river—from its confluence with the Dog Creek to the Virginia line—officially naming it a State Scenic River. The next year the secretary of the interior moved to designate the same stretch as a part of the National Wild and Scenic River System, and Congress followed suit to affirm the action, thereby prohibiting the construction of dams and reservoirs on the river.

Thus the New River State Park was born. The park covers not only a scenic and tranquil waterway, but three designated parkland areas as well. The pastoral fields and forests along the New River also have their own historic interest: Indian activity here has been documented from 10,000 years ago by archaeological excavations that uncovered pottery shards, arrowheads, stone axes, and other artifacts. This area of the New River Valley appeared to have served as a hunting ground for several neighboring tribes, Cherokee, Shawnee, and Creek Indians, on their way north to hunting lands along the Ohio River.

Today, New River State Park is a popular destination for outdoor recreation. You can picnic at the river's access areas and at tables sheltered by a grove of trees or beneath a bona fide roof or camp at the Wagoner Road access off

Highway 88. The New River's placid waters are perfect for canoeing, which makes it an extremely popular sport here. In fact the Alleghany County access area near the Virginia border can be reached only by canoe. This remote spot is bordered on one shore by an imposing rock face and on the other by a primitive camping area. Canoeing campers at this site must register at designated boxes or with a park ranger. Canoes may also be launched from the Wagoner Road access, the US 221 access in Ashe County to the south, and from numerous bridges that cross the New River.

You'll probably see more than one fisherman hip-deep in the well-stocked waters of this river. Area natives claim these waters provide some of the best bass fishing in the state. Anglers do need a license and should also be aware of fishing regulations of the North Carolina Wildlife Resources Commission. Check with park rangers for more information (and see our **Recreation** chapter).

A note of caution: During heavy rains, be aware that the New River is subject to heavy flooding. Park information and maps of the river's course are available at ranger stations. (See the Ranger Stations sidebar in this chapter.)

Park hours are 8 a.m. to 6 p.m. Nov to Feb; 8 a.m. to 7 p.m. in Mar and Oct; 8 a.m. to 8 p.m. during Apr, May, and Sept; and 8 a.m. to 9 p.m. June through Aug. Alleghany County access: by river only, near Sparta, SR 1549 and SR 1308. Ashe County access: near Jefferson, SR 1590 (Wagoner Road) and US Hwy. 221 off Hwy. 88 E.; 358 New River State Park Rd, Laurel Springs, NC; (336) 982-2587 (for both counties); ncparks.gov/new-river-state-park.

Stone Mountain State Park

Located in Alleghany and Wilkes County, 7 miles southwest of Roaring Gap, This area is a delight for the rugged outdoor types who scale mountains and face windstorms. Weathering action over eons of time has created a mini-moonscape on this dome-shaped granite mass. Climbers are invited and must register when entering the park. Bring your ropes and use the available bolts, but leave your metal gear at home as it is not permitted to drive new bolts into the rock.

Of the nine hiking trails most are noted as strenuous. They include the 4-mile Stone Mountain Loop, Summit Trail to the top for 0.75 mile, and the 2.5-mile Widow's Creek Trail. And now we find two that are listed as moderate. They are the Self-Guided Nature Trail for 0.5 mile and Middle Falls/Lower Falls Trail at 0.75 mile.

Bikes are not allowed, but horses are. There's a 5-mile Bridle Trail leading into the park. There are many comfort zones in the park as well: 75 picnic tables each with a grill, three picnic shelters with Chestnut and Dogwood each having eight tables and Hemlock with 12 tables. Pig cookers and portable grills are also permitted at the shelters, but in the grassy areas only. Some group camping is allowed through prearrangement. Toilet facilities are available, and drinking

Close-up

Boojum and Hootin' Annie

The folks at Haywood County's Lake Logan know for certain that the Boojum walk these mountains. There's an inscription in a cave at that site that tells the story.

This large creature has roamed these mountains since time began. The Boojum was apparently on friendly terms with the giant folks of the Cherokee. (They are buried in the Indian mound in Franklin, North Carolina, but that's another story.) As folks began to settle these parts, the Boojum was curious and watched their every move. With the arrival of newborn babies and livestock, the Boojum danced around the mountains with great delight. Some folks mistook the dancing for thunder.

The Boojum was misunderstood. He didn't mean to cause trouble, but being a big old ramblin' sort, he just kind of messed things up. Without meaning to, he'd trample crops, especially after a hailstorm, for example. So folks began to chase him away. This made him terribly distraught, and he formed lots of mountain streams with his big sad tears.

One day a sweet mountain girl named Annie happened upon the Boojum while he was sleeping. His great snoring was creating an infernal roar in the mountains, and his wheezing after each snore stirred up the biggest wind ever. Annie loved everyone and everything, so she had nary a fear of the big fellow.

"Howdy!" she said. The Boojum was used to folks throwing stones and sticks, so he tried to hide himself. This young gal wouldn't stand for that, however, and ran after him. Finally, possessing one of the best sets of lungs ever having come from Spivey,* Annie set up the sweetest hooting,

water can be obtained from the forest ranger. Backpack camping is permitted, and you can even roll your RV into the tent/trailer area, but no water or electric hookups are available. Clear flowing streams lure the angler, who must possess a current fishing license and trail stamp. "Fish for Fun" is offered at Bull Head Creek. It is a catch-and-release area. A fly rod, reel, barbless hook, and a net are required. The park is open year-round with seasonal adjustments for openings and closings. Give the ranger a call for more details and to register for the many opportunities: 3042 Frank Pkwy., Roaring Gap, NC; (336) 957-8185; ncparks.gov/stone-mountain-state-park.

which melted the heart of the Boojum. He slowly peeked out to see what it was all about.

The Big Boojum and sweet Hootin' Annie became the closest of friends that any two critters could be. Every day Annie would hoot for the Boojum. Every day he would come to her, and the two of them would dance from one mountain top to another. They'd start off at the Pisgahs, and the Boojum would whirl and jig until they got to the Balsams. They'd circle their partner and find their way to the Black Mountains. One day they even got as far as one could go dancing from the Grandfather all the way to the Great Smoky Mountains.

When they danced, the Boojum would roar with laughter. Annie would hoot with joy, and her clogging shoe taps would shoot sparks off the flint of the mountain. Not knowing any better, the folks in the valley thought they were besieged with thunder and lightning.

This tale saddened quickly when more folks moved into the mountains. Trains came through, big roads were built, and then everyone came. The Boojum went deeper into the mountains to escape all this. Annie would commence hootin' while looking for him. More and more she had to hoot longer and louder . . . until one day the Boojum didn't answer her. So she went deeper into the mountains on her search and she was never seen again.

Some folks claim that you can still hear them dancing, hootin', and roarin' with Annie's taps striking off the flint.

One other thing. Folks are strange. Even though they drove off the Boojum and Annie, whenever they get together for a good time in these parts, they fill tables with mountains of mouthwatering food, they fiddle and strum, and dance and sing . . . and they call it a "Hootin' Annie." Now doesn't that beat all!

Spivey is for Spivey Corners located in the eastern part of North Carolina, where a "Hollerin" contest is held annually.

STATE FORESTS AND GAME LANDS

DuPont State Forest

This is Western North Carolina's newest state forest. Its 7,600 acres in Henderson and Transylvania Counties were purchased in 1996 and 1997 from DuPont after the company sold its industrial operation and 2,700 acres of surrounding land holdings to Sterling Diagnostic Imaging. An acquisition in 2000 enlarged the forest to 10,300 acres. The forest is situated in an upland plateau of the Little River Valley with elevations that range from 2,300 to 3,600 feet.

Its gently rolling land is bordered by moderately steep hills and mountains that are topped by exposed granite slabs and domes.

Most of the forest trails are open for horseback riding and mountain biking. Registered as North Carolina game land, hunting in season is by lottery only, and no hunting is allowed on Sun. For fishing, streams here are classified as "wild." (Contact the North Carolina Wildlife Resources Commission, 512 North Salisbury St., Raleigh, NC 27604-1188; 919-733-3391 for more details on both hunting and fishing in this forest.) ATVs are forbidden in the forest.

At present the land is also open for hiking, and the forest has more than 80 miles of trail, ranging from easy to strenuous. (A detailed, hand-marked color map is available at the Henderson County Travel and Tourism office, 201 South Main St., Hendersonville, for $7.) For a short hike to 13-foot Hooker Falls, the site of a former gristmill, take DuPont Road (off Crab Creek Road) for about 3 miles until you see the Little River bridge at the bottom of a long hill. Park near the gated Hooker Falls Road on the right just before the bridge. Walk around the gate and along the dirt road, bearing left at the fork, and continuing parallel to the river. In a few minutes you will approach the top of Hooker Falls. Continue straight on the path to a good viewing location at the pool below. You won't want to miss the other three waterfalls: Triple Falls, High Falls, and Bridal Veil Falls.

If it's a hot day and you'd like to cool off, continue on up DuPont Road for another 2.6 miles until it dead ends into Cascade Lake Road (Buck Forest Road on some maps). Drive almost a mile to a wide parking spot on the right. Walk across the road and go around the gate on the marked Corn's Mill Road and continue on the road. Walk past the intersection of Big Rock Trail to a crossing over Tom's Creek. Continue on the graded road to a fork. Take the right fork, and after a short distance, take the left fork (you'll still be on Corn's Mill Road) until you reach a gentle waterslide and popular ford on the Little River where local residents have enjoyed swimming for years.

There are multiple ways to get to this mecca of land and forest, so ring up the forester to obtain directions that suit you. The park is located off Sky Valley Rd., Hendersonville, NC; (828) 251-6509.

Green River Game Lands

Over 10,000 rugged acres in Henderson and Polk Counties make up these state-owned gamelands. There are 15 miles of beautiful trails here ranging from easy to strenuous, but because of the nature of the terrain, it's recommended that you don't hike here alone. It's also wise to avoid the area during hunting seasons. Some of the trails offer great views of Tryon Peak and the Green River Gorge to the south. Others take you on a ridgeline next to the steep and dangerous Loobie Cliffs or for a view from Pace Cliffs. No vehicles or horses are allowed here. A brochure with a map and descriptions of the trails can be found at visitor centers in the area, or contact the North Carolina Wildlife Resources

Close-up

Big Tom Wilson

In 1835, University of North Carolina Professor Dr. Elisha Mitchell announced that his barometric measurements indicated that a mountain (which in time would bear his name) was the highest peak in the Appalachian chain. The measurement of 6,674 feet stood until 1857, when Thomas Clingman claimed that he had found a higher peak. Clingman and his team measured the peak, which stands on the North Carolina and Tennessee line. The summit is in Tennessee and is known as Clingmans Dome. But it proved to be at least 40 feet lower than Mount Mitchell.

Eventually Mount Mitchell was found to be even higher than Dr. Mitchell thought. Officially it stands at 6,684 feet. It is the highest point in the entire Eastern United States.

In response to Clingman's claim, Dr. Mitchell ascended the mountain alone to measure it. He did not return to his base camp at Black Mountain on schedule. After a search party failed to find any trace of Dr. Mitchell, they called upon Big Tom Wilson. Tom was known for his skill, knowledge, and prowess in the mountains. He was already legendary as a young man who had killed more than 100 black bears, which were a main staple in the life of the mountaineers.

Big Tom conducted the search with the help of a young lad of about 14 who carried a huge rope. As they ascended, the "smoke" of the Smokies, which some people might call fog, crowded in on them. Big Tom never faltered. Big Tom pointed out footprints of Dr. Mitchell that seemed to be going steadily up the mountain.

Approaching the summit and nearing the top of the waterfalls, Big Tom pointed out where Mitchell had misstepped. His footprints showed that he had stumbled on a rock or slipped off a log, evidenced by moss scraped off a rock, where Dr. Mitchell apparently tried to steady himself.

Reaching the top of the waterfall, the searchers saw brambles and brushes at the foot of the falls with a large, dark object floating underneath the mass. Big Tom lowered the boy with a rope, and the lad called up that indeed there was a body. He secured the rope to the body, and Big Tom pulled Dr. Mitchell from the pool and carried his body down off the mountain.

Mitchell is now buried at the summit of Mount Mitchell.

Big Tom has been immortalized by his great-great-great grandson, world class wood-carver David Boone. Standing in the museum at the parking lot on Mount Mitchell is the 6-foot 4-inch wood carving created by Boone.

Commission, 512 North Salisbury St., Raleigh, NC; 27604-1188; ncwildlife .org. It is also your source for information on hunting here. Green River Game Lands are located at 645 Green River Cove Rd., Saluda, NC; (919) 707-0010.

Holmes Educational State Forest

Well-tended trails loop through 235 acres of mountain forests at this pretty state forest. One of the most delightful, and educational, things about it is the Talking Trees Trail, which features different hardwood trees that, at the touch of a button, tell stories about themselves, their sites, and the forest history. Two other trails include the Soil and Water Trail, featuring a 300-foot boardwalk over a wetland area, and Crab Creek Trail, spotlighting firefighting equipment displays and a walk through a pine stand. (Crab Creek Trail was built with wheelchairs in mind.) There is also a Forest Demonstration Trail that teaches actual forest practices. The Forestry Center houses audiovisual exhibits, and a natural amphitheater is available for special sessions or groups.

Holmes also has picnic tables and a group picnic shelter with a massive stone fireplace. For the hardy there are walk-in tent sites in the forest that can be reserved with a phone call. This pleasant state forest is open from mid-Mar through mid-Nov. It is 8.5 miles from Hendersonville on Crab Creek Road (SR 1127), 1299 Crab Creek Rd., Hendersonville, NC; (828) 692-0100; ncesf.org/ holmes.

COUNTY AND CITY PARKS & RECREATION FACILITIES

When time allows, we mountain folk tend to head for the fabulous recreation offered by the 1.5 million acres of public lands in our area, often overlooking the many recreational opportunities right in our cities and towns. In this section we describe some of those recreational possibilities.

Northern Mountains

Alleghany County

CROUSE PARK, 60 Cherry St., Sparta, NC; (336) 372-4257; townofsparta .org. This city park provides a playground and covered picnic areas on the grounds of the Crouse House, the former home of one of Sparta's leading citizens. Basketball, volleyball, and horseshoes are also popular here. Various art and music fares take place here.

Ashe County

ASHE COUNTY PARK, Ashe Park Rd., Jefferson, NC; (336) 982-6185; asheparks.com. Centered in a lush green valley, Ashe Park is well equipped for fun with two tennis courts, two baseball fields, disk golf, horseshoe pits, and a nature trail. Find also two covered picnic areas, a barnlike covered building that can house groups up to 75, four bathrooms, plenty of parking, and a breathtaking view of Mount Jefferson. It's also home to the county's Old Time Fiddler's Convention celebrated each year.

WEST JEFFERSON PARK, 201 Church St., Jefferson, NC; (336) 246-3551; visitwestjefferson.org. West Jefferson's city park is a pleasant, grassy expanse on the rolling hills behind Main Street. Picnic tables are scattered by the creekside, and a basketball court crowns the hill. Lighted walking trail around the park for walking or jogging.

Avery County

SUNSET PARK, Beech Mountain Pkwy, 313 N. Pinnacle Ridge Rd., Beech Mountain, NC; (828) 387-3003; beechrecreation.org. A small park with trails and fantastic sunset views, true to its name. Check out the website for park hiking trails and dog park info.

TATE-EVANS PARK, 210 Park Ave., Banner Elk, NC; (828) 898-5398; townofbannerelk.org. The smallish park still has a walking trail, two playground areas—one area for smaller children and Fort VonCanon for more active children—plus wading pools, a volleyball court, picnic tables, and a covered picnic shelter. Restroom facilities are available from Apr through Sept. The amphitheater holds the Summer Concert Series each Thurs night beginning in June.

Watauga County

BLOWING ROCK MEMORIAL PARK, Main St., Blowing Rock, NC; townofblowingrocknc.gov. Picnic tables, a children's playground, and tennis courts fill this picturesque public park in the center of tiny Blowing Rock. Just off the main street, the park lends itself to outdoor lunches and ice-cream cone breaks. The park is also the center of village cultural events.

BOONE GREENWAY PEDESTRIAN WALKING AND BIKING TRAIL, Boone, NC. The access point for this ambling trail is adjacent to the university parking lot on Dale Street and the Watauga County Parks and Recreation Complex on Complex Drive.

BROYHILL PARK, 1504 Laurel Ln., Blowing Rock, NC; townofblowing rocknc.gov. This serene, beautifully landscaped city park, highlighted by a small, placid lake, is just behind Main Street in Blowing Rock. A walking path, beautiful gazebo, and ducks gliding across the water make this pleasant little park a favorite of local residents and visitors alike. A hiking path actually calls for some hearty climbing on the way back, during which you will pass leafy rhododendrons, a little waterfall, and forestation.

HOWARDS KNOB COUNTY PARK, 604 Howards Knob Rd., Boone, NC. Open from Apr 1 to Oct 31, this park is at the highest elevation in the city of Boone. To get to this pleasant little park, head west on King Street, turn right across from the Daniel Boone Inn, and proceed to the top of the hill. You'll find picnic tables, wildflowers, and a great view of Boone at this 5-acre park.

WATAUGA COUNTY PARKS AND RECREATION DEPARTMENT, 231 Complex Dr., Boone, NC; (828) 264-9511. The county parks and recreation department oversees a number of this area's recreational attractions. Countywide schools are home to a number of park facilities, such as lighted tennis courts, lighted athletic fields for football and soccer, outdoor basketball and volleyball courts, and numerous children's play areas. In an area where winter can bring a definite chill, the indoor, heated 25-meter pool, diving pool, and adjoining children's pool are welcome entertainment. It is open daily year-round, and the public is welcome. Modest fees vary according to age. Season passes are available. A changing schedule of Red Cross swimming instruction, aquacise, senior exercise, and scuba classes is available on request. Tot Lot Park, in front of the Watauga County Swimming Complex, is a play area for all children. A picnic shelter, volleyball court, and restrooms are nearby. An outdoor county pool with a capacity for 60 swimmers is open seasonally from Memorial Day through Labor Day at Green Valley School off Hwy. 194 E. Hours are noon to 6 p.m. Tues through Sat and 1 to 6 p.m. on Sun.

Central Mountains

Buncombe County

ASHEVILLE PARKS AND RECREATION, Asheville City Hall, 70 Court Plaza, Asheville, NC; (828) 259-5800; ashevillenc.gov. Asheville's parks and recreation facilities as well as greenways are scattered throughout the city and provide a multitude of recreational activities and cultural programs for all ages. Many of these are play areas, some with picnic tables and other amenities. The sites are open daily from 6 a.m. to 10 p.m. and can be used free of charge. Maps of park locations are available from the office of city parks and recreation. Outdoor public swimming pools are found in Malvern Hills (Sulphur Springs Road) and also on Walton Street. They are open June through Aug and charge a moderate admission. The pools offer Red Cross Learn to Swim classes, fitness, and lifeguard certification training. Approximately 20 public tennis courts dot the city for year-round use on a first-come, first-served basis. Some of these hard-surface courts are lighted for evening play.

BUNCOMBE COUNTY PARKS AND RECREATION, 46 Valley St., Asheville, NC; (828) 250-4260; bumcombecounty.org. This comprehensive county recreation program includes a multitude of services and recreation sites throughout the area, including softball, soccer, and tennis. The Aston Park Tennis Center on Hilliard Street (828-255-5193) offers memberships, clinics, private lessons, and regular tournament play. Lake Julian District Park off Long Shoals Road is a thermal lake, used as a cooling agent for the CP&L electric facility on its shore. The lake, south of Asheville in the Skyland area, is a family recreation park open year-round for fishing, canoeing, paddleboating, and outdoor games. A children's play area and picnic shelters are also available. Fishing is allowed from shore or by boat for a rental fee. Patrons must provide their own electric motor—gas motors are not allowed. North Carolina fishing laws are enforced, and a local lake permit is required. Hours are 8 a.m. to 6 p.m. Oct to Mar, in Apr from 8 a.m. to 8 p.m., from May through Aug 8 a.m. to 9 p.m., and in Sept from 8 a.m. to 8 p.m.

The Buncombe County Parks and Recreation Department operates a variety of recreational park sites along the French Broad River and at numerous other points in the county. There are also many athletic fields, community centers, and public pools.

FRENCH BROAD RIVER PARK, 508 Riverview Dr., Asheville, NC. One of Asheville's most beautiful parks, the park meanders alongside the tranquil French Broad River and features an area of open green space with old trees, a wildflower garden, a paved trail, a gazebo, picnic tables and grills, an observation deck, and a small playground. The dog park features a large fenced-in area so that dogs may run leash-free.

LAKE LOUISE, Weaverville, NC; weavervillenc.org. Just under a mile from Main Street lies Lake Louise, a human-made lake developed in 1911. The park once sported a dance pavilion on an island in the middle of the lake. Back then, a daily trolley line from the big city of Asheville brought dapper gentlemen and ruffle-skirted young ladies to Lake Louise for evening dance socials. Today, Lake Louise, with its central 40-foot-high fountain, offers a children's playground, an outdoor exercise facility, public restrooms, picnic shelters, and a 0.61-mile walking trail. Walkers on the popular lake path can observe an assortment of tree species cultivated by the Tree Board of the Town of Weaverville. You can identify more than 34 kinds, including sycamores, river birch, Japanese maples, flowering cherry, sugar maples, weeping willow, sweet gum, redbud, and Virginia Pine.

LAKE TOMAHAWK PARK, 401 Laurel Circle Dr., Black Mountain, NC; (828) 669-2052; bmrp.cdesk.com. This lovely little lake and 20-acre park in a residential area of picturesque Black Mountain was a WPA Depression-era project. Visitors can enjoy the scenic water view, well-trod 0.55-mile walking path around the lake, landscaping, and resident waterfowl. A community center, public pool, tennis courts, and play areas are part of Lake Tomahawk Park. The park opens around 5 a.m. and closes around midnight.

MARTIN LUTHER KING, JR. PARK, 50 Martin Luther King, Jr. Dr.; Asheville, NC. This park located near downtown pays homage to the great civil rights leader, Dr. Martin Luther King, Jr., with a life-size memorial statue set in a landscaped courtyard and includes a lighted ball field with concessions, playground, picnic shelter, restrooms, and parking.

Henderson County

BOYD PARK, 840 N. Church St., Hendersonville, NC; (828) 697-3007. This city park is within walking distance of downtown. It has a miniature golf course and an activity building used for meetings and events, such as local cat shows.

JACKSON PARK, 801 4th Ave. E., Hendersonville, NC; (828) 697-4884. As the largest municipal-owned park in Western North Carolina, Jackson Park offers activities and facilities for all ages, such as concession stands, mountain bike skills park, lighted tennis courts, nine lighted softball/baseball fields, two soccer fields, lighted basketball courts, playgrounds, covered picnic shelters (for 50 to 150 persons), 20 woodland picnic tables overlooking the playing fields, modern restrooms, a disc golf course, and 1.2-mile nature trail.

Polk County

POLK COUNTY RECREATION DEPARTMENT, 105 N. Peak St., Columbus, NC; (828) 894-8199. The Polk County Recreation Department, which is dedicated to serving citizens of all ages, offers programs in aerobics, youth basketball, youth volleyball, line dancing, men's basketball, and stretch-and-strengthen exercises at Stearns Gym on Walker Street. Gibson Park on Park Street boasts a baseball field and swimming pool. The pool, open from June through Aug, offers family passes, swimming lessons, and water aerobics.

Transylvania County

BREVARD COLLEGE, 400 N. Broad St., Brevard, NC; (828) 883-8292. Many of the recreation facilities at Brevard College, including the indoor swimming pool, are open to the public through inexpensive continuing education classes that include aerobics, water aerobics, beginning rock climbing, and even golf. The campus is also a popular place for runners and walkers.

SILVERMONT PARK, 364 E. Main St., Brevard, NC; (828) 884-3166; silvermont.org. Open seven days a week from 8:30 a.m. until 10 p.m., Silvermont has two lighted basketball courts, three tennis courts, a playground, a picnic shelter, and a walking path located on the grounds of a historic mansion. Mountain Music Night with a live local artist is free of charge every Thurs from 7:30 until 10 p.m.

SOUTH BROAD PARK, 335 S. Broad St., Brevard, NC; (828) 884-3156. The small picnic area found at this arboretum is a lovely place to bring a lunch. It's right next to a large multipurpose playing field.

Southern Mountains

Cherokee County

ANDREWS RECREATION PARK, 160 Park St., Andrews, NC; (828) 321-2135; visitcherokeecountync.com/parks. Andrews Recreation Park has a beach volleyball court, basketball and tennis courts, a softball field, playground equipment, and an area for horseshoe games. In addition there is a Little League baseball field, picnic areas, swimming pools, and the Andrews Community Center, which contains a large room with a stage, a smaller meeting room, and kitchen and restroom facilities. The park is wheelchair accessible.

HALL MEMORIAL PARK, 33 First St., Andrews, NC; (828) 321-2135; visitcherokeecountync.com/parks. Constructed in 1993, the small park next to the railroad in downtown Andrews provides benches, a gazebo used for many town events, picnic tables, and a grass area accented with flowers. The stage often hosts live music, plays, and festivals. From June to mid-Oct the park serves as host to the Andrews Farmer's Market, a place where local farmers sell their grown produce to the public. Andrews' Christmas tree lighting ceremony is held at this location every year.

KONEHETE PARK, 103 Konehete St., Murphy, NC; (828) 837-6617. This large city park offers a swimming pool, four lighted tennis courts, and four baseball/softball fields (three with lights). There are also areas for fishing, volleyball, two soccer fields, and outdoor basketball courts. Organized activities include swim teams, football, basketball, baseball, softball, and soccer leagues for children, youth, and adults. Wrestling, gymnastics, aerobics, line dancing, basketball, and other events are held in the park's Old Rock Gym. Runners and walkers can use the trail or sidewalks throughout Konehete Park or use the running track at Murphy High School.

Clay County

CLAY COUNTY PARK CAMPGROUND, 47 Clay Recreation Park Rd., Hayesville, NC; (828) 389-3532. This popular public park, not far from the 140-foot-high Chatuge Dam, is on Hwy. 175 on Lake Chatuge. The park has 25 campsites, picnic and swimming areas, a boat launch, and a ballpark.

Haywood County

TOWN OF CANTON RECREATION PARK, 77 Penland St., Canton, NC; (828) 646-3411. This city park, roughly 17 acres in size, contains three picnic sheds and numerous outside picnic tables, two outdoor basketball courts, four lighted tennis courts, play equipment both for small children and teenagers, and two Little League baseball fields. The park's swimming pool and wading pool are open from mid-May until the Sept 1. Canton also has an entertainment shelter and bandstand where summer programs are held. Around the park is a 1-mile walking and jogging trail along the banks of the Pigeon River. The parks department uses the sports fields at area public schools for team sports.

TOWN OF WAYNESVILLE RECREATION PARK, 550 Vance St., Waynesville, NC; (828) 456-2030; waynesvillenc.gov/recreation-park. There's plenty of action at this park, which consists of six hard-surface tennis counts, two outdoor basketball courts, a swimming pool, two picnic areas with shelters, a playground, three softball/baseball fields, two sand volleyball courts, a modified golf driving range, soccer fields, shuffleboard, a 0.25-mile track and fitness trail, a horse-show ring, and a recreation building. The City Parks and Recreation Department, which runs the complex, also sponsors all kinds of youth and adult team sports and special events that include an open tennis championship, a trout fishing festival, an Easter egg hunt, and judo and bridge tournaments. For senior citizens there are craft and exercise classes, trips, health programs, and meals. There's a full complement of fitness, hobby, and education classes for other adults and children, too.

Jackson County

RJ ANDREWS CAMPGROUND, 814 Ralph J. Andrews Park Rd., Glenville, NC; (828) 743-3923. Built on land near the Glenville dam donated to the county by the Nantahala Power Company, this 78-acre park offers full RV hookups, tent camping, picnicking, hot showers, and boat ramp access to Lake Glenville. To reach it go about 1.5 miles north of the Glenville Post Office until you come to Pine Creek Road on the left. Follow the signs to the park entrance, approximately 2 miles down the road.

Close-up

Finding Cold Mountain

Ever since Charles Frazier's *Cold Mountain*, a novel about a Civil War soldier's walk home to his beloved Ada, became a best-seller and its 2003 cinematic version was a box office hit, people have wanted to know how to find this 6,030-foot peak, located in Haywood County. There is a trail to the top, but only very experienced hikers should take it. It's steep, poorly marked, and according to how you go, 14 to 16 miles round-trip.

Those not so footworthy can take US Hwy. 276 from the Blue Ridge Parkway toward Waynesville. This roughly follows along Wagon Road Gap along the east side of the mountain. Near Cruso, turn onto US Hwy. 215, which will run along the western side of the peak. This 50-mile circle will take you past many of the coves, creeks, and churches mentioned in the book and bring you back to the Blue Ridge Parkway not very far south of where you left it.

If you haven't time for this wonderful tour, just stop at the parkway's milepost 420. The massive peak in the distance is Cold Mountain.

WESTERN CAROLINA UNIVERSITY, CAMPUS RECREATION CENTER, 245 Memorial Dr., Cullowhee, NC; (828) 227-7069; wcu.edu/experience/campus-recreation. Recreation facilities at the university include the Reid Health and Physical Education Building, Breese Gymnasium, A. K. Hinds University Center, and Ramsey Regional Activity Center. Among the indoor and outdoor sports available here are tennis, volleyball, basketball, swimming, bowling, handball, racquetball, softball, badminton, table tennis, and archery. The swim program is open to the public. Also open to the public are continuing education courses in yoga, t'ai chi ch'uan, hydrorobics, and other fitness classes.

Macon County

HIGHLANDS RECREATION PARK, 600 N. 4th St., Highlands, NC; (828) 526-3556. The recreation center here is open to the public from 8 a.m. to 10 p.m. Mon through Sat and noon to 6 p.m. on Sun. It offers swimming, a Nautilus room, tennis courts, and aerobics—all for a small fee. You can join a cardiovascular program or play softball, baseball, volleyball, basketball, bridge, and duplicate bridge here. Classes are taught in tumbling, rappelling, and wrestling. There is a picnic shelter with a playground nearby. The parks department also sponsors a Fourth of July Celebration, complete with a parade and fireworks, as well as a summer playground program, various bazaars, and a craft festival.

MACON COUNTY RECREATION PARK, US Hwy. 441 S., Franklin, NC; (828) 349-2090. The many attractions at this large and well-maintained park include softball fields, indoor and outdoor basketball courts, shuffleboard and tennis courts, horseshoes, a children's playground, a loop walking trail, a gymnasium, a swimming pool, two outdoor picnic shelters, and four conference/party rooms. The community building here is open from 8 a.m. to 5 p.m. daily.

> **i** As viewed from the Macon County Osage Overlook, the mountains seem to go on forever in shifting hues of blue and green. At certain times during the year, the mountains are totally shrouded in blue, which gives both the mountains and the Blue Valley Overlook their names. For a view you won't forget, drive 5.5 miles south of Highlands on Highway 106. Just a bit farther down this same highway, you'll come to the Osage Overlook with another great view of the Blue Valley.

Swain County

BRYSON CITY ISLAND PARK, 213 Bryson St., Bryson City, NC. As early as 1890 the editor of the *Swain County Herald*, the county's first newspaper, urged the county commissioners to strike a bargain for Island Park, as he called the 7-acre island in the Tuckasegee River, "where citizens may find a pleasant rendezvous far from the noise and bustle of city life." However it wasn't until 1986, almost a century later, that Bryson City's downtown island, reached by a swinging bridge, finally became a park. A lighted trail circles the island and tags identify many of the native plants and wildflowers along the trail. Boy Scouts who used the island for a camping site and headquarters in the 1930s and 1940s built the interpretive center. Island Park has a launching site for canoes and kayaks and areas for picnicking and fishing.

RIVERFRONT PARK, 101 Mitchell St., Bryson City, NC. This half-acre park that runs along the Tuckasegee is the site of the town's Riverfest. It also has a picnic area, including a covered pavilion and a walking trail. Another of Bryson City's parks, the small Ela River Park, also on the Tuckasegee, is used mostly for picnicking and fishing.

Swain County Recreation Park, 30 Recreation Park Dr., Bryson City, NC; (828) 488-6159; swaincountync.gov. This attractive 34-acre park has a lighted field for baseball and softball, four lighted tennis courts, a basketball court, two playgrounds, shuffleboard and volleyball courts, horseshoe pits, a pavilion and picnic area, and a jogging trail. There is also an outdoor swim complex with an Olympic-size pool, an intermediate pool, and a kiddie pool. The pools are open June through Aug for a small admission price. Season tickets are available. The list of organized activities includes several softball leagues, volleyball, soccer, aerobics, line dancing, tennis, and swimming lessons. Youth programs feature karate, winter ski instruction, ball programs, and a billiards league. The parks department also sponsors events such as the Christmas Extravaganza.

WATERFALLS

Whether it's the roar of a great cataract forming rainbows in its drenching spray or a slender, misty stream of water musically splashing in a shallow pool, there are few places where the call of the falls can be so fulfilled as in Western North Carolina. There are literally hundreds of waterfalls in these mountains, more than 250 in Transylvania County alone.

Nature and time have provided waterfalls throughout the mountains. Some are on private property, and others can only be reached by long and strenuous hikes though rugged country. Most of the ones we've chosen are just a short jaunt from a roadway, and some of these falls can be viewed simply by parking your car and taking a look. We have listed several worth the extra effort required to reach them, even though it sometimes means traveling on a narrow, curvy, graveled secondary road (SR) or Forest Service road (FR).

A few words of caution are in order: Water-drenched rocks are extremely treacherous, and a number of serious accidents and deaths occur each year to people who slip and fall from the tops of these falls or from the spray- and moss-slick rocks, steps, and trails nearby. (Even when fording mountain streams, extreme care is needed.) Use common sense and caution. Keep a sharp eye on children. Stay well away from the tops of falls and never try to climb or walk across them. Avoid tragedies.

Areas where nominal fees are collected include Sliding Rock, Dry Falls, and Whitewater Falls. A season pass costs under $20. However, one pass is needed for Sliding Rock and another is required for and provides access to Dry Falls and Whitewater Falls, as well as nearby Whiteside Mountain.

Northern Mountains

Avery County

ELK FALLS, off US Hwy. 19 E. Sixty-five-foot Elk Falls, just inside the Tennessee–North Carolina border, is one of the most beautiful waterfalls in the mountains. Its lovely pool, one of the largest and deepest around, makes this a super popular swimming hole, but beware of the fast water here.

Elk Falls is easily accessible; just go north on US 19 East to the town of Elk Park. A short distance up Main Street (SR 1303), turn right on Elk River Road (SR 1305), a residential street. Travel just over 4 miles to a parking area beside the Elk River. Here a short trail leads to the top and on down to the base of the falls.

Burke County

LINVILLE FALLS, Mile 316.5, Blue Ridge Pkwy. Well-known Linville Falls, at the head of Linville Gorge, pours downward in several stages into one of the deepest gorges in the eastern United States. You can reach the falls by hiking from the Linville Falls Visitors Center at milepost 316.5 on the Blue Ridge Parkway. For specific directions check the maps posted at the center. The trails to various overlooks of the falls range from easy to difficult.

> **i** Famous Linville Gorge and Linville Falls were named for William Linville and his son, John, who were killed by Indians in 1766. The Cherokee called the river eeseeoh or "river of many cliffs."

UPPER CREEK FALLS, off Hwy. 181. The main part of this cascade tumbles some 100 feet into a pool of thrashing water. This and the fact that it's moderately easy to get to make Upper Creek Falls a popular swimming and sunbathing area. To reach it, take Hwy. 181 south from the Blue Ridge Parkway for just more than 5.5 miles to a parking area on the left. A nearly mile-long, steep switchback trail descends through the woods to the falls.

Yancey County

CRABTREE FALLS, Mile 339.5, Blue Ridge Pkwy. This 70-foot waterfall, considered to be one of the most photogenic in the state, is in the Crabtree Meadows Recreation Area (elevation 3,700 feet) on the Blue Ridge Parkway, 8.4 miles south of the junction of Highway 226 at milepost 339.5. The steep, rocky trail makes for a moderately difficult hike from the parking lot in the Crabtree Meadows camping area (you can pick up a trail guide at the campground's entrance during the summer months). In winter, when the campgrounds are closed, you'll have to park outside the gate and walk in. A loop trail, lined with birch and hemlock and, in spring and summer, a great variety of wildflowers, leads to this beautiful 70-foot falls. To get to the falls by the shortest route, nearly a mile, descend the trail to the right. You can come back the same way for

ExploreAsheville.com

a trip of slightly less than 2 miles or continue on the 2.5-mile loop. If you do the latter, bear to the left to avoid trails leading into the campground.

SETROCK CREEK AND ROARING FORK FALLS, 3 miles off Hwy. 80 N. From the Blue Ridge Parkway, exit onto Highway 80 North (at milepost 344) and go approximately 2 miles north to F R 472. Make a left onto FR 472 and drive 4.7 miles to the Black Mountain Campground. Inside the campground you'll see a sign leading to the Briar Bottom group camp. Drive the short distance to a sign on the right that marks the way to this 75-foot cascade. When the trail forks, bear right. This is a round-trip excursion of a little more than a 0.5 mile. When you return to your car, continue your journey another 3.9 miles down FR 472 (when the road changes from gravel to pavement, it becomes SR 1205). At the busick work center sign, turn right and park at the gate. The trail, an old logging road to the right of the gate, will take you to Roaring Fork River. Turn right on a path at the river. You'll find the falls, which drop in beautiful 5-foot cascades, about a mile away.

The mossy rocks and leaves form alcoves worthy of the Garden of Eden! A trail running up the forested right side of the falls let you into a small pool at the top. Be very careful and use only the trail to get to the top.

WATERFALL ON BIG CREEK, off US 19 W. This gushing waterfall, which can be viewed from the road, is reached by taking US 19 out of Burnsville and then turning right on US 19 West toward the Tennessee border. Drive 17.5 miles to a marked pull-off on the left for a view of the 25-foot falls.

Central Mountains

Buncombe County

DOUGLAS (or Carter Creek) and **WALKER FALLS**, 5 miles south of Hwy. 197. A journey into Pisgah's Craggy Mountain Scenic Area to view Douglas Falls offers an added attraction: The falls are surrounded by a stand of rare virgin hemlock. To reach the area take US Highways 19/23 North out of Asheville for 13.5 miles and then go east on Highway 197 to Barnardsville. Turn south on Dillingham Road (SR 2173) about a half-block past the post office. About 4 miles down this winding road, veer to the left and continue until it becomes graveled FR 74; stop for a view of two-tier, 50-foot Walker Falls on the left.

Continue on another 5 miles or so until you dead-end at the Craggy Mountain Scenic Area parking area. Take the trail on the south end (right side) of the parking lot. It's a little more than 0.5 mile to a viewing area at the base of 70-foot Douglas Falls, named in honor of Supreme Court Justice William O. Douglas. Unless you are an experienced hiker armed with a good topographical map and compass, return the way you came. Most trail maps of this area are outdated and confusing. For the best viewing, visit both these falls after heavy rains.

GLASSMINE FALLS, Mile 361.1, Blue Ridge Pkwy. This waterfall is on private land, and its water flow can be thin when rain is scarce. (It's been known to dry up completely.) However after heavy rains, Glassmine Falls, with its immense slide downward, can be impressive. You can view the falls from Glassmine Falls Overlook at milepost 361.1 on the Blue Ridge Parkway. This overlook is about 200 feet from the parking area, which is 5.7 miles south of Highway 128, the road that leads to Mount Mitchell's summit. It will be on the left when driving south from Mount Mitchell and on the right when driving north. Look east to locate the fall's steep rock face (estimated at 800 feet), framed by stark skeletons of red spruce that have died from air pollution.

Polk County

PEARSON FALLS, off Pearson Falls Rd. (SR 1102). There is a small fee for adults and 50 cents for children 6 to 12 (children younger than 6 are admitted free) to Pearson Falls Park, which is owned and maintained by the Tryon Garden Club, and it's well worth the price. Take US Highway 176 South out of Saluda or north out of Tryon. Watch for a small sign on the Pacolet River side of the road that marks Pearson Falls Road (SR 1102). The entrance to the 250-acre park is slightly less than a mile down this road. This biologically rich glen with its profusion of wildflowers was purchased in 1931 and is now a North Carolina Natural Heritage Area. It's a great place for hiking, bird-watching, and picnicking. The park is open from 10 a.m. to 6 p.m. daily in the summer. From Nov 1 to Mar 1, it's closed on Mon and Tues and is only open from 10 a.m. to 5 p.m. the rest of the week.

SHUNKAWAUKEN FALLS, White Oak Mountain Rd., SR 1136. This cascade begins its tumbles practically from the summit of 3,102-foot White Oak Mountain, with the main portion measuring around 150 feet high. Though it's on private land, it can be viewed right from the roadside. From I-26 drive east on Highway 108 for just less than a half-mile and turn left on Houston Road (SR 1137). After another half-mile, take the fork to the left onto White Oak Mountain Road (SR 1136). You'll come to the waterfall in another 2 miles. There is a pull-off on the left just beyond it. If you continue on down the road for just a little more than 0.5 mile, you'll reach an overlook with a great view of Columbus and the surrounding area.

> **i** National Forest Service visitor centers often carry maps to waterfalls in the area.

Rutherford County

HICKORY NUT FALLS, inside Chimney Rock Park off US Hwy. 64 E. This waterfall spilling 404 feet over a granite face is just over the Henderson County line at Lake Lure and can be seen from quite a distance. Hickory Nut Falls are located in the privately owned Chimney Rock Park (see our Attractions chapter). Admission ($14 for adults and $6 for children 6 to 15; children under 6 are free) includes a 26-story elevator ride up through solid rock and access to nature trails offering unparalleled views of the falls (the best is from Inspiration Point). It also offers a smashing view of Lake Lure, craggy-faced Rumbling Bald Mountain, and the surrounding countryside. For a preview of the falls, you may want to rent the 1992 movie *The Last of the Mohicans*, which featured the majestic falls prominently. To reach the park, take US 64 E. off I-26 and drive approximately 15 miles through Bat Cave to the park.

Transylvania County

COURTHOUSE FALLS, off Hwy. 215. You'll have to walk a short distance to reach this waterfall, but it's one of our favorites and one of the most beautiful in the mountains. Take Highway 215 for 10.4 miles into Pisgah Forest from its junction with US 64 near Rosman. Turn right on FR 140 and drive approximately 3 miles to a small bridge that crosses a creek; you can park on the far side, on the right. Take the trail on the right for a few hundred yards to a narrow trail that bears left. This 300-foot, short, steep trail leads to the beautiful pool at the base of the falls.

DANIEL RIDGE FALLS, FR 475. Two other fine cascades—Cove Creek and Shuck Ridge Creek Falls—are in this general area, but Daniel Ridge, also known as Toms Spring Falls, is the largest and easiest to find. Drive 5.2 miles up US Hwy. 276 to FR 475 and go 3.9 miles to a parking area on the right. From there follow the logging road for less than a mile. You'll see the 150-foot falls on the left.

THE HORSEPASTURE RIVER FALLS, off Hwy. 281 S. The series of waterfalls here are some of the most awe inspiring in the region. To reach the falls from the intersection of US 64 and Hwy. 281 in Sapphire, turn south on Highway 281 and drive 1.8 miles to the Horsepasture River, 4.2 miles of which have been designated as part of the National Wild and Scenic River System. Find a parking spot along the guardrails near the bridge. Drift Falls, known to locals as "Bust Your Butt Falls," can be seen just downriver. It is privately owned and is not open to the public. The falls can still be viewed from the parking area. There's a pull-off on the right for about three or four cars next to the trailhead, marked by a small green sign on the guardrail. (Make sure your vehicle is completely off the road, or you may get ticketed.) From the trailhead descend the trail for 100 yards until it joins the trail paralleling the river. Privately owned Drift Falls will be to your right. Drop Off/Turtleback Falls, named for its domelike rock, is a few hundred feet farther on your left. Though it looks like a great place for some slide-and-swim fun, don't attempt it; the currents in this pool have caused a number of drownings, and it's dangerously close to the top of Rainbow Falls.

Viewing the other beautiful falls along this wide, deep gorge will require a 1.5-mile steep descent on a sometimes-strenuous trail with precipitous ledges.

Continue down the gorge to the top of roaring, 200-foot Rainbow Falls, where you can often see rainbows in the thunderous spray. Again, stay away from the brink of this waterfall! Instead take the trail to an upper overlook or descend to the lower overlook (if you don't mind a drenching) for a picnic or swim. Avoid these falls in winter; the spray freezes and it makes walking dangerous.

It's another fairly difficult half-mile trek to the base of Stairstep Falls, where the river tumbles down seven 10-foot-tall, river-wide steps. Only the most experienced and intrepid should continue down the strenuous and dangerous 1.3-mile trail to Windy Falls. That series of nine violent cascades plunges 700 feet so mightily that they create their own wind through the narrowing gorge. We definitely advise not attempting this one. There isn't even a viewing place to see all of Windy Falls. A final word of caution: When visiting this wild river gorge, one of the most beautiful and spectacular in the mountains, remember that accidents in the area have kept the local rescue squad busy through the years, and deaths have been a common occurrence.

LOOKING GLASS FALLS, US 276. You barely have to get out of your vehicle to enjoy the most visited of Transylvania County's many waterfalls. This rushing 30-foot-wide, 60-foot-high cascade is set alongside US 276, 5.5 miles into Pisgah Forest from its junction with US 64. A short flight of stone steps leads down to the base of the falls from a paved pull-off area right beside Looking Glass Creek.

MOORE'S COVE FALLS, 0.7 mile off US 276. One mile north of Looking Glass Falls on US 276, keep a sharp eye out for the first bridge ahead and pull off in the wide, unpaved area just before reaching the bridge. (When driving south, it's 1.6 miles from Sliding Rock.) A wooden pedestrian bridge will take you across Looking Glass Creek to the lovely, easy 0.7-mile-long Moore's Cove Trail, which is steep only for the first few hundred yards. At its end a small stream tumbles over a deeply recessed ledge that allows you to walk behind the free-falling, 50-foot falls. Avoid the steep path to the top of the ledge; it can be dangerous.

> **i** Due to the glare of sunshine on water, waterfall photos usually come out best if shot in the early morning, late evening, or on a cloudy day. If you can keep your camera lens dry, try shooting during light rain or fog for wonderful effects.

SLICK ROCK FALLS, FR 475B. To reach this watery attraction just a short distance up the road from Looking Glass Falls, follow the sign to the Pisgah Fish Hatchery (FR 475) on the left. Drive 1.6 miles and turn right on FR 475B. After 1.1 miles you'll come to a sharp bend in the road. Park at the small pull-off on the right, where a trailhead leads up to the summit of Looking Glass Rock. The small but pretty 30-foot-tall Slick Rock Falls, some 50 yards away, spills over a rocky ledge of this rugged mountain. This waterfall well deserves its name "slick," so please don't try to climb it or any other falls.

SLIDING ROCK, US 276. Just 1.6 miles farther up US 276 (or 7.6 miles from its junction with US 64) is Sliding Rock, one place where you're invited to "take the plunge" down a 60-foot slippery cascade into the 50- to 60-degree, 6-foot-deep pool below. If you don't care to make the slide, it's fun simply to watch the action from paved viewing areas at the top or bottom of this natural, exhilarating ride that's fueled by 11,000 gallons of water a minute. There's now a per-vehicle parking fee that helps pay for lifeguards, who are on duty from 10 a.m. to 6 p.m. from Memorial Day through Labor Day; the parking fee includes the use of a bathhouse.

The rock, while slick, can take the bottom out of an ordinary bathing suit, so old jeans or cutoffs are best for this fast ride. Also be careful while getting in and out of the water. The surface of the rock, even where the water isn't flowing, can be slick and accounts for some hard tumbles.

TOXAWAY FALLS, off US 64. In 1916 the first Lake Toxaway dam burst after a flooding downpour. The water from the lake washed away huge amounts of vegetation and soil and exposed a huge granite dome. As you drive over this dome on a bridge, you can see the once-mighty falls, just a small stream these days.

TWIN FALLS ON HENRY BRANCH, 2.2 miles off FR 477. Since we sometimes are able to take this lovely hike to Twin Falls without meeting anyone else along the trail, we almost hesitate to risk jeopardizing such solitude by writing about it. Note that at 4.4 miles for the round trip, this is the longest trek in this list. While it's not a particularly difficult trail, it does involve negotiating a number of log bridges, so we always equip ourselves with a long, sturdy walking stick to help keep our balance, a good idea almost anytime you're walking forest trails that often have slippery and eroded sections.

To reach these two 100-foot waterfalls, drive 2.2 miles north on US 276 from its junction with US 64. Turn right on FR 477 and travel just more than 2.5 miles to a small parking area on the right side at the sign to Avery Creek Trail. Take this yellow-and-blue-blazed path for slightly more than a mile, until Avery Creek Trail crosses orange-blazed Buckhorn Gap Trail, which you should take to the right. In a little more than a half-mile, you'll come to a Trail Falls Loop sign. It's just a short distance in either direction of the loop to Twin Falls (the left loop is usually less overgrown), which are formed by two separate streams. There is no trail to the very base of the falls. Don't try to make one. You'll only disturb the wonderful plants that live here.

WHITEWATER FALLS AND LAUREL FALLS, off Hwy. 281. At 411 feet, Whitewater Falls lays claim to being the highest unbroken falls in the Southeast. To reach it take US 64 to Hwy. 281 and travel south for approximately 9.5 miles. Turn left at the Whitewater Falls Scenic Area for the short drive to the parking area, where there is a $2 per vehicle fee. From there a 0.2-mile trail leads to the upper overlook. Be extremely careful when negotiating the steep trip down to a lower overlook for an even better view. An old roadbed leads to the top of the falls, but we don't recommend any close-up viewing, as a number of deaths occur in the area almost every year.

If you're in excellent shape, you can turn right on the trail that brings you to the middle overlook, and it will take you on a very strenuous hike of just less than a mile down to Laurel Falls, also known as Corbin Creek Falls. When the trees have shed their leaves, you can view this waterfall from Whitewater. It's made up of a series of broken cascades that tumble about the same distance as Whitewater, but only the lowest one, which drops approximately

75 feet, can be easily seen. It's much too dangerous to try to get a close-up view of the others.

Southern Mountains

Clay County

LEATHERWOOD FALLS, FR 340. Compared with some falls, 25-foot Leatherwood is not particularly grand, but Fires Creek, which rushes past the falls' base, is great for swimming and fishing. To find it go west out of Hayesville on US 64 for just short of 5 miles and turn right on SR 1302. After 3.7 miles turn left on SR 1344, which will become FR 340 as it enters the Nantahala National Forest. Drive 1.9 miles to the Leatherwood Falls parking and picnic area. You can view the falls from here or wade into the creek (it can be rushing and dangerous after heavy rains), or you can cross the bridge upstream and work your way back to the foot of the falls. Don't, however, be tempted to climb the cascade. It may not look dangerous, but it is. From the picnic area, paved trails provide access for fly-fishing from wheelchairs.

Haywood County

THE GRAVEYARD FIELDS FALLS, Mile 418.8, Blue Ridge Pkwy. Three waterfalls, Upper Falls, Second Falls, and Yellowstone Falls (the largest of the three), are in Graveyard Fields, a vast area left nearly treeless by a devastating forest fire in 1925. Second Falls can be seen from the parking area at milepost 418.8 on the Blue Ridge Parkway, but most people prefer a closer look and walk to the Graveyard Fields Loop Trail. The parking area is very crowded on weekends. Some parts of the trail are badly eroded, as are many side trails. Check the information board at the parking area for the most direct routes to the falls and be careful at the overlook at Yellowstone Falls, which can be treacherous (see our chapter on the **Blue Ridge Parkway**). As with all falls, stay out of the water at the top of the falls and stay on the trails.

MIDNIGHT HOLE AND MOUSE CREEK FALLS, 1.5 and 2 miles off Waterville Rd. Seeing these falls requires a 4-mile round-trip hike, but it's an easy walk on a graded road that runs along beautiful Big Creek. To reach Big Creek drive west on I-40 to the Waterville exit (just before you reach the Tennessee border). Turn left on Waterville Road, which will enter the Great Smoky Mountains National Park. After approximately 3 miles, 0.8 mile past the ranger station, the road will end at a parking area of the Big Creek Campground. (In winter the gate is closed at the ranger station, so you'll have to walk from there, adding 1.6 miles round-trip.) Take the road (Big Creek Trail) just a few feet back from the parking area. A little less than 1.5 miles along this easy route, an obvious path will lead to Midnight Hole, where small (7-foot) but gorgeous twin falls flow into a fantastic 80-foot-wide, 15-foot-deep swimming hole. Back on the road/trail, continue on slightly over another half-mile, and you'll see Mouse Creek Falls, which drop a total of 50 feet, rushing into the creek.

For those with the energy, there is another series of waterfalls called Gunter Fork Cascades. The longest one drops 100 feet, making it one of the tallest waterfalls in the park. They're 8.2 difficult miles from the parking area and are reached by a wonderful route that runs mostly along this beautiful creek then just over 2 miles up Gunter Fork Trail. That, however, is a hard 16.4-mile round-trip, and you'll have to make a number of wet-stream crossings. You should get a trail map and specific directions if you want to see these falls.

> **i** A self-guided, 1.5-mile loop trail will take you over the highest mountain in the Great Balsam Mountains, 6,410-foot Richland Balsam, and through a remnant of a spruce fir forest. Drive to the Haywood-Jackson County Overlook at milepost 431, just north of the highest point on the Blue Ridge Parkway. The trail begins at the upper end of the parking lot and is paved at its start.

Jackson County

HURRICANE FALLS AND GLASSY CREEK FALLS, Hwy. 107 and Norton Rd. (SR 1145). Hurricane and Glassy Creek Falls are both on private property, but they can be viewed from the roadside on the same trip. To reach Hurricane Falls drive north out of Cashiers on Highway 107 for 1.8 miles and turn left on Norton Road (SR 1145). It's just more than 0.5 mile to a pull-off where you can see the waterfall, which has an average height of 40 feet that varies according to the height of Lake Thorpe, into which it flows.

For Glassy Creek Falls return to Highway 107 and continue north for 8.6 miles to a pull-off on the left (because of the sharp curve at this location, pass the pull-off, turn around farther up the road, and come back to park). The 100-foot curling falls is formed by the Little River Creek. The river in front of the falls is the West Fork of the Tuckasegee.

SILVER RUN FALLS, Hwy. 107. Would you like a waterfall-fed pool to cool off in on a hot day? Then, from Cashiers drive south on Highway 107 for just more than 4 miles and park at a graveled pull-off on the left with a utility pole at its corner. Follow the short path over a fallen log that bridges the creek or wade the water to this picturesque 20-foot waterfall. Its lovely, sandy beach and pretty pool make it a relatively safe and popular swimming area.

Macon County

BIG LAUREL FALLS AND MOONEY FALLS, FR 67. Big Laurel Falls is a small but beautiful waterfall that plunges 30 feet in two stages into a tempting pool deep in the Southern Nantahala Wilderness Area. To get there take US 64 West out of Franklin for about 12 miles and turn left onto Old US 64. In slightly less than 2 miles, turn right on FR 67, which is only partly paved, and drive for just short of 7 miles to a marked parking area. Take the easy trail (it's less than a half-mile) to the falls, bearing to the right each time the trail forks. Mooney Falls, actually a series of falls, is just more than a half-mile farther up the road on FR 67. Park at the Mooney Falls sign and take the short trail for several different views of the falls. None of the cascades is more than 15 feet high, but the overall effect is exceedingly breathtaking.

BRIDAL VEIL FALLS, off US 64. Only a few dozen feet from US 64, 2.5 miles west of Highlands, you can see this 120-foot, ethereal cascade right from your car. US 64 used to run right behind the falls, but there was a problem with ice on the highway in winter, so the highway was moved. You can still use an old piece of the original highway to detour behind the falls. For a more leisurely view or to take a photograph, there's a pull-off just beyond the falls.

CULLASAJA FALLS, off US 64. The 250-foot Cullasaja Falls is one of the more majestic of the many cascades in the Cullasaja River Gorge, so it's unfortunate that US 64 is so busy, narrow, and dangerous at this point 8.8 miles west of Highlands, making more than a drive-by glimpse difficult. To get a good look, find a parking place in one of the narrow, frequently crowded, unmarked pull-offs on the highway's precipitous shoulder, keeping a careful eye on traffic when getting in and out of the car. Then be satisfied with a view and photo from the road. The primitive paths down to the base of the falls are much too dangerous to attempt.

DRY FALLS, off US 64. Less than a mile from Bridal Veil Falls, Dry Falls drops 80 feet; 40 feet of that distance is free fall. The neat thing about this falls is that an easy, paved path leads down from the parking lot, taking you inside the recessed ledge behind the roaring and sometimes-drenching waters for a view from the other side. There is a $2 per vehicle fee.

GLEN FALLS, SR 1618. There are several beautiful falls and accompanying cascades here that drop 640 feet in only a half-mile. So, though the well-maintained trail to the 70-, 60-, and 15-foot waterfalls in the Glen Falls Scenic Area is less than a mile long, it is steep and tough to hike back up. But it's worth it! In addition there are marvelous views of the Blue Valley as well as great picnic spots along the route. To reach the area take Highway 106 just south of

Highlands for less than 2 miles until you see the Glen Falls Scenic Area sign on the left and take SR 1618 immediately on the right. From there it's a mile to the trail that leads from a parking area.

Macon County: Slick Rock

Slick Rock is a granite rock outcrop on an eastward facing slope, the summit of which offers an impressive view of far-off mountains. From Highlands take Horse Cove Road to the end of the pavement, then take the right fork onto Bull Pen Road and drive about 1.5 miles. When you reach a sharp left curve, look for a pull-off and a steep, unmarked path on the right (if you pass a road that intersects Bull Pen on the right at a 45-degree angle, you've gone too far; turn around and go back). This timber sale road runs right beneath Slick Rock. The hike to the top is less than a quarter-mile, and it's a great place to watch a sunrise.

UPPER AND LOWER SATULAH FALLS, off Hwy. 28. Upper Satulah Falls, which looks like a steep waterslide, is on private property, but you can see it easily from the road. From Highlands drive south on Hwy. 28 for 2.3 miles and look to your left at the foot of the vast rock face of 4,543-foot Satulah Mountain. Park at the overlook a short distance farther on the right side of the road. Continue on Highway 28 for just more than a mile to view the high, narrow Lower Satulah Falls (also known as Clear Creek Falls). It's across the valley from a wide pull-off that also overlooks the Piedmont, including the Blue Valley, Rabun Bald, and Scaly Mountain. This 100-foot lower waterfall is best seen in the winter when the foliage is off the trees.

Swain County

JUNEY WHANK FALLS, TOMS BRANCH FALLS, and **INDIAN CREEK FALLS,** off Deep Creek Rd. All three of these popular falls in the Great Smoky Mountains National Park can be found by going out Deep Creek Road just outside Bryson City. However, you'll have to jog around several different streets as you pass through town to find this road, so the simplest thing is to go to Bryson City and ask directions to Deep Creek Road. You'll travel 2.2 miles up this road before you enter the actual park. From that boundary it's a little more than a half-mile to the parking area at the end of the road. The quarter-mile trail to 80-foot Juney Whank Falls begins about 100 yards from the picnic area.

To get to another 80-foot-drop cascade, Toms Branch Falls, go past the gate and take the gravel road (part of the park's popular Deep Creek Trail) a quarter-mile to the falls on the right. A half-mile upstream is the well-used tubing launch site, so expect to see hordes of tubers floating by in the summer.

Actually you can see the falls much better in the winter when the surrounding trees and bushes have lost their foliage.

Continuing on the Deep Creek Trail for less than a mile will bring you to Indian Creek Trail. The wide 25-foot waterfall known as Indian Creek Falls is just a few hundred yards down this path, where a side trail will take you to the base of the falls.

> **i** Some of the waterfalls listed here are deep in the area's forests, so be sure to take food and drink along with you and always wear comfortable shoes with nonskid soles. Packing a towel, a bathing suit, and a change of clothing also isn't a bad idea, but be warned: The water in any mountain pool will be chilly, to say the least. Make sure, too, that the pool you choose to swim in is absolutely safe. Currents near waterfalls can be treacherous. And as we've noted numerous times, never, ever wade above a waterfall, where a slip can be fatal.

MINGO FALLS, off Big Cove Rd. Mingo, on the Cherokee Indian Reservation, is one of the most fabulous falls in the whole Smoky Mountains area, though the landscape around it has been somewhat marred in the past few years by storm damage. To reach it take US Hwy. 441 out of Cherokee, where it becomes Newfound Gap Road once it enters the Great Smoky Mountains National Park. Just short of a mile after the junction with the Blue Ridge Parkway, turn right at the Jobs Corps Center sign. The road will end after a half-mile at Big Cove Road. Turn left and drive 3.3 miles to the Mingo Cove Campground and park. The trail is only a quarter-mile long, but the first part of it is very steep.

Festivals and Annual Events

Our North Carolina mountains are a celebration in and of themselves, and just living here seems to give rise to all manner of festivals. Here's a month-to-month sampling, broken down under the geographic regions of the Northern, Central, and Southern Mountains. The events are free unless we've noted an entry fee. Please note: While we update these events with each new edition, it's still best to check with the visitors centers and their online events calendars in each county to make sure events planned far ahead of time are still scheduled.

JANUARY

Northern Mountains

BLOWING ROCK WINTERFEST, Blowing Rock Chamber of Commerce, Blowing Rock, NC; (828) 295-7851. Typically the last weekend of Jan, events of WinterFest in Blowing Rock include the icy Polar Plunge in Chetola Lake, WinterFeast, WinterPaws Dog Show, WinterFashion Show, ice carving, a Winter Beer Garden, and more.

WINTERFEST, BEECH MOUNTAIN RESORT, 1007 Beech Mountain Pkwy., Beech Mountain, NC; (828) 387-2011; beechmountainresort.com. This town festival on Beech Mountain in the first week of Jan features an ice show, beer fest, and tubing and box races. Nominal entrance fees are charged for the various events.

Central Mountains

ANNUAL FRINGE ARTS FESTIVAL, times and locations vary, Asheville, NC; (828) 275-2627; ashevillefrienge.org. A week-long, multiple-venue arts festival that pushes the boundaries of performance and installation art. Limited entry is free, depending on venue (which range from bars to performance halls, galleries, and clubs), and full passes are $65 plus.

BIG BAND SWING AND DANCE WEEKEND, Omni Grove Park Inn, 290 Macon Ave., Asheville, NC; (828) 252-2711, (866) 238-4218. Evening concerts and dances featuring a headliner. The weekend includes dance instruction, afternoon tea dance, Sunday brunch, and guided history tours of the resort hotel. Admission is charged for concerts. Other venues are used around town as well.

MARTIN LUTHER KING JR. ANNUAL BIRTHDAY CELEBRATION; various locations, Asheville, NC; (828) 281-1624; mlkasheville.org. The MLK Association of Asheville & Buncombe County, Inc. organizes a variety of events in a five-day celebration at various locations around town honoring the birth and contributions of the famed civil rights leader. It all begins the third Mon of the month. Events include a peace march through town, singing, poetry readings, lectures, and music. The event is cosponsored by the city of Asheville.

FEBRUARY

Central Mountains

ARTS AND CRAFTS CONFERENCE, Omni Grove Park Inn, 290 Macon Ave., Asheville, NC; (828) 252-2711, (866) 238-4218; arts-craftsconference .com. Annual professional conference in praise of the Arts and Crafts Movement of Gustav Stickley and his contemporaries working in furniture, pottery, and metalware. The conference is usually held the third week in Feb.

ASHEVILLE MARDI GRAS PARADE, South Slope, Asheville, NC; ashevillemardigras.org. Believe it or not, there's an Asheville Mardi Gras celebration—with a parade and Queen's Ball afterword (actually *damanchegras*, since the parade and ball take place on the Sunday before actual Mardi Gras). Twelfth Night, Jan 6, begins the festivities with a King and Queen being crowned after King Cake is consumed by Asheville Mardi Gras members. The parade in downtown's South Slope typically occurs in early Feb.

MARCH

Central Mountains

COMEDY CLASSIC, Omni Grove Park Inn, 290 Macon Ave., Asheville, NC; (828) 252-2711 or (866) 238-4218. Always a sellout, this popular weekend features an exciting lineup of top professional talent. It is always scheduled for the first weekend in Mar.

APRIL

Central Mountains

ANNUAL EASTER SUNRISE SERVICE, Chimney Rock Park, 431 Main St., Chimney Rock, NC; (828) 625-9611; chimneyrockpark.com. Deep valleys and craggy ridges are an inspiring backdrop for this service conducted by a guest minister, a free, ongoing tradition for more than 50 years.

APPALACHIAN SPRING CELEBRATION, Cradle of Forestry, Pisgah National Forest; US Hwy. 276; (828) 877-3130. Starting the last week in Apr and running for a full month, the Cradle of Forestry celebrates our mountains' diversity of birds, wildflowers, and waterfalls with a variety of programs for children and adults, including guided bird and wildflower walks and a wild-flower photography contest. There is an entrance fee of $4 for adults and $2 for students.

BILTMORE BLOOMS, BILTMORE ESTATE, 1 Approach Rd., Asheville, NC; (828) 225-1333 or (800) 624-1575; biltmore.com. Not only is Mr. Vanderbilt's 250-room mansion a magnificent sight, but the grounds and gardens, designed by noted landscape architect Frederick Law Olmsted, are just as breathtaking. This month-long festival celebrates the exquisite beauty of the estate's wildflowers, formal plantings, and exotic blooms of the gardens. The mansion itself is arrayed in Victorian floral design, while live music serenades you in the house and gardens. The house is also open for Festival of Flowers Evenings by reservations on Fri and Sat during the event. The festival lasts from mid-Apr to mid-May, and the price is admission to Biltmore Estate.

THE BLOCK HOUSE STEEPLECHASE, 6881 NC Hwy. 9, Columbus, NC; tryon.coth.com/page/blockhouseraces. The Tryon Block House is the longest running steeplechase in North Carolina, occurring continuously since 1947. The National Steeplechase Association sanctions four of the races. It's located near Columbus, about 50 miles from Asheville. The Tryon Riding & Hunt Club (TR&HC) and Tryon International Equestrian Center (TIEC) have teamed up for the annual Steeplechase with a 1-mile track, attracting some 40 top-tier jockeys.

HISTORIC JOHNSON FARM FESTIVAL, 3346 Haywood Rd., Hendersonville, NC; (828) 891-6585. At the end of Apr, there are tours, an auction, demonstrations, arts and crafts, and food at this old tobacco farm, a heritage education center and farm museum now owned by the Henderson County Public Schools. It's 4 miles north of Hendersonville on Highway 191. The festival runs from 10 a.m. until 4 p.m.

PIONEER LIVING DAY, Zebulon B. Vance Birthplace, 911 Reems Creek Rd., Weaverville, NC; (828) 645-6706. Walk into the North Carolina mountains of yesteryear at the Zebulon B. Vance Birthplace. Pioneer Living Day at this state historic site is a fascinating event for the whole family, who can all become involved in demonstrations of the day-to-day life of early mountaineers at this country homestead, surrounded by meadows and mountains. Cooking, candle making, and spinning are just a few of the delights. This event occurs the third Sun in Apr.

Southern Mountains

RAMP FESTIVAL, various locations Robbinsville; (828) 479-3790. On the last Sun in Apr, the whole town celebrates the pungent ramp. This wild cousin of the onion is the star of this occasion sponsored by the local rescue squad. The day's activities feature a duck race, dinner with ramp-flavored dishes, and a craft fair.

Northern Mountains

SPRING ARTS FESTIVAL, Town Square, Burnsville, NC; (828) 682-7413 or (800) 948-1632. This festival at the end of May is usually held on a Sat from 10 a.m. to 4 p.m. in the town square. Meet the artists and see their works. Browse the booths for some creative gifts and fine art, while the children paint and draw to their hearts' content on the Expression Wall. Sponsored by the Toe River Arts Council and the Business Owners Association, this event is free.

SPRING STUDIO AND GARDEN TOUR, various locations, Spruce Pine, NC; (828) 765-9483 or (800) 227-3912. The first Fri and Sat in May, the artists and garden businesses of Yancey and Mitchell Counties open their studios and garden spots for informal viewing just before Mother's Day. Fine hand-crafted works and garden accoutrements make for a delightful shopping mixture. The tour runs from 10 a.m. to 5 p.m. and is sponsored by the Toe River Arts Council. Pick up a map of studios on the tour at the Mitchell County Chamber of Commerce at the North Carolina Museum of Minerals or at the *Mitchell News Journal* in downtown Spruce Pine.

Central Mountains

ANNUAL MAIN STREET ANTIQUE SHOW, Main St., Hendersonville, NC; (828) 692-9057. Seventy-five antiques dealers show their wares on Main Street from 9 a.m. until 5 p.m. This generally occurs the last week of the month or in early June.

CARL SANDBURG FOLK AND POETRY FESTIVAL, Connemara, 1928 Little River Rd., Flat Rock, NC; (828) 693-4178. One of the mountains' favorite people is the namesake and inspiration for this free entertainment. Carl Sandburg loved to sing, and music still graces Connemara, his farm, now a National Historic Site just outside Hendersonville. The last weekend in May, professional musicians and actors perform songs and poems from Sandburg's works from 10 a.m. until 5 p.m.

FOLK ART CENTER FIBER DAY, Mile 382, Asheville, NC; (828) 298-7928. The Folk Art Center, east of the city on the Blue Ridge Parkway, hosts a special day in the middle of the month to celebrate the fiber arts. The professional demonstrations attract large crowds, who get to watch how these folks spin thread and weave cloth out of the wool from sheep. This demonstration usually includes all the stages, from watching the sheep being shorn to the weaving on the loom.

GARDEN JUBILEE, Visitors Information Center, 201 S. Main St., Hendersonville, NC, (828) 693-9708, (800) 828-4244. The last week in May brings arts and crafts, a plant sale, garden talks, food, and more to the Visitors Information Center. The event is sponsored by downtown merchants, who hold sidewalk sales, treasure hunts, and a free flower drawing and bring in live music that day.

LAKE EDEN ARTS FESTIVAL, Camp Rockmont, 375 Lake Eden Rd., Black Mountain, NC; (828) 686-8742; theleaf.com. Lake Eden Arts Festival is an event celebrating the world of folk arts. On the sprawling grounds of a boys' summer camp, this fest features dancing and music, drumming and handicrafts, poetry and storytelling over the three-day Memorial Day weekend in May, then again in Oct. There are also spiritual and healing workshops, a farmers' market, ethnic food booths, massage and aromatherapy, and a vast and funky mixture of world music, folk, and country sounds, all running concurrently on four different stages. This is one very hip festival—call for a brochure with pricing. Camping during the festival is available.

MONTREAT KIRKIN' O' THE TARTANS, Montreat Scottish Society, Montreat, NC; (828) 669-8011. Memorial Day Sunday is when the 100 clans of the Scots at Montreat gather. At 10:30 a.m. the Montreat Pipe Band brings the tunes of Scotland to the mountains of Appalachia in front of the great stone building of Anderson Auditorium on the grounds of the Montreat Conference Center and Montreat College. At 11 on the hour, the pipers lead the standard bearers, 100 strong, into Anderson Auditorium for the traditional worship service and blessing of the tartans. Among the illustrious preachers has been Montreat's own resident, the Rev. Dr. Billy Graham.

SPRING HERB FESTIVAL, Western North Carolina Farmers Market, off I-26, Asheville, NC; (828) 689-5974. This event on the first weekend in May offers educational gardening programs as well as an opportunity to speak to herbalists and master gardeners. This festival is free, so you can save your money to buy herbs, books, and herbal products.

SUNDAY MELODIES IN THE PARK, Jackson Park Amphitheater, Hendersonville, NC; (828) 697-1745 or (800) 828-4344. A free summer concert series begins the second Sun of the month. The concerts range from beach music, soft rock and "Tuxedo Junction" tunes of the 40s to the 90s. Call for more information.

Southern Mountains

GREAT SMOKY MOUNTAIN TROUT FESTIVAL, Recreation Park, Waynesville, NC; (828) 456-3021, (800) 334-9036. This Memorial Day event held in Recreation Park honors the greatest catch in the mountains with exhibitions, contests, crafts, food, and entertainment. The Haywood County Chamber of Commerce sponsors this free event.

RAMP CONVENTION, various locations Waynesville, NC; (828) 456-3021 or (800) 334-9036. Early May brings a genuine mountain hoedown to again honor the ramp—a rare, wild onionlike plant—in downtown Waynesville. It adds zest to all the day's dishes. There'll be country and bluegrass music, square dancing, and clogging, too. But beware—it's been known to inspire a politician or two to make a speech.

JUNE

Northern Mountains

BLUE RIDGE MOUNTAIN FAIR CRAFT FESTIVAL, Crouse Park, Sparta, NC; (910) 372-5473 or (800) 372-5473. Crouse Park in Sparta is the setting for an old-time mountain fair of food, fun, crafts, and music held the last Sat of the month.

NORTH CAROLINA RHODODENDRON FESTIVAL, Mitchell Ave., Bakersville, NC; (828) 765-9483 or (800) 227-3912. For more than a half-century this festival has coincided with the blooming of the 600-acre Rhododendron Gardens atop Roan Mountain. A 10K road race, golf tournament, two pageants, historic tours, a car show, and a street dance round out the three-day weekend in the third week of June. These events are free.

SINGING ON THE MOUNTAIN at Grandfather Mountain, off Hwy. 221 (entrance of Grandfather Mountain) McRae Meadows, Linville, NC; (828) 733-4337. This traditional Southern gospel sing at magnificent McRae Meadows has been going strong since 1924. Drawing crowds in the tens of thousands, this event hearkens back to old-time preachin', when the message was delivered outdoors under the heavens and voices were lifted up to the skies. Lively gospel singing, entertainers, picnic lunches, preaching by well-known speakers, and wide-open vistas create a joyful good time for the entire family. This event, which takes place on the fourth Sun in June, is free.

YANCEY COUNTY CLOGGING–ART & CRAFT SHOW, Town Square, Burnsville, NC; (828) 682-7413 or (800) 948-1632. This dance festival runs for two days in mid-June. Burnsville's town square hosts a pig-pickin' the first night of the fest, serving succulent barbecue, while cloggers dance the traditional mountain jigs handed down through the generations. The first evening culminates in a street dance. Sat includes more clogging and arts and crafts booths.

Central Mountains

ASHEVILLE VEGANFAST, Pack Square Park, 80 Court Plaza, Asheville, NC; veganfest.bwar.org. Celebrating all things plant-based—foods, fashion, and a sustainable lifestyle. Vegetarians, vegans, conscientious consumers, fitness lovers, and passersby enjoy this festival with food and market booths.

THE BLUE RIDGE BARBECUE FESTIVAL AND NORTH CAROLINA STATE BARBECUE CHAMPIONSHIP, Harmon Field, Tryon, NC; (828) 859-6236. On a weekend in mid-June, the North Carolina state championship barbecue cook-off is held at Harmon Field, attracting even out-of-state barbecue specialists. There's nonstop bluegrass, Piedmont blues, rock and country music, crafts, and children's activities. There is an admission fee.

BREVARD MUSIC CENTER, 349 Andante Ln., Brevard, NC; (828) 884-2011 or (888) 384-8682. The notable music center's season opens mid-summer for its summer run of more than 80 concerts. Renowned director of the Boston Pops, Keith Lockhart, conducts on opening night. He was a former student of the Brevard Music Center and is now its director. The season continues through its final concert on Aug 8. Throughout the season the offerings are opera, symphony orchestra, symphonic band, and sinfonia.

Often a "Bach"s Lunch" concert is offered at noon for picnickers at no charge. Other concerts begin in the afternoon with featured attractions at 7:30 p.m. The grounds are open for early arrivals to share tables in the picnic area. You can bring your own or order from special menus prepared by local restaurants.

ICE-CREAM SOCIAL/SPRING KICKOFF, Silvermont Mansion, Main St., Brevard, NC; (828) 884-5255. This early June benefit for the Brevard

Little Theatre, held at the Silvermont Mansion on Main Street, gives participants a preview of the community theater's coming season. Admission is free.

FRENCH BROAD RIVER MONTH, various locations in Buncombe, Henderson, Madison, and Transylvania Counties; (828) 252-8474. June is French Broad River Month. This menagerie of events along the riverfront of the French Broad is sponsored by RiverLink, a nonprofit group devoted to improving the river and its banks. Boat races, a Bridge Party and Triathalon, white-water raft trips, biking, and rock climbing are all a part of this outdoors celebration. Activity charges vary, so call ahead.

MERMAID PARADE & FESTIVAL, Marshall, NC. Arts, crafts, silliness, and music 11 a.m. to 7 p.m., usually the second Sat of June. There's also a seafood cook-off and parade at 6 p.m. with costumes, water balloons, and squirt-guns.

RIVER DISTRICT STUDIO STROLL, River District, Asheville, NC; riverartsdistrict.com. Held the second full weekend in June (and Nov) from 10 a.m. to 4 p.m., the Studio Stroll is a chance to tour over 40 studios, meet with the artists, and purchase artwork.

XPAND FEST, South Slope, Asheville, NC. The second weekend in June, a street festival of some 40 vendors showcases the local arts community to promote positive self-growth for attendees. Art and food vendors and three stages center on Coxe and Buxton Avenues. It's presented by Xpand Your Vision, a creative arts nonprofit. Festival hours are noon until 10 p.m. Admission is free.

Southern Mountains

BLUEGRASS FESTIVAL, Happy Holiday Campground, US Hwy. 19 N., Cherokee, NC; (828) 864-7203 or (800) 438-1601; adamsbluegrass.com. You can join in the foot-stompin' that goes on during this three-day, late-June event at the Happy Holiday Campground.

TASTE OF SCOTLAND, Square and grounds of Burrell Building, Franklin, NC; (828) 524-7472; tasteofscotlandfestival.org. Since 1996, the town of Franklin has looked a great deal like "yon, bon bonnie banks of Scotland" on the Sat before Father's Day. This celebration of Scottish heritage is a joint venture of the Scottish Tartan Museum and the Franklin Chamber of Commerce. The day begins with a parade of bagpipe bands, followed by dancing, children's games and activities, a display of crafts, and food to please an eclectic taste—if it is Scottish.

JULY

Northern Mountains

CHRISTMAS IN JULY FESTIVAL, West Jefferson, NC; (336) 246-9550. This festival, which is held in mid-July, is heralded as a celebration of Ashe County's thriving Christmas tree industry. What better fun than to pretend it's Christmas in the heat of midsummer! Christmas crafts, from roping and wreaths to decorated trees, are on display along with traditional mountain crafts. Music to suit just about everyone's tastes, including bluegrass, gospel, and classic rock, fills the air. Helicopter rides, children's activities, and all kinds of mouthwatering food round out the fun. (The exact date of the festival varies from year to year, so call ahead of time.)

GRANDFATHER MOUNTAIN HIGHLAND GAMES AND GATHERING OF THE SCOTTISH CLANS, McRae Meadows, 4210 Mitchell Ave., Linville, NC; (828) 733-1333; gmhg.org. Expansive McRae Meadows on Grandfather Mountain is the gorgeous venue for a sea of kilts and tartans during the second full weekend in July. For more than 50 years, this gathering has brought Scottish hearts together for ancient games, traditional food, and bagpipes galore. Don't miss the spectacular Torchlight Opening Ceremony on Thurs evening, invoking the "spirit of the clans" upon the games. This stirring parade of torchbearers and traditional highland bagpipes and drums makes the centuries seem to fall away. A 5-mile foot race from the town of Linville to the top of Grandfather Mountain is also part of the opening night festivities. Evening activities continue throughout the weekend. Charges vary, so call for an informational brochure and for information about parking and the shuttle bus.

OLD-FASHIONED JULY 4TH CELEBRATION ON THE SQUARE, Town Square, Burnsville, NC; (828) 682-7413, (800) 948-1632. The picturesque Town Square is the scene of a Fourth of July like our grandparents enjoyed. Don't miss the wagon train parade, crafts, food, and mountain music. When twilight falls, you would swear it's still 1900.

Central Mountains

ASHEVILLE YOGA FESTIVAL, Pack Square Park and various locations in downtown Asheville, NC; ashevilleyogafestival.com. Since 2014, this weekend draws yogis and aficionados from around the nation for free classes as well as fee-based workshops for all things yoga with world-class instructors, musicians, motivating speakers, and a diversity of vendors in the festival's outdoor market space.

CRAFT FAIR OF THE SOUTHERN HIGHLANDS, US Cellular Center, Asheville, NC; (828) 298-7928; southernhighlandcraftguild.org. One of the most popular of the annual mountain crafts fairs, the Craft Fair of the Southern Highland Craft Guild features a juried craft exhibition, professional demonstrations, and fine traditional mountain music. It's held in the large downtown US Cellular Center on the third weekend in July and Oct.

COON DOG DAY, various locations Saluda, NC; saluda.com. This downtown celebration of the coon dog on the Fourth of July weekend is one of the more popular festivals in the region. It is a great day for both dogs and their people, with contests and judging for the dogs and crafts, live music, and a street dance for the people. "Coon" dog is the local term referring to dogs used for hunting raccoons. They range from Beagles to Fox Hounds, Blue Tick Hounds, Red Bones and more. This day includes a parade, 5K, and plenty of other diversions.

4TH OF JULY, Pack Square Park, Asheville, NC; ashevilledowntown.org. A spectacular shower of fireworks illuminates the skyline of historic City/County Plaza in downtown Asheville at dark. The Asheville Downtown Association hosts the Ingles Independence Day Celebration from 2 to 10 p.m. at Pack Square Park in downtown Asheville. Stages have a schedule of bands and dancing. You can also enjoy food and fun and craft booths, but leave your dog at home because pets not allowed. This event is produced in partnership with the City of Asheville and other sponsors.

SHINDIG-ON-THE-GREEN, Pack Square Plaza, Asheville, NC; folk heritage.org. Every Sat night in summer, starting the first weekend in July, old-fashioned mountain music thrives in the modern world on Asheville's central Pack Square Plaza. Musicians come from all over the area to be a part of the evening's entertainment.

> **i** Some towns won't allow dogs at their outdoor festivals, so be sure to find out the policy before you bring Fido, or he may end up in "doggie jail"—cages in the shade—while you attend the festival.

SWANNANOA CHAMBER FESTIVAL, Warren Wilson College, 701 Warren Wilson Rd., Swannanoa, NC. This annual festival of chamber music is a rarity and a delight. From the campus of Warren Wilson College, a visiting contingent of classically trained professional musicians produces a series of five marvelous concerts. Traveling workshops and concert series for the

Hendersonville and Waynesville communities are also part of this five-week-long musical celebration. The festival also combines lectures, demonstrations, and a benefit recital with the regularly scheduled program.

Southern Mountains

ANNUAL GEMBOREE, Robert C Carpenter Community Building, 1288 Georgia Rd., Franklin, NC; (828) 349-2090. The "Gem Capital of the World" shows off its rough and cut gems, minerals, fine jewelry, and equipment in late July. You can also shop for gem-related books and supplies, attend lectures, and maybe win a door prize. Admission is free.

ANNUAL 4TH OF JULY POWOW, Acquoni Expo Center, 1501 Acquoni Rd., Cherokee, NC; (828) 497-7128; visitcherokeenc.com. Authentic Native American music, dancing, food, and festivities, as well as dance competitions mark this three-day festival. The action-packed weekend includes colorful regalia, traditional dances, and music. Experience authentic tribal foods, browse traditional Indian crafts, and get an insider's look at a rich, ancient culture. Cost is $12 daily. Please note that this event is cash only. Children 6 and under are free.

ARTS ON THE GREEN, downtown Cashiers, NC; (828) 743-3434; villagegreencashiersnc.com. Arts on the Green is Cashiers' Plein Air Festival—a biennial event held to raise funds to enhance The Village Green. The week-long event allows artists to set up their easels in and around Cashiers to capture the landscape. The completed paintings are displayed for viewing and sale at The Village Green Commons. Other highlights include a special patrons' gala and auction as well as workshops and a lecture by the artists.

CASHIERS BENEFIT ANNUAL ANTIQUE SHOW, 95 Bobcat Dr., Cashiers, NC; (828) 743-9270; cashiersbenefitantiqueshow.com. Held mid-July, this juried show draws dealers from all over the Southeast. Come early: The place fills quickly, and people do come to buy!

FOLKMOOT USA, 112 Virginian Ave., Folkmoot Friendship Center, Waynesville, NC and other locations; (800) 334-9036; folkmootusa.org. An international folk festival the last two weeks in July, this event begins with a parade through downtown Waynesville. The mountains become the world's stage, as musicians and dancers from different countries gather in a celebration of music, dance, and culture. (See the "**Folkmoot**" Close-up.)

FOURTH OF JULY FREEDOM FEST, Town Square, Bryson City, NC; (828) 488-3681 or (800) 867-9246; greatsmokies.com. Independence Day in Swain County is celebrated with a bevy of live entertainment, food, crafts, and fireworks, of course.

JULY 4TH HERITAGE FESTIVAL, various downtown locations Robbins-ville, NC; (828) 499-3790. Join the downtown parade featuring local bands. The festival features lots of food and crafts, too.

AUGUST

Northern Mountains

BANNER ELK ART FESTIVAL, Old Cannon Hospital, Hickory Nut Gap Rd., Banner Elk, NC; (828) 898-5605; avercounty.com. These juried festivals feature hand-crafted wares from more than 90 vendors. Photography, paint-ings, jewelry, sculpture, and pottery are just some of the crafts on offer. It's sponsored by the Avery–Banner Elk Chamber of Commerce.

MINERAL AND GEM FESTIVAL, Pine Bridge Coliseum; 97 Pine Bridge Ave., Spruce Pine, NC; (828) 765-9483 or (800) 227-3912. A rock hound's dream come true, this weeklong event draws crowds to its displays and sales booths. More than 50 dealers descend during the first week in Aug.

MOUNT MITCHELL CRAFTS FAIR, Town Square, Burnsville, NC; (828) 682-7413; yanceychamber.com. Here's a spectacular slice of Americana on the grassy Town Square in the quaint village of Burnsville. A splendid array of tradi-tional mountain crafts, food, and music make for an enjoyable day in mid-Aug.

Central Mountains

BILTMORE VILLAGE ART & CRAFT FAIR, All Souls Cathedral Grounds, Historic Biltmore Village, Asheville, NC; (828) 274-2831; newmorning allerync.com. Historic Biltmore Village and the grounds of the Cathedral of All Souls, opposite the entrance to Biltmore Estate, come alive the first full weekend in Aug for this annual arts festival. More than 150 artists offer beauti-ful jewelry and fiber, pottery, and metalworks. Food and beverage sales benefit community charities.

LEAF DOWNTOWN ASHEVILLE, Pack Square Park, Asheville, NC. This world music festival at Pack Square Park downtown excites visitors with three stages of music, food trucks, and over 90 local and artisan vendors on Fri after-noon and all day Sat until 10 p.m. Local musicians perform as well as one headliner each evening for a big street dance. Free admission.

MOUNTAIN DANCE AND FOLK FESTIVAL, Lipinsky Hall, 300 Liberty Ln., UNCA, Asheville, NC; (828) 258-6101; folkheritage.org. This granddaddy of all US folk music festivals started informally back in 1927 as just "a little pickin' and a-grinnin' and a-steppin" at the home of Bascom Lamar Lunsford in

Close-up

Folkmoot

Dancers in traditional Kazakh headgear and flowing gowns, Turkish sword dancers with fezes, French stilt dancers in lambskin vests, New Zealand Maori in grass skirts, Bavarian oompah bands, and sombrero-wearing Mexican ensembles are only a few of the multicultural treasures you might encounter at Waynesville's world-renowned Folkmoot Festival.

For 10 days every July, this small mountain town transforms itself into a miniature United Nations, melding folk music, dance, and culture from around the world in an event much like one you would have to travel abroad to see. Each year 10 premier folk groups representing different parts of the world demonstrate their cultural heritages through colorful authentic and original reproduction costumes, lively dance, and music played on unique instruments that are often handcrafted. Through the years more than 70 countries have sent more than 130 groups to take part.

It's amazing to look back at the humble beginnings of this festival in 1984. America was in the midst of the Cold War, apartheid ruled South Africa, and yet in one mountain village we could speak to our Russian guests one-on-one or have them visit in our houses. Poles, Kazakhs, Turks, Germans, Lithuanians, Kenyans, and so many others joined together in song and dance, music being the common language. Even today the profound sense of "global family" that this festival evokes is hard to mistake. For more information on Folkmoot, including a performance schedule and admission costs, as well as year-round international events at the Folkmoot Friendship Center, call (828) 452-2997 or visit folkmoot.org. The Friendship Center is located at 112 Virginia Ave., Waynesville, NC 28786.

Turkey Creek in Buncombe County. Today it has evolved into one of the most revered folk music festivals of its kind in the country. Lunsford, the festival's founder, devoted his life to the perpetuation of our mountain music heritage. He died in 1973, but his festival still retains the naturalness and spontaneity that gave it life 90 years ago on that porch on Turkey Creek.

SOURWOOD FESTIVAL, various locations Black Mountain, NC; (828) 669-2300 or (800) 669-2301; sourwoodfestival.com. More than 150 art, craft, and food vendors set up in this picturesque town, a 15-minute ride east of Asheville. A music tent, battle of the bands, and carnival for children are just

FESTIVALS AND ANNUAL EVENTS

some of the fun in store Tues through Sun on the third week in Aug. Stroll the old-fashioned main street and peek into the numerous galleries and antiques stores. Many of them have special sales in conjunction with the festival. It features a lot of good old Americana—bring out the corndogs, watermelon, and, of course, the sourwood honey.

Southern Mountains

J. C. CAMPBELL ANNUAL AUGUST AUCTION, 1 Folk School Rd., Brasstown, NC; (828) 837-2775 or (800) FOLK-SCH; folkschool.org. Spend the first Sat of the month bidding on outstanding craft items. It's a great way to support this unique craft school.

QUALLA ARTS AND CRAFTS OPEN AIR INDIAN ART MARKET, 645 Tsali Blvd., Cherokee, NC; (828) 497-3103; visitcherokeenc.com. This Open Air Indian Art Market showcases traditional, handmade Cherokee arts and crafts. Come to shop for authentic and unique gifts but stay for the music, food, storytelling, and craft demonstrations. The outdoor event is held in the Cultural District of Cherokee at Qualla Arts and Crafts. Traditional Cherokee meals are available for purchase. General admission, though, is free to the public.

SMOKY MOUNTAIN FOLK FESTIVAL, Stuart Auditorium, Lake Junaluska, NC; (800) 334-9036; lakejunaluska.com. A freewheeling Labor Day celebration of the finest traditional and old-timey music and dance, this mountain festival is held in the cool, open-air Stuart Auditorium and on the surrounding grounds. There's even a separate show where kids can kick up their heels!

SEPTEMBER

Northern Mountains

MUSIC IN THE MOUNTAINS FESTIVAL, Toe River Campground Park, Hwy. 80, Burnsville, NC; (828) 682-7413, (828) 682-7215, (800) 948-1632. Mountain folk music and food at the Toe River Campground Park are a magical combination, especially with Mother Nature's beautiful backdrop. Various bluegrass and mountain music bands play at this all-day jamboree in late Sept, often jamming into the night with visitors who happen to bring along instruments. The small fee is usually under $5.

OVERMOUNTAIN VICTORY TRAIL CELEBRATION, Museum of North Carolina Minerals, 214 Parkway Maintenance Rd., Spruce Pine, NC; (828) 765-9483, (800) 227-3912; blueridgeheritage.com. Relive the lives of the "overmountain boys," who walked a trail toward history defending our rights and freedoms. Scheduled events are complemented by demonstrations of frontier cooking, leatherwork, beadwork, spinning, and other Revolutionary-era lifestyle skills. The celebration is held on the third weekend of the month at the North Carolina Museum of Minerals.

Central Mountains

CHOW CHOW, Pack Square, Asheville, NC; exploreasheville.com/chow-chow-culinary-festival. A multiday immersive food experience exploring the unique community of creative makers around the city's table—from growers and farmers to brewers and chefs to crafts people and artists.

GOOMBAY FESTIVAL, 20-40 Eagle St., Asheville, NC; (828) 257-4540; ymiculturalcenter.org. A vibrant celebration of music, food, and arts in conjunction with the YMI Cultural Center, celebrating African American heritage as it pertains to Asheville's traditional Afro-American community.

GREEK FESTIVAL, Holy Trinity Church, 227 Cumberland Ave., Asheville, NC; (828) 253-3754; holytrinityasheville.com. Asheville's Greek community has contributed richly to the multicultural fabric of the city for more than 100 years. This annual festival is a special treat for young and old alike. Greek music and crafts line the inside of the church's community building. A large tent allows for outdoor dining, dancing and celebrating. Spanakopita, gyros, baklava, lamb shanks—try one of everything! A cafe tent features Greek sweets and rich strong demitasses of finely ground Greek coffee.

FALL PIONEER LIVING DAYS AND MILITARY ENCAMPMENT, Zebulon B. Vance Birthplace, 911 Reems Creek Rd., Weaverville, NC; (828) 645-6706. The 1800s come alive at the Zebulon B. Vance Birthplace, a state historic site. Here mountain crafts and traditional cooking are demonstrated, and a 19th-century military encampment is reenacted on the grounds.

NORTH CAROLINA APPLE FESTIVAL, Main St., Hendersonville, NC; (828) 697-4557; ncapplefestival.org. For more than half a century this has been Henderson County's biggest event. It takes place from the first Fri through Mon in Sept and includes a huge street fair, food, crafts, entertainment, and sporting contests. There are over 40 individual events and 25 kinds of entertainment taking place all over town, including the Mountain Music Jamboree, Sunday in the Park, a bike tour, a 10K run, and the King Apple Parade.

Southern Mountains

FIREMAN'S DAY FESTIVAL, Town Square, Bryson City, NC; (828) 488-9416. Held on Town Square on the first Sat of the month, this is a day and evening of festivities in the mountain tradition with music, entertainment, and crafts.

HAYWOOD COUNTY FAIR, Haywood County Fair Ground, Lake Junaluska, NC; (828) 452-0152 or (800) 334-9036. There are barbecues, cotton candy, gospel singings under the tent, old-fashioned horse and tractor pulls, a man's biscuit-making contest, a petting zoo, food and craft exhibits, and more! The event takes place at the Haywood County Fair Ground in Lake Junaluska.

MOUNTAIN HERITAGE DAY, Western Carolina University, 1 University Way, Cullowhee, NC; (828) 227-3039; wcu.edu. Named one of the top 20 events in the Southeast, Mountain Heritage Day attracts more than 15,000 visitors to experience three stages of live entertainment, 130+ food and craft vendors, tons of family-friendly activities, interactive kids area and stage, along with performances and demonstrations celebrating the Southern Appalachian mountain culture. Admission and parking are free.

OCTOBER

Northern Mountains

MADISON HERITAGE ARTS FESTIVAL, various locations Mars Hill, NC; (828) 680-9031; madisonheritage.com. The first Sat in Oct, traditional mountain crafts such as rug braiding, basketmaking, spinning and weaving, and musical instrument making are among the exhibitions. This delightful, small college town opens up all of Main Street, serving a wonderful assortment of pies, cakes, breads, and home cooking. Forty craft booths, local musicians, clog dancers, storytellers, and shape-note singers add to the festivities.

SPRUCE PINE POTTERS MARKET, Historic Cross Building, 31 Cross St., Spruce Pine, NC; sprucepinepottersmarket.com. More than 30 potters show off their wares, functional, figurative sculpture, stoneware, and earthenware mid-Oct. This invitational market showcases artists of various ages utilizing different clay techniques and styles. This event allows artists to bring the privacy of their studios to a group setting. Admission is free and a couple of food booths are available.

TODD NEW RIVER FALL FESTIVAL, Walter and Annie Cook Park, 3977 Todd Railroad Grade Rd., Todd, NC; (828) 964-1362. Todd, a historic village in Ashe County, is the scene of a festival on the ancient New River in early Oct. Once a bustling train town, Todd is now a quiet hamlet frequented by the traveler who wants a different, more leisurely getaway. May festivities take place on the banks of the New River at Cook Memorial Park; features live music, storytelling, arts and crafts booths, a checkers playoff, special children's activities including face painting, and much more!

VALLE COUNTRY FAIR, 122 Skiles Way, Banner Elk, NC; (828) 963-4609; vallecountryfair.com. A premier arts, crafts, and mountain music event in the High Country, the fair draws upwards of 15,000 visitors annually for an entire weekend in mid-Oct. The event takes you back to simpler times when country fairs were the prime social events in the mountains. Every year more than 150 artisans unveil their handcrafted treasures. Mountain music is a highlight, too.

WOOLLY WORM FESTIVAL, Banner Elk, NC; (828) 898-5605 or (800) 972-2183; woollyworm.com. People gather high up in Banner Elk every year during the third weekend in Oct, just before the winds blow chill. Stripes on the woolly worm are traditionally inspected by town elders. Depending on the color, the elders can predict what kind of winter it will be. Along with the honored woolly worm, more than 120 craft artists, races, entertainment, and food make the festival a hit for the whole family.

Central Mountains

ANNUAL ANY AND ALL DOG SHOW, Harmon Field, Tryon, NC; (828) 859-6109. Calling all dogs! Bring your people and join in the fun the second weekend in Oct at 12:30 p.m. Categories include master and dog look-alike, most unusual tail, best trick, and more. Food and beverage vendors are on hand.

ANNUAL FOREST FESTIVAL DAY, Cradle of Forestry, 11250 Pisgah Hwy., Pisgah National Forest, Brevard, NC; (828) 877-3130; cradleof forestry.com. The Cradle of Forestry, a National Historic Site, celebrates our past and future forest resources with old-time demonstrations of carding, spinning, natural dyeing, weaving, whittling, basket making, crosscut sawing, fence rail splitting, and trail building. This popular event takes place the first week in Oct. Admission charged. Over 50 craftspeople, exhibitors, and entertainers take part.

CRAFT FAIR OF THE SOUTHERN HIGHLANDS, US Cellular Center, Asheville, NC; (828) 298-7928; southernhighlandcraftguild.org. One of the most popular of the annual mountain crafts fairs, the Craft Fair of the Southern Highland Craft Guild features a juried craft exhibition, professional demonstrations, and fine traditional mountain music. It's held in the large downtown US Cellular Center on the third weekend in July and Oct.

FARM CITY DAY, Jackson Park, Hendersonville, NC; (828) 697-4884. The free, daylong event, held in Jackson Park, includes tractor pulls, sheep herding, and shearing demonstrations. Here you'll find antique and modern farm equipment, square dancing, clogging, arts and crafts, and food booths. The festivities end with a Civil War reenactment. A special children's section features activities such as a greased pig contest.

HALLOWEEN FEST, various locations Brevard, NC; (828) 883-3700. What better place for a fun and scary Halloween than in Transylvania County? From 10 a.m. until 6 p.m., there are food vendors, crafters, a musical competition, a bicycle rodeo, and a mask-making workshop. In the afternoon participants can sacrifice their blood, not to a vampire, but to the Bloodmobile; join or watch a costume parade; trick-or-treat in the downtown area; compete in a pumpkin-carving contest; enjoy a kids' carnival; and much more.

HARD LOX FESTIVAL, Pack Square Park, Asheville, NC; hardloxjewish festival.org. Asheville's Jewish food and culture festival, usually held the second Sun of the month, with delectable deli-style food and baking booths, music, dancing, and other entertainment.

LEAF (LAKE EDEN ARTS FESTIVAL), Camp Rockmont, Black Mountain, NC; (828) 686-8742; theleaf.org. The Lake Eden Arts Festival is a fun event filled with dancing and music, drumming and handcrafts, poetry and storytelling. There are also spiritual and healing workshops and a farmers' market during the three-day weekend in late Oct and again in May. The first LEAF Festival premiered in 1996, and has become a tradition of concerts, camping, and food, whilst embracing world cultures, reflecting the creativity of the Asheville area, and complementing the surrounding landscape.

SOUTHEASTERN ANIMAL FIBER FAIR, WNC Agricultural Center, 1301 Fanning Bridge Rd., Fletcher, NC; (828) 891-2810. The end of Oct brings a fair that features hundreds of fiber animals, including llamas, Angora goats, rabbits, and many breeds of sheep. Demonstrations teach how to harvest and use such fiber "crops."

THOMAS WOLFE FESTIVAL, Thomas Wolfe Memorial and various locations, 52 N. Market St., Asheville, NC; (828) 253-8304; wolfememorial .com. The Thomas Wolfe Memorial Welcome Center and downtown Asheville host two days of events on the first weekend of Oct saluting Asheville's most famous writer. Included are readings, discussions, walking tours, a birthday party, music, and theater events. Most events are free.

Southern Mountains

CHURCH STREET ART AND CRAFT SHOW, Main Street, Waynesville, NC; (828) 456-3517; downtownwaynesville.com. Every Oct over 120 craft and food vendors descend on Main Street with artisans and crafts people displaying their works. This juried show takes place on Main Street, featuring two-dimensional and three-dimensional work such as pottery, jewelry, wood, fiber art, watercolors, and photography.

J. C. CAMPBELL FALL FESTIVAL, 1 Folk School Rd., Brasstown, NC; (828) 837-2775 or (800) FOLK-SCH. This is a two-day fair of food, crafts, children's activities, music, dance, and good company held the first weekend of the month.

PUMPKIN FEST, various locations Franklin, NC; (828) 524-2516; discoverfranklinnc.com. This street festival and celebration of autumn is for the whole family in Downtown Franklin. Bring a pumpkin (or buy one there) for the "World Famous Pumpkin Roll." A Costume Parade and Contest is another highlight of the day as well as the Pumpkin Pie Eating Contest, more than 80 vendors including mountain crafts, and some good food.

NOVEMBER

Northern Mountains

BLOWING ROCK CHRISTMAS, various locations, Blowing Rock, NC; (828) 295-7851; blowingrock.com/blowing-rock-holidays. The town of Blowing Rock begins the fun seasonal festivities on a late Nov weekend that continue through the end of Dec., including the holiday parade, "Christmas in the Park" with caroling in the town's Memorial Park, Christmas decorations throughout the town, and various day and evening activities that continue up until Christmas.

Central Mountains

CHRISTMAS AT BILTMORE ESTATE, 1 Approach Rd., Asheville, NC; (800) 411-3812; biltmore.com. This magnificent re-creation of a Victorian Christmas of a century ago begins just before Thanksgiving and continues through Dec. Daytime visits to George Vanderbilt's mansion are wonderful, but make a point to include on your agenda this nighttime delight—the Biltmore House bathed in the glow of candlelight and blazing hearth fires. It's exquisite, but it's by reservation only, so book early. The cost is admission to the estate, plus additional charges for additional tours.

HOLIDAY PARADE, Patton and Biltmore Aves., Asheville, NC; asheville downtown.org. This vibrant, rollicking parade begins the Christmas season in earnest. Always held before Thanksgiving, Asheville's Holiday parade is alive with colorful floats, energetic high school marching bands, tiny twirlers and local dance troupes, raucous clowns, and St. Nick himself showering the throngs with candy canes and peppermints. This parade is always well attended by young and old and swells downtown to bursting. Get there early to stake out your spot.

HOLLY JOLLY CHRISTMAS, Omni Grove Park Inn; 290 Macon Ave., Asheville, NC; (828) 252-2711 or (800) 438-5800. Here is a special place to fill your family with the Christmas spirit. In addition to beautifully decorated trees, there are gingerbread houses made by local and national bakers for this annual competition, storytelling, caroling, and craft demonstrations. Live holiday music in the Great Hall helps get you in the holiday mood and trees decorated through the main hallway wings inspire home decorating, as well. Holiday activities continue from late Nov through New Year's Day.

HOME FOR THE HOLIDAYS, various locations Hendersonville, NC and Flat Rock, NC; (828) 693-9708 or (800) 828-4244. Concerts, exhibits, tours, and special holiday events are scheduled beginning the day after Thanksgiving through Christmas. It starts with the mayoral downtown holiday lighting ceremony and includes tours of historic bed-and-breakfast establishments, Christmas carols, open house at the Curb Market, and much more.

RIVER DISTRICT FALL STUDIO STROLL, River District, Asheville, NC; riverartsdistrict.com. Held the second full weekend in Nov (and June) from 10 a.m. to 4 p.m., the Studio Stroll is a chance to tour over 100 studios, meet with the artists, and purchase artwork.

WINTER LIGHTS, North Carolina Arboretum, 100 Frederick Law Olmsted Way, Asheville, NC; (828) 665-2492; ncarboretum.org. Don't miss The North Carolina Arboretum's elaborate Winter Lights show, transforming the gardens into a nighttime wonderland with 500,000 lights! This magical walk through spectacular displays gardens is designed with an artistic aesthetic that enhances the natural beauty of the gardens as you celebrate the holidays.

Southern Mountains

ANNUAL HARD-CANDY ARTS AND CRAFTS SHOW, WCU Liston B. Ramsey Activity Center, 92 Catamount Rd., Cullowhee, NC; (829) 524-3406. You get a free stick of peppermint at this popular show, held just after Thanksgiving. The exhibitors are first class: There are apple crafts, a children's section full of dolls and doll houses, a host of angels, and other crafts reflecting the holiday spirit. Bring your Christmas list!

J. C. CAMPBELL ANNUAL BLACKSMITH AUCTION, 1 Folk School Rd., Brasstown, NC; (828) 837-2775 or (800) FOLK-SCH. Taking place on the second Sat of the month, this auction offers pieces by some the nation's greatest masters. Proceeds help keep the craft school's smithy one of the best.

TOWN LIGHTING, Highlands Town Hall and Main St., Highlands, NC; (828) 526-2112. Once again the population of Highlands swells with the guests joining the year-round folks for the lighting. It occurs on the Sat following Thanksgiving. This traditional event ushers in the excitement of the holiday season. The shops are adorned with seasonal decorations, subtle, yet beckoning. It's time to experience the holidays in a tasteful manner.

DECEMBER

Northern Mountains

BOONE CHRISTMAS PARADE, West King St., Boone, NC; (828)268-6280; joneshouse.org. The first Sat in Dec is set aside to herald the holiday season in this picturesque college town. The parade heads down West King Street, then visitors are invited to the Jones House for cider, cookies, and a potential visit from Santa, from noon to 4 p.m.

CHOOSE AND CUT WEEKEND, Ashe County, Sparta/Alleghany County, Watauga County; (800) 562-8789 or (828) 262-5826; ncchristmastrees.org. Choose and Cut Weekend provides the ideal opportunity to select the family Christmas tree. All locations offer tree-cutting festivities, including caroling and cider and cookie sampling in early Dec. After you tie the fir to the car roof, go have a mug of hot chocolate and join in the holiday events and festival fun. Christmas card memories!

SANTA COMES TO BEECH MOUNTAIN, 608 Beech Mountain Pkwy., Beech Mountain, NC; (828) 387-9283 or (800) 468-5506. A cute old-fashioned holiday visit with Santa happens in the lobby of the 4 Seasons at Beech Hotel in this cozy mountaintop ski village.

Central Mountains

THE BIG CRAFTY, Asheville Cellular Center, 87 Haywood St., Asheville, NC; thebigcrafty.com. At this spectacular community bazaar, a lively celebration of handmade commerce, local and regional artists and artisans ply their wares. Usually held the second weekend in Dec, the market boasts booths of crafted jewelry, art, letter-press stationary, hats and clothing, and hipster-to-high-end handcrafted gifts. It's a fun-for-all-ages event, held also in the summer.

BLACK MOUNTAIN CHRISTMAS PARADE AND COMMUNITY CANDLE LIGHTING, downtown Black Mountain, NC; (828) 669-2300; visitblackmountain.net. The unique village of Black Mountain just east of Asheville is the setting for a traditional parade down a picturesque Main Street to Lake Tomahawk, just a few blocks north of downtown. The event begins in late afternoon the first Sat in Dec and is capped by the lighting of candles and carol singing around the rim of luminaria-lit Lake Tomahawk (where Santa has been known to make an appearance).

CHRISTMAS AT CONNEMARA, Connemara, 1928 Little River Rd., Flat Rock, NC; (828) 693-4178; nps.gov/carl. Follow the luminaria-lined path up the hillside to the Carl Sandburg Home and savor a simple time of Christmas past just as the Sandburg family celebrated it. This one-day event, usually held the third week in Dec, charges a small fee but children younger than 16 are admitted free.

FESTIVAL OF TREES, 1 Brevard College Dr., Porter Center for the Performing Arts, Brevard College, Brevard, NC; (828) 884-8900 or (828) 883-3692. Resurrected after a five-year hiatus, this festival is back in a new venue, but still for buying or just enjoying exquisitely decorated trees, Christmas cakes, candies, cookies, and gifts prepared for this four-day event in early Dec that benefits the Children's Center. A raffle is also held.

HOLIDAY MAKERS SALE, Southern Highland Craft Guild, Folk Art Center, Mile 283, Blue Ridge Pkwy, Asheville, NC; (828) 298-7928; southernhighlandguild.org. The Southern Highland Craft Guild displays Christmas decorations and holiday craft exhibits at the grand showcase venue of the Folk Art Center at the Blue Ridge Parkway entrance just east of the city. Free holiday concerts are featured on weekends throughout Dec. The first two Saturdays of Dec, artists liquidate overstocks of select work at the Holiday Makers Sale, with 10 to 50 percent off retail from 10 a.m. to 4 p.m.

HOLIDAY TOUR OF HISTORIC INNS AND COOKIE CAPER, downtown Hendersonville, NC; (828) 697-3010 or (800) 828-4244. The Holiday Tour of Historic Inns and Cookie Caper is a self-guided afternoon tour of seven inns and the Cookie Caper part of the tour is a delicious Christmas treat at each inn.

TWILIGHT TOUR AND DICKENS ON MAIN, various locations Brevard, NC; (828) 884-3278; brevardnc.org. During this evening event on the first Sat in Dec, horse-drawn carriages transport revelers through the twinkling lights and luminaria-lit streets of downtown, past carolers, musicians, and food vendors. Most stores are open and serve free hot cider and cookies. This event, regardless of the weather, is extremely popular with local residents.

Southern Mountains

APPALACHIAN CHRISTMAS AT LAKE JUNALUSKA, Lake Junaluska, NC; (800) 222-4930; lakejunaluska.com. Over a long weekend mid-Dec enjoy holiday festivities including a Christmas Craft Show, a performance of

Handel's "Messiah" featuring a regional choir and orchestra, and self-guided tours of the newly-remodeled Lambuth Inn, all dressed for Christmas.

DILLSBORO FESTIVAL OF LIGHTS, various locations, Dillsboro, NC; (828) 586-3943; visitdillsboro.org. The first two weekends in Dec, all shops hold open houses with thousands of luminaria lighting up the streets and Christmas caroling filling the night. Complimentary refreshments are served.

HIGHLANDS OLDE MOUNTAIN CHRISTMAS PARADE, Main St., Highlands, NC; (828) 526-5841; highlandschamber.org. Jolly Old St. Nick has the key to the city gates and occupies the mayor's chair during this festive time. The parade winds its way through this mountain town on the first Sat in Dec. Bed-and-breakfasts and restaurants open their doors to guests, offering hospitality and Christmas-theme meals. The surrounding mountains offer the enchantment of the season and sleigh bells can be heard, especially if one listens carefully. Chestnuts are roasting on an open fire, and hot chocolate couldn't taste better. Highlands at the holidays is always special.

HOLIDAY TOUR OF HISTORIC HOMES, various locations, Canton, NC; (828) 646-3412, (828) 926-1686, (800) 334-9036. A tour of homes outfitted for the holidays in and around downtown Canton since the 1980s, this is a feast for the senses in old-fashioned homes decked out in their Christmas best. It takes place the first week in Dec and tickets may be purchased at the Canton Area Historical Museum.

J. C. CAMPBELL FIRESIDE SALE, 1 Folk School Rd., Brasstown, NC; (828) 837-2775, (800) FOLK-SCH; folkschool.org. This craft sale extravaganza on the first Sun in Dec is just one of many community events happening around the hearth and the big Christmas tree at the John C. Campbell Folk School.

APPENDIX:
Living Here

In this section we feature specific information for residents or those planning to relocate here.

Relocation

MOTOR VEHICLE INFORMATION

Driver licenses, learner permits, and IDs are issued from a central location and mailed to NC Division of Motor Vehicles (NCDMV) customers. Applying for a North Carolina driver license or ID will cancel any licenses or IDs from other states. Residents can receive a 60-day Temporary Driving Certificate, which can only be used for driving purposes and not identification; their license, permit, or ID will arrive before the certificate expires.

New residents of the North Carolina mountains must register their vehicle when their previous state registration expires (in 30 days, for most instances) or when residents obtain gainful employment accepted in North Carolina. Before a vehicle can be registered, the NCDMV requires a title. To title and register, residents can go to an NCDMV license plate agency or mail proof of title requirements. Vehicles can be titled and registered with a Temporary Driving Certificate so long as the resident has a valid out-of-state driver license and one of the following: a military ID, a student ID, a Form MVR-614, a court-ordered sale of the vehicle, or registration for a motor home.

Vehicle registrations must be renewed annually. Registration renewal fees and any vehicle property taxes are due at the same time, and can be paid online, by mail, or at an NCDMV license plate agency. Before renewing, the vehicle must undergo a safety and/or emissions inspection no more than 90 days before its license plate expires.

For more information, call NCDMV at (919) 715-7000 or visit the following NCDMV locations.

North Mountains (Alleghany, Ashe, Avery, Madison, Mitchell, Watauga, and Yancey Counties)

4469 Bamboo Rd., Ste. 103, Boone
116 North Main St., Burnsville
150 Government Cir., Ste. 2200, Jefferson
301 Cranberry St., Newland
115 Atwood St., Suite 508, Sparta
1032 Oak Ave., Spruce Pine

Central Mountains (Buncombe, Henderson, Polk, and Transylvania Counties)

1624 Patton Ave., Asheville
50 Commerce St., Ste. 4, Brevard

51 Walker St., Columbus
125 Baystone Dr., Hendersonville

Southern Mountains (Cherokee, Clay, Graham, Haywood, Jackson, Macon, and Swain Counties)

1440 Main St., Andrews
2650 Governors Island Rd., Bryson City
290 Lee Rd., Clyde
16 Patton Ave., Franklin
1 Riverside Cir., Hayesville
196 Knight St., Robbinsville (mobile unit location)
876 Skyland Dr., Suite 2, Sylva

VOTER REGISTRATION

A prospective voter must be a citizen of the United States, 18 years old by the time of the next general election, be residing in their county of registration for at least 30 days prior to the election, and not be serving a sentence for a felony conviction, including probation or parole. If a prospective resident has been previously convicted of a felony, their citizenship rights must be restored. To register to vote, newcomers must complete a voter registration application, which then must be mailed to the board of elections office in the county in which the prospective resident lives. Visit ncsbe.gov/voters for more information.

Northern Mountains (Alleghany, Ashe, Avery, Madison, Mitchell, Watauga, and Yancey Counties)

Visit alleghanyelections.com, ashecountygov.com, averycountync.gov, madison countync.gov, mitchellcounty.org, wataugacounty.org, or yanceycountync.gov for more information, or call the following numbers:

ALLEGHANY COUNTY: (336) 372-4557

ASHE COUNTY: (336) 846-5570

AVERY COUNTY: (828) 733-8282

MADISON COUNTY: (828) 649-3731

MITCHELL COUNTY: (828) 688-3101

WATAUGA COUNTY: (828) 265-8061

YANCEY COUNTY: (828) 682-3950

Central Mountains (Buncombe, Henderson, Polk, and Transylvania Counties)

Visit buncombecounty.org, hendersoncountync.gov, polknc.org, or transylvania elections.org for more information, or call the following numbers:

BUNCOMBE COUNTY: (828) 250-4209

HENDERSON COUNTY: (828) 697-4970

POLK COUNTY: (828) 894-8181

TRANSYLVANIA COUNTY: (828) 884-3114

Southern Mountains (Cherokee, Clay, Graham, Haywood, Jackson, Macon, and Swain Counties)

Visit cherokeecounty-nc.gov, claycountyboardofelections.com, grahamcounty .org, haywoodcountync.gov, jacksonnc.org, maconnc.org, or swaincountync .gov for more information, or call the following numbers:

CHEROKEE COUNTY: (828) 837-5527

CLAY COUNTY: (828) 389-6812

GRAHAM COUNTY: (828) 479-7969

HAYWOOD COUNTY: (828) 452-6633

JACKSON COUNTY: (828) 586-4055

MACON COUNTY: (828) 349-2000

SWAIN COUNTY: (828) 488-6177

UTILITIES

For natural gas, electricity, water, and telephone services in the North Carolina mountains area, visit ncuc.net or call one of the following:

Electricity/Renewables

DOMINION NORTH CAROLINA POWER, (877) 776-2427; dominion energy.com

DUKE ENERGY CAROLINAS, (844) 378-6352; duke-energy.com

DUKE ENERGY PROGRESS, (844) 378-6352; progress-energy.com

NEW RIVER LIGHT AND POWER, (828) 264-3671; nrlp.appstate.edu (Boone and surrounding area only)

NORTH CAROLINA ELECTRONIC MEMBERSHIP CORPORATION, (919) 872-0800 or (800) 662-8835; ncelectriccooperatives.com

Natural Gas

FRONTIER NATURAL GAS COMPANY, (336) 526-2690; frontiernatural gas.com

PIEDMONT NATURAL GAS COMPANY, (800) 752-7504; piedmontng .com

PSNC ENERGY/DOMINION ENERGY, (877) 776-2427; psncenergy .com

TOCCOA NATURAL GAS, (706) 886-8451; cityoftoccoa.com (Macon County only)

Telephone
Both Verizon and AT&T provide telephone services for the majority of North Carolina. Verizon's customer service may be reached at (800) 922-0204 or on their website, verizonwireless.com. AT&T may be reached at (800) 288-2020 or on att.com.

Water/Wastewater
Many counties have their own water and sewer commissions. Consult the telephone directory for their individual numbers, or go to ncwater.org to find your county's contact information:

NORTH CAROLINA DEPARTMENT OF ENVIRONMENTAL QUALITY, (877) 623-6748; ncwater.org

Retirement

North Carolina's mountain towns and cities have been at the top of leading publications' lists of "top places to retire" for some time now. It's no wonder—with cultural offerings in the cities and pastoral tranquility in the countryside—retirees can be as active or as relaxed as they want to be.

When moving to the North Carolina mountains, you won't feel like you are retiring, but rather beginning a second career of healthy recreation, travel, cultural enrichment, culinary arts, entertainment, and the discovery of nature. With all the cultural treats of the area—universities and music schools, museums and galleries, mountain craft schools and studios, unique shops and arrays of excellent restaurants, botanical gardens, and nearby forests and waterfalls—you would be hard pressed to find time to while away the hours sitting in a rocking chair.

If help is needed, it's available. Here is just a partial list of places you may call on for support systems, socializing, and just plain fun.

REGIONAL SERVICES

Northern Mountains

AREA AGENCY ON AGING COUNCIL OF GOVERNMENTS, 155 Furman Rd., Boone, NC; (828) 265-5434; regiond.org. This agency serves senior citizens in the seven northwestern counties of North Carolina. The agency directs a Long-Term Care Ombudsman Program for the region and serves as a funding and information resource for agencies involved in senior care, education, and public awareness in Alleghany, Ashe, Avery, Mitchell, Watauga, and Yancey Counties to the north. Senior centers in each of these locations offer a variety of programs that include group meals at the centers as well as home-delivered meals, In-Home Aide, recreational programs, legal services, health screening, and nutrition guidance. Transportation and adult day care are also provided through some locations. They also publish a helpful directory, listing agencies and telephone numbers.

LEGAL SERVICES OF THE BLUE RIDGE, 171 Grand Blvd., Boone, NC; (828) 264-5640, (800) 849-5666. Senior citizens can get advice for problems with Social Security, Medicaid and Medicare, food stamps, housing, institutional care, and consumer issues.

Alleghany County

ALLEGHANY COUNCIL ON AGING INC., Senior Center, Greyson and Whitehead Sts., Sparta, NC; (336) 372-4640. This organization oversees In-Home Aide, group meals, home-delivered meals, health promotion, Senior Games, AARP, recreation, and educational classes.

AMERICAN ASSOCIATION OF RETIRED PERSONS (AARP), Senior Center, Greyson and Whitehead Sts., Sparta, NC; (336) 372-4640. This branch of the national organization meets the fourth Tues of each month at 6 p.m. at the Alleghany Senior Center for discussion, support, counseling, and social time.

BLUE RIDGE OPPORTUNITY COMMISSION, 1747 US Hwy. 21 N., Sparta, NC; (336) 372-7284. The BROC provides information and referral, housing weatherization, and repair.

COOPERATIVE EXTENSION SERVICE, 90 South Main St., Sparta, NC; (336) 372-5597. This office provides advice on energy resources conservation, homemaking, and personal financial management counseling for Alleghany County senior citizens.

DEPARTMENT OF SOCIAL SERVICES, 182 Doctors St., Sparta, NC; (336) 372-2411, (336) 372-2414. The Department of Social Services can help you arrange for health support services, Medicaid, protective services, senior citizens transportation, emergency assistance programs, and nursing home placement. Food stamps are also available through this office.

Ashe County

ASHE SERVICES FOR AGING, INC., 180 Chatty Rob Ln., West Jefferson, NC; (336) 246-2461; asheaging.org. This agency oversees programs for transportation, In-Home Aide II, group and home-delivered meals, and educational classes. Senior Tar Heel discount cards, the Health Insurance Information Program, adult day care, and daily activity programs are some of the benefits available here for Ashe County's older residents.

BLUE RIDGE OPPORTUNITY COMMISSION, 169 Warrensville School Rd., Warrensville, NC; (336) 384-4543. The group offers assistance with weatherization and repair, housing and community action, and crisis intervention regarding fuel and electricity.

DEPARTMENT OF SOCIAL SERVICES, 303 East Main St., Jefferson, NC; (336) 246-1900. This public agency offers senior citizens resources, information, aid for medical expenses, adult protective services, food stamps, and (home-heating) fuel assistance.

Health Department, Senior Companion Program, 707 Ray Taylor Rd., West Jefferson, NC; (336) 246-4898. Companionship is key to the success of this in-home service that involves active senior citizens working with disabled or less-active senior citizens in the community and provides assistance with light house-keeping, meal preparation, laundry, bookkeeping, bill-paying, and transportation.

Avery County

AVERY COUNTY VETERANS OFFICE, 205 Administrative Building, Newland, NC; (828) 733-8211. This local office assists veterans with claims to the Veterans Administration for such things as education, medical care, insurance, and loans.

AVERY SENIOR SERVICES SENIOR CENTER, 165 Shultz Circle, Newland, NC; (828) 733-8220. Transportation, In-Home Aide I, group and home-delivered meals, and health promotion are a few of the many services Avery provides.

W.A.M.Y. COMMUNITY ACTION, 260 Estatoa Ave., Newland; (828) 733-0156. This group provides community center crafts, weatherization and home repair, job training, a garden program, and transportation assistance. (W.A.M.Y. stands for Watauga, Avery, Mitchell, and Yancey Counties.)

Madison County

MADISON COUNTY DEPARTMENT OF COMMUNITY SERVICES SENIOR CENTER, 462 Long Branch Rd., Marshall, NC; (828) 649-2722. This site is the central location for a network of centers that offers activities, health screening, chore services, nutrition information, and home-delivered meals, as well as congregate meals on site and information on other vital services of interest to Madison County senior citizens.

MARS HILL COLLEGE PROGRAMS FOR SENIOR CITIZENS, 100 Athletic St., Mars Hill, NC; (828) 689-1167. Mars Hill College participates with Elderhostel, a worldwide continuing education enrichment series for senior citizens. Programs from history and music to science and art are part of this learning opportunity offered 22 weeks each year. The college provides a regular continuing education program linked with the Mars Hill curriculum. The Summer Alternative Vacation Program and the Learning Institute for Elders (LIFE) have learning tours on a variety of subjects.

Mitchell County

COOPERATIVE EXTENSION SERVICE, County Building, Annex East, 10 South Mitchell Ave., Bakersville, NC; (828) 688-4811. This county extension service provides senior citizens with advice on energy resources conservation, financial management, and homemaking.

DEPARTMENT OF SOCIAL SERVICES, 271 Crimson Laurel Way, Bakersville, NC; (828) 688-2175. Senior citizens around Bakersville can find resource information, In-Home Aide services, food stamps, energy assistance, health support services, transportation, and home improvement assistance through this agency.

MITCHELL SENIOR CENTER, 152 Ledger School Rd., Bakersville, NC; (828) 688-3019. Transportation, In-Home Aide I, group and home-delivered meals, and health and nutrition assistance are some of the services provided by this center.

VETERANS SERVICE OFFICE, 130 Forest Service Dr., Ste. C, Bakersville, NC; (828) 688-2200. This local office assists veterans with claims to the Veterans Administration for such things as education, medical care, insurance, and loans.

W.A.M.Y. COMMUNITY ACTION, INC., 213 Oak Ave., Spruce Pine, NC; (828) 766-9150, (828) 765-9151. Transportation, weatherization and home repair, elderly nutrition, and gardening programs are some of the services provided by this office.

Watauga County

APPALCART TRANSPORTATION, 274 Winklers Creek Rd., Boone, NC; (828) 264-2280, (828) 264-2278. AppalCART provides county and town transportation service to seniors and the general public. Call for schedules and arrangements.

COOPERATIVE EXTENSION SERVICE, 971 West King St., Boone, NC; (828) 264-3061. Homemaking and housing information, as well as energy resources conservation and financial management counseling are provided through the county extension service.

DEPARTMENT OF SOCIAL SERVICES, 132 Poplar Grove Connector, Ste. C, Boone, NC; (828) 265-8100. Health support services are among the many types of aid available through this department.

VETERANS SERVICE OFFICE, Courthouse Annex, Rm. 100, Boone, NC; (828) 265-8065. This local office assists veterans with claims to the Veterans Administration for such things as education, medical care, insurance, and loans.

W.A.M.Y. COMMUNITY ACTION PROGRAM, 152 Southgate Dr., Ste. 2, Boone, NC; (828) 264-2421. Watauga County senior citizens benefit from the active participation of this office in the areas of weatherization and home repair, transportation for elderly, and job and gardening programs.

WATAUGA COUNTY PROJECT ON AGING, 132 Poplar Grove Connector, Ste. A, Boone, NC; (828) 265-8090; wataugacounty.org/aging. Transportation, In-Home Aide I and II, group and home-delivered meals, and health screenings are provided to Watauga County senior citizens.

Yancey County

COOPERATIVE EXTENSION SERVICE, 10 Orchard St., Burnsville, NC; (828) 682-6186. Financial management counseling, housing information, homemaking services, and information on energy resources conservation, agriculture, and home horticulture are offered by the county extension service.

DEPARTMENT OF SOCIAL SERVICES, 222 Lincoln Park Rd., Burnsville, NC; (828) 682-6148, (828) 682-2470. Health support services, transportation, and aid for medical expenses and family and veteran support services are some of the services of this department.

W.A.M.Y. COMMUNITY ACTION PROGRAM, 22 East Bypass, Burnsville, NC; (828) 682-2610. Above Pollard's Drug Store, the W.A.M.Y. program offers limited home repair assistance as well as elderly transportation.

YANCEY COUNTY COMMITTEE ON AGING, Senior Center, 10 Swiss Ave., Burnsville, NC; (828) 682-6011. This lively place offers In-Home Aide I, group and home-delivered meals, transportation, and health promotion like blood pressure and cholesterol checks. Senior Tar Heel Discount cards and the Seniors' Health Insurance Information Program (SHIIP) are also part of the services offered here.

YANCEY TRANSPORTATION AUTHORITY, Courthouse, 15 East Blvd., Burnsville, NC; (828) 682-6144. Yancey offers senior transportation assistance through a contract with the senior center.

Central Mountains

Buncombe County

BUNCOMBE COUNTY COUNCIL ON AGING, Community Services Center, 46 Sheffield Circle, Ste. 141, Asheville, NC; (828) 277-8288; coabc .org. This private, nonprofit corporation, a United Way agency, is composed of senior citizens groups and organizations providing services to Buncombe County senior citizens. Outreach services include friendly visitation, senior companionship, home repair, weatherization, and fan distribution. The agency coordinates various countywide programs that offer nutrition assistance, congregate meals at 17 locations, the Senior Tar Heel discount program, and volunteer opportunities for older citizens and other people.

BUNCOMBE COUNTY MOUNTAIN MOBILITY, 185 Coxe Ave., Asheville, NC; (828) 258-0186. This service provides door-to-door transportation services for the elderly, disabled, and transportation disadvantaged.

CENTER FOR CREATIVE RETIREMENT, COLLEGE FOR SENIORS, University of North Carolina Asheville, 1 University Heights, Asheville, NC; (828) 251-6140, (828) 251-6384; unca.edu. The University of North Carolina Asheville was one of the first to establish a college for seniors. Through the generosity of the Janirve Foundation the college found a home as the Center for Creative Retirement. This newest building on campus, known as the Reuter Center, is named for the founder of the foundation. This innovative university program, begun in 1988, offers learning, leadership, and community-service opportunities for older adults. Among these are the College for Seniors, a peer learning and teaching program; Schools and Campus Volunteer Programs, a variety of student/mentor learning experiences; Leadership Asheville Seniors, a series of daylong sessions geared toward community service; and a continuing program of research into issues concerning older adult education.

LAND OF THE SKY REGIONAL COUNCIL, 25 Heritage Dr., Asheville, NC; (828) 251-6622; landofsky.org. The following counties comprise Land of the Sky Regional Council: Madison, Buncombe, Henderson, and Transylvania. Its purpose is to provide total services for seniors in all these counties. Two of the Council's guide books that contain contacts for all services from health services to activity clubs and beyond are *Senior Adult Directory for Buncombe County* and *Madison County Senior Services Directory*.

Henderson County

AMERICAN ASSOCIATION OF RETIRED PERSONS (AARP), 314 Oklawaha Circle, Hendersonville, NC; (828) 697-0187. This organization offers a 55 Alive/Safe Driving Course for senior citizens and tax aid services. A member of the organization coordinates the Seniors' Health Insurance Information Program (SHIIP). It informs and educates seniors regarding relevant issues through speakers and literature and is one of the sponsors of the Widowed Persons Services (see below). It is an advocate for seniors' issues at the state and national levels.

COUNCIL ON AGING, 304 Chadwick Ave., Hendersonville, NC; (828) 692-4203. The council provides a variety of services that help older adults cope with physical, social, or other aging problems. Specific programs include Meals on Wheels, Service Advocates for the Elderly (SAFE), Elder Neighbors, minor home repairs, installation and repair of smoke alarms (Fire Alert), and an Information and Referral Helpline (828-697-4357). Other services include lending out heaters and fans, a hearing-aid bank, a thrift shop (213 South Church St., 828-693-7756), and living wills. The council also offers congregate meals at the Sammy Williams Senior Center located at Third Avenue West and Justice Street (828-692-3320), for those persons wishing to travel to the center.

LIFELINE PERSONAL EMERGENCY RESPONSE SYSTEM, Pardee Hospital/Lifeline, 2029A Asheville Hwy., Hendersonville, NC; (828) 692-9061. This program offers round-the-clock, professional monitoring of every emergency call for help direct to Pardee Hospital.

OPPORTUNITY HOUSE, 1411 Asheville Hwy., Hendersonville, NC; (828) 692-0575. This arts, crafts, and cultural center is a nonprofit organization that opened its doors in 1958. Now, as then, it continues to offer fellowship and learning opportunities to individuals of all ages and faiths. Activities include bridge, crafts, dance, golf, ladies club, seminars, and smoke-free bingo. The gift shop on the premises features many handcrafted items and is open to the public. Opportunity House is open Mon through Fri from 9 a.m. to 5 p.m., and visitors are always welcome. There is an annual membership fee.

PARDEE PAVILION (ADULT DAY CARE), 104 College Dr., Flat Rock, NC; (828) 696-7070. This adult day-care facility has planned activities to meet an individual's specific needs. It provides educational, recreational, social, diversional, and volunteer programs.

SENIORS HEALTH INSURANCE, PARDEE HEALTH EDUCATION CENTER, 1800 Four Seasons Blvd., Hendersonville, NC; (828) 692-4600. Personal insurance counseling provided by the Seniors' Health Insurance Information Program (SHIIP) is available at Pardee Hospital's Health Education Center in the Blue Ridge Mall. The trained SHIIP volunteers provide free counseling to older adults on long-term care insurance, Medicare, and Medicaid Supplement insurance.

WESTERN CAROLINA COMMUNITY ACTION, 526 Seventh Ave. East, Hendersonville, NC; (828) 693-1771. This organization develops and administers programs of interest to older adults that include weatherization, a heating appliance replacement and repair program (HARRP), FISH medical transportation answering and dispatch, a variety of transportation services, emergency assistance, emergency fuel, plastic for windows, a garden program, a food closet, job placement with supportive services, liquid nutrient supplement (Ensure), and Section 8 Housing Assistance, to name a few.

Polk County

THE MEETING PLACE, Jervey-Palmer Building; 330 Carolina Dr., Tryon; (828) 859-9707; polknc.org. This center serves both congregate and in-home lunches Mon through Fri. It also offers classes in exercise, quilting, and sewing, but one of its biggest draws is its ceramics workshop. The Meeting Place also has a pool room, a television lounge, and frequent games of cards, bingo, and checkers. It has its own library and is visited regularly by a bookmobile. There is also a regular Wed music session. Other services include regularly scheduled transportation for shopping and medical appointments, and special holiday trips are offered. Seniors may also take advantage of nutrition education programs, legal services, and tax services. There are satellite centers with many of the same services in both Saluda and Green Creek.

Transylvania County

BREVARD COLLEGE COMMUNITY EDUCATION, 400 North Broad St., Brevard, NC; (828) 884-8256; brevard.edu. Reaching beyond the college-aged population, Brevard has a wide variety of continuing education programs for adults. The Office of Community Education currently offers more than 200 courses annually, with an enrollment of nearly 2,000 participants, that include intellectual and academic subjects, cultural experiences, local orientation, hobbies and self-improvement, and health and physical fitness classes. Classes are noncredit. However, CEUs are offered for specific programs. In addition musical performances, dramatic presentations, art gallery exhibits, and lecture series are presented throughout the year and are open to the public. Computer courses are offered as well as a program that is lauded by the Transylvania newspaper as being one of the finest: the "Inside Transylvania" program. This course is designed for newcomers but open to all. Participants meet face to face with leaders in Transylvania County. It offers 3.0 CEUs. The Brevard College library is also an integral part of the intellectual life here.

KOALA ADULT DAY CARE, 19 Carolina Ave., Brevard, NC; (828) 884-2980; agingcare.com. Caregivers can leave loved ones here while they work or just take time for themselves. It offers its clients crafts, re-motivation, reminiscing, fun and games, medication, and a hot lunch. Call for information about the daily fee. Grants are available to those unable to pay the full amount.

MEALS ON WHEELS OF BREVARD, Transylvania Community Hospital; 260 Hospital Dr., Brevard; (828) 883-3743. Like so many other of these helpful programs, MOW provides hot, well-balanced noontime meals on weekdays to shut-ins without age or income restrictions. Volunteers deliver the meals and the cost is based on the client's ability to pay.

WESTERN CAROLINA COMMUNITY ACTION, 203 East Morgan St., Brevard; (828) 884-3219; wcca.org. A branch of the WCCA in Henderson County, Transylvania's office serves congregate lunches Mon through Fri at both Silvermont in Brevard and in Quebec on US Highway 64 West and provides transportation to both sites as well as out-of-county medical transportation. It joins with the AARP in providing trained tax preparers to assist with tax returns and oversees the Seniors' Health Insurance Information Program (SHIIP), job training for those older than 55, a weatherization program for both renters and homeowners with limited incomes, emergency assistance, liquid nutrient supplement (Ensure) program, plastic for windows, spring and fall garden supplies, a heating appliance repair and replacement program, and rental assistance. Program eligibility is based on income.

Southern Mountains

Cherokee County

CHEROKEE COUNTY SENIOR SERVICES, 69 Alpine St., Murphy, NC; (828) 837-2467; cherokeecounty-nc.gov. Many activities take place at the Penland Senior Citizens Center, including craft classes and exercise programs conducted by the health department. A Friendly Visitor Program visits homebound seniors for "cheers and chores," and there's a congregate meal program at the center Mon through Fri, as well as a home-delivered meals program. It also offers information and referrals to various community services. The organization's red vans offer regularly scheduled runs into each section of the county. Out-of-county trips are also scheduled for shopping, recreation, and medical appointments. SHIIP (Seniors' Health Insurance Information Program) is active here with trained counselors helping senior citizens with health insurance information.

Clay County

CLAY COUNTY SENIOR CENTER, 196 Ritter Rd., Hayesville, NC; (828) 389-9271. The center provides a congregate "Meals with Friends" and Meals on Wheels, Mon through Fri. It also holds classes in painting, wood carving, crocheting, and exercise, and has popular Thursday Morning Music Sessions.

Graham County

GRAHAM COUNTY SENIOR CENTER, 185 West Fort Hill Rd., Robbinsville, NC; (828) 479-7977. A congregate lunch is served at the center five days a week with home-driven meals to homebound seniors. There are also art and carving classes and bingo. Also offering Meals on Wheels.

Haywood County

CANTON SENIOR CENTER, Old Canton Armory; 1 Pigeon St., Canton, NC; (828) 648-8173; mountainprojects.org. The center promotes wellness in older adults through group socialization, special activities, crafts, speaking, educational opportunities, and organized trips. A meal is offered at 11:45 a.m., Mon through Fri. They also serve as a conduit for Meals on Wheels for the Department of Social Services.

COUNCIL ON AGING, 205 Hazelwood Ave., Waynesville, NC, (828) 456-9488; care.com. The council provides information and referral, resource directory, advocacy, coordination of services, special programs, and the Senior Games. The council is also the lead agency for CAP/DA, which serves elderly adults needing care in an in-home setting. Faith in Action provides aid to seniors with disabilities in installing railings and ramps and other devices necessary for well-being.

HAYWOOD SENIOR CENTER, 81 Elmwood Way, Waynesville, NC; (828) 356-2800; haywoodseniors.org. The center promotes wellness in older adults through group socialization, special activities, crafts, speaking, educational opportunities and equipping older adults to live in their own homes as long as possible.

INTENTIONAL GROWTH CENTER, 959 North Lakeshore Dr., Lake Junaluska, NC; (828) 452-2881, ext. 721, (800) 482-1442; intentional growthcenter.org. The center, an agency of the United Methodist Church, is a nationally accredited provider of continuing education courses and programs of clergy and laity. It also serves as a popular center for the national Elderhostel program and for church-related older adult events, such as Fall Flings and Christmas at Lambuth Inn.

MEALS ON WHEELS, DEPARTMENT OF SOCIAL SERVICES, 486 East Marshall St., Waynesville, NC; (828) 452-6620, ext. 377; haywoodnc.net. Meals are provided five days a week based on need. Fees are based on income.

RETIREMENT

MOUNTAIN PROJECTS, INC., 2251 Old Balsam Rd., Waynesville, NC; (828) 452-1447; mountainprojects.org. This organization is a community action agency serving Haywood and Jackson Counties. It operates numerous programs for low-income and disadvantaged persons. These currently include housing rehabilitation, Head Start, a congregate nutrition program, foster grandparents, a retired senior volunteer program, Section 8 rental assistance, Haywood Public Transit, employment and training programs, and in-home chore services for the elderly. The eligibility for program participation is determined by the particular grant funding the program.

WAYNESVILLE OLD ARMORY RECREATION CENTER, 44 Boundary St., Waynesville, NC; (828) 456-9207. Senior citizens meet here for lunch Mon through Fri. The center, which serves the entire community, also offers special activities, crafts, bridge, lectures, and organized trips.

Jackson County

GOLDEN AGE CLUB, 23 Central St., Sylva, NC; (828) 586-4944. This is one of the more active senior citizen centers in the mountains. Its 300 members enjoy classes in exercise, beginner and advanced line dancing, square dancing, tai chi exercise, wood carving, basic computer instruction, tennis, hiking, and creative writing.

JACKSON COUNTY DEPARTMENT ON AGING, 30 Central St., Sylva, NC; (828) 586-8562; aging.jacksonnc.org. This active agency provides programs and resources for county seniors. In addition to coordinating services with other agencies and councils, it provides information and referral services on a variety of subjects and health issues, initiates new services, and is a senior advocacy group. It also publishes a monthly newsletter, Jacksonian, with information about local senior events and happenings.

SYLVA SENIOR C.A.F.E., Community Services Building, 538 Scotts Creek, Sylva, NC; (828) 586-6710. A congregate lunch is served here Mon through Fri, and the Home-Delivered Meals Program delivers hot, nutritious meals daily to Jackson County's homebound elderly seven days a week. This center has a public access computer with Internet connection for seniors in the Sylva area, and instruction is available. It also offers occasional programs, including exercises, bingo, and adventurous outings, but simply socializing is one of the biggest attractions.

Macon County

CENTER FOR LIFE ENRICHMENT, PEGGY CROSS CENTER, 348 S. 5th St., Highlands, NC; (828) 526-8811; clehighlands.org. The center is aligned with four regional institutions of higher education: Western Carolina University, Southwestern Community College, Piedmont College, and Brevard College. Programs are offered for personal enrichment.

MACON COUNTY DEPARTMENT OF AGING, 108 Wyah St., Franklin, NC; (828) 349-2058; maconnc.org. The department is the only full-service agency to serve anyone older than 60 west of Hickory. A sampling of the services provided: congregate meals, home-delivered meals, chores, respite care services, in-home services, an Alzheimer's support group, an Alzheimer's day-care center, overnight respite, case management, information and referral, SHIIP, a lending library on dementia, and medical equipment for loan.

Swain County

STATE OF FRANKLIN SERVICES TO SENIOR CITIZENS, Courthouse-on-the-Square, Bryson City, NC; (828) 488-3047; maconnc.org. The Swain County Senior Center provides an Elderly Nutrition Program for people older than 60 at noon Mon through Fri as well as transportation to the center. Transportation is also provided for medical appointments and shopping. On certain days of the month, there are regularly scheduled trips for out-of-town medical appointments. Through the National Council of Senior Citizens, a Senior AIDES Program provides an employment service for people older than 55 for 20-hour-week jobs with nonprofit organizations and governmental positions.

RETIREMENT COMMUNITIES

Because Western North Carolina is so popular with retirees, it naturally follows that many retirement communities have sprung up here. Although most are concentrated in the Asheville-Hendersonville area, others are sprouting in surrounding areas. They offer everything from an independent living style to total life care. They also offer a wide range of options to fit various retirement needs and budgets: manufactured homes, cluster or attached homes, town houses, condominiums, apartments, and luxurious life-care facilities. Most counties have low-cost retirement apartments through their departments of social services that are priced according to income levels, though there is often a waiting list for these. Here are a few examples of what is available. For more information contact local chambers of commerce.

Central Mountains

COLLEGE WALK, 100 N. College View Ct., Brevard, NC; (828) 884-5800; collegewalkretirement.com. College Walk borders Brevard College and is convenient to the Brevard Music Center, shopping, and Pisgah National Forest.

This community offers two- and three-bedroom cluster homes; studio, one-bedroom, and two-bedroom apartments; and a state-licensed assisted-living facility. Fees include one meal daily, land lease, outside maintenance, security patrol, and use of the clubhouse, library, game room, auditorium, workshop, and other common areas.

DEERFIELD, 1617 Hendersonville Rd., Asheville, NC; (828) 274-1531, (800) 284-1531; deerfieldwnc.org. This pleasant Episcopal retirement community on Asheville's south end offers apartments and cottages for seniors. The attractively landscaped estate maintains a health center, a central formal dining room with wait service, and a community center with a host of amenities. Deerfield maintains Life Care assisted living and will be expanding over the next few years. Just off a main thoroughfare on Asheville's south side, Deerfield is close to shopping, restaurants, cinemas, and access to the Blue Ridge Parkway.

GIVENS ESTATE UNITED METHODIST RETIREMENT COMMUNITY, 2360 Sweeten Creek Rd., Asheville, NC; (828) 274-4800; givens estates.org. This United Methodist retirement community is spread over 160 wooded acres in south Asheville. The retirement village has residential options that include apartments, duplexes, and individual houses scattered across the campus. Asbury Hall, in the community's center, offers congregate living with dining and recreational facilities. Also within this facility is Sales Health Care Center, designed to provide domiciliary or skilled nursing care to residents who can no longer live alone. A campus nurse and 24-hour emergency call system and housekeeping are additional services.

GIVENS HIGHLAND FARMS RETIREMENT COMMUNITY, 200 Tabernacle Rd., Black Mountain, NC; (828) 669-6473; givenshighland farms.org. Highland Farms was one of the first retirement communities in Western North Carolina. This beautiful spot, nestled in the mountains in Buncombe County near the village of Black Mountain, has drawn retirees since the 1970s. Cluster homes, condominiums, apartments, individual homes, a residential lodge, a health care center, and a rest home are spread over a lovely campus with the mountains in view. A library, music area, art and craft studio, and even a vegetable garden keep those at Highland Farms active. Seminars and on-campus workshops foster a close relationship with the surrounding communities of Asheville and Black Mountain.

LAKE POINTE LANDING, 333 Thompson St., Hendersonville, NC; (828) 693-7800; centurypa.com/senior-living/lake-pointe-landing. The 32-acre complex has easy access to I-26 and is less than a mile from Hendersonville's restaurants, shopping, banks, and medical offices. The lush landscaping and one-plus-acre lake make it seem more a "country place." Lake Pointe is made up of patio homes known as the Villas, where retirees can enjoy 100 percent equity ownership. There are two- and three-bedroom units, each with a second-floor loft to use as a study or for extra storage. Both units come with two baths; a living room; a fully equipped, all-electric kitchen; a fireplace; a screened-in back porch; and an enclosed garage. For more space there are special homes with a lakeside view, retirement center proximity, or seclusion and privacy. Rental apartments are also available. Residents here have biweekly maid service and evening meals in a full-service dining room. All utilities except personal telephone service are included in the rental fee, along with maintenance and a full calendar of activities with scheduled transportation and use of the Club House. Special guest suites are available for family and friends when they come to visit. In addition there are assisted living apartments at the Inn at Lake Pointe Landing with a choice of alcove and one-bedroom apartments. A licensed staff provides help in monitoring medications, grooming, housekeeping, and access to transportation and other assistance. Lake Pointe Landing also offers an on-site, long-term-care facility, Life Care Center of Hendersonville. It provides rehabilitation, skilled, and long-term care services.

TRINITY VIEW, 2533 Hendersonville Rd., Asheville, NC; (828) 687-0068; trinityview.net. This Lutheran-sponsored planned community in Buncombe County has a variety of studio, one-bedroom, and two-bedroom apartment homes for retired seniors. Fine dining, housekeeping, and linen services are available here, as well as 24-hour security and transportation. Crescent View also offers assisted-living residences. On the south end of Asheville, it is close to major supermarkets, movie theaters, shopping, and easy access to the Blue Ridge Parkway.

TRYON ESTATES, 617 Laurel Lake Dr., Columbus, NC; (828) 894-3000, (800) 633-2718; actsretirement.org/communities/north-carolina/tryon-estates -columbus. Tryon Estates—owned and operated by ACTS, Inc., a not-for-profit corporation—lies on a 215-acre wooded site in Polk County's thermal belt. It offers one-, two-, and three-bedroom apartments and two- and three-bedroom villas with all buildings connected by covered walkways. Chef-prepared gourmet meals are served each day in an elegant central dining room. There are also private dining rooms. It has a regular activity schedule and a full-time activity director. Other amenities include a theater-style auditorium, library, woodworking shop, billiard room, an activity-craft room, a card room, a beauty/barber shop, a pharmacy, banking and postal services, a gift shop, and an indoor, heated swimming pool. Outside you'll find garden plots, walking and biking paths, a stocked fishing pond, croquet, and shuffleboard. Maid service is available.

Index